OF SKY, SEA, AND GROVE:
The Pantheon of the Deities in Greek Religion

M.L.RUSCSAK

Trient Press
3375 S Rainbow Blvd
#81710, SMB 13135
Las Vegas,NV 89180

Ordering Information:
Quantity sales. Special discounts are available on quantity purchases by corporations, associations, and others. For details, contact the publisher at the address above.
Orders by U.S. trade bookstores and wholesalers. Please contact Trient Press: Tel: (775) 996-3844; or visit www.trientpress.com.

Printed in the United States of America

Publisher's Cataloging-in-Publication data
Ruscsak, M.L.
A title of a book : Of Sky, Sea, and Grove: The Pantheon of the Deities in Greek Religion

ISBN
Hard Cover   979-8-88990-138-9
Paper Back   979-8-88990-139-6
Ebook   979-8-88990-140-2

Foreword

It is with great pleasure that I introduce to you "Of Sky, Sea, and Grove: The Pantheon of Nature Deities in Greek Religion." This comprehensive and scholarly work sets out to illuminate the rich tapestry of ancient Greek religious life by focusing on the intricate, captivating pantheon of deities that shaped it.

The book presents a fascinating journey through the dynamic spectrum of the Greek pantheon, from the grandeur of the Olympians to the primordial allure of the earliest gods, the quiet resilience of lesser-known deities, and the comforting presence of household and city gods. Each chapter invites the reader to delve deeper into the complex weave of narratives, rituals, and beliefs that framed the ancient Greeks' understanding of the world and their place within it.

At the heart of this exploration is a consideration of the deities' multilayered roles, from upholders of moral and societal order to embodiments of elemental forces and natural phenomena. The chapters meticulously dissect the interplay between these roles, the Greeks' daily life, and the broader societal norms and values.

What sets this book apart is its interdisciplinary approach, fusing historical, religious, and cultural perspectives to paint a nuanced picture of the Greek pantheon's importance. This is especially true in the chapter on the interactions between ancient Greek and African religions, providing a seldom-explored comparison that broadens our understanding of cross-cultural religious influences.

The final chapter on nature deities echoes our contemporary environmental discourse and spiritual traditions. Here, the ancient and modern worlds converge, offering readers an opportunity to reflect on the enduring influence of these ancient deities and their relevance today.

Supplementing the text are carefully designed exercises and discussion prompts that serve to deepen understanding and encourage critical thinking. These tools make this book a valuable asset not only for individual scholars but also for educators and students engaged in the study of ancient religions, mythology, and cultural studies.

"Of Sky, Sea, and Grove" is not just a study of ancient deities, it's an exploration of the human impulse to find meaning, negotiate identity, and seek connection—within the natural world, within our societies, and within ourselves. This book will form a pivotal component of "The Sacred Journey: Exploring Ancient Spiritual Traditions and their Influence on Modern Religions" course at AOW University, offering students a unique lens to examine the past and, in doing so, reflect upon the present.

Embark on this enlightening journey through the pantheon of Greek deities, and you will emerge with a broader understanding of the ways in which the divine, the natural, and the human intertwine, shaping cultures, belief systems, and our collective history.

ASSEMBLY OF
WANDERERS

Of Sky, Sea, and Grove

Chapter 1: Introduction to the Greek Pantheon: A broad overview of the pantheon concept, its origins, and its significance in Greek religion and culture.

Chapter 2: The Olympian Gods: Comprehensive examination of the twelve main gods of Olympus, their stories, roles, symbols, and their significance in ancient Greek religion.

Chapter 3: The Primeval Gods: Examination of the earliest gods in Greek mythology, often associated with elemental forces and the creation of the world.

Chapter 4: Interactions between Ancient Greek and African Religions: A Historical Overview

Chapter 5: The Lesser-Known Deities: A look at lesser-known gods, their roles, and the significance of these lesser deities in the daily life of ancient Greeks.

Chapter 6: Household and City Gods: An exploration of the deities related to domestic life and the city, like Hestia, and their religious and cultural importance.

Chapter 7: The Nature Deities: Overview of Pan, the nymphs, and other gods and spirits associated with natural phenomena and landscapes.

Of Sky, Sea, and Grove

Chapter 1: Introduction to the Greek Pantheon: A broad overview of the pantheon concept, its origins, and its significance in Greek religion and culture.

As we venture into the heart of ancient Greek spirituality, the pantheon of deities looms large, casting its multidimensional shadow over the landscape of cultural, societal, and individual practices. It is within this realm of divine entities that we begin our exploration, striving to comprehend the complex structure, rich mythology, and profound influences of these celestial beings upon the fabric of Greek civilization. This chapter, 'Introduction to the Greek Pantheon,' seeks to provide a broad and comprehensive overview of the concept of the pantheon, its origins, and its indelible significance in Greek religion and culture.

The term 'pantheon,' originating from the Greek words 'pan' meaning 'all' and 'theos' meaning 'god,' conjures a collective image of gods and goddesses. But it implies far more than a simple assemblage of deities. The pantheon represents a cosmology, a theological and philosophical structure reflecting the ancients' understanding of the cosmos, nature, and the human condition.

The origins of the Greek pantheon, steeped in the mists of antiquity, are a palimpsest of influences and evolutions. From primordial deities to the Twelve Olympians, the development of the pantheon mirrors the shifting tides of Greek society and its interactions with neighboring cultures.

One of the remarkable aspects of the Greek pantheon is its intricate hierarchical structure, a celestial bureaucracy of sorts, with deities presiding over various domains, both abstract and physical. This chapter will elucidate how these divine responsibilities provide insights into the ancient Greek understanding of natural phenomena, societal structures, and human attributes.

Furthermore, we will consider how the pantheon served as a cornerstone of religious practices, rituals, and festivals. The gods of the pantheon were intimately entwined with the ancient Greeks' daily lives, their society, and their identity, rendering a study of this divine structure invaluable in comprehending the broader picture of Greek culture.

Finally, we cannot overlook the critical role of the pantheon in myth and literature. Through epic tales of divine exploits and mortal interactions, we glean crucial insights into the nature of the gods and their relationships with humans. These narratives form an essential part of the pantheon's tapestry, embellishing our understanding of the ancient Greek worldview.

This chapter is an invitation to step into the ethereal realm of the Greek pantheon, to delve into the mysteries of its origins, structure, and influence, and to illuminate our understanding of the past. It beckons you to engage with the timeless tales of gods and goddesses, to reflect upon the echoes of ancient spirituality in contemporary practices, and to appreciate the intricate web that links the mortal and divine spheres.

Let us embark upon this intellectual odyssey, threading our way through the labyrinth of divine hierarchies, sacred rituals, societal implications, and epic narratives. By deciphering the enigma of the Greek pantheon, we begin to grasp the complexity and richness of Greek spirituality, laying a sturdy foundation for our deeper exploration of Hellenic religion and culture in the following chapters.

Definition of 'Pantheon'

As we embark upon the intricate journey of comprehending the Greek pantheon, it is incumbent upon us to initially define the concept of the 'pantheon.' Originating from the Greek words 'pan', meaning 'all', and 'theos', meaning 'god', the term pantheon is commonly construed as an assembly of all gods. Nevertheless, this rather simplistic interpretation belies the profound depth and complexity embodied in the pantheon concept.

To explicate the pantheon is to delve into an intricate matrix of divinity where each god and goddess, with their distinct domains and attributes, is not merely an isolated entity but an integral cog in an extensive divine machinery. The pantheon is thus a holistic structure encompassing a multiplicity of deities within a coherent system, each deity functioning within a hierarchical order and a network of relationships with other divine figures.

It is essential to discern that the pantheon is not a static construct, but rather a dynamic and fluid entity. It evolves in response to sociocultural changes, religious syncretism, and philosophical transformations, reflecting the mutable human understanding of the cosmos, nature, and societal structures. Thus, the pantheon can be perceived as a barometer of cultural and societal shifts, encoding within its divine framework the zeitgeist of different historical epochs.

Moreover, the pantheon extends beyond a mere catalog of deities. It encapsulates a cosmology, a worldview that shapes and is shaped by societal norms, cultural values, and philosophical ideas. The divine roles and interrelationships within the pantheon reveal the ancients' perceptions of natural phenomena, social order, and ethical principles. Each deity, with their specific purview, attributes, and narratives, is a facet of this cosmic understanding, illuminating the ancients' conceptualization of the universe and their place within it.

The pantheon, therefore, is far from being a mere theological concept. It pervades the realms of mythology, ritual, literature, and art, transcending the religious sphere to imprint upon the societal, cultural, and psychological facets of the ancient world. The pantheon, in essence, is a divine tapestry, woven with the threads of theology, cosmology, sociology, and psychology.

An exploration of the pantheon necessitates a multi-pronged approach, employing various methodologies such as textual analysis, archaeological interpretation, comparative religious studies, and historical contextualization. By embracing such an approach, we can begin to unravel the complex divine network that constitutes the pantheon and thereby gain profound insights into the rich and diverse tapestry of ancient Greek religion and culture.

In the subsequent sections, we will engage with the structure, origin, and evolution of the Greek pantheon, discerning the contours of this intricate divine landscape. As we navigate this celestial matrix, we will not only uncover the multifaceted aspects of the divine entities but also shed light on the intertwining relationships between religion, society, and culture in the ancient Greek world. Through this investigation, the pantheon will emerge as more than a collection of deities; it will reveal itself as a profound reflection of the ancient Greek worldview and a significant shaper of Hellenic identity.

Origin of the term.

The term 'pantheon', as we have established, designates an assembly of gods, incorporating both major and minor deities. The word itself originates from ancient Greek, combining 'pan' (all) with 'theos' (god). However, tracing the etymology of the term only scratches the surface of its inception and evolution. The pantheon concept is not merely a product of linguistic innovation; rather, it embodies a shift in religious perception, signaling a transition from localized worship of individual deities to a systemic organization of divine entities within a structured, hierarchical framework.

The origin of the pantheon concept, much like its defining characteristics, is fluid, rooted in the dynamic interplay between human understanding of divinity and evolving sociocultural structures. The genesis of the pantheon may be tracked back to prehistoric times when early humans, seeking to comprehend and navigate the mysteries of their natural surroundings, began to personify natural elements and forces, thus laying the rudimentary foundations of polytheism.

As societies grew more complex, so did their divine representations. Deities became associated with specific aspects of life, nature, and human experience, each assuming a distinct identity. This process of specialization led to the development of a multiplicity of gods, each ruling a particular domain. Yet, these gods were not perceived in isolation. They formed part of a complex web of relationships, interdependencies, and hierarchies, the understanding of which crystallized into the concept of the pantheon.

The genesis of the pantheon concept was not an isolated Greek phenomenon. It parallels developments in other ancient cultures, notably Egypt and Mesopotamia. In these civilizations, we find early instances of pantheonic structures, with gods organized hierarchically and forming an interconnected divine system.

It is essential to underscore that the Greek pantheon was not a rigid, universally accepted canon of gods but rather a flexible and regionally diverse collection of deities. Different Greek city-states had their local pantheons, reflecting the unique religious traditions, societal norms, and cultural values of their communities. The pantheon was thus an adaptable entity, capable of incorporating new deities, reflecting societal changes, and accommodating regional variations.

The concept of the pantheon represents an effort to systematize and comprehend the divine world, reflecting the human urge to impose order upon the seemingly chaotic cosmos. It also bears witness to the evolution of societal structures, echoing the complexities of human society in its divine mirror.

In the subsequent sections, we will delve deeper into the intricate framework of the Greek pantheon, its structure, its constituents, and its evolution, enriching our understanding of Greek religion and culture. Through this exploration, we will discern how the concept of the pantheon, in its dynamic complexity, encapsulates the richness of the Hellenic religious imagination, offering us a window into the ancient Greek understanding of the divine and the human.

How the concept of a pantheon applies to ancient Greek religion.

As we venture deeper into the rich tapestry of ancient Greek religion, we must grapple with the complexities of the pantheon concept and its manifestation within this particular spiritual landscape. The Greek pantheon is a complex constellation of deities, encompassing a vast array of divine figures, each with unique attributes, jurisdictions, and mythologies.

The Greek pantheon represents an intricate, fluid system wherein deities were neither isolated entities nor fixed in a rigid hierarchy. Instead, they were interconnected nodes within a vast network, with relationships, roles, and relative importance shifting according to various factors such as geographic location, historical period, cultural evolution, and societal needs.

To illustrate the dynamism of the Greek pantheon, consider the varying statuses of deities across different Greek city-states. For instance, Athens revered Athena as the city's patron deity, and thus, within the Athenian pantheon, Athena occupied a preeminent position. In contrast, Sparta held Ares, the god of war, in high regard due to their militaristic culture. This fluidity and regional variation are critical characteristics of the Greek pantheon, reflecting the diversity and dynamism of ancient Greek society itself.

Similarly, the roles of the deities within the Greek pantheon were not static. Over time, as societal values, cultural paradigms, and political structures evolved, so did the roles, attributes, and importance of various gods. Apollo, initially revered primarily as a god of music and poetry, evolved to embody prophetic wisdom, becoming associated with the famous Oracle at Delphi. Dionysus, the god of wine, ecstasy, and revelry, was not initially considered one of the twelve Olympian gods but was later incorporated into the pantheon, reflecting changes in religious practices and societal attitudes.

The Greek pantheon also showcases the concept of syncretism, which refers to the merging or assimilation of gods and their associated rituals and mythologies. Syncretism allowed the Greeks to incorporate foreign deities into their pantheon. For example, the Egyptian deity Isis was assimilated into the Greek religious landscape, and her worship was widespread, particularly during the Hellenistic period.

One cannot discuss the Greek pantheon without acknowledging the role of myth in structuring and communicating the divine system. Myths served as a narrative framework, encapsulating the relationships among the gods, their functions, and their interactions with the human world. Myths provided a common language and shared cultural reference, allowing the Greeks to comprehend, navigate, and negotiate their divine realm.

The concept of the pantheon, as applied to the ancient Greek religion, demonstrates an attempt to impose order upon the divine realm, mirroring the complexity and dynamism of human society. Its fluid, adaptive nature reflects the multifaceted, evolving reality of ancient Greek culture, underscoring the close interplay between religion and societal structures. The Greek pantheon is not merely a catalogue of divine figures; it is a reflection of the Greek worldview, encapsulating their understanding of the cosmos, their societal norms, and their cultural identity.

In the following sections of this chapter, we will examine the major and minor deities of the Greek pantheon, explore their unique attributes and functions, and consider their roles within the intricate web of Greek mythology. Through this exploration, we will further our understanding of the Greek religious psyche and the profound influence of the pantheon concept on the structure and practice of ancient Greek religion.

The Origins of the Greek Pantheon

The origins of the Greek pantheon are shrouded in the mists of antiquity, nestled within the intricate interplay of oral tradition, mythic narratives, and archaeological evidence. These elements weave together a multifaceted account of how the Greek pantheon took shape over time, reflecting the ever-evolving cultural, societal, and historical landscapes of the ancient Greek world.

To begin our exploration of the genesis of the Greek pantheon, we must step back into the Bronze Age, specifically the Minoan civilization that thrived on the island of Crete and the Mycenaean civilization on the Greek mainland. Both these civilizations, predating classical Greek culture, exhibited a rich religious life with an assortment of divine entities. The Linear B tablets of the Mycenaeans provide the earliest written evidence of names that would later feature prominently in the Greek pantheon, including Zeus, Hera, Poseidon, Hermes, and Artemis.

However, we must be cautious not to draw direct lines of continuity from these early appearances to their classical counterparts. The divine entities of the Mycenaean period may have possessed different attributes and societal functions, their identities being reshaped over the centuries as Mycenaean civilization gave way to the Greek Dark Ages, and eventually, the Archaic and Classical periods.

The Pantheon of the Deities in Greek Religion

As we traverse from the Bronze Age to the historical periods of ancient Greece, we encounter the pervasive influence of oral tradition, specifically in the form of epic poetry. The Homeric epics - the Iliad and the Odyssey - and the Theogony by Hesiod present a structured vision of the pantheon. In these epic narratives, a hierarchy of gods and goddesses emerges, each with distinctive jurisdictions and mythologies.

The Homeric epics, composed during the transitional period between the Dark Ages and the Archaic Period, offer not only a dramatic narrative of heroic adventure and warfare but also a theogonic (god-generating) and cosmogonic (world-generating) function. The epics depict the gods as deeply entwined with the human world, influencing events and embodying the forces that the ancient Greeks saw as shaping their world.

Hesiod's Theogony, composed around the same time, presents a more systematic account of the origin and genealogy of the gods. It narrates the primal cosmic events leading up to the establishment of Zeus's sovereignty over the world and the gods, thereby outlining a clear divine hierarchy. This literary work significantly shaped the Greek understanding of their pantheon and structured their religious praxis.

Nevertheless, while these literary works were instrumental in shaping the pantheon, the religious reality in ancient Greece was far from uniform. Regional variations were prevalent, and local cults often worshipped deities not included in the Homeric or Hesiodic pantheon. In the same vein, syncretism played a crucial role, leading to the assimilation of foreign deities, such as the Egyptian Isis and the Persian Mithras, into the Greek religious landscape, particularly during the cosmopolitan Hellenistic period.

Therefore, the origins of the Greek pantheon do not rest in a single point of inception. Instead, they unfold as a complex, nonlinear process, influenced by a multitude of factors ranging from the prehistoric religious practices of the Minoan and Mycenaean civilizations to the cultural interactions in the Hellenistic age. These diverse influences continually reshaped and expanded the pantheon, mirroring the dynamism and diversity of the ancient Greek world.

In the subsequent sections of this chapter, we shall embark upon a detailed exploration of the major and minor deities within the Greek pantheon. This exploration will allow us to further appreciate the intricacies and influences that shaped the Greek pantheon, providing us with deeper insights into the unique religious ethos of ancient Greece.

An overview of the earliest origins and influences on the formation of the Greek pantheon (Proto-Indo-European roots, influences from Near Eastern cultures, etc.).

The formative influences on the Greek pantheon are a rich and diverse tapestry, integrating elements from Proto-Indo-European roots, Near Eastern cultures, and intercultural exchanges within the ancient Mediterranean world. These disparate sources offer us a fascinating glimpse into the complex processes of cultural assimilation, synthesis, and adaptation that contributed to the Greek pantheon's formation and development.

The Greek pantheon's earliest origins can be traced back to the shared mythic heritage of the Proto-Indo-European peoples. Comparative linguistic and mythological studies suggest a range of deities and mythic motifs common to various Indo-European cultures, including the ancient Greeks. For instance, the sky father figure, exemplified by the Greek Zeus, finds parallels in the Roman Jupiter, the Norse Odin, and the Vedic Dyaus Pita. This suggests that such deities might be remnants of a common Proto-Indo-European pantheon.

However, while the Proto-Indo-European roots offer tantalizing hints, it is essential to approach them with caution. The complex process of linguistic evolution and cultural diffusion over millennia makes the direct tracing of such influences a highly speculative endeavor. Therefore, while these commonalities indicate a shared heritage, they do not delineate a direct lineage. Nevertheless, they deepen our understanding of the interconnected web of cultural influences that have shaped the Greek pantheon.

In addition to these deep-rooted Indo-European connections, the formation of the Greek pantheon was significantly shaped by interactions with Near Eastern cultures. The ancient Near East, comprising regions like Mesopotamia, Anatolia, and Levant, boasted a series of advanced civilizations, including the Sumerians, Hittites, and Phoenicians. The Mycenaean civilization, which predates classical Greece, had active trade and diplomatic connections with these Near Eastern entities, likely leading to significant cultural exchange.

Archaeological and textual evidence suggests that specific mythic narratives and divine attributes might have been adopted and adapted from these Near Eastern cultures. For instance, the myth of the Greek goddess Aphrodite shares striking similarities with the myths of the Mesopotamian goddess Inanna and her later counterpart, the Phoenician Astarte. Similarly, aspects of Zeus's character show resemblances with the Hittite weather god Tarhunt, further underlining these cultural interconnections.

The cultural exchanges continued well into the Archaic and Classical periods, with the Greek city-states' burgeoning maritime trade. Contacts with the Phoenician city-states led to the import of the Phoenician alphabet, which was adapted into the Greek alphabet, enabling the transcription of the Greek language and the immortalization of Greek myths and legends in written form. The cosmopolitan Hellenistic era, marked by increased contact with the wider Mediterranean world and Near East, further contributed to this syncretistic process, integrating various foreign deities into the Greek religious fabric.

Therefore, the Greek pantheon's formation was an extended, dynamic process marked by cultural assimilation, adaptation, and innovation. The influence of the Proto-Indo-European heritage, Near Eastern cultures, and other Mediterranean civilizations contributed to shaping a pantheon that was uniquely Greek yet bore the imprints of a shared ancient cultural heritage.

As we delve further into the individual deities of the Greek pantheon in subsequent sections, we will frequently encounter these formative influences. Appreciating these diverse influences and their role in shaping the Greek pantheon will enhance our understanding of the broader socio-cultural dynamics within the ancient Greek world and the wider ancient Mediterranean region.

Discussion on how the pantheon evolved over time, from the pre-Olympian deities to the Twelve Olympians and beyond.

When studying the Greek pantheon, one of the most fascinating aspects is its temporal evolution, a fluid and dynamic process that reflects the broader socio-cultural transformations within ancient Greek society. The pantheon's development, from the enigmatic pre-Olympian deities to the canonized Twelve Olympians and the incorporation of foreign deities in later periods, is an intriguing journey, reflecting the diversity and complexity of Greek religious thought.

In the earliest strata of Greek religious tradition, we encounter the enigmatic figures of the pre-Olympian deities, often referred to as the 'primordial' or 'proto-gods.' These entities, including Chaos, Gaia (Earth), Uranus (Sky), and others, embody elemental forces and cosmic principles. They represent a cosmogonic phase, laying the foundational mythic narrative of the universe's genesis. However, these entities' abstract and impersonal nature contrasts significantly with the later anthropomorphic deities, suggesting a shift in religious conceptualization over time.

The second wave in the evolution of the Greek pantheon is marked by the Titans, the offspring of Gaia and Uranus. Cronus, Rhea, Hyperion, and their siblings embody a more complex cosmology, with narratives revolving around power struggles, filial conflict, and primal fears. The mythic theme of the 'Titanomachy'—the battle and eventual overthrow of the Titans by their offspring, the Olympians—signifies a crucial transition in the Greek religious cosmos.

The advent of the Olympians heralds a new era in Greek religion, characterized by anthropomorphic deities exhibiting human-like behaviors, emotions, and flaws. This pantheon, with Zeus at its helm, is the most familiar aspect of Greek religion, profoundly influencing art, literature, and philosophical thought. The twelve principal deities—Zeus, Hera, Poseidon, Demeter, Athena, Apollo, Artemis, Ares, Hephaestus, Aphrodite, Hermes, and either Hestia or Dionysus—each had their distinct domains and mythic narratives, reflecting various aspects of human existence and natural phenomena.

However, it is worth noting that the Greek pantheon's configuration was not static or uniform. Regional variations existed, with certain deities assuming greater importance in specific locales due to local traditions or historical factors. For instance, Athena held a special place in Athens, whereas Artemis was the primary deity in Ephesus.

Moreover, the pantheon's boundaries were not rigid. Other deities, although not part of the canonical Twelve Olympians, played significant roles in Greek religion, including Asclepius, the god of medicine, and Persephone, associated with the Eleusinian Mysteries. Minor deities, nature spirits (like nymphs and satyrs), and heroic demigods further enriched the Greek religious landscape.

As Greek society expanded its geographical and cultural horizons during the Hellenistic period, the pantheon incorporated various foreign deities, reflecting the syncretistic tendencies of Greek religion. Isis, an Egyptian goddess, Cybele, a mother goddess from Phrygia, and Mithras, a Persian deity, found places in the Greek religious milieu, often synchronized with Greek deities or worshipped in their unique cults.

The evolution of the Greek pantheon, thus, is not merely a linear progression but a complex interplay of continuity and change, tradition and innovation, reflecting the pluralistic and adaptable nature of Greek religion. This dynamism, which allows for the integration of new deities and concepts while maintaining older traditions, underscores the Greek pantheon's richness and diversity, contributing to its enduring fascination for scholars and enthusiasts alike.

Structure of the Greek Pantheon

In Greek religion, the pantheon's structure displays an intricate interplay between hierarchy, domains, and religious functions, imbued with a complex cultural symbolism. The pantheon's structure is not merely a rigid taxonomic tool, but rather a dynamic framework that can provide significant insights into ancient Greek worldview and societal constructs.

A salient feature of the Greek pantheon's structure is the concept of hierarchy, with Zeus typically positioned at the apex as the "father of gods and men," signifying his role as the supreme arbiter and the keeper of cosmic order. However, this hierarchy was neither absolute nor static. Depending on geographical regions, specific local deities could be accorded prominence over Zeus. For example, Athena occupied a position of particular reverence in Athens.

The second structural layer consists of the remaining Olympians. They are divided into groups reflecting their familial relations, divine domains, and functions. While Hera, Poseidon, Demeter, and Hestia are Zeus's siblings, the remaining Olympians—Athena, Ares, Hephaestus, Aphrodite, Apollo, Artemis, and Hermes—are typically seen as his children, reflecting the complex interplay of family dynamics in the divine realm.

The division of divine responsibilities among these deities underscores the Greeks' conceptualization of the universe. Each god or goddess had a domain or set of domains over which they exerted influence, and their realms could encompass various aspects of the physical world, human life, and societal constructs. For example, Poseidon was the god of the sea and earthquakes, Athena was the goddess of wisdom and warfare, while Hermes was the god of commerce, thieves, and messengers.

Beyond the Olympians, the Greek pantheon included a wide range of lesser gods, demi-gods, and nature spirits, each with their respective spheres of influence. The Twelve Olympians were by no means the entirety of the Greek religious world. Diverse entities such as the Nereids (sea nymphs), Satyrs (companions of Dionysus), and the Muses (patrons of the arts and sciences) also held significant religious and cultural importance.

Importantly, the structure of the Greek pantheon was characterized by fluidity and adaptability. Deities could share, overlap, or encroach upon each other's domains, reflecting a holistic and interconnected view of the universe. Moreover, the Greek pantheon was open to foreign influences and capable of integrating new deities into its structure. For instance, the Egyptian goddess Isis and the Persian god Mithras were eventually absorbed into the Greek religious framework during the Hellenistic period.

In conclusion, understanding the structure of the Greek pantheon offers critical insights into Greek religion's complex and dynamic nature. It reveals a world that mirrored human society with its hierarchies, alliances, and conflicts, but also a world that encapsulated a profound sense of unity, with every element interconnected and every deity holding a crucial role in maintaining the balance and harmony of the cosmos.

Discussion on the hierarchical structure within the pantheon (Olympian gods, sea gods, underworld gods, etc.).

The hierarchy within the Greek pantheon reflects not only divine order but also societal norms, values, and cultural perceptions of the cosmos. As we delve into the intricacies of this structure, we must remember that it is a mirror reflecting both the cosmos' multilayered reality and the Greeks' nuanced understanding of that reality.

The Olympian gods, as the name suggests, resided on Mount Olympus and represented the pantheon's upper echelon. At the pinnacle stood Zeus, the sky god, who held sway over both divine and mortal realms. Zeus's supreme position was emblematic of his role as the enforcer of justice and order, a cosmic king of sorts, whose authority was acknowledged, albeit with varying degrees of acquiescence, by the other gods.

The other Olympian gods, including Hera, Poseidon, Demeter, Athena, Apollo, Artemis, Hermes, Aphrodite, Ares, Hephaestus, and Dionysus, occupied the next tier of the hierarchy. Each god possessed a distinct domain, denoting an aspect of the physical world or human experience. Notably, these gods' hierarchical position did not imply a divine autocracy; indeed, the Olympians were often depicted as a community bound by familial ties, shared responsibilities, and occasional strife.

Moving beyond Olympus, we encounter deities presiding over realms less immediately visible but no less significant. The sea gods, led by Poseidon and including a host of others like Nereus, Oceanus, and the fifty Nereids, were attributed control over the vast, unpredictable marine world. Here, we observe a parallel structure, with Poseidon at the helm, closely paralleling Zeus's position in the Olympian hierarchy.

The underworld gods, too, possessed a unique hierarchy. Hades, the god of the underworld, was a prominent figure, alongside Persephone, his queen, and various associated deities like Thanatos (Death), Hypnos (Sleep), and the Furies. Despite being less visible in everyday worship due to their association with death and the afterlife, these deities held significant importance within the larger Greek religious framework.

Furthermore, the Greek pantheon comprised an extensive array of minor deities, demi-gods, heroes, and nature spirits, each with their respective spheres of influence. This stratum was as integral to the Greek religious worldview as the upper tiers, reflecting a comprehensive, interconnected conception of the cosmos where every entity held a place and purpose.

However, while this hierarchical view provides a useful framework, it should not be interpreted too rigidly. There existed a certain fluidity in roles, domains, and even hierarchies, particularly when viewed across different regions or historical periods. Local deities could be elevated to higher positions, foreign gods could be adopted into the pantheon, and major gods could have different statuses in different city-states. For example, Athena, though an Olympian, was of paramount importance in Athens, reflecting local religious and civic pride.

In conclusion, the hierarchical structure within the Greek pantheon is a complex reflection of ancient Greek society and its understanding of the cosmos. It underscores the delicate balance between order and chaos, unity and diversity, universal and local—a harmony maintained through an intricate, ever-evolving dance of the divine and the mortal.

Exploration of the concept of domains and responsibilities among the gods.

To approach the Greek pantheon and to genuinely appreciate its profundity, one must delve beyond the hierarchy to the various domains and responsibilities associated with each god. This aspect is crucial as it not only clarifies the roles and jurisdictions of the gods, but it also sheds light on the manner in which the ancient Greeks perceived their universe.

Each deity in the Greek pantheon had a specific domain, essentially a sphere of influence or control, which often tied to elements of the natural world or facets of human experience. For instance, Zeus, the supreme Olympian god, was the lord of the sky and the enforcer of justice and order. As such, he commanded not only natural phenomena like thunderstorms but also regulated ethical norms within society.

Poseidon, Zeus's brother, held dominion over the sea, encapsulating the Greeks' deep respect and fear for the sea's capricious might. However, his role was not confined to the marine world. As the 'earth-shaker,' he was also associated with earthquakes, underlining the interconnectedness of natural phenomena in the Greek mind.

Demeter, the goddess of agriculture, and Dionysus, the god of wine and festivity, held sway over vital components of daily Greek life: grain and grape. Their importance extended beyond mere sustenance to societal and economic realms. Demeter's association with the Eleusinian Mysteries—a set of secretive religious rites—further expanded her domain to encompass esoteric spiritual dimensions.

The domains of the gods extended to more abstract aspects of life as well. Athena, the goddess of wisdom, warfare, and handicraft, and Apollo, the god of music, prophecy, and healing, encapsulated both the pragmatic and the sublime aspects of human existence. They were not just patrons of practical skills like strategy or archery, but also custodians of the intellectual and artistic pursuits, demonstrating the wide spectrum of their influence.

These domains were not static but possessed a certain dynamism, reflecting the evolving nature of human understanding and societal needs. With changing socio-political landscapes or cross-cultural interactions, gods could acquire new associations or even share domains. For instance, Hermes, initially a pastoral god, later evolved into the messenger of the gods, a psychopomp, and the patron of commerce and thieves.

Accompanying these domains were corresponding responsibilities. The gods were expected to oversee their domains, intervene when necessary, and respond to human prayers or sacrifices. However, these interventions were not always benevolent or straightforward, as myths often illustrated gods acting out of personal motivations or whims, reflecting the complex relationship between humans and the divine.

Yet, amidst this seeming capriciousness, the gods maintained cosmic order. They ensured the sun's rise, the seasons' change, the growth of crops, and countless other phenomena, both tangible and intangible. In turn, humans recognized these responsibilities, seeking the gods' favor through worship, offering, and observance of divine laws.

In essence, the domains and responsibilities of the gods reflect the ancient Greeks' multi-faceted understanding of their universe. They viewed their world as a complex, interconnected web of divine jurisdictions, reinforcing their relationship with the gods and the natural world, while also facilitating the construction of societal norms, moral frameworks, and cultural identities.

Role of the Pantheon in Greek Religion

The Greek pantheon's role in the fabric of the Hellenic religious ethos cannot be overstated. The pantheon, with its diverse assembly of deities, was the foundation upon which the religious, moral, and even socio-political structure of Greek society was established. Not only did the gods reflect the cosmological understanding of the ancient Greeks, but their intricate narratives and relationships also served to encode societal norms, guide moral judgments, and influence civic activities.

Religious Practices: The pantheon formed the backbone of religious practice in Greece. Each deity had a distinct cult, complete with its unique rituals, festivals, sacrifices, and sacred sites. These cults were not merely a reflection of personal devotion but were intrinsically linked to the social, political, and economic fabric of the community. For example, the City Dionysia, a festival dedicated to Dionysus in Athens, was not just a religious celebration but also a major civic event that saw the performance of tragedies, political proclamations, and even military parades.

Cosmology: The pantheon also embodied the Greek understanding of the universe's structure and operation. The gods' domain over various natural phenomena—from Zeus' command over thunderstorms to Poseidon's control over the seas—echoed the belief that the universe was a divine mechanism, with each deity playing a crucial role in its smooth functioning. This cosmological model was also reflected in the spatial organization of the pantheon, with gods of the sky, earth, and underworld representing different realms of existence.

Ethics and Morality: The pantheon had a significant influence on Greek morality and ethical thought. Deities like Zeus and Athena, who embodied justice and wisdom, respectively, provided moral exemplars that shaped societal norms and individual behavior. Even though the gods were not always paragons of virtue in myths, their actions still served as valuable lessons in morality, often illustrating the consequences of hubris, deceit, or disrespect towards the divine.

Culture and Art: The pantheon was a critical source of inspiration in Greek art and literature. From epic poetry and drama to sculpture and pottery, the narratives and iconography of the gods permeated various cultural expressions. These artistic renderings not only helped propagate the myths and ethos of the pantheon but also served to articulate complex human emotions, ideals, and dilemmas.

Politics: The role of the pantheon extended to political realms as well. Cities had patron deities—Athens with Athena, Corinth with Poseidon—whose favor was deemed crucial for the city's prosperity and protection. Often, political decisions, including warfare, were legitimized through divine signs or oracles, further underscoring the gods' pervasive influence.

Despite the significance of the pantheon in Greek religion, it is crucial to acknowledge the fluidity and diversity of religious belief in ancient Greece. Not all Greeks may have conceived of the gods in the same manner, nor would they have participated in all forms of worship equally. Additionally, the influence of foreign deities and cults, particularly during the Hellenistic period, introduced further complexities to the religious landscape.

Thus, while the pantheon provides a valuable lens to explore Greek religion, it is just one facet of a much broader and more nuanced religious tradition. The role of the pantheon is not a static or universally agreed-upon concept, but a dynamic and multifaceted phenomenon that continues to be a subject of scholarly interpretation and debate.

Exploration of how the pantheon reflects ancient Greek values and worldview.

The reflection of ancient Greek values and worldview in their pantheon presents a fascinating interplay between theology, philosophy, and culture. The structure, narratives, and dynamics within the pantheon offer profound insights into Greek society's moral, cosmological, and anthropocentric perspectives. It must be noted that Greek society was not monolithic, and thus the reflections of values and worldview in the pantheon can significantly vary based on geographical location, historical period, and social strata.

Values: The pantheon manifests key Greek values such as valor (ἀρετή), wisdom (σοφία), and justice (δίκη), among others. For instance, Athena, the goddess of wisdom, embodied the high regard Greeks held for intelligence and strategic acumen. Her prominent role in the pantheon underscores the value attached to intellectual pursuits in Greek society. Ares, the god of war, symbolizes the Greek admiration for bravery and martial prowess, while Zeus, in his capacity as the king of the gods, often serves as the embodiment of justice and the moral order. The narratives and rites associated with these gods encouraged individuals to imbibe these virtues in their lives.

Cosmology: The pantheon mirrored the Greek cosmological understanding, encompassing the celestial, terrestrial, and subterranean realms. The division of the universe among the sky gods (Zeus and his ilk), the earth gods (like Demeter), and the underworld deities (Hades and Persephone), reflects a hierarchical and structured view of reality. Such a cosmology, laden with personifications of natural elements, also hints at an attempt to make sense of and establish control over the natural world.

Anthropocentrism: The Greek pantheon, with its anthropomorphic deities, showcases an anthropocentric worldview. The gods, despite their immortal and powerful nature, exhibit a plethora of human traits and emotions. This anthropomorphism reflects the Greek tendency to humanize the divine and project their experiences onto the gods. This further allowed for a more relatable and accessible religious experience.

Societal Structure: The pantheon also mirrored the hierarchical societal structure in ancient Greece. Just as Greek society had its rulers, warriors, artisans, and farmers, the gods too had their domains of authority, often reflecting these societal roles. For example, Hephaestus, the god of blacksmiths and craftsmen, resonated with the artisan class of society. Similarly, the supremacy of Zeus in the pantheon parallels the societal respect for rulers and leaders.

Ethos of Struggle and Competition: The pantheon reflects the ethos of struggle and competition prevalent in Greek society. Mythological narratives often highlight gods vying for supremacy, such as the Titanomachy (the battle between the Titans and Olympians) or the Gigantomachy (the battle between the gods and the giants). These narratives, loaded with conflict and resolution, echo the competitive spirit of the Greek polis system and the constant struggle for power and prestige.

However, it is important to note the limitations and pitfalls of viewing the Greek pantheon merely as a reflection of societal norms and values. The pantheon, in its vast complexity and dynamism, is not merely a mirror but an active participant in shaping and influencing these values and worldviews. The pantheon, with its enigmatic gods and riveting narratives, continues to be a rich tapestry that weaves together the threads of divinity, humanity, and the cosmos in ancient Greek thought.

Discussion on the role of the pantheon in religious practices, rites, and festivals.

The ancient Greek pantheon played a central role in guiding the religious practices, rites, and festivals of the society. These practices are distinguished by their breadth and variety, and the role of the pantheon in them was manifold, reflecting the diversity of Greek religious expression.

Worship and Sacrifices: The principal form of religious practice in ancient Greece was the worship of the gods through sacrifices. Each deity in the pantheon received distinct offerings based on their specific domains and preferences. For instance, Zeus, the sky god, was typically offered burnt sacrifices of animals, while Demeter, the goddess of agriculture, was often venerated with offerings of grains and fruits. These sacrificial rites were essential in maintaining a beneficial relationship between humans and gods, wherein mortals offered gifts, and in return, expected divine favour or protection.

Divination and Oracles: Divination was another important religious practice that was intrinsically connected to the pantheon. Apollo, the god of prophecy, was the central figure in these practices. The most famous oracle was at Delphi, where Apollo's priestess, known as the Pythia, would deliver cryptic prophecies to seekers of divine wisdom. These oracles were considered to be the gods' answers to human inquiries, guiding individuals and polities in crucial decisions.

Mysteries: In the realm of mystery cults, certain gods held a significant role, like Demeter and Dionysus. The Eleusinian Mysteries, for instance, were rites dedicated to Demeter and her daughter Persephone, and they offered initiates unique religious experiences and hopes for a blessed afterlife. Dionysian Mysteries, focusing on the god Dionysus, involved ecstatic rituals that transcended the usual boundaries of social order.

Festivals: The Greek religious calendar was punctuated by numerous festivals dedicated to various gods. The city of Athens, for instance, observed the Panathenaia in honour of Athena, their patron goddess. This festival, involving athletic contests, musical competitions, and a grand procession, reflected the multifaceted nature of Athena's worship. Dionysia, honouring Dionysus, involved dramatic performances, revealing the interlinking of the theatrical tradition and religious practice in ancient Greece.

Hero Cults: Beyond the pantheon of gods, the ancient Greeks also venerated heroes, who occupied a liminal space between mortals and immortals. These heroes, like Heracles or Achilles, were often linked with the gods, either by blood or by divine favour. The hero cults incorporated rites of sacrifice, commemorative feasts, and games, which mirrored the practices associated with the gods.

Domestic Worship: It was also common for Greek households to have personal shrines dedicated to gods such as Hestia, goddess of the hearth, and Zeus Ktesios, protector of property. This form of domestic worship demonstrates the pantheon's permeation into everyday life and private sphere.

The inclusion of the pantheon in these religious practices underscores the reciprocal relationship between the divine and mortal spheres in ancient Greece. In the grand narrative of Greek religion, the pantheon served as a spiritual scaffold that helped humans navigate the complexities of existence, societal norms, and their relationship with the cosmos.

For the reader: To further understand the application of these practices, consider the following exercise: "Choose one major god or goddess from the Greek pantheon. Based on their domains and characteristics, devise a hypothetical festival in their honour. Detail the rituals, sacrifices, and other activities that might take place during this festival and explain their relevance to the chosen deity."

Pantheon and Ancient Greek Society

In the ancient Greek world, the pantheon of gods was not merely a spiritual or religious construct; it was intricately woven into the socio-cultural fabric of the society. The influence of the pantheon extended beyond religious rites and observances, permeating daily life, social norms, ethics, and even the political system.

Social and Moral Framework: The gods of the Greek pantheon often served as embodiments of moral and societal values. Athena, goddess of wisdom and warfare, exemplified the ideals of wisdom, courage, and strategic skill, values that were prized in the Athenian polis. Similarly, Artemis, as the goddess of virginity and the hunt, represented purity and self-reliance, values upheld particularly for women in certain societal contexts.

Politics and Governance: Greek political life was intrinsically tied to the pantheon. The gods were believed to confer legitimacy to rulers and political systems. For example, the concept of 'tuchē', or the favour of the gods, was often cited to explain a ruler's ascent to power. Even democratic Athens, often seen as a cradle of rational political thought, maintained the necessity of divine favour in political success.

City-states and Patron Deities: Each Greek polis (city-state) typically identified with a particular deity as its protector or patron. Athens, for instance, revered Athena as their patron, while Corinth was associated with Poseidon. The gods' statues and temples dominated the physical and cultural landscape of these city-states, reflecting the integration of the pantheon into the very identity of these independent entities.

Law and Justice: The pantheon also influenced Greek legal and justice systems. For instance, Zeus was regarded as the protector of social order and laws, while Nemesis, the goddess of retribution, embodied the principle of cause and effect in moral conduct. The concept of 'hubris', or the crime of arrogance against the gods, often featured in legal discourses, underscoring the interplay between divine will and human law.

Literature and Arts: The pantheon's influence extended to the flourishing arts and literature of ancient Greece. From Homer's epic poems to Aeschylus's tragedies, Greek literature abounds with references to the pantheon, exploring their relationships with mortals, their ethical dilemmas, and their elemental forces. In visual arts, too, depictions of gods and goddesses were common, appearing on everything from monumental temple sculptures to everyday pottery.

Education and Philosophy: The myths and stories of the gods served as educational tools, imparting moral lessons and societal norms to the young. Furthermore, philosophical discourse often engaged with theological questions related to the gods, such as the problem of divine justice or the nature of divine power, as seen in the works of Plato and other philosophers.

In summary, the Greek pantheon was deeply integrated into the social and cultural matrix of ancient Greek society, informing and shaping it in profound ways. Understanding this relationship is crucial in comprehending the lived reality of the ancient Greeks and their world.

To stimulate further thinking on this topic, consider the following exercise: "Choose one aspect of ancient Greek society (e.g., law, politics, education). Discuss how the Greek pantheon might have influenced this aspect, citing specific gods and myths where possible. What values or ideas might the pantheon have imparted in this context?"

Examination of the pantheon's influence on social structure and daily life in ancient Greece.

In the civilization of ancient Greece, the influence of the pantheon on social structure and daily life cannot be overstated. The gods and goddesses were not distant entities, relegated to lofty, celestial spheres, but were a constant, palpable presence in the minutiae of everyday existence. This chapter aims to delve into the myriad ways the Greek pantheon influenced and shaped the social structure and everyday life of ancient Greek society.

Household Worship: The Greek pantheon played a significant role in the daily lives of individuals and families. Household worship of gods was common and each family usually had an altar at home dedicated to Zeus Herkeios (Zeus of the Fence), protector of the household, and Hestia, the goddess of the hearth. The hearth itself was considered sacred and was the central place of domestic worship and familial gatherings.

Rituals and Sacrifices: Daily routines were infused with religious rituals and practices. From starting a journey with a prayer to Hermes, the god of travel, to invoking the Muses at the commencement of a poetic recitation, the gods permeated everyday activities. Sacrifices, both grand and modest, were made regularly to the gods, and it was not uncommon for a Greek citizen to participate in several religious ceremonies in a single day.

Births, Marriages, and Deaths: The gods played critical roles during significant life events. Births were overseen by Eileithyia, the goddess of childbirth; weddings involved ritual offerings to Hera, the goddess of marriage; and the journey into the afterlife was associated with Hades, the god of the underworld. These rites of passage were deeply entrenched in the society's fabric, providing cohesion and commonality among its members.

Gender Roles: The pantheon also had implications for gender roles in Greek society. Deities such as Hera and Demeter represented certain aspects of womanhood, while gods like Ares and Apollo were associated with traditional masculine roles. Moreover, certain goddesses like Athena and Artemis, who transgressed conventional gender roles, may have offered a form of subversive potential within a largely patriarchal society.

Social Hierarchy and Slavery: The pantheon justified and upheld the social hierarchy, with Zeus, the king of the gods, mirroring the terrestrial monarch or chieftain. The institution of slavery, an integral part of ancient Greek society, found support in the existence of Hephaestus's mythical automata, and the punishment meted out to Prometheus for challenging the divine order.

Seasons and Agriculture: The pantheon was directly linked to the agricultural cycle, which dictated the rhythm of rural life. Demeter and her daughter Persephone were integral to the changing seasons and the success of crops. Festivals, such as the Thesmophoria, were centered on agricultural cycles and the fertility of the earth.

Commerce and Industry: Even areas such as trade and industry were under the gods' patronage. Athena was not only the goddess of wisdom and warfare but also of weaving and crafts. Hephaestus was the god of blacksmiths and artisans, while Hermes was considered the patron of commerce and financial gain.

In summary, the Greek pantheon's influence seeped into every facet of ancient Greek society, from the personal to the public, and from the mundane to the monumental. The deities provided a structure, a form of order, a means of understanding the world, and a way of relating to it. In the next chapter, we will examine the role of mythology in Greek society.

Here is an exercise to help consolidate the understanding of this topic: "Pick two gods from the Greek pantheon and discuss how their domains could have influenced daily life in a typical ancient Greek household."

Discussion on the connection between gods and cities, professions, and other societal structures.

The Greek pantheon was thoroughly interwoven into the societal fabric of ancient Greece, influencing not only personal lives but also larger societal structures such as cities, professions, and other socio-cultural institutions. This section will elucidate the profound connection between the gods and these structures.

Patron Deities of Cities: Ancient Greek cities typically had a patron deity to whom they owed special allegiance and worship. Athens, for example, was famously dedicated to Athena, the goddess of wisdom, warfare, and crafts. In her honor, the monumental temple known as the Parthenon was built on the Acropolis. Likewise, Corinth was associated with Poseidon, god of the sea and earthquakes, and Olympia with Zeus, the king of the gods. The patron deity's festival often became the city's major holiday, and the deity's symbols frequently appeared on the city's coins and seals.

Gods and Professions: Deities were also linked to various professions. Athena was the patroness of weaving, crafts, and other skilled work, embodying the city-dwelling artisan's ideals. Apollo, the god of music, was revered by musicians and poets. Hephaestus, the god of blacksmiths and metalwork, embodied the spirit of creation and craftsmanship. Hermes, the god of commerce, was revered by merchants. These affiliations provided the professions with a sacred connection and allowed the professionals to seek divine favor for success in their work.

Gods and Military: Ares, the god of war, was invoked by soldiers and generals before battles. Athena, too, was a deity of strategic warfare, while Nike was the personification of victory. In a society where warfare was a significant aspect of statecraft, these gods' reverence reflected the intersection of religious belief and military necessity.

Gods and Societal Institutions: Even societal institutions like marriage and funerary rites had specific deities associated with them. Hera, the queen of the gods, presided over marriage, and Hades, the god of the underworld, oversaw the journey of souls into the afterlife. The Erechtheion, a temple in Athens, was dedicated to both Athena and Poseidon and was associated with mythic kings of the city, thus demonstrating the close connection between the pantheon, royalty, and civic identity.

The intertwining of gods and societal structures served multiple purposes. Firstly, it sanctified these structures, thus granting them a form of legitimacy and divine approval. Secondly, it provided a common religious and cultural framework that fostered social cohesion. Lastly, it contributed to the sense of civic pride and identity, particularly in relation to patron deities of cities.

In summary, the gods of the Greek pantheon were not merely superhuman entities residing in the distant realms of Olympus. They were deeply integrated into Greek society, influencing various facets of life, from personal habits to larger societal structures such as cities and professions.

Exercise for critical thinking: "Choose one Greek god or goddess and explore how the attributes and domains associated with this deity might have shaped the societal structures related to them."

Pantheon in Myth and Literature

Greek mythology and literature offer an extensive, although often contradictory, portrait of the pantheon's complex relationships, power dynamics, and influence over human affairs. An understanding of these sources is vital to grasp the cultural and religious values of ancient Greek society.

The Gods in Myth: The Greek pantheon's myths are a rich tapestry of narratives. They illuminate divine-human interactions, illustrate the gods' domains, and provide moral and philosophical lessons. For example, the myth of Persephone's abduction by Hades explains the cycle of seasons, emphasizing Demeter's association with agriculture and fertility. The Trojan War myth, encapsulated in Homer's Iliad, showcases the gods' involvement in human affairs and their relations with each other.

Epics: Epics, particularly Homer's Iliad and Odyssey, offer detailed portrayals of the gods' personalities and spheres of influence. In the Iliad, the Olympian gods take sides, with Athena supporting the Greeks and Ares the Trojans, reflecting their roles as deities of war. The Odyssey delineates the role of the gods in guiding, assisting, or hindering humans. Here, Poseidon is the divine antagonist, while Athena is the patron and helper, underlining their contrasting domains and attitudes towards humans.

Tragedies: Tragic plays often deal with the interaction between humans and the gods, and their sometimes catastrophic outcomes. For instance, in Sophocles' Oedipus Rex, Apollo's prophecy drives the plot, and the king's attempt to circumvent his fate results in his downfall, illustrating the notion of divine fate and its inescapability.

Hesiod's Theogony: Hesiod's Theogony offers a cosmogonic myth that outlines the genealogy of the gods, tracing their lineage from primordial entities to the Olympians. This narrative serves as a foundational text for understanding the structure of the Greek pantheon.

Homeric Hymns: The Homeric Hymns are a collection of poems praising various gods, providing insight into their specific domains and the veneration they received from ancient Greeks.

Orphic Texts: These texts give alternative versions of myths and provide unique perspectives on the gods, particularly Dionysus, highlighting the diversity of ancient Greek religious thought.

The pantheon's portrayal in myth and literature offers a comprehensive understanding of the gods' nature, their relationships, and their engagement with the world. Moreover, it reflects societal values and conceptions of divinity, destiny, morality, and the cosmos.

Dissenting Opinions: It is worth noting that our understanding of the pantheon through myth and literature can be challenging. These sources were not intended as literal, historical accounts, but as religious, moral, and philosophical narratives. Consequently, they often contain contradictory portrayals of gods and events, reflecting the diverse perspectives of their authors and the societies they originated from. Moreover, as the texts that have survived to the present day represent only a fraction of ancient Greek literature, our perception of the pantheon may be inherently incomplete or skewed.

Exercise for critical thinking: "Select a myth or piece of literature that features an interaction between gods and humans. Analyze how it portrays the gods and reflects ancient Greek values."

Brief overview of the role of the pantheon in ancient Greek myths and literature.

The ancient Greek pantheon served as a powerful narrative force in myths and literature, encapsulating societal norms, belief systems, and existential ponderings within its complex structure. This amalgamation of divine characters, each embodying distinct traits and domains, provided a flexible framework for creative narratives and moral expositions.

Myths typically center around the gods' interactions with each other and humans, illustrating the complexity of divine politics and morality. For instance, in Homer's Iliad, the interplay among the Olympians during the Trojan War provided a cosmic backdrop to human conflict. Similarly, the myth of Pandora, first presented in Hesiod's Works and Days, underlined the themes of transgression, punishment, and hope within the human condition.

Literature, both epic and dramatic, offered a more intricate exploration of the pantheon's influence over mortal life. In the epic tradition, Homer's Odyssey depicted the gods as powerful yet capricious entities shaping Odysseus's perilous journey home. The gods' direct and indirect interventions underscored their domains and human dependence on divine favor.

In the realm of drama, the gods' role is often less tangible but no less impactful. Aeschylus's Prometheus Bound showcased the god Prometheus's punishment for aiding humanity, posing profound questions about justice and authority in the divine and human realms. Sophocles's Antigone hinged on the conflict between divine and royal edicts, underscoring the tension between societal and religious obligations.

Furthermore, lyric poetry, such as the works of Pindar, often referenced the gods to praise human achievement, highlighting the perceived interconnection between divine favor and mortal success. Philosophical texts, like Plato's Dialogues, utilized myths and gods as metaphors to probe the nature of reality, morality, and knowledge.

However, while the pantheon plays a significant role in Greek myths and literature, it's important to remember that these portrayals are not always consistent or literal, reflecting the fluid nature of ancient Greek religious thought.

Counterargument: While the pantheon's presence in literature and myth is undeniable, scholars like Martin P. Nilsson argue that these portrayals often reflect literary traditions and philosophical debates rather than the popular religion practiced by the average ancient Greek. The interpretations of these texts should be nuanced, considering both their artistic and religious dimensions.

Exercise: "Compare the portrayal of a selected god in two different genres of ancient Greek literature (e.g., epic poetry and tragedy). How does each genre present the god and his/her influence on human affairs?"

Analysis of how these narratives contribute to our understanding of the pantheon.

The rich narratives embedded within ancient Greek myths and literature are more than mere storytelling; they serve as essential interpretive lenses, offering profound insights into the understanding of the pantheon. These tales offer us vivid depictions of divine personalities, moral paradigms, societal norms, and intricate cosmologies that illuminate the complex architecture of the pantheon and its function within the Greek worldview.

Firstly, myths and literature give form and substance to the abstract attributes of the gods. For example, in the Iliad, the character of Athena extends beyond her formal designation as the goddess of wisdom and war strategy. The narrative depicts her as fiercely loyal to her chosen, such as Odysseus, and uncompromisingly wrathful to those who defy her, as Paris did. Thus, literary portrayals add dimension to divine characters, highlighting their complexities and contradictions.

Secondly, the narrative interplay between gods and humans is an exploration of morality and ethics. In the tragedy of Sophocles's Oedipus Rex, the prophecy from Apollo sets the tragic fate in motion. This underlines the notion of divine ordination and inevitability of fate, a concept central to the Greek religious thought.

Furthermore, narratives often reveal societal values and expectations through the lens of the divine. In Hesiod's Works and Days, the myth of Pandora offers a commentary on human curiosity, disobedience, and the resulting consequences— reflections of societal norms and values. Similarly, the divine patronage of certain cities in the Iliad, such as Athena's protection of Athens, reflects the real-world social and political affiliations, revealing the intertwining of religion, politics, and social identities.

Lastly, narratives often present the cosmological order and the hierarchical structure within the pantheon. For example, the opening of the Theogony by Hesiod narrates the creation of the cosmos and the genealogy of the gods, placing the Olympians at the apex of the divine order.

Counterargument: Some scholars, such as Walter Burkert, caution that interpreting these narratives too literally can result in misconceptions about the nature of the gods and ancient Greek religion. For instance, the gods' humanlike behavior in myths often serves narrative or allegorical purposes, rather than representing theological doctrines.

Exercise: "Analyze a Greek myth or literary work of your choosing. Discuss how the narrative contributes to your understanding of the role and characteristics of a particular god/goddess within the pantheon."

Summary

This chapter presented a comprehensive introduction to the concept of the Greek Pantheon, tracing its origins and highlighting its significance in ancient Greek religion and culture. The chapter began with an exploration of the word 'pantheon', its etymology, and the broad theoretical framework within which it is employed, underlining its utility as a collective term for the assembly of Greek gods.

Thereafter, the concept of domains and responsibilities among the gods was meticulously scrutinized. The Greek Pantheon was revealed to be an organized system, where each deity presides over specific realms and spheres of influence. These divine jurisdictions, in many instances, echoed the social, political, and natural divisions within the human world, thereby linking the celestial and the terrestrial.

Further, the Pantheon was explored in the context of its pivotal role within the Greek religion. It was emphasized that the Pantheon was not merely a catalogue of divine entities, but a dynamic, interactive complex central to religious practices, rites, and festivals.

Next, the reflection of ancient Greek values and worldview within the Pantheon was analyzed. The divine attributes, conflicts, and alliances within the Pantheon encapsulate the ancient Greek ethos, offering us profound insights into their understanding of honor, justice, and the nature of the universe.

The influence of the Pantheon on social structure and daily life in ancient Greece was also meticulously examined, demonstrating how religion, social organization, and cultural practice were inextricably intertwined in this ancient civilization. This was further extended to a detailed discussion on the connection between gods and cities, professions, and other societal structures.

The chapter concluded with an exploration of the role of the Pantheon within the corpus of ancient Greek myths and literature. It was postulated that these narratives are not only enthralling tales, but also intricate tapestries that portray divine personalities, societal norms, moral paradigms, and cosmological concepts, thereby deepening our comprehension of the Pantheon.

Chapter 1 has laid the foundation for a comprehensive understanding of the Greek Pantheon, its complex structure, and its central role within Greek religion and culture.

As we progress to Chapter 2, titled "The Olympian Gods", we shall delve into an in-depth examination of the twelve main gods of Olympus. We will explore their stories, roles, symbols, and their significance within the fabric of ancient Greek religion. We will journey through the myths and legends, discover their idiosyncrasies, divine attributes, and unearth the layers of meanings encapsulated within their narratives. This next chapter forms the heart of our exploration, shining light on the most significant and influential entities within the Greek Pantheon.

Chapter 2: The Olympian Gods: Comprehensive examination of the twelve main gods of Olympus, their stories, roles, symbols, and their significance in ancient Greek religion.

As we venture further into the heart of ancient Greek religion, we now turn our attention to the most esteemed entities of the pantheon—the Olympian gods. Dwelling atop the mythical Mount Olympus, these divine beings were at the pinnacle of the celestial hierarchy, wielding great power and dominion over various facets of the cosmos and human life.

The term 'Olympian' traces its roots back to Mount Olympus, the highest peak in Greece, and is emblematic of the elevated status of these deities in the ancient Greek belief system. Mount Olympus was perceived as a place of absolute sanctity, and its lofty peaks were believed to breach the celestial sphere, thus serving as a divine residence far removed from the mortal realm. Consequently, 'Olympian gods' denotes not merely a geographical association, but a hierarchical positioning that placed these gods at the zenith of the pantheon.

Twelve is a figure of note within this celestial cadre. Although variations occur in different literary sources and regional traditions, twelve Olympian gods are most commonly acknowledged. This divine dozen consists of Zeus, Hera, Poseidon, Demeter, Athena, Apollo, Artemis, Ares, Aphrodite, Hephaestus, Hermes, and either Dionysus or Hestia. Notably, these deities exhibit a remarkable blend of diversity and unity, embodying various elements of nature and human life while being united by their shared abode and familial ties.

In this chapter, we shall embark upon a comprehensive exploration of these twelve Olympian gods. Each god will be examined from multiple perspectives. We will delve into their individual narratives, drawing upon ancient texts and myths that shape their identities. Furthermore, we will probe their distinct roles and responsibilities within the pantheon and the symbols associated with them. We shall strive to understand not merely who these gods were, but what they represented within the multifaceted tapestry of ancient Greek religion.

Understanding these Olympian gods is paramount to our exploration of Greek religion and culture, for they were not merely figments of mythology, but integral components of societal dynamics. They wielded influence over all facets of life, from the grand workings of the universe to the everyday affairs of individuals. Their stories, symbols, and significance permeated all levels of ancient Greek society, sculpting the spiritual landscape of the time.

As we journey through this chapter, I invite you to view these gods not as isolated entities, but as part of a divine continuum. Each god, with their unique portfolio, contributes to a holistic understanding of the Greek pantheon's influence and reach. As we examine each Olympian, we shall endeavor to appreciate their distinctiveness, as well as their role within the larger divine assembly.

Let us commence this fascinating journey through the annals of the divine, beginning with the highest amongst them all, the omnipotent sky god and the ruler of the Olympians—Zeus.

Definition and description of the term 'Olympian'

To appreciate the significance of the Olympian gods in ancient Greek culture and religion, it is indispensable to grasp the nuances of the term 'Olympian'. The word, deriving from 'Olympus', the highest mountain in Greece, bears connotations that are much more profound than a mere geographical affiliation.

Mount Olympus, reaching an elevation of nearly 3,000 meters, was considered the celestial abode of the gods, its peaks thought to penetrate the ethereal realm, thereby facilitating a junction between the terrestrial and the divine. Thus, the appellation 'Olympian' is laden with symbolism, embodying both the physical elevation and the divine elevation that these gods enjoyed over other entities in the pantheon.

When the term 'Olympian' is employed in reference to a god, it signifies that this god belongs to the supreme echelon of the pantheon, that they reside on Mount Olympus, and are members of the divine council, the convocation of gods that held sway over the cosmos. These gods held jurisdiction over diverse aspects of the universe and human existence and wielded authority that was superior to other celestial beings.

However, it is crucial to recognize that the designation of 'Olympian' is not static or unchanging. Several ancient sources differ in their identification of the twelve Olympians, illustrating that this group was not rigidly defined and was susceptible to regional and temporal variations. For instance, while Dionysus is commonly recognized as an Olympian in many traditions, other sources replace him with Hestia, the goddess of the hearth and home. Therefore, it is critical to approach the term 'Olympian' with a degree of fluidity, appreciating its core implications while acknowledging its variations.

The Olympian gods are an embodiment of the ancient Greeks' attempts to personify and comprehend the diverse and complex facets of existence. Each Olympian was assigned specific realms of influence, embodying abstract concepts, natural phenomena, and human activities. Consequently, the Olympians as a collective represented a comprehensive framework through which the Greeks interpreted and navigated their world.

In sum, the term 'Olympian' refers to a god's high hierarchical standing, divine abode, and role within the divine council. These gods are the focal points of numerous myths, rituals, and artistic depictions, reflecting their central role in the religious and cultural imagination of ancient Greece.

Brief overview of the twelve main gods of Olympus

In ancient Greek religion, the number twelve holds a particular significance, often associated with completeness and unity. The twelve Olympian gods, presided over by Zeus, form the core of the Greek pantheon and exemplify this principle. However, it must be noted that the identity of these deities varies according to different sources and traditions, demonstrating the complexity and richness of Greek mythology. For the purposes of this discussion, the most commonly recognized Olympians shall be considered: Zeus, Hera, Poseidon, Demeter, Athena, Apollo, Artemis, Ares, Aphrodite, Hephaestus, Hermes, and Dionysus.

Zeus: As the king of the gods, Zeus holds dominion over the sky and weather. He is the dispenser of justice and order, an embodiment of the patriarchal authority.

Hera: The queen of the gods and Zeus's wife, Hera is the goddess of marriage, childbirth, and familial bonds. She represents the ideal of matronly virtue and the sanctity of the marital bond.

Poseidon: The god of the sea, earthquakes, and horses, Poseidon's power is as tumultuous as the seas he governs. He exemplifies the might and unpredictability of nature.

Demeter: The goddess of agriculture, grain, and fertility, Demeter personifies the Earth's abundance and the cyclical rhythms of nature.

Athena: The goddess of wisdom, war, and crafts, Athena represents the harmonious blending of intellect and action. She is the patroness of the city of Athens.

Apollo: The god of music, prophecy, and healing, Apollo embodies the ideals of beauty, harmony, and reason.

Artemis: The goddess of the hunt, wilderness, and childbirth, Artemis symbolizes independence, virginity, and the untamed aspects of nature.

Ares: The god of war, Ares personifies the brutal and violent aspects of conflict, contrasting with Athena's strategic aspect of warfare.

Aphrodite: The goddess of love and beauty, Aphrodite embodies physical attraction, romance, and desire.

Hephaestus: The god of fire and metalworking, Hephaestus symbolizes the transformative power of fire and the human capacity for creativity and craft.

Hermes: The messenger of the gods, Hermes is the god of travel, commerce, and communication. He represents the fluidity of boundaries and the power of discourse.

Dionysus: The god of wine, ecstasy, and theater, Dionysus embodies the liberating, intoxicating, and transformative power of the vine.

Together, these twelve gods preside over a vast range of human experiences and natural phenomena, providing the ancient Greeks with a comprehensive lens to interpret and navigate their world. By exploring their myths and significance in Greek religion, one gains insights into the ancient Greeks' perceptions of the universe, their cultural values, and their quest for meaning in the face of life's complexities.

Zeus: King of the Gods

Considered the supreme ruler of the Olympian gods, Zeus held a central and dominant role in the ancient Greek pantheon. Born to the Titans Kronos and Rhea, he emerged victorious from a cosmic power struggle and thereafter established his reign over the cosmos.

Origins and Rise to Power

Zeus's rise to power, as narrated in Hesiod's Theogony, is a tale of intergenerational conflict. The prophecy foretold that Kronos, Zeus's father, would be overthrown by one of his offspring, much as he had dethroned his own father, Ouranos. In an attempt to prevent this, Kronos swallowed each of his children as they were born. However, when Zeus was born, Rhea concealed him and presented Kronos with a swaddled stone, which he swallowed in the belief that it was his son. Zeus, thus saved, later compelled Kronos to regurgitate his siblings, leading to a cataclysmic battle known as the Titanomachy. The victory of Zeus and his allies ended the reign of the Titans and began the age of the Olympian gods.

Symbolism and Representations

Zeus is often depicted holding a lightning bolt, his weapon of choice, symbolizing his control over the skies and weather. His other symbols include the eagle, a creature known for its power and majesty, and the oak tree, representing Zeus's role as a provider of justice and protector of oaths. These symbols embody Zeus's authority, strength, and his function as the upholder of social and cosmic order.

Roles and Associations

As the ruler of the Olympian gods, Zeus presided over numerous domains. His primary realm was the sky and weather, and he was often invoked as a rain-god, nourishing the earth and ensuring agricultural fertility.

Furthermore, Zeus was associated with kingship, law, and social order. He was revered as the protector of hospitality, a crucial aspect of ancient Greek society. As Zeus Xenios, he watched over travelers and ensured that the sacred laws of guest-friendship were upheld. He was also recognized as Zeus Horkios, the keeper of oaths, maintaining the integrity of social and political contracts.

Finally, Zeus's numerous love affairs and liaisons with goddesses and mortal women, resulting in many offspring, symbolize the generative power associated with sky gods in Indo-European traditions. This procreative aspect further underlines his role as the patriarchal figure of the pantheon.

Cult and Worship

Zeus was venerated across the Greek world, with major cult centers at Olympia and Dodona. The Olympic Games, held in his honor every four years at Olympia, were a significant religious event, drawing participants from across the Greek world. At Dodona, in Epirus, an ancient oracle of Zeus provided counsel and predictions, underlining Zeus's role as a dispenser of wisdom.

In summary, Zeus, in his multifaceted roles, governed the physical, moral, and social laws that regulated the Greek world. His narratives and cults offer profound insights into the concepts of power, authority, and order in ancient Greek society.

Biography and mythological narratives

The narrative arc of a deity's life can often provide an interpretative framework for their functions and spheres of influence. For the purposes of this chapter, we shall examine these narratives focusing on their mythic and symbolic aspects.

Creation Narratives

✧   A Universe in Flux: The Birth of the Olympians

Within the Greek cosmogonic narrative, the creation of the Olympian gods represents an important shift from chaos to cosmos—an order. This shift is best embodied in the rise to power of Zeus. The ancient Greeks believed that before the reign of the Olympians, the universe was ruled by the Titans, led by Kronos. It was a time of primal, untamed forces and unregulated might.

The myth recounts that Kronos, warned by his parents Gaia (Earth) and Ouranos (Sky) that he was destined to be overthrown by one of his offspring, swallowed each of his children as soon as they were born. Rhea, Kronos' wife, distraught by the loss of her children, managed to hide the youngest, Zeus, and gave Kronos a stone wrapped in swaddling clothes to swallow instead. When Zeus reached maturity, he freed his siblings from Kronos' stomach and incited a ten-year war known as Titanomachy. The Olympians, led by Zeus, emerged victorious, marking the shift from the primordial rule of the Titans to the structured, ordered rule of the Olympians. This narrative of transition underscores the concepts of power, cunning, and ultimately, order, that are associated with Zeus.

✧   The Birth of Athena: Wisdom Emerges Fully Formed

Another illuminating creation narrative is that of Athena. According to the myth, Zeus, having swallowed the Titaness Metis (Cunning Intelligence) to prevent a prophecy that her child would overthrow him, suffered an unbearable headache. Hephaestus, the blacksmith god, split Zeus's head open with an axe, and Athena emerged fully grown and armed. The unconventional birth of Athena from the head – the seat of wisdom – of Zeus visually reinforces her associations with intellect, strategic warfare, and crafts.

Furthermore, being born fully grown and clad in armor symbolizes Athena's immediate readiness to partake in the responsibilities and conflicts of the Olympian order. This iconography reflects the attributes for which Athena is revered: wisdom, courage, inspiration, civilization, law and justice, strategic warfare, mathematics, strength, strategy, the arts, crafts, and skill.

Such creation narratives serve to provide symbolic insights into the characteristics and roles that each deity would come to embody in the ancient Greek religious understanding. They provide an interpretative lens through which the ancients understood the functions and realms of influence of these divinities. Each narrative, imbued with symbolism and metaphor, sheds light on the inherent nature of the deity it pertains to, offering a rich tapestry of interwoven stories and meanings.

Mythic Narratives

   ✧   Persephone: The Cycle of Seasons

A vibrant part of the Olympian pantheon's biographic repertoire resides within the mythic narratives — the tales of adventures, relationships, and conflicts that unfolded in their divine existences. Such narratives, fraught with drama, served to explain natural phenomena, moral codes, and societal norms. The myth of Persephone, the daughter of Demeter and Zeus, serves as an emblematic instance of such.

Persephone, the goddess of vegetation, was abducted by Hades, the god of the underworld, while she was picking flowers in a meadow. Demeter, the goddess of agriculture and fertility, and Persephone's mother, was stricken with grief and despair, causing all vegetation on Earth to wither and die. The plight of the Earth compelled Zeus to negotiate Persephone's return. However, since Persephone had eaten pomegranate seeds — the food of the underworld — she was bound to spend a part of the year in the underworld with Hades. This corresponds to the barren winter months, during which Demeter mourns Persephone's absence. The rest of the year, when Persephone is with her mother, corresponds to the fertile and productive seasons.

This narrative, while providing a biography of Persephone's dual role as the queen of the underworld and the goddess of vegetation, also offers an ancient Greek explanation for the cyclical pattern of seasons. The tale encodes a natural phenomenon into the life story of a deity, providing a theologically laden understanding of the world.

✧   Zeus and Europa: The Abduction and Its Ramifications

A similarly instructive narrative involves Zeus and the Phoenician princess Europa. Zeus, enchanted by Europa's beauty, transformed himself into a tame white bull and mingled with her father's herds. Europa, intrigued by the gentle and beautiful creature, climbed onto his back. Seizing the opportunity, Zeus, still in his bull form, darted across the sea and carried Europa to Crete.

The mythological abduction of Europa is not merely a tale of divine passion and cunning. It had profound geopolitical implications in ancient Greek mythology. The abduction of Europa led to the establishment of a new lineage of kings on Crete, including Minos, a semi-divine ruler known for his justice and wisdom. Minos, as Zeus's son, often conferred with the king of gods on matters of justice, thus infusing the mortal world with divine wisdom and order.

Furthermore, this narrative plays into the Greek conceptual framework of the barbarian 'other'. By establishing the Phoenician princess Europa as the matriarch of an esteemed Cretan lineage, the Greeks traced a part of their cultural heritage to the Near East, reinforcing a sense of shared history and interconnectedness.

In sum, these mythic narratives, which are intrinsically bound to each deity's character, offer a complex and rich view into the roles, relationships, and attributes associated with the gods. They provide a context to interpret natural phenomena, social order, cultural connections, and the interplay of divine and mortal realms. The deities, through these narratives, are personified and their domains of influence in the mortal world are illustrated.

Relationships and Lineages

In studying the pantheon of the Olympian gods, we observe an intricate tapestry woven from the threads of divine relationships. These associations are not merely a reflection of familial connections, but often denote the spheres of influence, attributes, and roles of the gods in the cosmological order. The relational map of the gods can thus be perceived as a grand metaphor of interconnected powers, duties, and domains that govern the cosmos and human life.

✧   The Hieros Gamos: Zeus and Hera

One of the most renowned divine unions is the marriage of Zeus, the king of the gods, and Hera, the queen of the gods. This marriage, referred to as 'Hieros Gamos' or the sacred marriage, signifies a cosmic union of paramount forces. Zeus, the sky god who wields the thunderbolt, is the emblem of the celestial domain and divine authority. Hera, often associated with the earth, signifies the nurturing, terrestrial sphere, and oversees aspects of fertility, marriage, and childbirth.

Their marital bond exemplifies the union of the heavens (sky) and the earth, integral to the existence and continuity of life. This cosmic matrimony encapsulates the harmony and balance in the universe, underlining the reciprocal influence of sky and earth, male and female, authority and nurture. However, their turbulent marital life, marked by Zeus's numerous extramarital affairs and Hera's vengeful plots, also represents the dynamism and conflicts inherent in the cosmos, further humanizing the gods and making them relatable to their worshippers.

✧　Athena and Hephaestus: Virginity and Craftsmanship

The relationship between gods can also highlight distinct characteristics and virtues. Consider the bond between Athena, the virgin goddess of wisdom, warfare, and craft, and Hephaestus, the divine blacksmith. Though Athena rebuffed Hephaestus's marital advances, the association between them emphasizes their shared domain over arts and craftsmanship.

Athena's virginity, a significant aspect of her identity, is indicative of her independence and the Greek respect for intellectual and moral integrity. Hephaestus, with his craftsmanship, embodies the application of wisdom and strategy (areas Athena governs) into tangible artifacts. Their connection delineates the harmonious coexistence of cerebral ingenuity (Athena) and manual dexterity (Hephaestus) — two indispensable facets of human civilization.

In conclusion, the exploration of divine relationships provides crucial insights into the Olympian gods' roles, attributes, and their interactions with each other and the cosmos. These relationships are metaphorical representations of natural elements, societal virtues, and the various facets of life and culture. They reveal the Greek penchant for personifying and deifying the world around them, thereby creating a pantheon that reflects the complexities of the universe and human existence.

Death and Transition Narratives

In the context of the immortal Olympian deities, the concept of death is inherently absent. However, narratives encapsulating transitions, transformations, and changes in status are a recurring motif in Greek mythology. The mythic tales of apotheosis — the elevation of a mortal to divine status — or the converse, exile or demotion, offer fascinating insights into the dynamics of the divine world and the interplay between mortal and divine realms.

✧ Heracles: The Hero's Apotheosis

One of the most celebrated narratives of apotheosis in ancient Greek mythology is the tale of Heracles, famously known for his Twelve Labours. Born a mortal, albeit as Zeus's son, Heracles was renowned for his exceptional strength and heroic deeds. Upon his death, caused by the treachery of his wife Deianira, he was subjected to a funeral pyre. Yet, instead of descending to Hades like other mortals, Heracles ascended to Mount Olympus in a blaze of fire, signifying his transition from the mortal to the divine.

This transition was not only an acknowledgement of Heracles's heroic feats but also a reflection of his dual heritage, being the son of Zeus. His apotheosis symbolized the potential for mortals to transcend their human limitations, given extraordinary courage, strength, and virtue. Consequently, Heracles came to be revered as the paragon of heroism, valor, and endurance in the face of adversity.

✧ Prometheus: The Exiled Titan

In stark contrast stands the narrative of Prometheus, a Titan renowned for his intellect and for stealing fire from the gods and giving it to humans. In defiance of Zeus's directive, Prometheus's transgression was an act of compassion towards humanity, but it incurred the wrath of Zeus. As punishment, Prometheus was chained to a rock in the Caucasus Mountains, where an eagle, Zeus's emblem, would eat his ever-regenerating liver each day.

Prometheus's tale is one of demotion and exile, signifying the repercussions of defying divine authority. However, his story also presents a nuanced perspective on his punishment. While he was punished for his disobedience, Prometheus was also celebrated as the champion of humanity, the bringer of fire and knowledge, essential elements for the progress of civilization.

Thus, through these transition narratives, Greek mythology provides a complex portrayal of divinity, exploring themes of heroism, rebellion, punishment, and elevation. These stories imbue the gods with multifaceted characters, making them relatable figures to their mortal worshippers, while simultaneously emphasizing the gods' authority and the order of the cosmos.

Roles, responsibilities, and symbols

As we delve into the intricate tapestry of Greek mythology, we find that each deity in the pantheon of Olympian gods is not merely a divine personality but represents an embodiment of various aspects of life, natural phenomena, virtues, vices, and human experiences. The roles, responsibilities, and symbols associated with each god provide a complex system of understanding that reflects the ancient Greeks' worldview, values, and apprehensions.

Roles and Responsibilities

The roles and responsibilities of Zeus, as king of the gods and lord of the sky, encompassed a vast array of spheres within the cosmos, society, and the realm of abstract concepts. As the figurehead of the Olympian pantheon, Zeus exemplifies the archetype of divine kingship, symbolizing authority, order, and power. His multifaceted roles and responsibilities manifest in multiple layers, reflecting his preeminence and universal significance in Greek mythology.

✧   Ruler of the Universe and Weather Phenomena

In his most prominent role, Zeus was recognized as the supreme deity, governing the cosmos and all of its inhabitants. This role is intrinsically linked to his victory over the Titans, after which he was established as the ruler of the gods. His jurisdiction extended not only over his divine counterparts but also over humanity and the natural world, signifying his ultimate sovereignty and omnipotence.

Zeus's connection with weather phenomena, particularly lightning and thunder, was another vital aspect of his divine portfolio. As the lord of the sky, he controlled the weather and wielded the thunderbolt, a symbol of his celestial power and authority. His control over meteorological conditions represents an aspect of his wider cosmic jurisdiction, further enhancing his status as the supreme deity.

✧   Guardian of Justice, Hospitality, and Oaths

On an abstract level, Zeus was intimately connected with the moral and ethical framework of Greek society. He was perceived as the guardian of justice, affirming his role as the ultimate arbiter and keeper of balance. He ensured the enforcement of divine and moral law, particularly vindicating those who were wronged.

Moreover, Zeus was the divine guarantor of hospitality, or xenia, a social code of conduct that played a significant role in ancient Greek society. Xenia governed the relationship between hosts and guests, reinforcing mutual respect and generosity. This association with hospitality underscores Zeus's moral authority and reflects the societal values and norms of the time.

Furthermore, Zeus was regarded as the god of oaths, emphasizing his role as the overseer of societal transactions and agreements. Swearing by Zeus was considered the most binding oath, underlining his status as the upholder of truth and integrity.

✧   Protector and King

Zeus also held a protective role, often invoked as a protector of cities, homes, and individuals. He was seen as a paternal figure, providing safety and blessings to his worshipers. His protective capacity reflects his nurturing aspect, offering a more personal and immediate connection with his devotees.

Additionally, as a symbol of political power, Zeus's image was often used to legitimize earthly kingship. His iconography was a common feature in regal contexts, reinforcing the link between divine and mortal rule.

In essence, the roles and responsibilities of Zeus are emblematic of his expansive and dominant influence in the Greek pantheon. His multifaceted nature, spanning cosmic, societal, and ethical domains, illustrates the comprehensive significance attributed to him in Greek religion and culture.

Symbols

Symbols are integral components of the divine persona in ancient Greek religion. They act as extensions of the deity's character, reflecting their attributes, authority, and associations. For Zeus, his associated symbols - the thunderbolt, the eagle, the bull, the oak tree, and the Aegis - provide insight into his multifaceted role and personality within the pantheon.

✧   Thunderbolt

Perhaps the most recognized symbol of Zeus is the thunderbolt, an emblem of his dominion over the sky, his ruling authority, and his role as the bringer of justice. The thunderbolt epitomizes his control over weather phenomena and emphasizes his potent ability to maintain cosmic order. Its fearsome destructive power signifies Zeus's wrath, highlighting his capacity to mete out divine retribution.

In the visual arts, Zeus is often depicted wielding the thunderbolt, a testament to his celestial authority and his role as the executor of justice. This symbol is also significant in literature, where it frequently serves as a metaphor for divine intervention and power.

✧   Eagle

The eagle, a bird renowned for its majesty and power, is another central symbol of Zeus. This noble creature, soaring high in the sky, embodies the lofty status of Zeus as the supreme ruler of the gods. Its keen eyesight is symbolic of Zeus's all-seeing nature, reinforcing his role as the omniscient overseer of the universe.

In mythology, the eagle often acts as Zeus's messenger or agent, carrying out his commands. In some narratives, Zeus himself takes the form of an eagle, further solidifying the connection between the god and this bird.

✧   Bull and Oak Tree

The bull, another of Zeus's symbols, underscores his virility and strength. In several mythological tales, Zeus assumes the form of a bull, most notably in the abduction of Europa. This association with the bull underscores his masculine fertility and potency.

The oak tree, sacred to Zeus, was considered a symbol of his presence. The ancient oracle of Zeus at Dodona was famed for its sacred oak, and votive offerings were often hung from the branches of oak trees. The enduring and mighty oak tree represents Zeus's enduring authority and strength.

✧   Aegis

The Aegis, the shield often associated with both Zeus and Athena, symbolizes protection and power. This divine piece of armor was thought to instill fear in the hearts of enemies, thereby serving as a symbol of divine authority and protective power.

In conclusion, the symbols associated with Zeus—each bearing its own layers of meaning—further elucidate his roles, authority, and influence. They offer an enriched understanding of this paramount figure, providing a lens through which to explore his multifaceted character and the breadth of his divine dominion.

The Interplay of Roles and Symbols

It is noteworthy that the roles and symbols of the gods often intersect, providing a multilayered understanding of the deities' characters and functions. For instance, Apollo, the god of the sun, is also associated with music, poetry, and healing. His symbols include the lyre, a musical instrument, and the laurel tree, associated with victory and honor, reflecting his various roles.

The deities' intricate web of roles, responsibilities, and symbols provides an invaluable insight into the ancient Greeks' understanding of the world, human nature, societal norms, and the divine. By examining these attributes, we can comprehend the essential functions of the gods within the Greek pantheon, enriching our understanding of their mythology and culture. These multi-dimensional divine figures reveal a worldview where the divine and mortal realms intertwine, where the gods reflect human traits and experiences, and where every aspect of life and nature holds divine significance.

Zeus in ancient Greek religion

Zeus held an overarching position in ancient Greek religion, embodying not just the sovereign of the Olympian gods but also the upholder of divine and moral law, a figure revered and petitioned by the mortals.

Worship and Rituals

The veneration of Zeus took many forms, reflecting his multifaceted persona. Temples dedicated to Zeus were prevalent across Greece, with the most prominent one being the Temple of Zeus at Olympia. In addition to serving as places of worship, these temples were also sites of communal interaction and societal cohesion, anchoring the social, political, and religious lives of ancient Greek communities.

One of the primary forms of worship was sacrifice, typically involving the killing of an animal (most commonly a bull), which was then offered to the deity. These rituals, often performed at altars in or near the temples, were an integral part of religious festivals, personal supplication, and communal gatherings. The grandeur of these sacrificial rites, particularly during state festivals, underscored the high status of Zeus within the pantheon.

Zeus was also the focal point of the Olympic Games, a major event held every four years in Olympia. Athletes from different Greek city-states competed in various sporting events to honor Zeus, reinforcing his stature as a panhellenic deity.

Cults of Zeus

Zeus's cults were numerous and diverse, reflecting his wide-ranging associations. For instance, Zeus Xenios was venerated as the patron of hospitality and protector of strangers, upholding the sacred rules of guest-friendship (xenia). Zeus Horkios was invoked as the keeper of oaths, emphasizing the importance of truth-telling and the maintenance of social and legal contracts.

In a more localized context, Zeus was often syncretized with local deities and worshipped under various epithets. These local cults of Zeus, although fundamentally connected to the larger panhellenic tradition, often highlighted specific aspects of his divine persona, responding to regional needs and cultural landscapes.

The Theophany of Zeus

The theophany of Zeus, or his manifestation to mortals, is a recurring theme in Greek mythology and religion. Whether through the symbolism of the thunderbolt and the accompanying thunder, the appearance of an eagle, or even transformation into a bull, Zeus made his presence known in both subtle and overt ways. Such divine appearances underscored his pervasive influence and further confirmed his status as the paramount deity.

In summary, the central role of Zeus in ancient Greek religion cannot be overstated. He was deeply entwined in the religious consciousness of the ancient Greeks, impacting every sphere of their lives - from personal morality to communal solidarity, from the upholding of sacred laws to the interpretation of divine signs.

Hera: Goddess of Marriage and Birth

One cannot delve into the study of the Olympian gods without considering the prominent figure of Hera, the queen of the gods and the wife of Zeus. Hera's role in ancient Greek mythology and religion transcends the traditional domestic sphere, extending to realms of power, hierarchy, and cosmic balance. Her aspects as the patron of marriage, childbirth, and kingship speak to her pervasive influence in both private and public domains of Greek life.

Biography and Mythological Narratives

Hera is the daughter of the Titans Rhea and Kronos, making her a sibling of Zeus. In the mythic narrative, Zeus pursued Hera ardently, and their courtship culminated in a secret marriage. Despite the frequent marital conflicts narrated in mythology, primarily due to Zeus's numerous extramarital affairs, the divine couple represented the sanctity and the challenges of the marriage bond.

Many myths surrounding Hera emphasize her vengeful nature against Zeus's lovers and illegitimate children. One notable example is her relentless persecution of

Heracles (Hercules in Roman mythology), Zeus's son by a mortal woman. Yet, this narrative may be seen not simply as a testament to her jealousy but also as an assertion of her authority and a protest against marital infidelity.

Roles and Responsibilities

As the goddess of marriage, Hera was the divine embodiment of the wife and the protector of married women. She presided over the rites of marriage, symbolizing the social and religious sanctity of the union. Her role extended to the realm of childbirth, offering divine aid to women during labor.

Beyond these personal and domestic domains, Hera was also recognized as the queen of the gods and a patroness of royalty, reinforcing social hierarchies and the institution of kingship. She represented the power behind the throne, emphasizing the crucial role of the queen in maintaining the balance of power and ensuring the legitimacy of succession.

Symbols

Just as Zeus is associated with the thunderbolt, Hera too has her distinctive symbols that highlight her divine attributes. The peacock, with its resplendent beauty, is often associated with Hera, representing her majesty and her role as the queen of the gods. The pomegranate, a symbol of fertility and marriage, is another emblem frequently linked to Hera.

Hera in Ancient Greek Religion

Hera's worship was widespread throughout ancient Greece. The primary center for her veneration was the city of Argos, which held the Heraia, a festival and athletic competition dedicated to Hera, paralleling the Olympic Games dedicated to Zeus.

Her temples, most notably the Heraion of Argos and the Heraion of Samos, were not just religious centers but also served as important socio-political spaces. The celebration of Hera's sacred marriage to Zeus, known as hieros gamos, was a significant event often enacted in her cult practices, symbolically reasserting social and cosmic order.

In conclusion, Hera's intricate and multifaceted divine persona serves as an insightful reflection of the complexities of marital relations, social hierarchies, and power dynamics in ancient Greece. Through a comprehensive study of Hera, we can gain a deeper understanding of Greek societal structures and the interplay between the divine and the human in shaping those structures.

Biography and mythological narratives

Exploring the biography and mythological narratives of Hera provides an indispensable understanding of the ideological structures of ancient Greek society, especially regarding marriage, hierarchy, and the feminine divine.

Creation Narrative

Hera, like her Olympian siblings, hails from the lineage of the Titans — the second generation of divine beings, preceded by the primordial deities, in the cosmogonic schema of ancient Greece. Her parents, Kronos and Rhea, were among the leading figures of the Titans. This generation came to an abrupt end when Kronos, prompted by a prophecy that he would be overthrown by one of his children, swallowed each of them whole at their birth.

This egregious act of cannibalism, however, was subverted by Rhea when Hera's younger brother Zeus was born. Through an elaborate ruse, Rhea tricked Kronos into swallowing a stone wrapped in swaddling clothes, thus sparing Zeus. Zeus was clandestinely whisked away to the island of Crete, where he grew to maturity under the protection and guidance of the nymphs Adrasteia and Ida, the divine goat Amalthea, and the warrior-like Kouretes.

On reaching adulthood, Zeus confronted Kronos and coerced him into disgorging the children he had swallowed. Thus, Hera, along with her siblings Poseidon, Hades, Hestia, and Demeter, were 'reborn', marking the genesis of the Olympian pantheon. Unlike her brother Zeus, who is frequently associated with storms, or her sister Athena, who was famously born from Zeus's forehead fully armed, Hera's birth and subsequent 'rebirth' are devoid of natural phenomena or extraordinary circumstances. This relative modesty of Hera's birth narrative arguably reflects her future role as the goddess of marriage and social institutions, which require stability and predictability, unlike the constantly changing weather or the chaos of war.

The exploration of Hera's creation narrative not only contributes to the rich tapestry of Greek mythology but also provides a metaphorical view of the sociocultural norms of ancient Greek society. It encapsulates the importance of familial relationships and societal roles among the deities, reflecting similar values in the human world. In the next sections, we will delve deeper into the different mythic narratives and roles associated with Hera.

Mythic Narratives

Hera's myths frequently intersect with those of her husband, Zeus, revealing the interplay of power, fidelity, and retribution that characterizes their relationship. As the goddess of marriage, Hera's stories primarily focus on her marriage to Zeus, an embodiment of the ideal social institution. Yet, their relationship is fraught with Zeus's numerous infidelities, casting Hera in the role of the jealous wife. This jealousy, however, should not be trivialized or dismissed as petty. Rather, it is representative of Hera's fierce commitment to the sanctity of her marital bond, a value she enforces as the goddess of marriage.

One of the most compelling examples of Hera's pursuit of retribution is her persecution of Heracles, the son of Zeus and the mortal woman Alcmene. Heracles, whose name ironically means "glory of Hera," was the target of Hera's wrath from the moment of his birth. She sent two serpents to kill him in his cradle, but the infant Heracles strangled them, demonstrating his extraordinary strength. Later, in Heracles' adult life, Hera induced a madness in him that led to the murder of his wife and children, resulting in the hero's twelve labors as penance. This relentless hostility towards Heracles exemplifies Hera's vengeful response to Zeus's infidelity.

Hera's involvement in the Trojan War offers another dimension to her mythic biography. Slighted by Paris in the Judgment of Paris, who awarded the golden apple to Aphrodite as "the fairest" over Hera and Athena, Hera held a deep grudge against the Trojans. She, along with Athena, consistently supported the Greek side during the Trojan War, often intervening in battles to assist the Greek heroes. The Iliad vividly illustrates her active role in the war, including an instance when she seduced Zeus to distract him and allow Poseidon to aid the Greeks in battle.

These stories emphasize Hera's role as a deity who upholds societal norms and institutions, yet is not averse to engaging in manipulation and vengeance when these norms are violated. This aspect of her character resonates with the cultural expectations of the ancient Greeks, who viewed the gods as enforcers of societal and moral order but also as beings whose actions frequently paralleled human flaws and desires. In the following section, we will explore the relationships, roles, and responsibilities of Hera, further illuminating her intricate character and significant influence in the divine and mortal realms.

Death and Transition Narratives

In the realm of the immortal, traditional narratives of death are inherently absent. Nevertheless, tales of transition, punishment, and rebirth are common among the ancient Greek pantheon, and Hera is no exception to this rule. While she never experiences a corporeal death, she does encounter moments of intense hardship, often in the form of punishment meted out by Zeus, her husband and the king of the gods.

The most notable of these incidents occurs when Hera, in collusion with Poseidon and Athena, attempts to rebel against Zeus. Discontented with Zeus's autocratic rule, the trio of deities sought to bind Zeus and thus assert their own power. The plot, however, was foiled, and Zeus's retribution was swift and severe. Hera, the primary instigator of the plan, was suspended from the cosmos with golden chains, left to dangle between heaven and earth as a warning to others who might consider a similar course of action.

This story marks a significant transition point for Hera. On the one hand, it underscores her ambition and desire for shared governance among the gods, even in the face of possible retribution. On the other hand, it highlights her subjugation and the uncompromising nature of Zeus's sovereignty.

Another narrative of interest is the temporary ousting of Hephaestus, Hera's son, from Mount Olympus. In one version of the myth, Hera, repulsed by Hephaestus's physical deformity, throws him off Olympus. In another, it is Zeus who hurls Hephaestus down in retaliation for the latter's attempt to intervene in a quarrel between Zeus and Hera. In both versions, Hephaestus eventually returns to Olympus, signifying a reconciliation or, at the very least, an acceptance of his place in the divine realm. This narrative, while not directly involving Hera's transition, underscores the themes of conflict, reconciliation, and the constant flux of power dynamics within the divine family.

The exploration of Hera's death and transition narratives provides a fascinating insight into the power dynamics, conflicts, and reconciliations of the Olympian gods. These narratives, while involving divine beings, mirror the struggles, aspirations, and compromises that are part of human societal structures. Such stories serve as a reminder of the complexities of the ancient Greek divine world, where the gods, despite their immortality and supreme powers, bear characteristics profoundly influenced by human society and its values.

Roles, responsibilities, and symbols

The Multifaceted Roles of Hera

As in any complex societal structure, the ancient Greek pantheon was not without its hierarchies and divisions of labour. The goddess Hera, in particular, stands as an emblem of the essential roles that women were believed to play, both in the divine realm and in human society. As the wife of Zeus, she is bestowed with the title of the queen of the gods, underscoring the status she enjoyed within the divine hierarchy. However, her roles extend far beyond her marital association.

Firstly, Hera is universally recognized as the goddess of marriage. She personifies the sanctity and the binding nature of the marital bond. The sacredness Hera assigns to the institution of marriage is evident in the mythology surrounding her relationship with Zeus, where she is frequently portrayed as being deeply affected by Zeus's numerous infidelities, often seeking to punish his illicit lovers and their offspring. This role of Hera illuminates the societal norms and expectations attached to the institution of marriage in ancient Greece, where fidelity and commitment were profoundly valued.

In addition to being the goddess of marriage, Hera also presides over childbirth and, more broadly, the realm of women's fertility. She is often invoked as the protector of women in labour, reflecting the inherent risks associated with childbirth in ancient times and the consequent necessity for divine protection. This role places Hera as a central figure in the critical phases of a woman's life—marriage and childbirth—highlighting the societal importance of these life stages.

Symbols and their Significance

Symbols, as visual or contextual representations of divine attributes, played an indispensable role in ancient Greek religious practices. They facilitated the connection between the divine and the mortal, acting as metaphors that encapsulated the characteristics and spheres of influence of the gods.

Hera's symbolic representation is no exception to this. The peacock, with its grandeur and beauty, is perhaps the most widely recognized symbol associated with Hera. The bird's resplendent display aligns with Hera's status as the queen of the gods, and its protective nature over its young resonates with Hera's role as the protector of women and childbirth.

Another symbol associated with Hera is the pomegranate, a fruit often linked with fertility and marriage rites in the ancient world. The pomegranate, with its numerous seeds, symbolizes abundance and fertility, thus reflecting Hera's association with marriage and childbirth.

Furthermore, Hera is often depicted holding a scepter or a staff, the symbols of her royal status and her authority within the divine hierarchy. The presence of these symbols in depictions of Hera is a testament to her power and influence as the queen of the gods.

The exploration of Hera's roles, responsibilities, and symbols presents an intriguing insight into the societal structures, norms, and values of ancient Greece. These roles and symbols offer an interpretive framework for understanding the status of women, the sanctity of marriage, and the perilous nature of childbirth within that historical context. This exploration also underscores the dynamic nature of mythology, where the divine and the mortal realms continually interact and reflect upon each other.

Hera in ancient Greek religion

Cults and Worship of Hera

The role of Hera in ancient Greek religion extends beyond her mythological narratives, transcending into the domain of religious practices and rituals. As the queen of the gods and the patroness of marriage, childbirth, and women, Hera occupied a central place in Greek religious life. Her worship was widespread across the Greek world, with several important cults dedicated to her.

In Argos, Hera was venerated as Hera Argeia, the preeminent deity of the city. The Heraion of Argos, one of the oldest sanctuaries in Greece, dedicated to her, bears testimony to her significance in this region. Hera's annual festival, the Heraia, marked by a procession and sacrifices, was a major event in the religious calendar of Argos.

On the island of Samos, the Heraion of Samos, another prominent sanctuary, was built in her honor. It is significant that both these sanctuaries predate the establishment of the cult of Zeus, underscoring the antiquity and importance of Hera's worship.

In Athens, while Zeus enjoyed a more prominent position, Hera was revered as the protector of women, and rituals associated with marriage often invoked her presence and blessings.

Hera and the Social Order

Hera's religious significance is closely tied to her roles within the social order. As the goddess of marriage, she legitimized the social institution that formed the cornerstone of Greek society. Marriage was not merely a personal affair but held wider societal implications—it established political alliances, ensured the lawful transfer of property, and maintained the purity of the citizen body. Therefore, Hera's oversight of this realm was integral to the preservation of social order.

Similarly, her role as the protector of childbirth underscores the perilous nature of childbirth in antiquity and the importance of divine intervention for a successful delivery. Given that the survival and continuity of the family and the city-state rested heavily on childbirth, Hera's role was again central to the societal structure.

Iconography and Representations

The representations of Hera in Greek art and iconography further accentuate her roles and attributes. She is often depicted as a mature, stately woman, veiled to denote her marital status, and frequently accompanied by symbols like the peacock or the pomegranate, signifying her association with royalty, marriage, and fertility. These visual representations served to reinforce her attributes and her cult, aiding devotees in their religious practices.

The influence of Hera in ancient Greek religion is far-reaching, extending across various aspects of life—social, religious, and personal. The veneration of Hera underscored the value the ancient Greeks placed on marriage, women, childbirth, and familial continuity, reflecting their societal norms, beliefs, and structures. At the same time, it illuminated the complex and nuanced character of the divine in the Greek religious imagination, where gods were deeply entwined with the mortal realm.

Poseidon: God of the Sea

Biography and Mythological Narratives

✧   Poseidon: Son of the Titans

Poseidon, one of the primary deities of the Olympian pantheon, was a son of the Titans Kronos and Rhea. His father, Kronos, fearful of a prophecy that stated he would be overthrown by one of his own children, swallowed each of them as they were born. However, when Zeus was born, Rhea tricked Kronos by offering him a stone swaddled in clothes, which he swallowed believing it to be his son. Zeus would later force Kronos to regurgitate his siblings, including Poseidon, who then sided with Zeus in the great battle against the Titans, known as the Titanomachy. Their victory marked the ascendancy of the Olympians as the new pantheon of gods.

✧   Poseidon: Ruler of the Sea and Earth-Shaker

Poseidon's domain extended beyond the sea to encompass earthquakes and horses, earning him titles such as the Earth-Shaker and Tamer of Horses. As the

Earth-Shaker, Poseidon wielded the formidable power of the earth. He could induce tremors in the earth, reflecting the violent shaking of the sea during a storm. Earthquakes, quite common in the Mediterranean region, were thought to be caused by his anger or displeasure, a testament to his control over the forces of nature.

✧   Poseidon and Athena: The Contest for Athens

A significant myth involving Poseidon revolves around his rivalry with Athena, the goddess of wisdom, for the patronage of the city that would become Athens. Both deities presented the city with a gift: Poseidon struck his trident into the ground, creating a spring of salty water, signifying naval power. Athena, on the other hand, offered an olive tree, symbolizing peace and prosperity. The citizens, deciding in Athena's favor, named the city after her. This story not only emphasizes Poseidon's competitive spirit but also underscores his connection with maritime power and water.

✧   Poseidon: Creator of Horses

In his attempts to woo Demeter, the goddess of the harvest, Poseidon created the first horse, displaying his inventive faculties. He was henceforth associated with these majestic creatures, with his control extending to horse breeding and chariot racing. This association further cements his connection with elements of nobility and power, as horses were seen as symbols of status and wealth.

In conclusion, Poseidon's narratives offer a multi-faceted view of his character, from his inventiveness and association with nature's raw power to his volatile temperament, reflecting the sea's unpredictability. Through these stories, we see the Greeks' attempts to understand and explain their world—a world where the sea played a crucial role, horses symbolized wealth and status, and earthquakes were potent signs of divine displeasure.

Roles and Responsibilities

✧   Poseidon: Master of the Seas

Given his dominion over the seas, Poseidon wielded enormous influence over the lives of the ancient Greeks, a civilization intimately tied to the sea. Their economy, military strength, and cultural exchange were all largely dependent on sea voyages, making Poseidon a critical deity to propitiate. Sailors sought his favor for safe travels, and offerings were made to him in hopes of calm seas. Fisherfolk, too, would pray to Poseidon for abundant catches, affirming their livelihoods.

✧   Poseidon: The Earth-Shaker

Poseidon's realm was not limited to the seas. Known also as the Earth-Shaker, he wielded the power to cause earthquakes. The seismic activity in the region made earthquakes a significant and recurrent event in the lives of the ancient Greeks. Thus, Poseidon was propitiated with rituals and sacrifices, particularly in areas prone to seismic disturbances, to prevent his wrath from causing destruction. The magnitude of his power and the fear it incited underscore his importance in Greek religious life.

✧   Poseidon: The Tamer of Horses

An aspect of Poseidon that is not as widely known as his control over the seas is his connection with horses. In fact, one of his epithets was Hippios, or "of horses." Horse breeding was a prestigious activity in ancient Greek society, and chariot racing was a significant event at religious festivals, including the Olympic Games. Poseidon's association with these creatures and activities linked him with elements of nobility, strength, and wealth.

In summary, Poseidon's roles and responsibilities, spanning the seas, the earth, and horses, highlight the diverse nature of his influence and power. This diversity is reflective of the multiplicity of elements in nature and society that the ancient Greeks revered and feared. Whether as a seafaring deity, a powerful earth-shaker, or a noble tamer of horses, Poseidon held a multifaceted and influential role in ancient Greek religion and life.

Symbols

The symbolic representation of deities is a significant aspect of ancient Greek religion, and Poseidon is no exception. His symbols not only emphasize his divine roles and responsibilities but also serve as iconic identifiers in art and literature.

Trident

The most identifiable symbol associated with Poseidon is undoubtedly his trident. This three-pronged spear is not just a weapon, but a symbolic representation of his dominion over the sea. In Greek art and mythology, Poseidon is often depicted wielding this powerful tool to command the sea, stir up storms, cause earthquakes, and create springs of water.

Fish and Dolphin

Given Poseidon's jurisdiction over the oceans, it is unsurprising that marine creatures, such as fish and dolphins, serve as his symbols. These creatures underscore his command over the sea and its inhabitants, illustrating the depth and breadth of his influence. The inclusion of these symbols in various artistic and literary works reinforce the ancient Greeks' recognition of Poseidon's role as the master of the sea.

Horse

Interestingly, another of Poseidon's symbols is the horse. This connection originates from the myth where Poseidon, in an attempt to woo Demeter, created the first horse. This story not only demonstrates Poseidon's creative power but also symbolizes his status as the divine patron of horse breeding and chariot racing. As such, the horse becomes a symbol of Poseidon's influence over these esteemed activities in Greek society.

In summary, the symbols associated with Poseidon - the trident, fish, dolphin, and horse - serve to articulate his multifaceted roles and influence, spanning the sea, the earth, and the realms of horse breeding and chariot racing. These symbols, whether in art, literature, or religious rituals, provide a powerful visual and symbolic language through which the ancient Greeks understood and revered the complex nature of Poseidon.

Poseidon in Ancient Greek Religion

The cult of Poseidon was widely spread across the Greek world. His major sanctuaries include the Isthmus of Corinth, Onchestus in Boeotia, and Helike in Achaea. These temples served as centers for his worship and the celebration of various festivals and games, often involving horse and chariot races, in his honor.

As a deity, Poseidon encapsulates the ancient Greeks' reverence and fear of the sea and its unpredictable might. His volatile character, capable of both generosity and wrath, reflects the dual nature of the sea—as a source of sustenance, adventure, and wealth, but also as a site of danger, destruction, and death. Understanding Poseidon and his myriad roles and representations offers profound insights into the Greek perception of the natural world and their attempts to negotiate their existence within it.

Demeter: Goddess of the Harvest

In the pantheon of ancient Greek deities, Demeter, the goddess of the harvest, held a significant place due to her association with agricultural bounty and the life-giving aspect of nature. Her overarching dominion over fertility and the harvest rendered her an essential figure in a society where agriculture formed the backbone of sustenance and economic activity.

Biography and Mythological Narratives

The biography of Demeter is a compelling narrative that aligns with her vital role as the goddess of agriculture and the cycles of life. As the offspring of the Titans Kronos and Rhea, she shares her lineage with other key Olympian deities, including Zeus, Poseidon, Hades, Hera, and Hestia. The meaning of her name, often interpreted as "Earth-Mother", underscores her profound connection with the earth and its bounty, situating her as a maternal figure who nurtures the soil and promotes the growth of crops.

One of the most pivotal narratives in Demeter's mythic corpus revolves around the abduction of her daughter Persephone by Hades, the god of the underworld. This narrative, often referred to as the "Homeric Hymn to Demeter", provides an explanation for the cyclical pattern of the seasons.

According to the myth, Hades, captivated by Persephone's beauty, kidnaps her and takes her to his realm in the underworld. The loss of her daughter sends Demeter into a state of profound grief and despair. She roams the earth in search of Persephone, neglecting her divine responsibilities in the process. As a result, the earth becomes barren, and a harsh, unyielding winter sets in, representing a period of death and stagnation.

Zeus, alarmed by the earth's desolation, intervenes and orders Hades to release Persephone. However, before leaving the underworld, Persephone consumes a few seeds of a pomegranate given by Hades, binding her to return to the underworld for a portion of each year. In the ancient Greek world, this myth served to explain the seasonal cycle. When Persephone rejoins her mother on the surface, Demeter's joy restores her divine powers, bringing about spring and the fruitful summer. However, Persephone's periodic return to Hades plunges Demeter back into sorrow, leading to the barrenness of autumn and winter.

This narrative underscores the intricate relationship between the divine and natural worlds in Greek mythology, highlighting the Greeks' understanding of natural phenomena through mythic narratives. Moreover, the Persephone myth provides an emotive portrayal of a mother's love and its powerful influence, a theme which resonates universally across time and cultures.

Roles and Responsibilities

In her role as the goddess of the harvest, Demeter occupied a central place in ancient Greek religion and life. She was perceived as the divine overseer of the earth's abundance, presiding over all facets of agriculture. This encompassed not only the planting and harvesting of crops, but also the cultivation of fruit trees, vineyards, and the keeping of bees for honey, showcasing the breadth of her influence over agrarian life. As the bestower of grains, she was the provider of the primary sustenance for both humans and livestock, positioning her as a life-giving figure.

However, the remit of Demeter's responsibilities extends beyond the sphere of agriculture and food production. She was also associated with the sanctity of marriage and the social institution of the family. Just as she nurtures the earth to yield its produce, she was seen to preside over the fertility and prosperity of the family unit. This made her an integral part of marriage rituals and ceremonies, reinforcing the societal norms of ancient Greek society.

Additionally, Demeter had a role in upholding the sacred law and the established order of things. She was often invoked in legal contexts, signifying her role as a protector of rights and justice. This connection between Demeter and law is manifest in the Thesmophoria, a festival held in her honor. The festival's name derives from thesmoi, which denotes laws or customs, suggesting that Demeter's worship was closely linked to social and legal order.

Furthermore, Demeter's involvement in the cycle of life and death — evident in the Persephone myth — imbued her with a significant role in the Greek understanding of mortality and the afterlife. Her alternating states of joy and sorrow, corresponding to the changing seasons, mirrored the human experience of life's ebb and flow.

These manifold responsibilities of Demeter were not confined to the literal germination and reaping of crops; rather, they encapsulated the broader notions of fertility, prosperity, and the cyclical nature of existence. Thus, Demeter's favor was sought not merely for fruitful harvests, but also for human fertility, economic prosperity, societal harmony, and the equilibrium of the natural world. In this way, the goddess Demeter permeated various facets of Greek life, from the everyday sustenance to family, societal order, and existential concepts of life and death.

Symbols

Demeter's iconographic representations and associated symbols underscore her deep-rooted ties with the earth, fertility, and the nourishing bounty of the harvest. Let us take a closer look at these symbols to understand the nuances they bring to our understanding of the goddess.

Scepter: The scepter, a common attribute of royalty and divinity, symbolizes Demeter's authority and her role as an Olympian goddess. When depicted in her hand, it reasserts her power and control over the earth's fertility and the cycle of seasons.

Torches: Demeter is often seen bearing a pair of torches, a symbol that has its roots in the myth of Persephone's abduction. In the narrative, Demeter is said to have used the light of torches in her relentless search for her lost daughter. The torches, therefore, symbolize her unwavering determination, her maternal devotion, and the enduring hope that eventually leads to Persephone's partial return to the world above.

Cornucopia: The cornucopia, or the "horn of plenty," is perhaps one of the most fitting symbols for Demeter. Often depicted as a large horn overflowing with fruits, grains, and other harvest produce, the cornucopia represents the abundant gifts of the earth. As such, it is a potent emblem of Demeter's role in ensuring agricultural abundance and nourishment.

Wheat Ears: Wheat ears are another recurring symbol associated with Demeter. Given that wheat was a primary food source in ancient Greece, its symbolic connection with the goddess reaffirms her crucial role in sustaining life. Wheat ears can often be seen in artistic representations of Demeter, further solidifying her identity as the life-giving goddess of agriculture.

Poppies: Poppies, while perhaps less immediately associated with sustenance, carry rich symbolic value. Commonly grown alongside barley, another staple grain, poppies are emblematic of both the beauty of growth and the cyclical nature of life and death – themes that align with Demeter's mythic narratives. In some interpretations, poppies are also linked to sleep and rest, possibly alluding to the dormant phase of the earth during winter, while Persephone resides in the underworld.

These symbols, whether wielded by or associated with Demeter, offer a richer, multifaceted understanding of the goddess. Each enhances our perception of her, illuminating her nurturing essence, her authority, and her integral role in the rhythms of natural and human life.

Demeter in Ancient Greek Religion

Demeter's importance in ancient Greek religion is reflected in the numerous festivals held in her honor, the most famous being the Eleusinian Mysteries. This annual festival was one of the most important religious events in ancient Greece. It centered around the myth of Persephone's abduction and return, signifying the cyclical nature of life and death, and by extension, the agricultural seasons. The mysteries held at Eleusis were enveloped in secrecy, but it is believed that they provided the initiated with hope for a blessed afterlife, highlighting Demeter's overarching control over life's cyclicity.

The cult of Demeter and Persephone had widespread influence, with its reach extending beyond Eleusis to multiple parts of the Greek world. Devotees worshipped Demeter as the bringer of seasons, and the rites performed in her honor were believed to ensure her favor and, consequently, a prosperous harvest.

In summary, the study of Demeter provides profound insights into the ancient Greek understanding of nature's cyclicity, agricultural practices, and notions of life, death, and afterlife. Through the worship and celebration of this goddess of the harvest, the ancients showcased their deep-rooted reliance on the land and their gratitude for the natural world's cyclical renewal and abundance.

Athena: Goddess of Wisdom

Athena, recognized as one of the most influential figures within the Greek pantheon, holds various epithets reflecting her many domains and characteristics. Born fully armored from the forehead of Zeus, she is the embodiment of wisdom, courage, inspiration, civilization, law, justice, strategic warfare, mathematics, strength, strategy, the arts, and skill. This wide-ranging scope of influence warrants a comprehensive exploration of Athena's complex character and her multifaceted role in ancient Greek religion and mythology.

Biography and Mythological Narratives

Athena's extraordinary birth mythology distinguishes her from her Olympian brethren, imbuing her with unique characteristics and associations. As per the narratives, Zeus, the king of gods, swallowed his first wife Metis, the goddess of wisdom and craft, when he learned that their offspring would eventually dethrone him. However, Metis was already pregnant with Athena. In due course, Zeus was seized with an excruciating headache, leading to Hephaestus splitting open his forehead with an axe, from which Athena emerged, fully grown, armored, and ready for battle. This remarkable birth story has been subject to manifold interpretations throughout history, and has been theorized to symbolize various attributes associated with the goddess.

One of the prevalent interpretations is that Athena, born directly from Zeus's head, signifies a mind's intellectual progeny. As the daughter of Metis (Wisdom) and Zeus (King of the Gods), Athena embodies divine wisdom and strategic warfare. Her emergence, fully grown and armored, signifies wisdom's immediate, decisive quality and the readiness for intellectual and physical challenges. As a virgin goddess, Athena's narrative underscores a self-sufficient existence, unencumbered by romantic liaisons. This celibacy can be seen as a metaphor for a clear, undistracted focus on intellectual and strategic pursuits.

Athena's contest with Poseidon for the patronage of Athens is a classic illustration of her wisdom and the value the Greeks placed on it. This myth shows a competition of practicality and strategic offering. Poseidon struck his trident into the Acropolis, producing a saltwater spring, while Athena planted an olive tree. While Poseidon's gift was powerful, dramatic, and immediate, Athena's gift was practical, offering sustenance, fuel, and raw materials for various crafts. The selection of Athena's olive tree symbolizes the preference for long-term strategic gains, sustainable resources, and the values of peace and prosperity. This mythological narrative not only underscores Athena's wisdom but also highlights the ancient Greeks' pragmatism and forward-thinking approach.

The narrative of Arachne, who was transformed into a spider by Athena, provides valuable insight into the nature of divine and human interactions and the ancient Greek understanding of hubris. Arachne, a gifted mortal weaver, claimed her skills surpassed Athena's and challenged the goddess to a contest. The resultant transformation into a spider underscores the narrative's moral—recognizing divine authority and the limits of human abilities. It emphasizes the importance of maintaining respect for the gods and serves as a reminder of the consequences of excessive pride or self-confidence, known as hubris, in Greek culture. This narrative also underlines Athena's domain over crafts, asserting her supremacy in areas under her patronage.

Roles and Responsibilities

Athena's patronage spans several crucial domains of ancient Greek life, underscoring her status as an influential and multifaceted deity. As a goddess of wisdom and strategic warfare, Athena represents the intellectual and rational mind, embodying insight, forethought, and astute judgment. As a result, her counsel was highly valued in both personal dilemmas and broader societal affairs, particularly in those requiring strategy and foresight. Warfare, a significant part of the Greek city-states' existence, particularly showcased her role as a guide and counselor. Renowned heroes, such as Odysseus and Perseus, benefited from her wisdom, allowing them to navigate complex situations and overcome formidable adversaries.

Apart from her role in strategy and warfare, Athena is also revered as the goddess of crafts, marking her influence over the productive and creative aspects of society. The act of crafting — transforming raw materials into objects of utility or beauty — requires a blend of technical skill, creativity, and foresight, attributes that align closely with Athena's characteristics. Her patronage of crafts such as weaving, pottery, and sculpture underscores her role in fostering societal development and refinement. Through her guidance, raw materials were transformed into essential goods or works of art, symbolizing the transition from nature to culture, chaos to order.

Furthermore, Athena's influence extends to the realm of justice and law, again highlighting her connection with wisdom and rationality. Ancient Greek society placed high value on the rule of law and justice as stabilizing forces in the community. Athena, embodying principles of fairness, righteousness, and moral wisdom, therefore held an essential role in maintaining social order and harmony. She was often depicted in art and literature meting out justice or guiding others towards fair resolutions, further accentuating her image as a civilizing force. Through these diverse roles and responsibilities, Athena emerges as a complex and vital figure in the Greek pantheon, embodying attributes central to the functioning and advancement of society.Symbols

Athena is frequently depicted with an owl, a creature emblematic of wisdom in ancient Greek culture. The owl's ability to see in the dark metaphorically refers to Athena's capacity to discern truth and provide insight in even the most obscure situations.

Her Aegis, a protective shield, often bears the head of Medusa, serving as a potent deterrent to enemies and embodying Athena's martial aspect. The olive tree, another symbol associated with Athena, represents peace and prosperity, reiterating her role as a civilizing force.

In art, she is often portrayed wearing a helmet and holding a spear, underscoring her strategic prowess and readiness for battle.

Athena in Neopaganism, Magic, and Ecospirituality

In contemporary neopagan practices, particularly within Wicca, Athena's attributes of wisdom, strategic thought, independence, and valor continue to reverberate profoundly. Adherents often invoke Athena for her strength and strategic acumen, seeking her guidance during decision-making processes or at moments requiring courage and resilience. They draw upon the symbolisms and narratives associated with her to develop personal spiritual paths that resonate with the goddess's energy and attributes.

The olive tree, sacred to Athena, holds an esteemed position in contemporary ecospirituality. This tree, which Athena was believed to have given to the city of Athens, symbolizes peace, wisdom, and resilience, aligning closely with Athena's characteristics. The tree's ability to withstand harsh conditions and still produce its fruit—a source of nourishment, medicinal use, and even light in the form of oil—reinforces its symbolism. Ecospiritual practitioners revere the olive tree, incorporating it into various rituals and practices aimed at promoting harmony with nature, resilience in face of adversity, and attainment of inner wisdom.

Within the realm of ancient Greek magic, practitioners sought Athena's wisdom and insight to unravel the mysteries of the universe. Divination, a common practice in ancient Greek society, relied on invoking Athena's insight to interpret the will of the gods or to foresee future events. Symbols associated with Athena, such as the owl (symbolizing wisdom and insight) and the olive branch (symbolizing peace and prosperity), were employed in these divinatory practices. These symbols also found use in protective rituals and as amulets, believed to summon Athena's protection and bestow upon the wearer the goddess's wisdom and strategic insight.

The enduring influence of Athena, stretching from ancient times to contemporary spiritual and eco-conscious practices, reaffirms her as a potent and enduring deity. This continuity testifies to the goddess's versatility, her multi-faceted nature making her relevant across different cultural and temporal contexts. The narratives and attributes of Athena continue to inspire and guide individuals, offering a blueprint for cultivating wisdom, strategic insight, resilience, and independence. Athena's powerful and complex persona embodies a blend of strength, wisdom, and creative productivity, all of which are universally valued qualities, thus explaining her enduring relevance and influence.

Exercise and Discussion Questions

Discuss the significance of Athena's unconventional birth from the forehead of Zeus. How does it contribute to her association with wisdom and strategy?

How does the contest between Athena and Poseidon for the city of Athens reflect on their contrasting domains and the values of ancient Greek society?

Explore Athena's role as a virgin goddess. How does her independence factor into her personality and her areas of influence?

Discuss the representation of Athena in contemporary spiritual practices. How do her ancient attributes translate into modern contexts of neopaganism, Wicca, and ecospirituality?

Analyze the story of Arachne in the context of the relationship between mortals and gods in ancient Greek culture. How does the narrative reinforce the notions of respect for the divine and recognition of human limitations?

Apollo: God of Light and Prophecy

Apollo, a multi-faceted deity in the Greek pantheon, embodies several roles and principles, ranging from the prophetic to the artistic. This Olympian god, the son of Zeus and the Titaness Leto, is a key figure in Greek mythology and religion, where he is celebrated as the god of light and prophecy, among other attributes.

Biography and Mythological Narratives

Apollo's birth on the island of Delos unfolds as a narrative of struggle and perseverance. As the story goes, Leto, impregnated by Zeus, was targeted by Hera's wrath. In her jealousy, Hera forbade Leto to give birth on any landmass - any place under the sun that was stable or solid. Exiled and weary, Leto found solace on Delos, which was then a floating rock and not considered 'terra-firma' in the strictest sense. It was there that she was finally able to give birth to her twins: Artemis and Apollo. This tale of Apollo's birth resonates with themes of endurance, resilience, and eventual triumph over adversity, echoing through Apollo's many roles and characteristics.

One of the most pivotal stories from Apollo's mythology involves the slaying of Python. Python was a monstrous serpent that dwelled at the center of the Earth, at Delphi, which was considered the navel of the world in ancient Greek thought. This beast was the child of Gaia (Earth), and was regarded as a chthonic creature, symbolizing the chaotic and primal forces. Apollo's defeat of Python, thus, was not merely a heroic feat, but a symbolic assertion of Olympian order over the primeval chaos. By slaying Python, Apollo further claimed Python's oracle at Delphi as his own, becoming the god of prophecy and establishing his authority over this significant site.

Thereafter, Apollo was closely associated with Delphi, and the oracle at this site became one of the most prestigious in the ancient world. The Pythia, or priestess of Apollo at Delphi, would deliver prophecies believed to be inspired by Apollo himself. The utterances of the Pythia were considered Apollo's words and were highly esteemed as divine wisdom.

In honor of Apollo and his victory over Python, the Pythian Games were instituted, taking place every four years at Delphi. Comparable to the Olympic Games, the Pythian Games comprised not only athletic competitions, but also musical and poetic contests. This celebration was an affirmation of Apollo's myriad attributes - not only his physical strength and heroism but also his patronage of music, poetry, and the arts. Through the narrative of Python's slaying and the Pythian Games, we see the confluence of Apollo's various roles, symbolizing order, prophecy, and the arts.

Roles and Responsibilities

Apollo, in his capacity as the god of light, embodies both the literal and metaphorical aspects of illumination. On a literal level, his association with the Sun underscores his significance in the physical realm. As the Sun is fundamental to life on Earth, vital for the growth of crops and human well-being, so too is Apollo's role essential in the ancient Greek worldview. His connection with light is a testament to his influence over nature's cycles and the sustenance of life.

However, Apollo's link to light transcends the material world and ventures into the realm of intellect and truth. Light, in this sense, represents the illumination of the mind, clarity of understanding, and the revelation of truth. Apollo, as such, is not merely a physical illuminator but also a divine entity that guides mankind towards knowledge and enlightenment. This intellectual aspect of Apollo converges with his role as the god of prophecy.

Apollo's prophetic function, most notably manifested at the oracle of Delphi, held a critical position in Greek religious life. The Delphic Oracle was Apollo's most significant oracular shrine, where he was believed to convey divine prophecies through the Pythia, the high priestess of his temple. Individuals, city-states, and even kings sought these prophecies, as they were considered divine decrees and guided people in making critical decisions. Therefore, Apollo's role as a prophetic deity served as a bridge between the divine and mortal realms, facilitating communication between gods and humans.

Yet, Apollo's sphere of influence is not confined to light and prophecy. He also presides over the artistic and intellectual domains, emblematic of his patronage of the arts. As the leader of the Muses, the nine goddesses who presided over various forms of arts and sciences, Apollo's authority extends over music, poetry, and dance, among other disciplines. His attributes further reflect this artistic patronage. The lyre, a musical instrument often depicted in Apollo's hand, is symbolic of his affinity for music and his ability to create harmonious and enchanting melodies. This artistic aspect of Apollo highlights his multifaceted nature - he is a deity who brings not only physical light and divine insight but also the joy of artistic creativity and intellectual pursuit.

Symbols

In the realm of symbols, Apollo's attributes are as varied as his domains of influence. The lyre, a stringed musical instrument, is one of the most potent symbols associated with him. As the patron of music and arts, Apollo is frequently depicted holding or playing a lyre. The melodious sound of this instrument was believed to embody the harmony and rhythm of the cosmos, and Apollo, as the master of the lyre, was considered the divine maestro orchestrating this celestial symphony. Thus, the lyre not only emphasizes Apollo's artistic patronage but also symbolizes his control over the harmonious order of the universe.

The laurel wreath is another significant symbol linked to Apollo. This wreath was awarded as the prize in the Pythian Games, which were held in his honor every four years at Delphi. The laurel wreath, therefore, represents victory and honor. This symbol has its roots in the myth of Daphne and Apollo, in which Daphne, a nymph, was transformed into a laurel tree to escape Apollo's pursuit. Despite the tragic end, Apollo declared the laurel as his sacred tree, and hence, the laurel wreath became a symbol of his enduring love and loss.

Apollo's association with the sun is a prominent aspect of his iconography. He is often identified with Helios, the personification of the sun, even though in early Greek mythology, these were separate entities. The sun, as a symbol, represents light, clarity, truth, and enlightenment - aspects that are central to Apollo's identity as a solar and intellectual deity.

The animal symbols related to Apollo further illustrate his diverse roles and attributes. The dolphin and the crow hold particular importance in Apollo's mythology. The dolphin is a nod to Apollo's navigational guidance and his association with ports and seafarers. According to one myth, dolphins guided Apollo's priests to Delphi, marking it as a site for his worship. The crow, on the other hand, is connected to Apollo's prophetic and oracular aspect, often seen as a messenger of the god.

In summary, these symbols—the lyre, the laurel wreath, the sun, the dolphin, and the crow—provide a nuanced understanding of Apollo's complex nature. Each symbol adds a layer of meaning to Apollo's divine persona, underlining his roles as the god of arts, prophecy, light, and healing.

Contemporary Relevance and Associations

The influence of Apollo, the god of light, prophecy, and the arts, extends beyond antiquity, permeating into the tapestry of contemporary spirituality, creative pursuits, and ecospiritual practices. His multivalent attributes are reflected in varied domains of human experience and continue to inspire people in different ways.

The light that Apollo personifies symbolizes enlightenment, knowledge, and truth. This association aligns him with intellectual and academic pursuits, where the quest for wisdom and understanding is a central goal. Scholars, researchers, and students might, therefore, look to Apollo as a symbol of intellectual clarity, seeking divine inspiration in their search for knowledge. His connection with the sun, as a life-giving and energy-providing entity, further strengthens this association, symbolizing vitality, growth, and illumination.

In the realm of arts, Apollo's patronage continues to inspire contemporary musicians, poets, dancers, and artists. His skill with the lyre and leadership of the Muses underscore the creative process's divinity, fueling artistic expressions and performances. The laurel wreath, a token of honor and victory, motivates artists to strive for excellence in their crafts, symbolizing the potential glory of artistic achievement.

The prophetic aspect of Apollo finds resonance in neopagan traditions, where divination and spiritual insights hold significant importance. Practitioners invoke Apollo's wisdom for clarity and guidance in their divinatory rituals, drawing from his ancient role as the overseer of the Delphic Oracle. His symbols, such as the crow and the laurel, are incorporated into these rituals, acting as potent tools for spiritual connection and prophecy.

Furthermore, Apollo's solar association has significant implications for ecospiritual practices. Reverence for the sun as a life-sustaining force aligns with environmental consciousness, where the natural elements are respected for their crucial role in the Earth's ecosystem. Apollo, as a solar deity, symbolizes the power and importance of renewable energy sources, urging a shift towards sustainable living and respect for the environment.

In conclusion, Apollo's domains—light, prophecy, arts, and healing—demonstrate their timeless relevance and universality through their continued influence in contemporary contexts. Whether through the pursuit of knowledge, the creation of art, spiritual divination, or environmental conservation, Apollo's attributes echo in the human quest for understanding, expression, insight, and harmony with nature. His enduring influence is a testament to the dynamic interplay of myth, symbol, and human experience that continues to shape our world.

Artemis: Goddess of the Hunt

Artemis, the goddess of the hunt, wilderness, and moon, occupies a unique place within the Greek pantheon. The twin sister of Apollo, she was born to Leto and Zeus on the island of Delos. As an eternal virgin, she is the epitome of independence, a trait echoed in the narratives surrounding her, where she often repels attempts to control or manipulate her.

Artemis's domain encompasses both the nurturing and destructive aspects of nature. As the goddess of the hunt, she embodies the primal instinct for survival and the pursuit of sustenance. She presides over wildlife, particularly the animals that were hunted in ancient Greece, such as the stag and the boar. Artemis is also revered as the protector of young animals, underlining her role as the nurturer of the wild.

Simultaneously, Artemis is associated with childbirth and the protection of young girls up to the age of marriage. This may seem contradictory given her association with hunting and her status as a virgin. However, this dichotomy reinforces her multifaceted nature – she is both the hunter and the protector, the wilderness and the homestead, the maiden and the matron.

Narratives associated with Artemis underscore her fierce independence and formidable nature. The tale of Actaeon, a hunter turned into a stag by Artemis for peeping at her while she bathed, exemplifies the consequences of violating her privacy and autonomy. Another legend involves Niobe, who boasted of having more children than Leto, Artemis's mother. In retaliation, Artemis and Apollo slew Niobe's children, illustrating the dire consequences of hubris and disrespect towards the divine.

Artemis's symbols are reflective of her dominions and attributes. The bow and arrow are her primary symbols, representing her mastery over hunting. Animals, such as the deer, bear, and boar, are associated with her, echoing her connection with the wild. The moon, as a nocturnal and feminine symbol, aligns with her status as a virgin goddess and a protector of women.

In contemporary neopaganism and Wicca, Artemis's fierce independence, connection with nature, and feminine power continue to inspire. She is invoked for courage, self-reliance, and protection, particularly in the context of nature and wildlife. As a virgin goddess, she embodies autonomy and self-determination, qualities revered in feminist spiritualities. In eco-spiritual practices, Artemis's connection with the wild is celebrated, her narratives and symbols employed in rituals promoting environmental consciousness and respect for wildlife.

In ancient Greek magical practices, Artemis was invoked for protection, particularly for women and children, and in matters relating to childbirth and female health. Her symbols were used in amulets and charms, believed to bring protection and blessings to the wearer.

Artemis's enduring influence testifies to the continuing relevance of her domains, which span the spectrum from the wild and untamed to the protective and nurturing. Her representation in art, literature, and spiritual practices underscores her status as a powerful symbol of independence, strength, and respect for nature.

Ares: God of War

Ares, often described as the personification of violent and physical warfare, holds a unique and somewhat ambiguous position in the pantheon of Greek gods. Son of Zeus and Hera, Ares embodies the more brutal and bloody aspects of conflict, standing in contrast to Athena, who represents strategic and principled warfare.

In contrast to many other Olympian gods, Ares is seldom portrayed in a favorable light within Greek mythology. Homer, in his epic poem the "Iliad," presents Ares as a disruptive and destructive force, a deity whose thrill for battle and bloodshed often instigates chaos rather than serving a constructive purpose. This negative characterization is further emphasized in his frequent defeats at the hands of other gods, including Athena and Hercules, suggesting a certain level of disapproval of his belligerent nature in the ancient Greek consciousness.

Yet, despite this predominantly negative depiction, Ares does possess a multifaceted persona. In addition to his role as the god of war, he is also associated with courage and the primal instinct for survival in the face of life's battles. As the father of Fear (Phobos) and Terror (Deimos), his influence extends to the psychological aspects of warfare, reflecting the terror and stress induced by the horrors of war.

In terms of symbolism, the most apparent emblems of Ares include the spear and the helmet, items representative of a warrior's accoutrements. The vulture, a creature that thrives in the aftermath of battle, and the dog, known for its aggressiveness, are considered sacred to Ares.

In contemporary contexts, Ares has been subjected to various reinterpretations. In neo-pagan and Wiccan traditions, for instance, Ares's characteristics have been somewhat redefined, with a greater emphasis placed on his connection with physical strength, personal courage, and determination. His traditional role as a war deity has also been expanded to represent the struggles and conflicts encountered in modern life, not just those on the battlefield. Hence, he is invoked for courage and strength during trying times, reflecting a shift from external to internal battles.

In the realm of magic and witchcraft, Ares's power and assertiveness are harnessed for protection, especially against enemies and negative energies. His symbols, particularly his spear, are often used in rituals aimed at fortification and defense.

In the sphere of ecospirituality, while Ares might not have a direct correlation, his association with primal and raw forces of nature could potentially symbolize natural disasters or the more destructive aspects of the environment, offering a unique angle to ecological interpretation.

Ares, despite his controversial status within Greek mythology, remains an intriguing figure. His association with war, both physical and psychological, offers considerable room for exploration and reinterpretation, especially in a world that continues to grapple with conflict and strife on various fronts. This provides fertile ground for engaging discussion and critical thinking, allowing students to explore and challenge traditional views while drawing parallels with contemporary contexts.

Aphrodite: Goddess of Love

Aphrodite, the celebrated Greek goddess of love, beauty, and fertility, presents an exquisite blend of sensuality, attraction, and creative life force. As one of the key figures in the Greek pantheon, Aphrodite's influence spans far beyond romantic love, encompassing a broad range of affections and creative processes.

Born from the sea foam generated by the severed genitals of Uranus (thrown into the sea by his son Cronus), Aphrodite's unique birth narrative alludes to her association with both the primal forces of the universe and the life-giving properties of the sea. This remarkable origin story underscores her role as a conduit of potent creative energy and fertility.

Aphrodite's mythology is replete with stories of passion, allure, and transformation. One notable narrative involves her love affair with the war god Ares, a relationship that yielded Harmonia (goddess of harmony) and Eros (god of erotic love), and thus symbolizing a profound connection between love, war, harmony, and desire. Her role in the tale of the Trojan War, where she offered the fairest woman in the world to Paris, underscores the destructive potential of unbridled desire and vanity.

Aphrodite is commonly depicted with several symbols, including the dove, rose, mirror, and girdle. The dove and rose denote love and beauty, while the mirror signifies vanity and the enchanting power of beauty. The girdle represents irresistible allure and desire. These symbols enhance our understanding of Aphrodite as a complex deity wielding considerable influence over human emotions, relationships, and creative processes.

As the goddess of love, Aphrodite oversees all forms of love, ranging from spiritual love to sexual desire. Her purview extends to the realm of beauty, encompassing both physical attractiveness and the aesthetic appreciation of beauty in all its forms. Aphrodite also holds sway over procreation, symbolizing fertility and the perpetuation of life.

In contemporary interpretations, Aphrodite's energy resonates strongly in the realm of love, beauty, and creativity. She is frequently invoked in Wiccan and neopagan rituals celebrating love, beauty, and fertility. The practice of Aphrodisian spirituality, focusing on self-love and acceptance, draws heavily on her influence.

In divination and magic, Aphrodite's symbols are employed in rituals designed to attract love, enhance beauty, foster creativity, and promote harmony in relationships. Her energy is invoked to cultivate love (romantic, platonic, and self-love) and to stir the creative life force within individuals.

In the realm of ecospirituality, Aphrodite's association with the sea denotes her connection to the waters that nourish life on Earth. As such, she is revered as a symbol of life-giving water and is invoked in rituals aimed at water conservation and reverence for aquatic ecosystems.

Throughout the ages, Aphrodite has remained a vibrant symbol of love, beauty, and the potent forces of attraction that ignite creativity and perpetuate life. Her enduring relevance across diverse domains underscores the universality of these concepts and their intrinsic value to human existence. The exploration of Aphrodite's multifaceted persona invites engaging discussions, encourages introspection, and fosters a deep appreciation of the complexities of love, beauty, and creativity.

Hephaestus: God of Fire and Forge

Hephaestus, the Greek god of fire, blacksmiths, and craftsmanship, stands out in the Greek pantheon with his unique connection to the practical and transformative aspects of fire and technology. Despite his physical impairment, a rarity among Greek gods, Hephaestus's narrative is rich with symbolic undertones of resilience, creativity, and transformation.

Hephaestus was the son of Hera, the queen of the gods. According to one version of his birth narrative, Hera conceived him alone in retaliation to Zeus giving birth to Athena independently. However, Hephaestus was born lame, and this imperfection led to his rejection. In one well-known myth, he was thrown from Olympus by Hera, while in another version, it was Zeus who hurled him down for intervening in a quarrel between his parents. Regardless of the teller, Hephaestus's fall from Olympus is a recurring theme, linking him to the motif of suffering and resilience.

Once on earth, Hephaestus turned adversity into advantage by becoming a master craftsman. He created many marvelous artifacts, tools, and weapons for the gods and heroes of Greek mythology, including the thunderbolts of Zeus, the aegis of Athena, and the invisibility helmet of Hades. His creations, often imbued with magical properties, were not just functional but were also works of immense artistic merit. One of his most famous creations is Pandora, the first woman, whom he fashioned from clay on Zeus's orders.

Hephaestus is commonly depicted holding a blacksmith's hammer, signifying his mastery over metallurgy and craftsmanship. Fire is another primary symbol associated with him, signifying transformation, creativity, and the vital force that drives technological advancement. His sacred animals are the donkey, the crane, and the guard dog, all of which are related to labor and craftsmanship.

In the context of ancient Greek religion, Hephaestus held an important role as the patron of blacksmiths, artisans, and craftsmen. His temples, notably the Hephaesteum in Athens and the Temple of Hephaestus in Thasos, were centers of worship and artisanal guilds. He was honored with annual festivals known as Hephaestia, where the ritual kindling of fire was a significant feature.

In modern interpretations, Hephaestus's energy resonates in domains that value skill, creativity, and transformation. His overcoming of personal adversity to master his craft is seen as an embodiment of resilience and resourcefulness. In neopagan and Wiccan traditions, Hephaestus is revered as a god of craftsmanship, and his aid is invoked in rituals related to skill enhancement, creative endeavors, and transformation.

His association with fire places him within the realm of ecological consciousness, where fire is recognized for its role in ecological succession and nutrient recycling. Thus, Hephaestus also finds a place in ecospiritual practices.

In ancient Greek magical practices, Hephaestus's symbols, particularly fire, were used in spells and rituals aimed at transformation, creative inspiration, and skill enhancement. Today, he continues to inspire those who seek to transform raw materials into functional and artistic forms.

The exploration of Hephaestus's narrative and symbolism provokes reflection on the themes of resilience, creativity, and transformation, offering rich opportunities for discussion and critical engagement in the understanding of these timeless human experiences. By delving into the persona of Hephaestus, we can glean valuable insights into the human capacity for turning adversity into advantage, the role of craftsmanship in societal development, and the transformative power of technology.

Hermes: Messenger of the Gods

Hermes, renowned as the herald and messenger of the Olympian gods, constitutes an intriguing figure within the Greek pantheon. His roles are manifold, reflecting his associations with communication, travel, trade, and cunning, among other attributes. The narratives surrounding Hermes offer profound insights into the values of agility, wit, and versatility in ancient Greek society.

Hermes was the son of Zeus, the king of the gods, and Maia, a nymph and one of the Pleiades. His birth story accentuates his cunning and resourcefulness, as Hermes is said to have invented the lyre from a tortoise shell and stolen Apollo's herd of sacred cows, all within the first day of his life. When confronted by Apollo, Hermes cleverly placated his half-brother by offering him the newly crafted lyre, hence earning Apollo's forgiveness and demonstrating his skills in negotiation and appeasement.

As the divine messenger, Hermes serves as the link between mortals and the divine, capable of traversing the realms of the gods, humans, and the underworld with ease. He is also the protector of travelers, guiding souls to the underworld and safeguarding those embarking on earthly journeys.

Additionally, Hermes's patronage extends to commerce and trade, reflecting his knack for negotiation and wealth acquisition. In some narratives, he is also portrayed as a trickster, highlighting his clever, cunning, and playful nature.

Hermes is often depicted wearing a winged helmet and sandals, symbolizing his swiftness and ability to travel between realms. He holds the caduceus, a staff intertwined with two serpents and topped with wings, emblematic of his role as a messenger and mediator. Other symbols associated with Hermes include the tortoise, representing wisdom and perseverance, and the rooster, a symbol of the new day and a herald of sorts.

Within ancient Greek religion, Hermes held a central role due to his function as a divine messenger and mediator. His statutes, known as Hermae, were erected at boundaries and crossroads, functioning as markers and protectors for travelers. His worship extended throughout Greece, and festivals called Hermaia were held in his honor, particularly in Athens.

In the field of ancient Greek magic, Hermes was often invoked for his cunning and resourcefulness. His ability to move between realms made him a significant figure in rituals related to travel, communication with the divine, and transitions.

The contemporary relevance of Hermes extends into various facets of modern spirituality and societal functions. In neopagan and Wiccan traditions, Hermes is invoked for his swiftness, adaptability, and his ability to guide through transitions and journeys, both literal and metaphorical.

In the modern context, with rapid advancements in communication technology and the growth of global trade, Hermes's attributes resonate profoundly. His ability to mediate, negotiate, and facilitate exchange across different realms finds echoes in diplomacy, international relations, business, and in the digital communication era.

The study of Hermes provides a lens through which to explore the complex intersections between communication, travel, commerce, and cunning, thereby fostering critical thinking and engagement with these multidimensional aspects of human society and individual psyche. The narrative of Hermes thus offers a rich tapestry of ancient beliefs and practices that continue to find resonance in contemporary times.

Dionysus: God of Wine

Dionysus, the Greek god of wine, ritual ecstasy, and theater, embodies a fascinating and paradoxical deity within the Greek pantheon. His association with both jubilation and profound despair symbolizes the Greek comprehension of the dual nature of life and human emotions.

According to mythological narratives, Dionysus was the son of Zeus and Semele, a mortal woman. His birth was wrought with tragedy, as Hera, Zeus's wife, orchestrated Semele's death out of jealousy. Zeus, however, managed to rescue the unborn Dionysus, sewing him into his thigh until he was ready to be born, hence Dionysus's epithet, "twice-born." Dionysus's narratives frequently depict him introducing the art of winemaking to mankind and his journeys across the world, followed by his ecstatic female followers, the Maenads, and the satyrs.

As the god of wine, Dionysus symbolizes the intoxicating power of nature and its potential to free individuals from their everyday selves through the divine ecstasy of drink and dance. His patronage over theater further underscores his connection to the exploration and expression of the human condition in all its variegated emotions and experiences.

Dionysus's symbols reflect his nature and patronage. The thyrsus, a fennel staff topped with a pine cone, represents both his connection to nature and the ecstatic aspect of his cult. Ivy, grapevines, and wine cups are also frequently associated with Dionysus, underscoring his dominion over wine and revelry. The panther and the bull, both animals known for their strength and untamed natures, are often associated with him, symbolizing the raw, potent, and often dangerous force of nature he embodies.

In ancient Greek religion, the cult of Dionysus held a prominent position. Dionysian rituals often involved the consumption of wine and ecstatic dancing, serving as a form of catharsis and a way to transcend mundane reality. His festivals, notably the Dionysia, provided the platform for the performance of tragedy and comedy plays, contributing to the development of ancient Greek drama.

In the domain of magic and divination in ancient Greece, Dionysus was invoked for his transformative and liberating attributes. Rituals associated with Dionysus often aimed at personal liberation, channeling the ecstatic and transformative powers associated with him.

The legacy of Dionysus permeates contemporary spiritual and cultural practices. His connection to wine, ecstasy, and the arts makes him a symbol of creativity, liberation, and the transformational power of nature. In neopagan traditions, Dionysus is revered for his association with nature's potent forces and his ability to blur the ordinary boundaries of existence through ecstasy.

In the broader cultural context, Dionysus's influence is evident in our understanding of theater as a space for exploring the human condition. The Dionysian influence also pervades our association of wine with conviviality and its role in social and religious rituals.

An in-depth study of Dionysus offers not only a view into the multifaceted nature of divine representations in ancient Greek religion but also insights into the Greek understanding of life, nature, and human emotions. His narrative, marked by joy and tragedy, provides a rich platform for exploring themes of transformation, liberation, and the human experience's complexity.

Hestia: Goddess of the Hearth

Hestia, the Greek goddess of the hearth, home, and domestic life, holds a unique and vital position within the Greek pantheon. Although not as flamboyantly depicted in mythologies as some other deities, her role is of profound significance in Greek religious life and provides a critical understanding of the domestic sphere's importance in ancient Greece.

Hestia was the eldest child of Cronus and Rhea, and in many accounts, she was the first swallowed by Cronus and the last to be regurgitated, making her both the oldest and youngest of the Olympians. Her biography is largely devoid of the turbulent narratives and passionate affairs that define other Greek deities. Hestia remained a virgin goddess, rejecting marriage offers from both Poseidon and Apollo, choosing instead to maintain her position at Olympus's hearth, signifying the central place of the home and hearth in Greek culture.

In terms of roles and responsibilities, Hestia's domain was the hearth and domestic life. As the goddess of the hearth, Hestia symbolized the comfort and blessings of a well-ordered home and family life. Each city, too, had a public hearth dedicated to Hestia, where the fire was kept continuously burning. If a colony was to be established, it was a fire from the city's public hearth, representing Hestia, that would ignite the hearth in the new city, symbolizing continuity and the spread of civilization.

Key symbols associated with Hestia include the hearth and the flame, both symbolizing the home's comfort, warmth, and security. The circle is also often associated with Hestia, representing the completeness and unity of the family unit. The donkey, a hardworking domesticated animal, is often linked with Hestia as an emblem of domesticity and humble service.

In ancient Greek religion, Hestia was widely revered, and while there were few temples specifically dedicated to her, she had an essential place in every home and public institution. Her flame in both the family hearth and the town prytaneion (public hearth) were never allowed to go out. The first part of every meal was offered to her, affirming her role in daily domestic life.

In the field of magic in ancient Greece, rituals associated with Hestia often aimed at protection of the home and the family and the promotion of harmony within the household. The lighting and tending of fires were imbued with symbolic meaning, and the hearth functioned as a sacred space within the home.

Today, Hestia's legacy endures in neopagan practices and domestic traditions where she is revered as a goddess of the home, hearth, and familial unity. Her influence permeates the concept of the home as a sanctuary and the hearth or fireplace as a gathering place for family. In broader cultural contexts, the phrase "Hestia's hearth" has become a metaphor for a peaceful, well-managed household.

In conclusion, Hestia, while relatively modest and understated compared to some of her Olympian counterparts, embodies the vital importance of the hearth and the home, the central pillars of both personal and civic life in ancient Greece. She offers rich insights into Greek values and the sacredness attributed to domesticity and familial harmony. A study of Hestia serves to underline the critical role of what is often considered the mundane or ordinary, highlighting its place in the sacred sphere.

Conclusion: The Pantheon's Collective Influence

The pantheon of ancient Greek gods, headed by the twelve Olympians, served as a grand cosmic model of an intricate web of power dynamics, relationships, and principles. These divine figures, each with unique characteristics, responsibilities, and domains, together formed an integral part of the ancient Greek religious landscape, shaping the society's moral, ethical, and spiritual perspectives.

The roles and significance of the Olympian gods cannot be understated. Zeus, as the king of the gods, embodied the principles of justice, law, and order, exercising control over the sky and weather. His brothers Poseidon and Hades ruled the sea and the underworld, respectively, symbolizing the Greek world's tripartite division. Hera, as Zeus's wife and the goddess of marriage and childbirth, underlined the importance of the family unit, and Athena, as the goddess of wisdom and warfare, denoted the Greeks' reverence for intellect and strategic prowess. Apollo and Artemis, as the god of light and the goddess of the hunt, represented illumination, both literal and metaphorical, and nature's wild aspects. Ares, the god of war, symbolized the tumultuous aspects of conflict, while Aphrodite, the goddess of love, highlighted the potent power of beauty and desire. Hephaestus, the god of fire and forge, underlined the value of craftsmanship, and Hermes, the messenger of the gods, represented communication and commerce. Dionysus, as the god of wine and revelry, symbolized ecstasy and the loss of self, while Hestia, the goddess of the hearth, emphasized the sanctity of the home.

Together, the Olympian gods had a profound collective impact on ancient Greek religion, embodying the values, fears, and hopes of Greek society. Their stories reflected the world's complexities and uncertainties as perceived by the ancient Greeks. This pantheon also served as a guiding framework for understanding the universe and human existence, offering narratives that explored the interplay of power, morality, destiny, and the human condition.

Religious rituals, festivals, and oracles centered around these deities played a critical role in establishing social cohesion, defining the civic identity, and promoting ethical behavior. The gods' interrelationships, often marked by conflicts and reconciliations, mirrored the dynamics within human society, providing models of conduct, albeit frequently cautionary.

Moreover, these gods had their distinct sacred sites, priesthoods, and cult practices, fostering a multifaceted, decentralized religious system. This diversity allowed various city-states and regions to have their local preferences and traditions, creating a rich tapestry of religious expression across the Greek world.

In the realm of magic and divination in ancient Greece, the gods' influence was paramount. Their symbols, narratives, and powers were invoked in rituals, and their favor was sought through sacrifices and offerings. Divination, in particular, was viewed as receiving insights from the gods, underlining their integral role in such practices.

Even today, the influence of the Greek pantheon transcends academic discussions, permeating modern culture, arts, and spiritual practices. In neo-pagan traditions, such as Wicca and various forms of modern witchcraft, the Greek gods often serve as archetypes invoked in rituals. Ecospirituality draws on gods like Gaia, Demeter, Artemis, and Dionysus to embody the respect for and interconnectedness with nature.

To conclude, the collective influence of the Olympian gods on ancient Greek religion and beyond underscores the enduring power of these myths and the human desire to understand and relate to the world. Far from being a static set of beliefs, the Greek pantheon exemplifies a dynamic system that evolved and adapted over time, offering rich insights into the human psyche, societal values, and our relationship with the natural world and the divine.

Recapitulation

This chapter offered an in-depth exploration of the Olympian gods and their roles within the context of ancient Greek religion. It highlighted their unique domains and the values they embodied, the narratives that surrounded them, and their profound impact on religious practices, societal norms, and cultural identities. The Olympians were revealed as multidimensional entities, embodying a myriad of concepts ranging from order, justice, and wisdom to love, war, and revelry, reflecting the complexities of the human condition.

Key takeaways from the chapter include:

The Olympian gods served not only as divine entities but also as representations of various aspects of life, the world, and societal values, thereby deeply influencing the societal structure, moral code, and worldview of the ancient Greeks.

The ancient Greek religious system, centered around the pantheon of gods, was multifaceted and decentralized, accommodating local traditions and regional variations.

The influence of the Olympian gods transcended religious practices, permeating every aspect of ancient Greek life, from political decisions to daily chores. Their stories, often allegorical, provided an understanding of the world, human nature, and the cosmic order.

The interaction between the gods and humans in mythological narratives highlighted the concept of hubris and the idea of divine retribution, acting as cautionary tales.

The Pantheon of the Deities in Greek Religion

The symbols and narratives of the Olympian gods played significant roles in the practices of magic, divination, witchcraft, and shamanism in ancient Greece.

The impact of the Olympian gods extends beyond antiquity, resonating in modern practices, interpretations, and neo-pagan traditions.

While the focus thus far has been on the Olympian gods, this exploration has paved the way for delving into the mysteries of the earliest divine entities in the Greek mythological cosmos.

Upcoming in Chapter 3, we will shift our focus from the Olympian gods to the primeval deities of Greek mythology. Often associated with elemental forces and the creation of the world, these deities represent a more abstract and fundamental layer of the divine in the ancient Greek worldview. The examination of primeval gods, including Chaos, Gaia, Uranus, and the Titans, will offer further insights into the Greeks' understanding of the universe's origins and structure, the interplay of order and chaos, and the cyclic nature of time and existence. These narratives provide valuable context for the rise of the Olympians and further illuminate the rich tapestry of Greek mythology and religion.

Chapter 3: The Primeval Gods: Examination of the earliest gods in Greek mythology, often associated with elemental forces and the creation of the world.

In the intricate tapestry of Greek mythology, an essential narrative thread is woven by the Primeval Gods. These deities form the cornerstone of the cosmos, the elemental forces from which all life emerged. In this chapter, we will embark on an in-depth examination of these earliest gods, and trace their profound influence on Greek mythological and religious practices.

Primeval Gods occupy the prehistoric stage of Greek mythology, their existence predates the creation of the world itself. Their narratives embody ancient Greeks' efforts to elucidate the mysteries of existence, the natural world, and the cosmos. To understand Greek mythology and its subsequent pantheons, it is indispensable to comprehend the role and significance of these primeval forces.

These entities include the primordial deities like Chaos, the void from which everything sprang, and Gaia, the Earth Mother who bore the sky, the sea, and the mountains. It also includes elemental forces such as Tartarus, the deep abyss used as a torturous underworld for the wicked, and Eros, the personification of love and procreation. These gods, along with others, formed the backdrop against which the Greek world was created and organized.

The narratives of these primeval gods provide deep insights into the ancient Greeks' understanding of the world's fundamental elements. These narratives, intricate and at times conflicting, reflect a culture wrestling with the mysteries of life, death, existence, and the universe. The earliest mythological tales sought to provide structure and meaning in a chaotic universe, portraying the world as a product of divine actions and interactions.

As we proceed with this chapter, we will explore the mythology surrounding each of these primeval deities, examining their unique roles and their relationships with other deities. We will delve into their symbolism, their influence on ancient Greek religion, and their enduring impact on modern spiritual practices, particularly within the context of contemporary neo-paganism, witchcraft, and ecospirituality.

In this journey, we shall uncover the rich layers of the narratives of these ancient deities, their profound roles in the cosmos, and their pervasive influence on the pantheon that succeeded them, the Olympian gods. Our exploration of the Primeval Gods will lay a strong foundation for understanding the evolution of Greek mythology and its enduring resonance in the modern world.

Brief overview of the primeval gods

The Primeval Gods, often referred to as Protogenoi (meaning "first-born" in Greek), encompass a group of deities representing the raw, elemental forces of the universe. To the ancient Greeks, these entities were the substance of the universe itself, each god an embodiment of a specific elemental aspect or concept. Although they were not anthropomorphized to the same extent as their Olympian counterparts, they were nonetheless deemed vital to the world's foundation and ongoing function.

Chaos: In Greek mythology, the story of the universe commences with Chaos, the yawning void, the primeval emptiness from which all existence sprang. Often described as a void or chasm, Chaos represents the state of the universe before creation. It gave birth to the first divine entities: Gaia, Tartarus, Eros, Erebus, and Nyx.

Gaia: Often referred to as the Earth Mother, Gaia is the personification of the Earth. She emerged from Chaos, embodying all aspects of terrestrial life. Gaia's role is central to many creation myths, including the birth of the sky (Uranus), the sea (Pontus), and the mountains (Ourea).

Uranus: The embodiment of the sky, Uranus was borne from Gaia. He is the primeval god of the heavens, the divine representation of the sky. Uranus' union with Gaia produced the Titans, the Giants, and the Cyclopes, among other beings.

Tartarus: Personified as a divine figure, Tartarus is also a place—the deep abyss used as a dungeon of torment for the wicked and a prison for the Titans. It is a primordial force akin to Chaos, residing far beneath the earth.

Eros: The primeval god of procreation, Eros was the force behind the propagation of beings in the universe. Though often confused with the later, more anthropomorphic god of love, this original Eros represented the driving force of attraction that compelled entities to combine and reproduce.

Nyx and Erebus: Representing night and darkness respectively, Nyx and Erebus are two more primeval deities born from Chaos. They were parents to Aether (light) and Hemera (day), embodying the cosmic balance between light and darkness, day and night.

Pontus: The primeval god of the sea, Pontus, born from Gaia, embodies the sea's mystery, depth, and power. Though less mentioned in myths, he sired ancient sea gods and sea monsters.

By comprehending these earliest deities' nature, one gains critical insights into the ancient Greeks' efforts to rationalize their surroundings, interpret natural phenomena, and understand the essential constituents of life and existence. This understanding provides a necessary foundation for delving into the subsequent generations of gods, who, despite their anthropomorphism, continued to bear the influence of these elemental beginnings.

The significance of the primeval gods in Greek cosmogony

To comprehend the importance of the Primeval Gods in Greek cosmogony, one must first understand the context of their genesis. According to the ancient Greeks, the cosmos was not created ex nihilo, or from nothing. Instead, the universe arose from a pre-existing entity: Chaos. This differs markedly from many monotheistic creation narratives in which a divine being crafts the universe from nothing.

In the case of Greek cosmogony, the universe arose from a transformation of what already existed in another form—Chaos. Chaos, in Greek understanding, did not denote disorder, but rather referred to an unfathomable emptiness or abyss. This elucidates the concept that the universe's genesis was not a process of crafting from void, but a matter of forming order from pre-existing elements.

Emerging from Chaos, the first deities—Gaia, Uranus, Tartarus, Eros, Nyx, and Erebus—were embodiments of the world's basic elements. Gaia personified Earth, Uranus the sky, Tartarus the depths or the underworld, and Eros signified the propulsive force of love or desire. Nyx and Erebus represented night and darkness, elemental aspects of the natural world.

Their importance lies not only in their primordial status but also in the notion that these gods were the world. They were not simply in the world, as were later deities, but were of the world, each representing a piece of the cosmic puzzle. Greek cosmogony, thus, is fundamentally an anthropomorphic exercise—an effort to humanize or personify the natural world and its forces.

The narrative sequence of their birth also reflects the Greeks' understanding of the cosmos's logical structure. The universe evolves from less differentiated (Chaos) to more differentiated (Earth, Sky, Underworld), and from inanimate (Chaos, Earth) to animate (the birth of Eros). This progression exhibits an emergent order from an undifferentiated state, which may reflect the Greeks' observations of natural processes and phenomena.

Moreover, these deities' roles extend beyond mere representation. Their relationships and interactions—marriages, births, and conflicts—establish the context for subsequent mythical narratives involving Titans and Olympians. For example, Uranus' fear and suppression of his offspring led to his castration by his son Cronus, initiating the era of the Titans and setting the stage for the Olympians' ascension.

In summation, the Primeval Gods play an instrumental role in Greek cosmogony. They serve as the physical and metaphorical foundation of the world, embody the natural and supernatural order, provide explanation for natural phenomena, and set the stage for the pantheon of gods that followed. Their existence and narratives underscore a fundamental facet of Greek religious thought—the intimate connection between the divine and the natural world.

Chaos: The Void from Which Everything Emerged

Chaos, in ancient Greek cosmogony, occupies a central place in the genesis of the universe. The word Chaos derives from the Greek "χάος," indicating "gap," "chasm," or "void." According to Hesiod's Theogony, Chaos, the dark void, existed before all things. This idea proposes that before the creation of the universe, there was not simply nothingness, but a vast, undifferentiated, and infinite chasm.

Contrary to contemporary perceptions, Chaos in ancient Greek understanding did not imply disorder or confusion. Instead, it represented the unfathomable depths of the void from which all life originated, a realm of infinite potentiality, embodying the first primordial state from which all beings emerged.

Within this abyss, the first divine entities were born. From Chaos came Gaia (Earth), Tartarus (the abyss), Eros (Love), Erebus (Darkness), and Nyx (Night). These entities did not originate from Chaos in a biological sense, but they arose or spontaneously generated from it, affirming the primeval god's role as the progenitor of the cosmos.

However, we must exercise caution against understanding Chaos merely as a deity. In Hesiod's cosmogony, Chaos represents a physical location and a state of being. The ambiguous nature of Chaos, simultaneously representing a deity, a place, and a condition, epitomizes the fluidity of the divine in ancient Greek religion.

One might draw parallels with other cosmological narratives, where the universe is birthed from a primordial abyss. For instance, in the Egyptian cosmology, the notion of Nu or Nun—the primordial waters from which the world emerged—bears striking resemblance with Chaos.

Understanding Chaos as the original void from which everything emerges prompts us to consider the dynamic nature of the cosmos in Greek thought. It embodies the philosophical concept of "ex nihilo nihil fit" (nothing comes from nothing), reinforcing the understanding that the universe's existence necessitates an antecedent entity or condition.

An exploration of Chaos' role prompts profound reflections upon the creation myths across cultures and their implications for understanding the origins and nature of the cosmos. It underlines the human longing to comprehend the universe's origin, embodied in the cosmogonical narratives of ancient civilizations.

Exercise: Reflect upon the concept of Chaos in relation to modern scientific theories about the origins of the universe, such as the Big Bang theory. In what ways do these ancient and contemporary narratives intersect, and how do they diverge? How do these different narratives reflect the specific cultural and historical contexts in which they were formulated?

Further reading: Hesiod's Theogony offers a seminal narrative on the role of Chaos in Greek cosmogony. For a comparative analysis, consider the Enuma Elish from Mesopotamia or the creation myths from the Coffin Texts of ancient Egypt.

Explanation of Chaos and its role in Greek cosmogony

To comprehend the role of Chaos in Greek cosmogony, it is imperative to delve into the narrative's philosophical underpinnings and contextual nuances. As previously mentioned, Chaos is not merely a deity in the traditional sense but also a place and a primordial condition of existence, encapsulating the boundless void from which the cosmos and its entities emerged.

According to Hesiod's "Theogony", Chaos, alongside Gaia (Earth), Tartarus (the abyss), and Eros (Love), was among the initial entities that appeared at the inception of the universe. In this narrative, Chaos exists not only as a precursor to creation but also as the primordial entity from which various deities such as Erebus (Darkness) and Nyx (Night) originated.

The interpretation of Chaos as a formless, infinite void—uncharacterized by matter or energy—parallels the void state prior to the Big Bang in modern cosmological theories. In both cases, the cosmos is viewed as evolving from an initial singularity or 'nothingness', challenging the very limits of human comprehension.

From a symbolic perspective, Chaos stands as a powerful testament to the ancient Greeks' conceptualization of existence and the cosmos' inherent unpredictability. The world was born from Chaos and is constantly subject to changes that often elude human understanding, echoing the elusive and unfathomable nature of the Chaos entity itself.

Chaos' role in the Greek cosmogony underscores the ancient Greek belief in the universe's cyclical nature, where dissolution and rebirth are intrinsic components of existence. This is mirrored in the annual agricultural cycle, the human life cycle, and the astral patterns that the Greeks observed. Chaos, as the primeval void, underscores the universe's fluid and dynamic nature, suggesting an ongoing process of creation and dissolution.

In synthesizing these perspectives, we discern that Chaos, in Greek cosmogony, symbolizes the primal state of potentiality from which all elements of the cosmos emerged. Chaos' inscrutable nature prompts humans to confront the universe's inherent complexities and the limits of human understanding, fueling the ceaseless quest for knowledge and wisdom.

Exercise: How does the role of Chaos in Greek cosmogony influence the philosophical outlook of ancient Greeks towards the cosmos and existence? Draw parallels between the concept of Chaos and modern scientific theories about the universe's origins. How do these ancient and contemporary narratives both diverge and intersect in their explanations of cosmic origins?

Further reading: For an in-depth analysis of Chaos and its role in Greek cosmogony, consult Hesiod's "Theogony". Additionally, consider other cosmogonies, such as those found in the Rig Veda of ancient India or the Popol Vuh of the Maya, for a comparative study.

Exploration of the concept of 'chaos' in Ancient Greek understanding

In our ongoing study of primeval deities, we have encountered the enigmatic figure of Chaos, recognized as both a deity and a state of pre-existence. To further enhance our understanding of this concept, we shall delve into its etymology and its place in Ancient Greek cognitive and perceptual frameworks.

The term 'Chaos' hails from the Greek word 'Khaos,' which denotes an open chasm or abyss. However, in the context of ancient cosmology, 'Chaos' signifies more than a simple void or emptiness. It carries connotations of the unfathomable, the disordered, and the illimitable potentiality from which all existence sprang.

The concept of Chaos underscores the ancient Greeks' awareness of the inherent volatility and unpredictability of the universe. The primordial state of Chaos was neither tranquil nor static but teemed with potential for change and transformation. This ontological outlook resonates in the turbulence of the deities born from Chaos, such as Erebos, the embodiment of darkness, and Nyx, the personification of night.

Paradoxically, Chaos also implies the potential for order. Within its void, elements coalesced to form the structured universe, providing a framework for the ancient Greeks' nuanced understanding of the cosmos. Thus, Chaos represents the equilibrium between order and disorder, both fundamental aspects of existence.

The ancient Greeks perceived the world not as an entity with rigid, immutable rules, but as a dynamic process subject to alterations and irregularities. They appreciated that order and chaos were not binary opposites, but rather, two dimensions of the same reality. Such perspectives are reflected in the Greeks' polytheistic beliefs, where a multitude of deities, each with their own domains, temperaments, and interests, govern various aspects of the world.

In conclusion, the notion of 'Chaos' in the Ancient Greek worldview encapsulates an understanding of the universe as a vast, enigmatic, and continually evolving entity. The cosmos emerged from Chaos and remains in a state of constant flux, reflective of the eternal dance between order and disorder. This ancient perspective echoes contemporary scientific paradigms such as quantum mechanics and chaos theory, where the unpredictable and the probabilistic are integral components of existence.

Exercise: Reflect on the duality represented by Chaos, considering its implications as both the originator of disorder and the progenitor of order. How does this understanding of Chaos relate to the dichotomy of order and chaos in your own life?

Further reading: For a deeper understanding of the concept of 'Chaos' in the ancient Greek context, refer to Pierre Vidal-Naquet's "The Black Hunter: Forms of Thought and Forms of Society in the Greek World". Comparatively, the role of chaos in creation narratives in other ancient civilizations can be studied from Mircea Eliade's "Myth and Reality".

Gaia: Mother Earth

Proceeding in our discourse on primeval deities, we arrive at Gaia, the Ancient Greek embodiment of the Earth. Renowned as one of the first beings to emerge from Chaos, Gaia is a deity of profound importance, representing not only the physical planet but also the inherent fertility and nurturing qualities attributed to motherhood.

The name 'Gaia', or 'Ge' in earlier transliterations, is suggestive of a more profound, elemental force, rather than merely a divine personality. This etymological analysis provides an insight into the ancient Greek perception of the world as being intrinsically alive, a testament to the prevalence of animistic thought patterns in early societies.

Gaia's role within Greek cosmogony is of paramount importance. As Hesiod recounts in the 'Theogony', Gaia gave birth, without male intervention, to the sky (Uranus), the mountains, and the sea (Pontus). In this context, Gaia embodies the principle of parthenogenesis, the ability to reproduce without fertilization, emphasizing her status as the ultimate source of all life.

Moreover, Gaia, through her union with Uranus, brought forth a host of divine entities, the Titans, the Cyclopes, and the Hecatoncheires, further affirming her prolific nature. In some respects, Gaia serves as a symbol of nature's inexhaustible creativity, underlining the ancient Greeks' respect for and understanding of the fecundity inherent in the natural world.

Simultaneously, Gaia's narrative is not devoid of strife. In her relationships with her children, particularly the Titans, one can discern themes of rebellion, overthrow, and familial discord. Such narratives lend depth to Gaia's character, depicting her as a figure of authority and resilience, unwilling to countenance injustice even when perpetrated by her progeny.

In modern discourse, Gaia's name has been invoked in the Gaia Hypothesis proposed by James Lovelock. This hypothesis suggests that Earth functions as a self-regulating system, similar to a living organism, reinforcing the ancient view of Gaia as the sentient embodiment of our planet.

Exercise: Consider the various roles Gaia embodies – as mother, creator, and nurturer, but also as a force of justice. How do these varied aspects shape our understanding of Gaia as a deity and the Earth as an entity?

Further reading: For a more comprehensive exploration of Gaia and her significance in Greek mythology, refer to "The Gods of the Greeks" by Karl Kerenyi. Additionally, for an examination of the Gaia Hypothesis and its implications, consider "Gaia: A New Look at Life on Earth" by James Lovelock.

Analysis of Gaia's role in Greek mythology

Upon a closer inspection of the narratives, we discern that Gaia's role is multifaceted, revealing her as a deity of extraordinary influence and power. This discourse intends to illuminate the nuances of Gaia's role and significance within the context of Greek mythology.

Primarily, Gaia's representation as the earth itself distinguishes her from other deities. She is not a mere entity governing over a specific aspect of existence but is the embodiment of existence itself, making her a foundational force in the Greek cosmological narrative. This position situates Gaia as a primordial entity, one whose existence predates the familiar pantheon of Mount Olympus, and further amplifies her importance in the narrative of creation.

Moreover, Gaia's role as a mother is not confined to producing offspring. Rather, she is also seen as a protector and nurturer. This maternal aspect manifests most strikingly in her reactions to the ill-treatment of her children, which is depicted as not only triggering her wrath but also activating her sense of justice. When Cronus, one of her Titan children, seizes power and incarcerates his siblings, Gaia aids in orchestrating his overthrow by his son Zeus. This instance portrays Gaia as an advocate for cosmic order, suggesting a dimension of morality attached to her role.

Gaia also plays a critical role in Greek eschatology, or the study of the end times. According to Hesiod, it is prophesied that Gaia, along with her daughter Thalassa (the sea), will join the Titans in a cataclysmic war against the Olympian gods, leading to a period of destruction and chaos before the birth of a new age. This aspect not only cements her significance in the narrative but also presents her as a deity beyond mortal and divine control, capable of altering the course of existence itself.

From these instances, it is evident that Gaia occupies a dual role in Greek mythology, both as the creatrix and the final arbiter of existence. She is simultaneously a force of nurturing love and righteous retribution. Gaia's narrative invites us to consider the interconnectedness of creation and destruction, love and justice, pointing to a complex and nuanced understanding of these concepts in ancient Greek thought.

Exercise: Analyze Gaia's role as both a nurturing mother and an entity capable of retribution. How does this dual aspect of her character illuminate ancient Greek understandings of morality, justice, and the natural world?

Further Reading: For an in-depth study of Gaia's narrative and its implications, students are encouraged to read "The Goddesses in Greek Mythology" by Noel Robertson. Also, "The Theogony of Hesiod" provides direct access to one of the primary sources of Gaia's myth.

Gaia's role as a mother figure and her progeny

Gaia, as the primal Greek Earth Goddess, enjoys a unique place in the Greek mythical canon. However, it is her role as a mother figure and the examination of her progeny that truly distinguishes her, offering a rich, nuanced perspective on familial relationships and power dynamics within Greek mythology.

In Hesiod's cosmogony, Gaia generates her children asexually, birthing Uranus (Sky), Ourea (Mountains), and Pontus (Sea) directly from herself. Yet it is her relationship with her first-born, Uranus, that truly defines the initial generations of Greek mythology. She becomes the consort of Uranus, and together they generate the first pantheon of divine beings, including the Titans, Cyclopes, and the Hecatonchires.

The maternal aspect of Gaia's role is thus twofold. First, she gives life to the fundamental elements of the universe. Her offspring are not merely beings but the very constituents of existence itself. As such, Gaia is the matrix from which all creation springs, encapsulating an ideal of motherhood as both biological and cosmic genesis.

Secondly, Gaia's role as a mother extends to a deep sense of protective care for her children. When her mate Uranus turns tyrannical, imprisoning her offspring within her womb, Gaia experiences a profound sense of injustice. Her love for her children spurs her into action, leading to her crafting a sickle of adamant and planning the dethronement of Uranus. This defiance against Uranus speaks volumes about her as a mother: not only a creator but also a protector of her progeny.

Furthermore, Gaia's response to the imprisonment of her children, namely the assistance she provides to Cronus in castrating Uranus, is a compelling insight into the extent of her protective instincts. It is not merely personal affront or rage that motivates Gaia, but a profound sense of motherly duty, of ensuring safety and justice for her progeny.

Lastly, it is worth contemplating how Gaia's relationship with her children echoes throughout Greek mythology. Even as the generations of gods shift from Titans to Olympians, echoes of Gaia's influence and her role as the primeval mother reverberate. Whether it is through her direct interventions in the Titanomachy and Gigantomachy or through the continued reverence paid to her as the all-mother, Gaia's status as the maternal figure of the cosmos is indelible and undeniable.

Exercise: Compare Gaia's portrayal as a mother with representations of motherhood in other mythologies or cultures. Consider the implications of her willingness to rise against Uranus to protect her children.

Further Reading: For deeper insights into Gaia's role as a mother and the dynamics of her divine family, see "The Greek Myths" by Robert Graves. For primary source material, refer to Hesiod's "Theogony."

Uranus: The Sky God

The narrative of Greek mythology plunges into deeper complexities with the advent of Uranus, the personification of the Sky, born directly from Gaia, the Earth. As a foundational deity within the Greek cosmological framework, Uranus's mythos is vital for understanding the intricate mesh of power dynamics, cycles of violence, and cosmic balance in Greek mythology.

Uranus, or Ouranos, meaning 'sky' or 'heaven', is conceived by Gaia alone, solidifying her capacity for parthenogenesis, or asexual reproduction. In Hesiod's Theogony, Uranus is described as the equal of Gaia, encircling her on all sides to become her consort and the enveloping sphere of the heavens. This duality and interaction between Earth and Sky form the basis of the archaic cosmology of the ancient Greeks, a cosmic yin and yang that, together, gave birth to the world as we know it.

However, the union of Gaia and Uranus results in a complex family dynamic that is emblematic of the Greek mythical narrative's cyclical nature of violence and revolt. Together, Gaia and Uranus birth the Titans, the Hecatonchires, and the Cyclopes. Yet, Uranus proves to be a malevolent father. Fearing their power, he confines his children to the dark abyss of Tartarus within Gaia, causing her great pain.

This action incites the first generational conflict of the Greek pantheon, as Gaia, enraged and suffering, incites her children to rebel against their oppressive father. Uranus's downfall comes from his own lineage – Cronus, one of the Titans, using the adamantine sickle Gaia has crafted. The dismemberment of Uranus represents a cosmic coup d'état, symbolizing the tumultuous shift of power from one generation to the next.

The story of Uranus highlights several fundamental themes of Greek mythology. Firstly, it underscores the complex interplay between creation and destruction, love and violence that lies at the heart of these myths. Secondly, the narrative of Uranus provides a precedent for the succession myth, a motif that recurs with Cronus and his son, Zeus.

From an eco-spiritual perspective, Uranus can be seen as representing the often tumultuous relationship humanity has with the 'heavens', whether it be the unpredictable and sometimes destructive weather patterns or the vast and mysterious expanse of space.

Exercise: Reflect on the representation of father figures in mythology. Compare Uranus's role as a father with other father figures in different mythological contexts.

Uranus in mythological narratives

The figure of Uranus extends beyond the early cosmogonic narratives, maintaining his influential presence throughout Greek mythology. His depiction as the primordial Sky God, his role in the cycles of violence and succession, and his continuing significance in myth and symbol contribute to a more profound comprehension of the Greek cosmological worldview.

In Hesiod's Theogony, one of the most comprehensive sources for Greek cosmogony, the narrative of Uranus is one of high drama and profound symbolism. It illustrates the overthrow of an older, primordial power, embodying the sky by a younger, more organized deity, representing the more tangible and earthly. As we delve into the specifics of this narrative, Uranus appears not just as a divine entity but also as a character laden with symbolic meaning.

Uranus's dethronement by his son Cronus stands as a paragon of the succession myth, a common motif in various mythologies. The graphic imagery of his castration by Cronus symbolizes a shift of power from the primordial to the Titan generation. His severed genitals falling into the sea and leading to the birth of Aphrodite embody the intricate links between violence, creation, and beauty that frequently surface in Greek myths.

The father-son conflict between Uranus and Cronus finds echoes in the subsequent struggle between Cronus and Zeus. This pattern reinforces a cyclical understanding of time in Greek cosmology, where the son overthrowing the father becomes an almost inevitable cosmic recurrence. It introduces a thematic exploration of patricide, power dynamics, and the paradox of the 'tyrannical father' who sows the seeds of his own downfall.

However, Uranus's influence is not confined to violent rebellion or generational struggle. He also serves as a symbol of the boundless sky, representing the cosmos's celestial aspect. In later Hellenistic astrology, Uranus becomes associated with the zodiac, reaffirming his link with the heavens and astral phenomena. Furthermore, Uranus is invoked in magical rites and spells in the Greek Magical Papyri, underscoring his enduring cultural resonance.

To conclude, Uranus is more than a character in a narrative sequence; he is a personification of elemental forces and cosmic principles. His narrative arcs help elucidate various aspects of the human condition, like power, rebellion, paternity, and the cosmos's awe-inspiring enormity.

Discussion Question: Consider the cyclical pattern of power dynamics seen in Greek mythology, starting with Uranus. What are the implications of such a pattern in terms of understanding Greek views of leadership and power?

Further Reading: For an extended study of Uranus's role in Greek mythology, refer to "The Gods of the Greeks" by Károly Kerényi. For a philosophical interpretation of Uranus, see Friedrich Nietzsche's "Thus Spoke Zarathustra", especially the section titled "On the Three Metamorphoses", which uses Greek mythology for allegorical purposes.

The relationship between Gaia and Uranus

The symbiotic relationship between Gaia, the Mother Earth, and Uranus, the Sky Father, forms a central motif in the narratives of Greek cosmogony. This relationship not only manifests the quintessential unification of the earth and the sky but also presents a dynamic spectrum of gender roles, familial bonds, power dynamics, and conflict within the primal divine order.

One can discern in the association of Gaia and Uranus a fundamental cosmological principle: the marriage of the earth and the sky. As told in Hesiod's Theogony, Gaia, in her solitude, births Uranus, her equal, to cover her entirely, providing a celestial counterbalance to her terrestrial mass. Their union generates the initial set of divine beings, including the Titans, Cyclopes, and Hecatoncheires, thereby instigating the process of creation. Thus, the relationship between Gaia and Uranus symbolizes the necessity of balance between the terrestrial and celestial realms for the cosmos's functional coherence.

However, the symbiosis of Gaia and Uranus transcends the mere binary of earth and sky. It is also a narrative about power, conflict, and liberation. When Uranus, in his paranoia, imprisons Gaia's offspring within her womb, the maternal earth deity instigates the rebellion against the tyrannical sky deity. Here, Gaia's resourcefulness and strategic ingenuity are highlighted as she aids her son Cronus in dethroning his father. Such actions exhibit the dynamic qualities of these deities, challenging any simplistic perceptions of gendered passivity or domination.

Moreover, the story of Gaia and Uranus illustrates the destructive potential of power when unbridled by ethical considerations. Uranus's repressive rule incites the cycles of violent rebellion and patricide that come to characterize the successive divine generations. This narrative thread anticipates the turbulent history of the gods, presenting a foundational parable of power's cyclical abuse and upheaval.

In summation, the relationship between Gaia and Uranus offers a fertile ground for various thematic explorations. Their union and conflict serve as a microcosm of broader cosmological principles, power dynamics, and ethical dilemmas. Moreover, the repercussions of their interactions provide the impetus for the unfolding mythic history of the Greek gods.

Discussion Question: Reflect on the roles of Gaia and Uranus in the creation myth. How do their actions and interactions reflect the ancient Greeks' understanding of creation, power, and rebellion?

Further Reading: For a detailed analysis of the relationship between Gaia and Uranus, refer to "The Marriage of Heaven and Earth: A Visual Representation of the Greek Cosmogony in Archaic Art" by Nanno Marinatos. For a comparative study of creation myths, see "Creation Myths of the World: An Encyclopedia" by David A. Leeming.

The Titans: The Elder Gods

The Titans, an integral part of Greek mythology, represent a fascinating chapter of divine history. Descending from Gaia and Uranus, these 'elder gods' were pivotal figures in the cosmogonical narrative and played a substantial role in establishing the pantheon's complex hierarchy and dynamics.

The Titans comprised twelve principal deities: Oceanus, Tethys, Hyperion, Theia, Coeus, Phoebe, Cronus, Rhea, Mnemosyne, Themis, Crius, and Iapetus. These deities were associated with vast natural phenomena, ranging from celestial bodies to oceanic depths. As such, they personified the ancient Greeks' understanding and reverence of the natural world. For example, Oceanus and Tethys, the Titan pair who ruled over the world-encircling river, epitomize the interconnectedness of water bodies, a vital element in Greek geographical consciousness. Similarly, Hyperion and Theia, associated with the heavenly luminaries, reflect ancient celestial observations and the importance of heavenly bodies for temporal reckoning.

However, the Titan mythos is not confined to these elemental associations. Their narratives are steeped in themes of power, succession, and revolt. Cronus, the youngest of the Titans, famously overthrows his father, Uranus, only to meet a similar fate at the hands of his son, Zeus. This cyclical pattern of patricide and usurpation underscores the tumultuous struggle for power among the divine beings and the inexorable transience of rulership. The Titanomachy, the ten-year war between the Titans and the Olympians, is a testament to this ceaseless quest for supremacy, demonstrating the raw, primal forces at play in the cosmos' governance.

Furthermore, in analyzing the Titans, one cannot overlook the significant role of the female deities. Titanesses like Rhea, Themis, and Mnemosyne played pivotal roles in the cosmogonical narrative. They often served as mediators, custodians of wisdom, and nurturers, embodying a host of societal virtues and expectations. The prominence of the Titanesses in the Greek pantheon underscores a nuanced approach to divine femininity in Greek religious thought.

Ultimately, the Titans embody a raw, primordial power and play a critical role in establishing the cosmos and defining divine order. They represent both the awe-inspiring grandeur of nature and the capricious volatility of divine politics.

Discussion Question: Reflect on the role of the Titans in Greek cosmogony. How do their narratives contribute to the understanding of power dynamics and natural phenomena in ancient Greek society?

Further Reading: For more information about the Titans, please consult "The Gods of the Greeks" by Carl Kerenyi. For a comparative perspective on the Titans within the larger scope of ancient mythologies, refer to "The Oxford Companion to World Mythology" by David Leeming.

The Transition from Primeval to Titan Gods in Greek Cosmogony

Understanding the transition from primeval to Titan gods necessitates a deep dive into the mythological narratives in Greek cosmogony, primarily as narrated in Hesiod's "Theogony." According to this source, the primeval gods - Chaos, Gaia, Tartarus, and Eros - were the first entities to emerge at the universe's creation. Following these entities, Gaia gave birth to Uranus, the Mountains, and Pontus. In this context, Gaia and Uranus represent Earth and Sky, respectively, and their interaction heralds the beginning of a complex and somewhat tumultuous generational progression of divine beings.

Uranus, the Sky, mates with Gaia, the Earth, leading to the birth of the twelve Titans - Oceanus, Coeus, Crius, Hyperion, Iapetus, Theia, Rhea, Themis, Mnemosyne, Phoebe, Tethys, and Cronus. Thus, the Titans were born from the union of two primeval gods, representing a new generation of divine entities.

However, Uranus, fearing that his progeny might usurp his rule, confined them within Gaia's depths. Gaia, distressed by this action, plotted with her youngest Titan son Cronus to overthrow Uranus. Armed with a sickle gifted by Gaia, Cronus castrated his father Uranus, casting the severed genitals into the sea. The Titans were hence freed, and Cronus assumed dominion over the cosmos, marking the end of the reign of the primeval gods and the beginning of the age of the Titans.

Thus, it was not a peaceful handing over of power but rather an act of cosmic rebellion that led to the succession of the primeval gods by the Titans. This cyclical narrative of parent-child conflict, symbolic castration, and subsequent usurpation is a recurrent theme in Greek mythology, highlighting the ancient Greek understanding of power's transient nature, the struggle for dominance, and the inevitability of generational succession.

Exercise: Reflect on the transition from primeval gods to Titans. How does this change of power inform the themes of conflict, power, and rebellion in Greek mythology?

The significance of the Titans in Greek mythology

The Titans, these majestic elder deities, hold a pivotal place in Greek mythology. Being among the first generations of divine beings, they offer rich insights into the cosmogonical narrative and ancient Greek conceptions of the universe. However, the significance of the Titans extends far beyond their creation-oriented roles, imparting profound implications on socio-cultural, religious, and philosophical fronts.

One of the crucial aspects of the Titans' significance lies in their foundational role in establishing the cosmos. Their narratives evoke the primordial chaos and the subsequent structuring of the universe. As such, they are emblematic of the awe-inspiring, raw forces of nature. For instance, Oceanus personifies the endless waters encircling the earth, and Hyperion embodies the celestial light, demonstrating how the Titans were conceptual vehicles for the ancient Greeks to navigate their understanding of natural phenomena.

Moreover, the narratives surrounding the Titans serve as rich metaphoric explorations of power dynamics and cyclical time. The succession myth, involving Uranus, Cronus, and Zeus, frames a cycle of usurpation that represents an ancient perspective on political power's transient and cyclical nature. Such narratives, replete with familial conflicts and generational curses, hold a mirror to human society, presenting an exaggerated reflection of earthly power struggles.

Furthermore, the Titanomachy, the great war between the Titans and Olympians, symbolizes the conflict between old and new orders, chaos and cosmos, and stagnation and progress. It provides a mythological framework for the progression of ages, hinting at a primitive perception of historical change and societal development. This battle can also be interpreted as an allegorical representation of overcoming one's ancestral inheritance and shaping a new era—a potent narrative that would have resonated deeply within an ever-evolving Greek society.

In addition, the Titanesses such as Rhea, Themis, and Mnemosyne embody an array of societal and moral virtues—from motherhood and justice to memory. Their prominent roles in various myths reflect a multi-faceted approach to divine femininity, significantly influencing cultural constructs of gender roles.

Lastly, the Titans' narratives serve a vital religious function. They provided ancient Greeks with a means to understand their place in the world, connecting them with a divine past and offering a tangible link to the divine order. Moreover, with their elemental associations, they likely played an essential role in ancient nature worship and early animistic beliefs, precursors to more structured Hellenic religious practices.

In conclusion, the Titans' significance in Greek mythology transcends their cosmogonical function. They are not merely actors in a divine drama but embodiments of deep-seated societal structures, natural phenomena, and philosophical concepts. Their narratives shed light on the ancient Greeks' worldview, making them a subject of enduring relevance and intrigue.

Discussion Questions: How do the Titans' narratives reflect the societal norms and philosophical ideas of ancient Greece? In what ways do these narratives continue to hold relevance in contemporary discussions around power, conflict, and nature?

Key Titans and their roles (e.g., Cronus, Rhea, Hyperion)

The Titan generation of gods in Greek mythology encompasses an array of deities each associated with unique functions and roles. Among these, Cronus, Rhea, and Hyperion stand out due to their critical importance in various mythological narratives.

Cronus - The Quintessential Titan

Cronus, as depicted in Hesiod's "Theogony," is one of the most prominent Titans. His role is twofold: he serves as a progenitor, fathering several Olympian deities, and as a usurper, overthrowing his father Uranus. Cronus is most notably associated with time and harvest, a linkage that underscores the themes of cyclical nature, destruction, and regeneration. He signifies the inescapable passage of time and the inevitability of change, underscoring the transient nature of power.

However, Cronus's rule is marked by his fear of being overthrown, leading to the grotesque act of swallowing his offspring. This narrative accentuates themes of power and its abuses, and the cyclical nature of retribution. By illustrating Cronus's downfall, the ancient Greeks explore the consequences of hubris and the inexorable force of cosmic justice.

Rhea - The Mother of Gods

Rhea, Cronus's sister and wife, is another significant figure among the Titans. As the mother of key Olympian deities—Zeus, Hera, Poseidon, Hades, Demeter, and Hestia—she plays a pivotal role in the Greek pantheon's formation. Her fertility and maternal attributes contribute to her identity as the 'Mother of Gods'. Rhea's significance also lies in her crucial act of saving her son Zeus from Cronus, setting in motion the events leading to the Titanomachy. Thus, she symbolizes maternal instinct, fertility, and the concept of protective love, underscoring the power and cunning often associated with motherhood.

Hyperion - The Pillar of Light

Hyperion, another Titan, embodies celestial light and wisdom. As the father of Helios (Sun), Selene (Moon), and Eos (Dawn), his association with celestial bodies and illumination is prominent. He represents the primal cosmogonical principle of light, an essential force in the structuring of the universe. Thus, Hyperion's role extends beyond his physical associations to encapsulate enlightenment and knowledge, themes central to ancient Greek culture.

In conclusion, the roles and significance of these Titans—Cronus, Rhea, and Hyperion—are multilayered, embodying a range of natural phenomena, societal roles, and philosophical concepts. Their narratives, rich with symbolisms, offer profound insights into the ancient Greek worldview.

Discussion Questions: How do the stories of Cronus, Rhea, and Hyperion reflect ancient Greek values and fears? How do their roles contribute to our understanding of the cosmogonical narrative?

The Titanomachy: War of the Titans

The Titanomachy, or the War of the Titans, holds a pivotal place in Greek mythology and offers a fertile ground for examining conflict, power, and the evolution of divine leadership. It represents a cataclysmic struggle, the effects of which resonate through Greek cosmogony and reverberate in the many tales that ensued.

According to Hesiod's "Theogony," the Titanomachy transpired over ten grueling years, serving as a fulcrum for the transfer of power from the second to the third generation of gods. The progenitor of this conflict was the Titan Cronus, who, after overthrowing his father Uranus, came to rule over the cosmos. His reign was marked by fear, as he had been prophesied by Gaia and Uranus to be dethroned by his own child, mirroring the fate he had inflicted upon his father.

Driven by this forewarning, Cronus devoured each of his offspring at birth, a tactic intended to prevent their maturation and, thus, any threat to his dominion. However, when his sixth child, Zeus, was born, his wife, the Titaness Rhea, hid the newborn away on the island of Crete, offering Cronus a stone wrapped in swaddling clothes, which he consumed in the belief that it was his child. Zeus thus escaped his father's destructive grasp and grew in secrecy, later returning to free his swallowed siblings, the future Olympians: Poseidon, Hades, Hestia, Demeter, and Hera.

With the stage set for revolt, the Titanomachy ensued, a conflict that pitted the Titans, led by Cronus, against the younger gods, the Olympians, marshaled by Zeus. Titans and Olympians clashed in fierce, monumental battles. The war swayed when Zeus freed the Cyclopes and the hundred-handed Hecatoncheires, powerful entities who had been imprisoned by Uranus and remained confined during Cronus' reign. In gratitude, the Cyclopes bestowed upon Zeus his signature thunderbolts, alongside other potent gifts for his siblings.

Thus armed, the Olympians launched a decisive attack against the Titans, casting them into Tartarus, a deep abyss located at the cosmos' edges. With this victory, the Olympians, under Zeus, ascended to power, marking the dawn of a new era and the commencement of Olympian hegemony.

The Titanomachy, while reflecting a mythical clash of divine beings, also encapsulates many aspects of the human condition and societal evolution, such as the fear of generational shift, power dynamics, rebellion, and change. It underlines the inherent transience of power and underscores the age-old adage: "just as fathers are overthrown by sons, so too are sons destined to be overthrown by their progeny."

Exercise: Analyze the Titanomachy in terms of its representation of power dynamics and generational conflict. What does this mythological conflict reveal about the ancient Greek understanding of leadership, change, and the cyclical nature of power?

Other Elemental Forces: From Eros to Nyx

In Hesiod's cosmogony, the Greek pantheon consists not only of Titans and Olympians but also encompasses a multitude of elemental forces, each manifesting distinct aspects of the universe and life within it. Among the most prominent are Eros, the primordial embodiment of love and attraction, and Nyx, the personification of night. Delving into these archaic figures offers illuminating perspectives on the Greeks' worldview and their comprehension of natural phenomena and universal truths.

Eros: The Primeval Force of Attraction

Eros, one of the earliest entities born from Chaos in Greek mythology, is a primal deity that represents love and desire. While the modern term 'erotic' draws from his name, underscoring his association with passionate love, a deeper exploration reveals that Eros is more than the god of love as commonly conceived in a romantic or sensual sense. In Greek cosmogony, Eros signifies a broader, more universal principle: the intrinsic force that drives attraction and connection at the most fundamental levels of existence.

Hesiod's "Theogony" presents Eros as a pivotal figure in the fabric of the cosmos. He emerges as a cosmic force capable of initiating creation and fostering connections. This deity embodies the drive towards unity and cohesion, functioning as a universal adhesive that binds the cosmos together. This yearning for unity and order is as evident in the grand dance of celestial bodies as it is in human relationships and the process of procreation.

Eros also plays a role within individuals, driving them towards wholeness. Plato's "Symposium" depicts Eros as a fundamental force that stimulates individuals' quest for self-completion. This portrayal of Eros underscores its role as a catalyst for self-improvement and self-realization, enabling the pursuit of philosophical and spiritual ideals.

As time passed, the portrayal of Eros shifted. Hellenistic and Roman depictions presented him as Cupid, a mischievous child with a bow and arrow, a portrayal that focused on the unpredictable and capricious nature of romantic desire. However, this more humanized depiction should not eclipse the profound significance of the primeval Eros, a cosmological principle of attraction and connection that transcends the interpersonal dimension of love.

In the intricate web of Greek cosmogony, Eros instigates the connection between Earth (Gaia) and Sky (Uranus), sparking a cycle of creation that includes divine entities such as the Titans and Giants. Eros, in essence, underpins the cosmos's order, ensuring the interrelatedness of beings and promoting continuity and growth. This principle is also apparent in the relationships between the gods and their offspring, including the births of Aphrodite from the foam formed by Uranus' severed genitals and Dionysus from Zeus' thigh. These instances of creation from the union of different entities symbolize the workings of Eros on a divine level.

In conclusion, Eros, transcending the simplistic notion of a god of romantic love, serves as a cosmic catalyst in Greek cosmogony. It represents a powerful, primal force that binds entities together, instigating a continuous cycle of creation and contributing to the cosmos's constant evolution. This broad concept of Eros provides profound insight into the ancient Greeks' understanding of the universe, where love and attraction are integral aspects of existence, unifying and diversifying the cosmos.

Nyx: The Enigmatic Darkness

In Greek cosmogony, Nyx, the embodiment of night, emerged directly from Chaos as one of the first entities to populate the cosmos. Born of Chaos, this elusive goddess personifies not merely the absence of light, but the multifarious aspects of night: mystery, rest, trepidation, and even death. Through her, we gain insight into the Greeks' understanding of natural forces as inherently dualistic, their night viewed as a time of uncertainty and potential danger, yet also a period of rest and renewal. The duality embodied by Nyx is a testament to the Greeks' perceptions of the cosmos and their position within it.

Hesiod's "Theogony" presents Nyx as a potent entity, birthing a host of personified phenomena such as Hypnos (Sleep), Thanatos (Death), Oneiroi (Dreams), and the Moirai (Fates), without male involvement. This lineage underscores her pervasive influence on every aspect of existence and reflects the night's protean nature, varying in significance according to different contexts and perspectives. Nyx's role within Greek cosmogony is significant, highlighting human attempts to grapple with and comprehend the vast array of life experiences, from the mundane to the mystical.

Each of Nyx's progeny embodies aspects of the night and human existence. Hypnos represents the rest and rejuvenation that night brings, but also oblivion and vulnerability. Thanatos stands as the stark reminder of mortality's inevitable end, while the Moirai symbolize the inexorable progression of life and the interplay of destiny and chance. Their varied natures illustrate the broad spectrum of life experiences and existential concerns encapsulated by the night.

Despite her enigmatic nature, Nyx's role in the Greek cosmic narrative is further explored in "The Cambridge Companion to Greek Mythology". This exploration offers a more profound comprehension of how the ancient Greeks perceived the cosmos and their place within it. Nyx, through her progeny, exerts her influence on the cosmic order, despite her lack of direct interactions. These offspring hold key roles in the lives of both gods and mortals, indicating the profound reach of the night goddess.

Hypnos, for instance, has the power to induce sleep in both gods and humans, thereby altering the course of significant mythological events, such as the Trojan War. Thanatos, meanwhile, personifies death, which holds an unavoidable sway over mortals, and the Moirai, controlling destiny, wield one of the greatest powers in the Greek cosmos. Thus, even though Nyx herself is an enigmatic figure, her influence is felt through her progeny.

The study of Nyx and her children thus offers invaluable insight into the Greeks' perception of the cosmos, revealing their philosophical exploration of universal principles such as attraction, unity, duality, and the interplay between light and dark, life and death, consciousness and the unconscious.

Exercises:

Evaluate the roles of Eros and Nyx in the context of Greek cosmogony. How do they contribute to our understanding of the ancient Greeks' perception of the cosmos? How do their roles reflect the cultural and philosophical perspectives of ancient Greece?

Reflect on the implications of Nyx's progeny on how the Greeks viewed the night. What does this suggest about their understanding of the cosmos and human existence?

Reflect on the symbolism of Nyx's offspring (Sleep, Death, and Fates). How do these entities reflect different facets of the night and its implications for humans and gods alike?

Reflect upon the roles of these elemental deities in major mythological narratives. How do these interactions enhance your understanding of Greek cosmogony?

Brief overview of other elemental deities and their roles

The Greek cosmogony, replete with a rich assortment of deities and primordial entities, portrays a world where elemental and divine forces coalesce to govern the cosmos's fabric. Four such significant elemental forces are Eros, Erebus, Tartarus, and Nyx. Their roles, while variegated, are essential in the broader context of Greek mythology and the interpretation of ancient cosmological beliefs.

Erebus: The Personification of Darkness

In the realm of Greek mythology, Erebus stands as a symbol of darkness and obscurity. Emerging from Chaos itself, Erebus is a primordial force that speaks to the ancient Greeks' conceptualization of life, knowledge, and the cosmos. This understanding is deeply rooted in a matrix of dualities and cycles, with Erebus offering a contrast to the realm of light.

Erebus, however, is not merely an abstract representation of darkness or shadow. This deity's essence is intimately tied to a specific realm - the underworld, a territory shrouded in mystery that serves as the dwelling place for the dead. The world of Erebus is one of profound darkness, lying beneath the earth and only penetrable by those who have passed from the mortal world. This intricate association of Erebus with the underworld demonstrates the deity's function as a marker of borders - between life and death, the known and unknown, the visible and invisible.

The essence of Erebus extends beyond the physical representation of darkness and delves into the metaphysical realm. This deity embodies the unknown, the unfathomable, thereby symbolizing human awe and fear of the unseen and unexplored. The obscurity that Erebus personifies extends from the depths of the earth to the vast abyss of the night sky. Consequently, this deity provides a valuable insight into the Greeks' understanding of human knowledge's limits and the profound mysteries that lie beyond these boundaries.

Interestingly, the cosmogonic narrative surrounding Erebus provides further depth to its symbolism. Erebus, in conjunction with Nyx, the personification of night, gives rise to Aether, the heavenly light, and Hemera, the light of day. This detail underscores the Greeks' understanding of the cyclical interchange between light and dark. This duality indicates the Greeks' philosophical conception that knowledge and ignorance, light and darkness, are interdependent. Neither can exist or be comprehended without the other, and their cyclical interchange is integral to the rhythms of life and the cosmos.

Erebus's representation also offers critical insights into the Greek attitudes towards death. The strong association of Erebus with the underworld manifests a perception of death as a journey into the unknown. It is a transition from light into the unfathomable darkness, marking the end of mortal existence and the beginning of an enigmatic journey in the realm of Erebus.

In summary, Erebus's role within Greek cosmogony underscores the deity as more than just an embodiment of darkness. It epitomizes the enigma of the unknown and the primordial fear associated with it. However, through its progeny, Erebus facilitates the cyclical transition to light and knowledge, thus exerting influence on the cosmic order and progression. As such, Erebus emerges as a profound symbol in the Greek cosmogonical narrative, illuminating the Greeks' perception of life, death, knowledge, and the cosmos.

Exercise: Reflect on the philosophical implications of the relationship between Erebus and his progeny. How does this familial dynamic echo broader themes within Greek cosmology and philosophy?

Exercise: Consider the role of Erebus within the Greek perception of the underworld and the afterlife. How might the symbolism of Erebus have shaped or reflected ancient Greek funerary practices and beliefs?

Exercise: Analyze the connections between the attributes of Erebus and contemporary attitudes towards the unknown. How might these ancient conceptions of darkness and obscurity resonate within modern contexts, such as attitudes towards death, knowledge, and the exploration of outer space?

Tartarus: The Deep Abyss

As a location, Tartarus is as far beneath the earth as the earth is from the sky, a depiction that conveys its role as a formidable prison, the ultimate symbol of retribution for severe transgressions against divine and natural laws.

In the intricate narrative of Greek cosmogony, Tartarus holds a significant place. Its role, beyond being the primeval depth of the universe, extends to being the manifestation of divine justice. This understanding of Tartarus echoes in the ancient Greek ethos, particularly encapsulating the principle of 'dikē,' the equilibrium of justice and moral order.

Tartarus is not a mere repository of the wicked mortal souls; it is also the confinement of those divine entities guilty of upsetting the cosmic balance. The primeval Titans, dethroned by the Olympians during the cataclysmic Titanomachy, find their eternal prison within Tartarus, as does the monstrous Typhoeus. These narratives underscore the primordial concept of justice in Greek cosmology: not even beings of divine origin are immune to the consequences of their transgressions against the cosmic order.

Moreover, Tartarus, in its capacity as both a deity and a place, enhances our understanding of the Greek cosmological imagination. This dualistic nature depicts an interconnected cosmos where entities and their domains are not separate but parts of a larger, harmoniously interwoven whole.

Exercise: Analyze the symbolism of Tartarus within the context of Greek societal norms and justice systems. How does Tartarus, as the embodiment of ultimate retribution, reflect the ancient Greeks' understanding of law, justice, and punishment?

Tartarus: The Ultimate Boundary

In Greek cosmogony, Tartarus holds a unique dual status, personifying the vast, impenetrable abyss while also embodying the ultimate prison, the farthest boundary and end of all things. As such, Tartarus serves as a potent symbol of divine retribution, its existence vital to maintaining cosmic balance.

The notion of Tartarus speaks volumes about the Greek perception of justice, moral order, and the nature of evil. By confining those guilty of severe transgressions to this impenetrable abyss, Tartarus embodies the principle of 'dikē.' This principle signifies an inherent equilibrium that must be maintained in the cosmos, necessitating severe retribution in cases of profound violations.

The profound significance of Tartarus is evident in various Greek myths. The Titans, for example, who committed the hubris of challenging the Olympians, were banished to Tartarus, underlining the unforgiving nature of divine justice. Similarly, Typhoeus, a monstrous storm giant, found his eternal punishment within the depths of Tartarus. These narratives underscore the infallibility of the cosmic order and the severe consequences faced by those who dare to disrupt it.

Exercise: Discuss the role of Tartarus within the framework of ancient Greek philosophies. How does its embodiment of justice and retribution correlate with philosophical teachings on ethics and morality?

The Primeval Gods in Ancient Greek Religion

The primeval gods, or the Protogenoi, in ancient Greek religion represent the elemental aspects of the cosmos. They embody fundamental principles of existence, such as Earth, Sky, Sea, Darkness, Night, and Love. Their ontological status in Greek cosmogony sets the stage for the entire creation narrative. To comprehend their roles, interactions, and influence on the cosmos, we need to delve into each of these primeval gods and their associated elements.

Gaia: The All-Nourishing Earth

As one of the first primordial deities springing from Chaos, Gaia embodies the fertile Earth from which all life burgeons. Depicted as the omnipresent provider, the nurturing maternal figure, she is held in high regard for her unending generosity in bestowing sustenance to all. Her pervasive presence underscores the intricate relationship between the inhabitants of Earth and their environment, which was particularly salient in ancient Greek society, given their reliance on agriculture and natural resources.

The etymology of Gaia, traced back to the Proto-Indo-European '*ǵʰehₗ-', meaning 'to increase' or 'to nourish', underscores her role as the life-sustainer. She is often depicted as a serene matron or as the Earth itself, a testament to her role as a nurturing figure. In Hesiod's "Theogony", Gaia is an autonomous entity who, without the need for a masculine counterpart, gives birth to Ouranos (the Sky), Ourea (the Mountains), and Pontus (the Sea). This act of parthenogenesis is indicative of Gaia's supreme power, demonstrating her capacity to create and shape the cosmos single-handedly.

Moreover, Gaia's ability to bring forth the Sky, the Sea, and the Mountains signifies the symbiosis between different aspects of the natural world. The Greeks envisioned their universe as an orderly, harmonious system, where each element, while distinct, is interconnected. The offspring of Gaia represent various elements of the cosmos, denoting her as the original source from which the diversity of the universe unfolds.

Gaia's narrative extends beyond creation. She plays a crucial role in the succession myth, where she assists her son, Cronus, in overthrowing Ouranos, and later aids her grandson, Zeus, in defeating Cronus. This cyclical narrative of rebellion and usurpation underscores the inherent instability of power and the ceaseless change in the cosmos.

In summary, Gaia's embodiment as the all-nourishing Earth highlights the Greeks' perception of the earth as a reliable provider and a powerful entity capable of creation and destruction. Her story encapsulates themes of fertility, rebellion, and cyclical change, offering insights into the dynamic nature of the cosmos and the Greek understanding of their world's inherent interconnections.

\

Ouranos: The Vast, Starry Sky

Emerging from the fertile earth of Gaia, Ouranos, the Sky, symbolizes the celestial expanse. As Gaia's offspring and consort, Ouranos embodies the vast, starry cloak enveloping the Earth, stretching from horizon to horizon, where the earth and the heavens meet. He represents the boundless limits of the cosmos, the sublime space where the divine drama unfolds, shaping the Greek cosmogonic narrative.

The Greeks envisioned Ouranos as an embodiment of celestial order and majestic grandeur. As the infinite dome enclosing the world, Ouranos symbolizes an ordered cosmos, where celestial bodies follow predictable paths, inspiring the Greek understanding of cosmic harmony and regularity. The etymology of Ouranos, associated with the Proto-Indo-European root for "rain," suggests a possible role as a rain-giver, reflecting the Sky's fertility aspect that, coupled with Earth's productivity, nurtures life.

As the personification of the Sky, Ouranos also shares a deeply intimate relationship with Gaia. Their union, representing the confluence of earth and sky, signifies the primal creative act, resulting in the birth of the first generation of the Titans, the Cyclopes, and the Hecatoncheires. The mythology thus depicts Ouranos as both an overarching entity and a progenitor, affirming his role in shaping the genealogical tree of the Greek deities.

However, despite his celestial majesty and paternal role, Ouranos is remembered in Greek mythology as a tyrant. He imprisons his offspring, the Hecatoncheires and the Cyclopes, within Gaia, causing her great pain. This act catalyzes the first instance of divine rebellion, as Cronus, the youngest Titan, guided by Gaia, castrates Ouranos, thereby separating the Earth and Sky.

This narrative not only underscores the theme of intergenerational conflict and succession but also symbolizes the separation of different cosmic domains. This act is a defining moment in the cosmogonic narrative, indicating the transition from an undifferentiated cosmos to a structured universe with clearly defined realms: the Heavens, the Earth, and the Underworld.

In summary, Ouranos' characterization as the vast, starry sky reflects the ancient Greeks' attempts to comprehend the grandeur of the cosmos. His narrative represents the unifying celestial dome, the primal creative force, the divine patriarch, and the despotic ruler. These aspects elucidate the dynamic interplay between order and chaos, unity and differentiation, and stability and change in Greek cosmogony.

Pontus: The Unfathomable Sea

Pontus, born from Gaia without a consort, personifies the sea in its boundless and tumultuous majesty. As one of the primeval deities in Greek cosmogony, Pontus symbolizes the chaotic, untamed, and unpredictable forces of nature that counterpoise the stability represented by Gaia, the Earth, and Ouranos, the Sky. This deity illustrates the Greek understanding of the sea as a vital, albeit chaotic, component of the cosmos, an element that complements and contrasts with the terrestrial and celestial realms.

The sea, as embodied by Pontus, encapsulates paradoxical aspects. It is both life-sustaining and treacherous, enabling maritime travel, trade, and fishing, while simultaneously posing significant threats with its volatile storms and enigmatic depths. This duality reflects the Greek perception of the sea as a potent but unpredictable entity, a provider and destroyer, intrinsically connected to human life but forever beyond complete human control.

Pontus' genealogy further underscores his association with the world's turbulent and enigmatic aspects. His union with Gaia begets the ancient sea gods Nereus, Thaumas, Phorcys, Ceto, and Eurybia. These deities and their descendants, which include formidable sea monsters and beautiful Nereids, signify the diverse, marvelous, and often terrifying creatures believed to inhabit the maritime realm. This divine and monstrous progeny underscores the sea's multifaceted symbolism, reflecting its capacity to inspire both awe and fear.

One of Pontus' notable offspring is Nereus, often referred to as the "Old Man of the Sea". Nereus embodies the more benevolent and navigable aspects of the sea and is a symbol of the sea's wisdom and tranquility, in stark contrast to his sibling Typhoeus, a monstrous storm giant. The stark differences between Pontus' children highlight the sea's paradoxical nature, teeming with dangers and wonders, mysteries and revelations.

Moreover, it is worth noting that Pontus, despite being a primordial entity, does not feature prominently in Greek myths as an active character. His role is primarily generative, and his character remains largely undefined, which might mirror the Greek view of the sea: ever-present, profoundly influential, but elusive in its vast expanse and fathomless depths.

In summary, Pontus, the personification of the sea, provides a lens to explore how the ancient Greeks understood and interacted with the marine environment. The deity's character and lineage embody the sea's dual aspects: its capacity to nurture and destroy, its unpredictable moods, and its abundant yet often enigmatic life forms. Understanding Pontus thus enriches our comprehension of the Greek cosmos, underscoring the essential, dynamic, and often volatile relationship between humans and the natural world.

Conclusion: The Interconnectedness of the Primeval Gods

The primeval gods and their elemental representations are interconnected, each playing a significant role in shaping the universe and maintaining cosmic balance. Their complex interactions provide a narrative for the creation, progression, and operation of the cosmos, influencing the subsequent generation of gods and humans alike.

Discussion Questions :

Reflect on the anthropomorphizing of natural elements in Greek cosmogony. What might have led ancient Greeks to personify these elements as deities?

Explore the philosophical implications of the roles and interactions of the primeval gods. How do they reflect ancient Greek understanding of existence and the cosmos?

Delve into the narrative role of the primeval gods in Greek myths. How do their personalities and conflicts drive the stories and provide deeper meanings?

Influence on ancient rituals, magic, and divination

The concept of Tartarus, deeply embedded in Greek mythology and cosmology, has had significant impact on ancient rituals, magic, and divination practices. This influence spans a vast spectrum, from ritualistic behaviors aimed at appeasing the divine and avoiding a fate akin to Tartarus, to divination methods seeking guidance from the deities, and magical practices intended to wield or counter supernatural forces.

Tartarus and Ritual Practices

Ritual practices in ancient Greece, designed to communicate with or appease the gods, were significantly influenced by the concept of Tartarus. Fear of divine retribution, exemplified by the Tartarus myth, was a potent motivating factor behind the performance of these rites. The underlying belief system emphasized adherence to a moral and cosmic order to avoid punitive justice.

Take, for instance, the act of animal sacrifice, a prevalent ritual in ancient Greek religion. Such sacrifices were not only expressions of devotion but were also seen as measures to ensure divine favor and avoid divine wrath. The notion of Tartarus, with its implication of severe punishment for transgressions against the divine order, certainly informed the seriousness with which these rituals were conducted.

Exercise: Analyze the role of fear of divine retribution, as embodied by Tartarus, in the execution of ancient Greek rituals. Does this fear predominantly manifest in a particular type of ritual?

Influence on Magic and Witchcraft

The concept of Tartarus also found resonance in the magical practices and witchcraft of ancient Greece. The punishment meted out to those who violated cosmic laws, as embodied by Tartarus, served as a cautionary tale within these practices. Magic and witchcraft, often seen as tools to manipulate or influence the natural and divine order, had to be exercised with caution, lest the practitioners meet a fate similar to the Titans.

Moreover, the stories revolving around Tartarus were woven into magical incantations and spells as a form of sympathetic magic. An individual might, for instance, use a spell invoking the names of the Titans trapped in Tartarus to bind or incapacitate an enemy.

Exercise: Investigate the intersection of Greek mythology and magic. How does the narrative of Tartarus and its inhabitants influence the practice and theory of witchcraft in ancient Greece?

Tartarus and Divination Practices

Divination, the practice of seeking knowledge or guidance from the divine, was another area influenced by the concept of Tartarus. The idea that divine entities, such as the Titans, could be punished for transgressing the cosmic order underscored the power of the gods and the necessity to understand their will.

Augury, interpreting the flight patterns of birds, and extispicy, examining the entrails of sacrificed animals, were common forms of divination. Both methods sought to discern the will of the gods to avoid displeasing them and risking a fate comparable to Tartarus. The ominous nature of Tartarus also likely contributed to the somber gravity with which these divination practices were approached.

Exercise: Discuss the psychological impact of the Tartarus myth on divination practices. How might the threat of divine punishment influence the approach and mindset of ancient Greek diviners?

In essence, the specter of Tartarus, as a symbol of divine retribution and cosmic justice, loomed large over ancient Greek rituals, magic, and divination. Its influence underscored the need for respect and adherence to the divine order, a concept that permeated various aspects of Greek spiritual and sociocultural practices.

Comparison between Primeval and Olympian Gods

The pantheon of ancient Greek mythology is home to an array of deities, demigods, and monstrous creatures, all of whom contribute to the richness and complexity of the Greek cosmological imagination. Central to these are two classes of deities: the Primeval Gods and the Olympian Gods. Although both groups hold significant roles within the mythological narrative, their responsibilities, narratives, and power dynamics are fundamentally distinct.

Key Differences in Roles, Responsibilities, and Narratives

✧   Primeval Gods

The Primeval Gods, also known as the Protogenoi, represent the very elements of the cosmos - sky, earth, sea, and even abstract concepts like time and love. As personifications of natural and cosmic phenomena, their roles are intrinsic to the fundamental structures of the universe. For instance, Gaia represents the Earth itself, Uranus the Sky, and Chronos stands for Time.

These deities are the genesis of Greek mythology, birthing the Titans, Giants, and many monstrous beings. They are more associated with the creation of the universe than with human affairs, and their narratives often involve grand, cosmic events, such as the birth of the world or the creation of the heavenly bodies.

✧   Olympian Gods

In contrast, the Olympian Gods, while also powerful, are more anthropomorphic, possessing human-like characteristics and emotions. They are the offspring of the Titans, themselves children of the Primeval Gods, and are seen as the ruling deities of the cosmos, residing on Mount Olympus.

The Olympians have specific roles and responsibilities akin to a societal structure, reflecting various aspects of human life and culture. For instance, Athena is the goddess of wisdom and warfare, Hermes is the messenger of the gods and patron of commerce and thieves, and Dionysus is the god of wine and festive revelry.

Unlike the narratives surrounding the Primeval Gods, those of the Olympian Gods often involve human interactions, moral lessons, and tales of honor, treachery, love, and revenge.

The Transition of Power from the Primeval to the Olympian Gods

The transition from the rule of the Primeval Gods to the Olympian Gods is a critical theme in Greek mythology, encapsulating a power shift from elemental forces to more relatable, human-like entities. This transition is characterized by a series of violent struggles, the most significant of which are the Titanomachy and the Gigantomachy.

✧ Titanomachy

The Titanomachy is a ten-year-long conflict between the Titans, led by Cronus, and the Olympians, led by Zeus. The Olympians emerged victorious, resulting in the overthrow of the Titans and their incarceration in Tartarus, the cosmic abyss.

This clash symbolizes the struggle between the old, primeval order and the new, more structured Olympian order. It is a narrative that emphasizes the dynamic nature of the cosmos, the inevitability of change, and the harsh consequences of resisting that change.

✧ Gigantomachy

The Gigantomachy is another significant battle, this time between the Olympians and the Giants, monstrous offspring of Gaia, a Primeval deity. Again, the Olympians were victorious, further cementing their rule over the cosmos.

These power transitions highlight a shift from chaos to order, from the elemental to the humanistic. They suggest an evolution in the Greek understanding of divinity, reflecting perhaps the evolution of societal structures and norms.

Exercise: Analyze the symbolism behind the transition of power from the Primeval Gods to the Olympian Gods. What societal changes might this transition reflect?

In conclusion, while both the Primeval and the Olympian Gods are central to Greek mythology, they represent different stages of the cosmological order. Understanding their roles, responsibilities, narratives, and the transitions between them is essential to a nuanced understanding of Greek mythology.

The Legacy of the Primeval Gods

In tracing the chronicles of time, it becomes evident that the Primeval Gods, despite their displacement from the central narrative of Greek mythology by the Olympian Gods, have left an enduring impact. Their legacy can be found within the realms of literature, philosophy, and spiritual practices, extending from ancient Greece to modern neo-pagan traditions.

The Influence of the Primeval Gods on Later Greek Literature and Philosophy

✧   Influence on Greek Literature

In the realm of Greek literature, the Primeval Gods occupy a position of utmost importance. Their narratives form the basis for many epic poems, plays, and hymns. Homer, in his epic poems "The Iliad" and "The Odyssey," makes numerous references to the Primeval Gods, often invoking their elemental powers to underline the majesty and might of the natural world.

Hesiod's "Theogony," an account of the origins and genealogies of the gods, extensively chronicles the birth, life, and rule of the Primeval Gods, thereby immortalizing them in the annals of literature.

✧   Influence on Greek Philosophy

Greek philosophers often incorporated elements of myth, including those relating to the Primeval Gods, into their philosophical discourses. Plato, for example, made use of the cosmogonic myth in his dialogue "Timaeus," discussing the formation of the world by a divine craftsman, drawing parallels with the acts of the Primeval Gods.

The concept of Chaos, the first of the Primeval Gods, was of particular interest to philosophers as a philosophical concept, leading to discussions about the nature of the cosmos, order, and the metaphysical.

The Impact of Primeval Gods on Modern Spiritual Practices and Neo-pagan Traditions

✧   Influence on Modern Spiritual Practices

In the realm of modern spiritual practices, the Primeval Gods continue to hold sway. Their raw, elemental power and association with the fundamentals of the universe make them appealing figures for those seeking a deeper connection with nature and the cosmos.

The Primeval God Gaia, for instance, is often invoked in ecological movements and practices, seen as the personification of the Earth Mother. Similarly, Uranus, the primeval god of the sky, is invoked in astrological and cosmological discourses.

✧   Influence on Neo-Pagan Traditions

In neo-pagan traditions, the Primeval Gods have found a new wave of followers. Practices such as Wicca, Hellenism, and Druidry often honor these deities in their rituals and celebrations, seeing in them the embodiment of natural forces and cosmic principles.

The reverence of the Primeval Gods offers neo-pagans a chance to honor the foundational aspects of existence, symbolizing a return to the roots, the elemental, and the primal.

Exercise: Analyze the enduring legacy of the Primeval Gods in contemporary literature, philosophy, and spirituality. How have these deities been reinterpreted in modern contexts?

In conclusion, the legacy of the Primeval Gods is robust and enduring, extending from the realm of ancient literature and philosophy to modern spiritual practices and neo-pagan traditions. Despite the passing of millennia, their elemental power continues to resonate, underscoring their timeless relevance in understanding the cosmos and our place within it.

Chapter 4: Interactions between Ancient Greek and African Religions: A Historical Overview

In the variegated landscape of the ancient world, interactions between different civilizations were inevitable. From the Mediterranean's azure shores to the expansive Saharan dunes, ideas, practices, and beliefs crossed geographic, cultural, and temporal boundaries. It is within this context that we begin our exploration of the interaction between ancient Greek and African religions, a topic that yields a rich tapestry of shared traditions, syncretic deities, and reciprocal cultural exchanges.

The chapter commences with an analysis of the historical circumstances fostering these interactions. Geographic proximity played a significant role, with the North African region sharing the Mediterranean Sea's basin with ancient Greece. Key historical events—such as the Greek colonization of Cyrene, the establishment of the Ptolemaic dynasty in Egypt, and the expeditions of Alexander the Great—provide pivotal moments for a chronological evaluation of the exchanges and influences between these two realms.

Following the chronological framework, we delve into an examination of shared religious themes and syncretic deities. A notable example is the fusion of Greek and Egyptian religions resulting in deities like Serapis, a god who combined aspects of Osiris and Apis from the Egyptian pantheon with Hellenistic features. The concept of Isis, the Egyptian goddess, evolved and gained immense popularity in the Hellenistic world, embodying the shared cultural and religious sentiments of the era.

Next, the focus turns to the interaction between ancient Greek and sub-Saharan African religions. Although direct interactions were less due to geographic constraints, evidence suggests a certain degree of indirect influence through intermediary civilizations. The exploration of such interactions provides an intriguing avenue to appreciate the diffusion of religious ideas and practices.

Finally, the chapter concludes with an analysis of the enduring legacies of these interactions in the modern world. From the modern spiritual practices that draw upon these syncretic traditions, to the enduring impact on art, literature, and philosophy, the influence of these interactions continues to reverberate through the ages.

Throughout this chapter, we will adhere to a balanced and objective approach, acknowledging that in the study of historical interactions, different interpretations may arise due to the diversity of sources and the complexities of cultural transmissions. It is our hope that the ensuing discussions will foster an appreciation for the complex tapestry of interactions between these ancient civilizations and stimulate further inquiry into this fascinating subject.

Exercise: Reflect on how cultural exchanges, particularly in the sphere of religion, can influence and shape civilizations. Consider both the ancient context of Greek and African interactions and its resonance in the modern world.

The importance of understanding cross-cultural interactions in the study of ancient religions.

Cross-cultural interactions, in the broad panorama of human history, have served as crucial vectors in the dissemination of ideas, belief systems, and religious practices. Recognizing the significance of these interactions becomes an indispensable asset when one embarks upon the study of ancient religions. This chapter aims to highlight the criticality of understanding these interactions and seeks to explain how they contribute to a more nuanced and in-depth appreciation of ancient religions' nature, evolution, and influence.

A substantive exploration of ancient religions cannot be limited to an isolated examination of individual cultures or regions. Instead, it demands a broader perspective—one that acknowledges the porous boundaries of ancient societies and recognizes that ideas and beliefs traversed those boundaries, influenced by, and influencing, the societies they entered. It is this intercultural interplay that enriched, diversified, and redefined religious practices and beliefs across the world.

Drawing upon specific examples, such as the interactions between ancient Greece and Egypt, we can observe the tangible impact of these cultural exchanges. The syncretism of deities such as Serapis and the Hellenistic interpretation of Isis offer evidence of the profound influence that these interactions had on religious thought and practice. Additionally, the cross-pollination of ideas led to the transformation of theological constructs and religious rituals, enhancing their complexity and broadening their scope.

Further, cross-cultural interactions have also played a role in the proliferation of various forms of spirituality, including magic and divination, across different societies. The transmission of these practices, often adapted to suit local contexts, underscores the dynamic nature of spiritual beliefs and the role of intercultural communication in facilitating their spread.

These examples exemplify how understanding cross-cultural interactions can enrich the study of ancient religions. By acknowledging these exchanges, we not only gain a more comprehensive understanding of individual religions but also of the broader religious landscape of the ancient world. Furthermore, these cross-cultural interactions can also shed light on the societal, political, and economic contexts that framed these exchanges.

In conclusion, the importance of understanding cross-cultural interactions in the study of ancient religions is twofold. First, it provides an avenue to appreciate the fluidity and adaptability of religious beliefs and practices, highlighting the dynamic nature of religion. Second, it underscores the interconnectedness of ancient societies, challenging narratives of isolation and reinforcing the idea of the ancient world as a complex network of cultural exchange and mutual influence.

Exercise: Consider the role of cross-cultural interactions in shaping your understanding of a specific ancient religion. How does acknowledging these interactions change or broaden your perspective on that religion? Consider both the direct and indirect influences in your reflection.

The recognition of the historical links between Ancient Greece and Africa, specifically Egypt, through trade, warfare, migration, and diplomacy.

The historical ties between Ancient Greece and Egypt, the jewel of the African continent, have been complex, multifaceted, and critical in shaping both civilizations. The cross-pollination of ideas and practices between these two ancient cultures was facilitated through various conduits, notably trade, warfare, migration, and diplomacy. This chapter delves into the exploration of these historical links and aims to illustrate their profound influence on the Greek and Egyptian societies.

Trade between Ancient Greece and Egypt: Trade has long been a driving force behind cultural exchanges, and it was no different in the case of these two civilizations. Egyptian grain, papyrus, gold, and other goods made their way to Greek cities, influencing Greek economy and lifestyle. On the other hand, Greece, with its strategic location, served as a gateway to the broader Mediterranean world for Egyptian goods, enabling the economic expansion of Egypt. More significantly, this commercial interaction also facilitated the exchange of religious ideas and philosophical concepts, leading to a remarkable synthesis of Hellenistic and Egyptian traditions.

Warfare and its implications: Military conflicts often led to shifts in power dynamics and cultural intermixing. The Greco-Persian Wars, in which Egypt and Greece found themselves on opposite sides, brought Greek soldiers and mercenaries to Egypt, leading to an exchange of military techniques, strategies, and even ideologies. More notably, the conquest of Egypt by Alexander the Great resulted in the creation of the Ptolemaic Dynasty, which brought about a fusion of Greek and Egyptian customs, beliefs, and governance styles.

Migration and its cultural impact: Migration, either forced or voluntary, played a significant role in the exchange of ideas and practices. The settlement of Greeks in Egypt, particularly in the city of Alexandria, resulted in the merging of Greek and Egyptian ways of life, seen in the evolution of architectural styles, religious practices, and even languages.

Diplomacy and its outcomes: Diplomatic interactions between Greece and Egypt, especially during the era of the Ptolemaic Dynasty, forged alliances and facilitated peace treaties. These diplomatic efforts often involved cultural exchanges as gestures of goodwill, including the exchange of scholars, artifacts, and religious practices.

In sum, the historical links between Ancient Greece and Africa, specifically Egypt, were substantial and multifarious. Understanding these connections provides valuable insights into the processes that led to the cultural and religious syncretism evident in these civilizations. This analysis underscores the importance of trade, warfare, migration, and diplomacy as conduits for cultural exchange and as significant catalysts in the evolution of ancient societies.

Exercise: Reflect on a historical event that exemplifies the link between Ancient Greece and Egypt. How did this event influence the cultural, political, or religious landscape of these civilizations? How does this event reflect the broader patterns of cultural exchange in the ancient world?

The Hellenistic Period: A Time of Intense Cross-Cultural Exchange

The Hellenistic period, ushered in by the conquests of Alexander the Great in the 4th century BCE and lasting until the rise of the Roman Empire in 31 BCE, stands as a testament to the breadth and depth of cross-cultural exchange that can occur when diverse societies intersect. This epoch is characterized by an intense blending of

Greek (Hellenic) culture with those of the Near and Middle East and Northeast Africa.

Greek political control under Alexander and his successors, the Diadochi, initiated a process of Hellenization, wherein Greek cultural and intellectual life permeated the conquered lands. However, it was not a unilateral process; the Greek settlers, soldiers, and administrators were themselves transformed by their contact with the rich tapestry of cultures they encountered. The Hellenistic period, therefore, is remarkable for its cultural syncretism.

In Egypt, the Ptolemaic Dynasty upheld a dualistic policy that aimed at integrating Greek and Egyptian traditions. Alexandria, the new Greek capital of Egypt, became an intellectual beacon, housing the famed Library and the Mouseion, attracting scholars from across the Hellenistic world. Egyptian gods were integrated into the Hellenic pantheon, with Serapis, a fusion of the bull-god Apis and Osiris, with attributes of Greek gods, serving as a prominent example.

The Hellenistic era also saw the dissemination of Greek language, a crucial tool of administration and commerce. The use of Koine Greek, a simplified and homogenized form of the language, spread beyond ethnic Greeks, facilitating communication and aiding in the exchange of ideas. This linguistic shift allowed for the fusion of philosophical and religious thoughts, such as the blending of Greek Stoicism with Eastern mysticism.

While the Hellenistic kingdoms in Asia and Africa maintained their political autonomy for nearly three centuries, they remained in close contact with the Greek mainland, importing sculpture, pottery, and other goods, while also sending their own products—textiles, spices, and precious metals—to Greece. These trade interactions fostered a further exchange of ideas and cultural practices.

Nonetheless, the process of Hellenization was complex and uneven, faced with resistance and adaptation by local populations. The conquered cultures, while absorbing elements of Greek culture, retained their distinct identities, adapting the Greek elements to their own needs and traditions. The resulting cultural hybridity of the Hellenistic world demonstrates the capacity of societies to maintain their uniqueness even while they share and adapt to foreign influences.

The Hellenistic period thus stands as a testament to the dynamism and complexity of cultural interaction in the ancient world. It underscores the potential for cross-cultural exchange to foster innovation and transformation in diverse areas of life—political, linguistic, artistic, philosophical, and religious.

Exercise: Reflect on the concept of cultural syncretism as evidenced in the Hellenistic period. How did this cultural syncretism manifest in the art, philosophy, or religion of the era? Can you find parallels in contemporary society where cultural exchanges have led to similar phenomena of fusion or syncretism?

The background and significance of the Hellenistic period in relation to the cultural interaction between Greece and Egypt.

To appreciate the importance of the Hellenistic period, one must first understand the profound historical transformations that led to this era. The period is bookended by the conquests of Alexander the Great in 336 BCE, which toppled the mighty Persian Empire, and the annexation of the last Hellenistic kingdom by Rome in 31 BCE. This era not only heralded a new geopolitical order but also birthed a vibrant cultural exchange that transformed the Mediterranean and Near Eastern world.

The cross-cultural interaction between Greece and Egypt during this time is a crucial component of Hellenistic history. Prior to the Hellenistic period, Greece and Egypt maintained an extensive network of diplomatic, trade, and cultural ties. Yet, the scale of Greek presence and influence in Egypt dramatically escalated after Alexander's conquest in 332 BCE, and the subsequent establishment of the Ptolemaic Dynasty.

Egypt, with its ancient civilization and religious traditions, and Greece, with its philosophical and scientific advancements, interacted closely, leading to significant cross-pollination of ideas, practices, and aesthetics. It is pertinent to note that this was not a process of one-sided Hellenic imposition, but a symbiosis, a coalescence of cultures that each took and gave in their own manner.

The Ptolemaic rulers adopted the pharaonic title and performed traditional religious duties, even while promoting Greek culture. Alexandria, the newly established capital, embodied this fusion, with its grand Hellenistic buildings and institutions, such as the famed Library and the Mouseion, co-existing with ancient Egyptian temples.

The emergence of syncretic cults, such as that of Serapis, demonstrated the extent of religious intermingling. A conflation of Greek and Egyptian gods, Serapis symbolized unity and harmony, appealing to both Greek settlers and native Egyptians.

Greek scholars in Alexandria showed a keen interest in Egypt's historical and religious heritage. Manetho, an Egyptian priest who wrote in Greek, composed the

'Aegyptiaca', which organized the chaotic chronology of Egyptian pharaohs into the system of dynasties still used today. Meanwhile, Hellenistic poets, like Callimachus and Theocritus, were drawing inspiration from Egyptian mythology.

In visual arts, the 'Egyptianizing' style became popular, as seen in the statues of Ptolemaic rulers with pharaonic motifs. Similarly, the use of Greek in official inscriptions and the widespread adoption of the Koine dialect attested to the linguistic blending.

Nevertheless, it is essential to remember that the process of cultural exchange was not homogenous nor without tensions. Local populations often resisted Hellenization, maintaining their customs and language. Hence, the Hellenistic period in Egypt saw a parallel existence of Greek and Egyptian societies, overlapping yet distinct.

The Hellenistic period, therefore, marks an epoch of remarkable cultural dynamism, spurred by the interaction of two of antiquity's greatest civilizations. Its legacy continued well into the Roman period and beyond, shaping the development of the Mediterranean world in myriad ways.

Exercise: Analyze the factors that contributed to the coalescence of Greek and Egyptian cultures during the Hellenistic period. How did the rulers of the Ptolemaic Dynasty facilitate this process? Can you identify any counterexamples of resistance or rejection of the Hellenistic culture by the local Egyptian population?

An exploration of how the conquest of Egypt by Alexander the Great set the stage for a synthesis of cultural and religious ideas.

The conquest of Egypt by Alexander the Great in 332 BCE is a seminal event in the annals of history that set in motion a dynamic process of cultural and religious amalgamation between two of antiquity's most influential civilizations: the Hellenic and the Egyptian. To comprehend this cross-cultural synthesis, one must delve into the factors that preceded, accompanied, and succeeded Alexander's conquest.

Alexander's arrival in Egypt, which had chafed under Persian rule, was welcomed. Unlike his approach in other regions, he showed respect for Egypt's ancient religion and traditions, perhaps recognizing the cultural resilience and spiritual fervor of the Egyptians. Alexander's strategic decision to portray himself as a liberator and to adopt the mantle of the Pharaoh ingratiated him with the local population and priesthood, thus paving the way for a more receptive atmosphere to Greek influence.

The founding of Alexandria was a milestone in this cultural blending. Located at the crossroads of the Mediterranean and the Nile, it quickly became a bustling cosmopolis, drawing immigrants from across the Hellenistic realms and the Near East. The city embodied the Greek notion of 'polis', while also incorporating facets of Egyptian urban design. Alexandria, with its grandiose Library and Mouseion, served as a beacon of Hellenistic culture, attracting philosophers, scientists, and artists. At the same time, it was home to temples dedicated to Egyptian deities, including the Serapeum, housing the syncretic god Serapis.

The post-Alexandrian period, specifically the reign of the Ptolemies, also played a substantial role in nurturing this synthesis. While the Ptolemaic rulers were of Macedonian-Greek origin, they deftly balanced their dual identity as Hellenistic monarchs and Egyptian Pharaohs. They promoted the Greek language and customs among the administrative and military elites. Yet, they also performed traditional Pharaonic religious rituals, built temples in the Egyptian style, and even adopted the practice of dynastic intermarriage.

It was this fusion at the political and religious level, endorsed by the rulers themselves, which catalyzed the process of cultural syncretism. Notably, this fusion was not limited to the elites but permeated various strata of society. For instance, 'koine', the lingua franca of the Hellenistic world, found its way into the lives of common people in Egypt, as evidenced by papyri, ostraca, and inscriptions.

In the realm of religion, the emergence of hybrid deities, such as Serapis (a fusion of Osiris and Apis with Hellenic gods), Isis (who was increasingly Hellenized), and Hermanubis (a combination of Hermes and Anubis), symbolizes the intertwining of the spiritual outlooks of these two cultures. These cults often combined Greek and Egyptian rituals, providing a shared religious framework that transcended ethnic and linguistic boundaries.

The artistic and architectural domains also mirrored this confluence, with the creation of the 'Ptolemaic style'—a blend of Hellenistic techniques and Egyptian motifs. Conversely, Egyptian iconography and stylistic elements influenced Greek art, giving birth to the 'Egyptianizing' style.

In conclusion, Alexander's conquest was a catalyst for a transformative interaction between Greece and Egypt. However, the resulting cultural synthesis was not a simple imposition of Greek culture on Egypt. It was rather a two-way process, with both cultures borrowing, adapting, and melding into a unique Hellenistic-Egyptian cultural milieu that left an indelible imprint on the history of the Mediterranean world.

Exercise: Analyze Alexander the Great's approach towards Egypt's native culture. What role did Alexandria play in facilitating the Greek-Egyptian cultural synthesis? Discuss the importance of syncretic cults in bridging cultural divides during the Hellenistic period.

Shared Cosmological Concepts

Cosmology, the study of the structure, origin, and evolution of the universe, forms a vital core of any religious or philosophical tradition. This chapter aims to delve into the shared cosmological concepts between Ancient Greece and Africa, particularly Egypt, illustrating the profound exchanges and similarities that existed in their perceptions of the universe.

Creation Myths

The creation myths of both Ancient Greece and Egypt, while being unique and distinct in their details, do possess certain commonalities. They serve as complex and elaborate interpretations of the origin of the cosmos, showcasing the intricacies of human imagination and the quest for understanding the universe's genesis.

✧ Greek Cosmogony: Theogony

In Ancient Greece, one of the primary sources that provides insights into their cosmogony is Hesiod's Theogony. This seminal work is a genealogy of the divine, detailing the origin and generations of the gods, which simultaneously becomes a narrative of the universe's birth.

Theogony opens with Chaos, often represented as a yawning void or chasm, from which emerge the primeval entities: Gaia (Earth), Tartarus (the underworld abyss), Eros (Love), Erebus (Darkness), and Nyx (Night). These were not gods in the classical sense but personifications of elements and phenomena.

From these initial entities, the world gradually develops. Gaia, on her own, gives birth to Uranus (Sky), who then becomes her consort, symbolizing the union of Earth and Sky. The Titans, the next generation of divine entities, were born from this union. Eventually, the narrative evolves to the birth and rule of the Olympian gods, marking the cosmos's current form.

✧   Egyptian Cosmogony: Nun and the Sun God

Unlike the relatively uniform Greek cosmogony, Egyptian cosmogonies exhibit significant variations, reflecting regional differences. However, they share a broad agreement on certain cosmological concepts. Central to these myths is the primordial watery abyss known as 'Nun', symbolic of a state of disorder or non-existence before creation.

From this chaotic Nun, a mound or hill emerges spontaneously, symbolizing the first tangible matter. Upon this mound, the sun god manifests, denoting the dawn of creation. Depending on the regional variant, the sun god might be Atum (in Heliopolis) or Ra (in Thebes). This sun god then creates other gods and beings, culminating in the ordered universe, aligning with the principle of Ma'at.

✧   Shared Themes: Chaos, Emergence, and Order

Analyzing these myths, one cannot help but notice shared themes. Both start with a state of formless chaos—Chaos in Theogony and Nun in Egyptian myths. There is also a marked process of 'emergence,' where Earth arises from Chaos, and a mound surfaces from Nun.

Lastly, both myths underscore a transition from disorder to order, mirroring the human yearning for order in the universe. In Theogony, this is manifested through generations of gods from the primeval to the Olympian. In Egyptian myths, this order is tied to the principle of Ma'at, established as the sun god initiates creation.

Through these shared themes, creation myths offer a profound understanding of how ancient civilizations grappled with existential questions, seeking to explain the origin of the universe in a manner reflective of their cultural and religious milieu.

Exercise: Analyze the motif of 'emergence' in both Greek and Egyptian creation myths. How does this theme relate to the larger cosmological picture in both traditions? How do the narratives handle the transition from disorder to order? Reflect on the role of primeval entities in these myths and their significance in the subsequent pantheon.

Divine Order - Ma'at and Themis

The role of divine order is paramount in understanding any religious system. It represents a sacred blueprint that directs both the cosmos's functioning and the moral conduct of individuals within society. Among the numerous shared themes between Ancient Greek and Egyptian religious systems, the concepts of Ma'at and Themis present an intriguing convergence, encapsulating the divine order's notion in these two civilizations.

✧ Ma'at: The Foundation of Egyptian Cosmology and Ethics

In the pantheon of Ancient Egyptian religion, Ma'at stands as an indispensable figure, embodying the principles of truth, justice, and cosmic balance. This complex notion was both a philosophical concept and a deity, indicating its substantial role in Egyptian cosmology and ethics.

Ma'at represented the divine order established at the universe's creation, persisting as the cosmic balance governing natural phenomena. Concurrently, Ma'at was also the moral code directing human actions, intertwining the ethical and cosmological dimensions.

The responsibility of upholding Ma'at lay primarily on the Pharaoh, the earthly representative of the gods. Ensuring Ma'at's continuance was vital for societal and cosmic harmony, as any disruption could lead to chaos, reverting the universe to its primordial state.

✧ Themis: Divine Order and Prophecy in Greek Religion

In the Ancient Greek context, Themis, one of the Titanesses, personified divine order, custom, and law. Unlike the personal code of ethics expressed by other concepts such as 'dikē' (justice) and 'eunomia' (good order), Themis represented a more universal law—the divine ordinance that governs the world.

Themis was also a prophetic deity, serving as an oracle at Delphi before Apollo's tenure. She could discern the divine will, much akin to Ma'at's role in understanding the gods' intentions in the Egyptian context.

The role of the ruler in the Greek context was not as religiously ordained as the Pharaoh's role in Egypt. However, it was implicitly understood that upholding laws and ensuring societal order were among his primary responsibilities.

✧ Ma'at and Themis: Parallel Concepts in Different Civilizations

While Ma'at and Themis emerged from distinct cultural and religious contexts, they exhibit remarkable similarities, emphasizing the universality of certain religious and philosophical ideas. Both concepts represent the divine order governing the cosmos and ethical norms, ensuring the universe's smooth functioning and societal harmony.

However, the difference in their representation—Ma'at as a goddess with a distinctive iconography and Themis often considered an abstract personification—reflects the unique cultural milieu in which these concepts were formulated.

Through comparative analysis of Ma'at and Themis, we gain valuable insights into how different societies perceived and portrayed divine order, reflecting their unique understandings of cosmology and ethics.

Exercise: Examine the concepts of Ma'at and Themis in the context of their respective societies. How does each concept reflect its civilization's understanding of the cosmos and ethics? Consider the societal role of the Pharaoh in Egypt and the ruler in Greece in upholding Ma'at and Themis, respectively. Reflect on the differences in the portrayal and personification of these concepts.

Cosmological Entities

One of the most profound aspects of ancient religions is the deification and personification of natural phenomena and celestial bodies. This anthropomorphization seeks to explain the inexplicable aspects of nature and the cosmos by attributing them to the actions of divine beings. In the intricate pantheons of both the Greeks and the Egyptians, the Sun, Moon, Earth, and Sky are represented as deities, reflecting the significance of these entities in these civilizations' cosmological understanding.

✧   Solar Deities: The Lifegiving Sun

The Sun, as the most prominent celestial entity, personifying life's sustenance, occupies a crucial place in many religious traditions. In Greek mythology, the Sun was represented by Helios, a titan who drove the chariot of the Sun across the sky. However, with time, Helios was largely conflated with Apollo, the Olympian god of light and the Sun.

Egyptian religion revered the Sun god Ra, who was considered the king of the gods and the creator of all life. Ra was believed to traverse the sky during the day, descending into the underworld at night to battle forces of chaos and re-emerge victorious every morning.

These solar deities not only signify the Sun's physical presence and its role in sustaining life but also symbolize the triumph of light over darkness, order over chaos.

✧   Lunar Deities: Mysteries of the Moon

The Greeks personified the moon in the form of Selene, a Titaness who, like her brother Helios, drove a chariot across the sky. Selene was associated with the peaceful passage of time and the rhythm of life, mirroring the moon's cyclic nature.

In Egyptian mythology, Thoth, the god of wisdom, writing, and the moon, was a significant deity. The moon's waxing and waning were connected with Thoth's role as the recorder of time. Thoth was also considered the arbitrator of godly disputes and the scribe of Ma'at, establishing him as a deity of balance and order, akin to the moon's role in establishing earthly rhythms.

✧   Earth and Sky: The Divine Foundation

The Earth and Sky, the two most evident aspects of the natural world, were deified in both cultures. The Greeks regarded Gaia as the Earth goddess, mother of the Titans, and the entire cosmos. Ouranos, the sky, was her consort, and their union produced the first generation of Titans.

Similarly, in Egypt, Geb and Nut represented the earth and sky, respectively. Geb was the judge of human deeds, linking the earth with moral conduct. Nut was the barrier between the ordered cosmos and chaos, often depicted arching over Geb.

The deification of these entities demonstrates an understanding of the interdependence between different natural elements and their roles in maintaining the cosmos's balance.

Through the lens of these cosmological deities, we can glimpse into how ancient civilizations sought to comprehend and articulate their experiences of the natural and cosmic world around them, highlighting the awe, respect, and understanding they had towards these forces.

Exercise: Compare and contrast the roles and characteristics of corresponding Greek and Egyptian deities. Consider how these civilizations' geographical and climatic conditions might have influenced their cosmological concepts. Reflect on the symbolic meanings associated with these deities and how they contributed to their societies' moral and ethical constructs.

Eschatology

The fascination with death and the afterlife has been a universal feature of human societies, leading to the development of eschatological doctrines in many religious systems. The ancient Greeks and Egyptians were no exception, each harboring complex beliefs about the afterlife, encapsulating their views on morality, justice, and the universe's ultimate fate.

✧   Judgement and the Afterlife: The Egyptian Perspective

Egyptian eschatology emphasized a post-mortem judgement, in which the deceased's heart was weighed against the feather of Ma'at, symbolizing truth and balance. This event occurred in the Hall of Two Truths, presided over by Osiris, the god of the underworld and resurrection. If the heart was lighter or equal to the feather, the soul could enter the Field of Reeds, a paradisiacal realm mirroring their earthly life. However, if the heart was heavier, it was devoured by the demoness Ammut, leading to a second death.

The Egyptians' elaborate burial customs, including mummification and grave goods, underscore their beliefs in the afterlife's materiality. These practices ensured the Ka (vital essence) could recognize and reunite with the body, facilitating its journey in the afterlife.

✧   Elysium, Tartarus, and the Asphodel Meadows: The Greek View

In contrast, ancient Greek eschatological beliefs were more diverse, reflecting their polytheistic and regionalized religious system. Nevertheless, some commonalities existed. Upon death, the soul crossed the river Styx guided by Charon, the ferryman, to reach Hades, the realm of the dead.

Depending on their earthly actions, souls could end up in various places. The virtuous were rewarded with the Elysian Fields, a paradise resembling the Egyptian Field of Reeds. Those guilty of heinous crimes were punished in Tartarus, a deep abyss of torment. Ordinary souls, who were neither particularly virtuous nor wicked, resided in the Asphodel Meadows, a monotonous, neutral place.

These beliefs were not as uniformly held or ritualized as in Egypt, reflecting the ancient Greeks' diverse philosophical traditions and regional practices.

✦ Morality, Balance, and Eschatology

Both cultures incorporated the concept of moral recompense in their eschatological systems. In Egypt, the heart's weighing encapsulated the concept of Ma'at, mirroring their societal values of truth, balance, and justice. For the Greeks, the distinction between Elysium and Tartarus reflected a moral dichotomy, although the criteria for judgment were less systematized.

In conclusion, these cultures' eschatological beliefs underscore the universal human concern with morality, justice, and the mystery of what lies beyond death. These doctrines provide profound insights into their societal values, cosmological views, and the ways they grappled with existential questions.

Exercise: Discuss the significance of judgment in both Egyptian and Greek eschatology. How do these beliefs reflect the respective cultures' societal values and ethical systems? Consider the role of burial practices and rites in supporting beliefs about the afterlife. Reflect on how the conceptions of the afterlife might have influenced behavior and attitudes during earthly life in these societies.

A comparative study of the cosmogonical narratives from Ancient Greece and Egypt, emphasizing the personification and deification of natural elements and phenomena.

A society's cosmogony, or origin story, provides a lens through which to understand its worldview, particularly the manner in which it conceptualizes and interacts with the natural world. In this respect, the ancient Greeks and Egyptians offer rich examples of how diverse societies personified and deified natural elements within their cosmogonical narratives.

Cosmogony in Ancient Greece: A Hierarchical Universe

✦ Hesiod's Theogony: Emergence from Chaos

The cosmogonical narrative of Ancient Greece, as articulated in Hesiod's Theogony, commences with the universe emerging from Chaos, a chasm of emptiness and confusion. From this yawning void, the first entities - Gaia (Earth), Tartarus (the Underworld), Eros (Love), Erebus (Darkness), and Nyx (Night) - sprung into existence.

In this early phase of creation, natural elements such as Earth (Gaia), Sky (Ouranos), and Sea (Pontus) are personified and endowed with divinity, setting the stage for the birth of the cosmos. The divine personification of these elements, each with distinct characteristics and realms of influence, illustrates the Greeks' inclination to comprehend the universe in terms of distinct entities embodying various natural phenomena.

✧ Divine Lineage and the Personification of Natural Phenomena

The narrative of Theogony unfolds as a complex genealogy of deities, reflecting the Greeks' conception of a universe ordered in a hierarchical structure. The primordial deities—Gaia, Ouranos, and Pontus—engage in complex relations that birth new entities, establishing a divine lineage that further personifies natural phenomena.

One notable instance is the union of Gaia (Earth) and Ouranos (Sky), which results in the creation of the Titans, a generation of gods symbolizing various facets of the natural world. Among the Titans, we find Oceanus (Ocean), Hyperion (Sun), and Selene (Moon), each embodying crucial aspects of the observable environment.

✧ Hierarchical Universe and Its Implications

The personification of natural elements and phenomena in the divine genealogy highlights the Greeks' understanding of the cosmos as an interconnected, yet hierarchical, system. This hierarchy is not merely a social construct but echoes in the natural world's perceived order. As the narrative of Theogony unfolds, successive generations of gods usurp their predecessors, mirroring patterns of natural succession, such as day following night or seasons changing in cyclic patterns.

Moreover, the Greek cosmogony underscores a belief in divine justice maintaining cosmic order, embodied by Themis, the Titaness of divine law and order, and her daughters, the Moirai or Fates. These deities control the destiny of gods and humans alike, emphasizing that the cosmos, despite its chaotic origins, is bound by order and predictability.

The Greek cosmogony, therefore, presents an intricate web of divine entities symbolizing the natural world, reflecting an ordered and hierarchical worldview that shaped Greek religion, philosophy, and social structure.

Exercise: Examine the role of natural elements in Hesiod's Theogony and their personification as divine entities. How does this cosmogony reflect the Greek understanding of the universe as a structured and hierarchical system? Consider the importance of divine justice in maintaining cosmic order. How does this worldview resonate in other aspects of Ancient Greek culture, such as their philosophy, religion, or social structure? Reflect on the broader implications of this cosmogony for our understanding of the Ancient Greek worldview and its influence on subsequent Western thought.

Egyptian Cosmogony: A Fluid and Dynamic Cosmos

✧   Predominant Narratives: Heliopolis and Hermopolis

The cosmogonical narratives in ancient Egypt, while varying in details, commonly conceived of the universe as a fluid and dynamic entity. Unlike the Greek notion of a strictly ordered and hierarchical cosmos, Egyptian cosmogony exhibited a more fluid and multifaceted understanding, as evident in the divergent cosmogonies stemming from Heliopolis and Hermopolis.

✧   Heliopolitan Cosmogony: Emergence from the Primordial Waters

The Heliopolitan cosmogony revolves around the primordial waters of Nun, symbolizing a state of inert potentiality and unlimited possibilities. In this narrative, a mound, known as the benben, rises from the Nun, a metaphorical representation of the emerging ordered cosmos from the chaotic primordial waters. The sun god, Atum, is said to have emerged or created himself on this mound, subsequently giving birth to the rest of the gods and the cosmos.

In this cosmogony, the sky is personified as Nut, and the earth as Geb, portraying these fundamental elements as divine entities. This depiction reflects the interconnectedness of the cosmos, symbolizing the dynamic relationship between earth and sky.

✧   Hermopolitan Cosmogony: The Ogdoad and the Primeval Chaos

On the other hand, the Hermopolitan cosmogony emphasizes the primeval chaos preceding the cosmos's establishment. The concept of the Ogdoad, a group of eight gods, is central to this cosmogony. These gods, presented in four male-female pairs, personify aspects of the pre-cosmic state: the primeval waters, darkness, infinity, and hiddenness.

The gods of the Ogdoad are portrayed as frogs (males) and snakes (females), creatures associated with the chaotic and unformed. This depiction underscores the

Egyptians' view of the cosmos as an ordered system that arose from a state of chaotic potentiality.

✧   The Concept of Ma'at and Its Implications

In both Heliopolitan and Hermopolitan cosmogonies, the concept of Ma'at, embodying truth, balance, order, law, morality, and justice, plays a crucial role. Ma'at is not only an abstract concept but also personified as a goddess, embodying the principles that govern the cosmos and human conduct. The establishment of Ma'at signifies the transition from chaos to order, from the unformed to the formed, reflecting the Egyptians' understanding of the cosmos as a dynamic system, continuously regenerated and sustained by this divine order.

Exercise: Examine the Heliopolitan and Hermopolitan cosmogonies and their representation of the universe. How do these narratives portray the cosmos as a fluid and dynamic system? Consider the role of Ma'at in these cosmogonies. How does the concept of Ma'at resonate in other aspects of Ancient Egyptian culture, such as their religion, morality, or social structure? Reflect on the broader implications of these cosmogonies for our understanding of the Ancient Egyptian worldview and its distinctness from the Greek perspective.

Shared Themes and Distinctive Approaches

✧   Deification and Personification of the Natural World

Despite the cultural and temporal distance separating Ancient Greece and Egypt, there are intriguing parallels in their cosmogonical narratives, particularly in their personification and deification of the natural world. In both cultures, cosmogonical narratives are teeming with anthropomorphic and theriomorphic representations of the cosmos and its various elements.

These representations are not mere flights of fancy, but sophisticated philosophical and theological constructs designed to elucidate the nature of the cosmos. They symbolize a range of cosmological principles, and their interactions dramatize various cosmic phenomena. For instance, the union of the sky (Ouranos) and the earth (Gaia) in Greek cosmogony or the sky (Nut) and the earth (Geb) in Egyptian cosmogony symbolize the intricate connection between these natural elements.

This shared aspect of personification and deification underscores the human urge to comprehend and narrate the cosmos's intricate workings, even in cultures vastly separated by time and space.

✧ Greek Cosmogony: A Hierarchical Universe

Despite these shared themes, the Greek and Egyptian cosmogonies reveal different conceptions of the cosmos and its operations. In Greek cosmogony, the cosmos is depicted as a structured, hierarchical universe, with successive generations of gods asserting control and shaping it.

This hierarchical structure reflects the Greek understanding of the cosmos as an ordered system, ruled by divine entities, each with their specific sphere of influence. For instance, in Hesiod's Theogony, the cosmos is born from Chaos, followed by the Earth (Gaia), Sky (Ouranos), and Sea (Pontus), forming the basis of a divine hierarchy that maintains the cosmos's order.

✧ Egyptian Cosmogony: A Fluid and Cyclic Cosmos

On the other hand, Egyptian cosmogony offers a contrasting perception of the cosmos. The Egyptians envisioned a more fluid and cyclic cosmos, where order and chaos were not opposites but part of an ongoing process of creation and renewal.

In the Heliopolitan cosmogony, the cosmos emerges from the primeval waters of Nun, representing a state of chaotic potentiality. Yet, from this chaos, order is established, embodied in the concept of Ma'at. Similarly, the Hermopolitan cosmogony emphasizes the role of the Ogdoad, gods representing the pre-cosmic chaos, from which the cosmos is born and sustained.

This understanding of the cosmos as fluid and cyclic reflects the Egyptians' broader cultural and religious beliefs, where death and rebirth, chaos and order, were part of the eternal cycle of existence.

Exercise: Compare the Greek and Egyptian cosmogonies, focusing on their shared themes and distinctive approaches. How do these narratives personify and deify the natural world, and what do they reveal about each culture's understanding of the cosmos? Reflect on how these narratives relate to other aspects of Greek and Egyptian cultures, such as their religious practices, moral beliefs, and social structures. How might these cosmogonies have shaped their respective worldviews and cultural identities?

Examination of the similarities and differences, while noting the risks of reductionism and oversimplification in comparative religious studies.

Avoiding Reductionism and Oversimplification

While comparative religious study can yield valuable insights, it is essential to approach this enterprise with caution, mindful of the potential pitfalls. Reductionism, the tendency to oversimplify complex religious phenomena, is one such risk. For instance, while it may be tempting to reduce Egyptian and Greek cosmogonies to a dichotomy of 'cyclic' versus 'hierarchical,' such an approach risks eliding the richness and complexity of these traditions.

Cultural and Historical Contextualization

Moreover, a comparative study must be sensitive to the unique cultural, historical, and geographical contexts that shape religious narratives. While certain motifs may appear similar, their meanings and implications can significantly vary across different cultural contexts.

Respecting the 'Otherness' of Religious Traditions

Finally, it is important to recognize and respect the 'otherness' of religious traditions. That is, while comparing, one must avoid projecting one's cultural assumptions onto the other. The objective is not to make the 'other' familiar but to appreciate the distinctiveness and intricacies of each tradition.

Exercise: Reflect on the advantages and pitfalls of comparative studies in religion. How can we avoid the risks of reductionism and oversimplification while examining the similarities and differences in Greek and Egyptian cosmogonies? Discuss the importance of cultural and historical contextualization in comparative religious studies. How does the recognition of the 'otherness' of religious traditions contribute to a more nuanced and respectful comparative approach?

Syncretism and Cultural Exchange

Syncretism and cultural exchange constitute essential phenomena in the historical development of human societies, shaping their religions, philosophies, and cosmologies. Syncretism denotes the amalgamation of different, often contradictory, religious beliefs or schools of thought, into a new, cohesive system. Cultural exchange, on the other hand, refers to the mutual sharing and assimilation of cultural elements between societies, either through peaceful interaction or conquest.

These processes play a pivotal role in the evolution of cosmogonical narratives, leading to overlaps, similarities, and diffusion of specific elements, motifs, or entire narratives.

Syncretism and Cultural Exchange in Greek and Egyptian Cosmogonies

Given their geographical proximity and significant periods of interaction, Ancient Greece and Egypt experienced considerable cultural exchange, impacting their cosmogonical narratives. One prominent example is the syncretization of gods, where deities from one culture are identified with those from another due to perceived similarities in their functions or attributes.

During the Hellenistic period (323–30 BCE), following Alexander the Great's conquests, Greek and Egyptian cultures intermingled extensively. This interaction led to notable instances of syncretism. For instance, Zeus, the sky god and king of the Greek pantheon, was often syncretized with Amun, a significant deity in the Egyptian pantheon, creating the hybrid deity Amun-Zeus.

Similarly, the deified elements in both cultures, such as sky, earth, sun, and moon, often underwent a process of identification or equation. For instance, the Greek goddess of the sky, Ouranos, was often associated with the Egyptian sky goddess, Nut, in interpretatio graeca.

However, it's critical to avoid over-generalization and remain cognizant of the cultural specificities that endure despite such processes of syncretism and cultural exchange.

Exercise: Examine the syncretic phenomena that occurred between Greek and Egyptian cosmogonies during the Hellenistic period. Discuss the impact of these syncretic processes on the personification and deification of natural elements in both cultures. Can you identify any potential problems or limitations in assessing syncretism and cultural exchange in ancient cosmogonies?

Examples of syncretism in the Hellenistic period, such as the identification of Greek and Egyptian gods .

The Hellenistic period (323-30 BCE) was a pivotal era marked by significant cultural and religious syncretism between Greek and Egyptian cultures. This syncretism resulted from Alexander the Great's conquests, which led to extensive interactions and mutual influence between these two ancient civilizations. In the realm of religion, this led to the identification and merging of Greek and Egyptian gods based on shared attributes or functions. This process is often known as "interpretatio Graeca" (the Greek interpretation), a term coined by historians to denote the tendency of Greek writers to equate foreign gods with members of their pantheon.

Zeus-Amun: A Syncretic Deity

✦ The Confluence of the Divine: Zeus and Amun

The fusion of Zeus and Amun into the syncretic deity of Zeus-Amun serves as a poignant example of Hellenistic syncretism. Both Zeus and Amun held analogous positions within their respective pantheons: Zeus was the king of the gods in Greek mythology, ruling over the sky and thunder, while Amun was a powerful deity in the Egyptian pantheon, often associated with creation and kingship.

However, the assimilation of these two deities was not merely a simple alignment of similar roles. Rather, it represented a complex negotiation of religious and cultural identities, where the distinctive attributes of each deity were not subsumed but enriched through their confluence.

✦ Zeus-Amun: A Manifestation of Power and Authority

The syncretic deity of Zeus-Amun assumed a crucial role in the assertion of power and authority, particularly by Hellenistic rulers. The identification of Alexander the Great as the son of Zeus-Amun during his visit to the Oracle of Amun at the Siwa Oasis exemplifies this. By aligning himself with this powerful hybrid deity, Alexander effectively asserted his divine lineage, simultaneously reinforcing his sovereignty over the lands he conquered.

✦ Cultural Significance of Zeus-Amun

Beyond its political implications, the figure of Zeus-Amun also had profound cultural significance. The amalgamation of Zeus and Amun represented a blending of

Greek and Egyptian cosmologies, emphasizing commonalities and fostering mutual respect and understanding. Consequently, the worship of Zeus-Amun became a symbol of cultural and religious unity in the Hellenistic world.

Conclusion

The emergence of Zeus-Amun, therefore, encapsulates the transformative effects of Hellenistic syncretism. By combining the central deities of two distinct pantheons, Zeus-Amun not only challenged and reshaped religious boundaries but also symbolized the profound shifts in power, identity, and understanding that characterized this era.

Exercise: Reflect on how the syncretic deity of Zeus-Amun could have impacted the daily religious practices and beliefs of individuals living during the Hellenistic period. How might this fusion of deities have affected their understanding of the divine and the cosmos? Consider the different perspectives that might have existed, such as those of Greek settlers in Egypt, native Egyptians, and Hellenistic rulers.

Hermes-Thoth: The Union of Wisdom

✧ The Fusion of the Wise: Hermes and Thoth

Syncretism in the Hellenistic period manifests prominently in the unification of Hermes, the Greek deity of eloquence, travel, and boundaries, with Thoth, the Egyptian god of wisdom, writing, and the moon. Both gods commanded respect as deities of wisdom and knowledge. Hermes, often portrayed as an intermediary between the divine and human realms, was renowned for his shrewdness and cunning. Thoth, on the other hand, was revered as the inventor of writing and the arbitrator of divine disputes, a reputation that underscored his wisdom and impartiality. These overlapping portfolios provided a robust foundation for their confluence.

✧ Hermes-Thoth: A Synthesis of Philosophical and Religious Thought

Hermes-Thoth was not simply a figure of worship but became a significant influence on philosophical and religious discourse. The combined figure gave rise to Hermes Trismegistus, or "Thrice-Greatest Hermes," who was credited with a corpus of writings known as the Hermetic corpus. This body of work, grounded in the fusion of Greek philosophical thought and Egyptian religious traditions, formed the basis of Hermeticism. This esoteric tradition emphasized the pursuit of gnosis—knowledge of the divine—and highlighted the potential for human beings to attain divine status.

✦   The Cultural Impact of Hermes-Thoth

The cultural ramifications of Hermes-Thoth were profound. The fusion of Hermes and Thoth facilitated the creation of a unique intellectual and religious milieu that absorbed and reframed elements from both Greek and Egyptian cultures. The figure of Hermes-Thoth served as a potent symbol of this dynamic synthesis, fostering cross-cultural dialogue and understanding.

Conclusion

The convergence of Hermes and Thoth into Hermes-Thoth exemplifies the transformative power of syncretism in the Hellenistic period. The combination of these gods, each respected for their wisdom, resulted in an entity that transcended cultural boundaries and spurred a unique philosophical and religious tradition. This underlines the capacity of syncretism not merely to blend distinct entities but also to generate novel and influential cultural phenomena.

Exercise: Consider the cultural implications of Hermes-Thoth and the philosophy of Hermeticism. Reflect on how the amalgamation of Greek and Egyptian elements might have shaped the views and values of individuals in Hellenistic Egypt. How might the Hermetic tradition have contributed to changing perceptions of the divine, the cosmos, and the potential of human beings? Consider both the perspectives of those who adhered to Hermetic teachings and those who did not.

Analysis of the implications of such syncretic practices on the religious landscapes of both Greece and Egypt.

The Broader Pantheon and Cross-Cultural Worship

✦   Emergence of a Multicultural Pantheon

The syncretic practices that unfolded during the Hellenistic period had profound implications on the religious landscapes of Greece and Egypt. The identification of gods across cultures, such as Zeus-Amun and Hermes-Thoth, fostered an environment of religious inclusivity and mutual recognition. The result was an expanded, more diverse pantheon, incorporating deities from both Greek and Egyptian traditions. Gods traditionally associated with Greek mythology found their place within Egyptian temples, while Egyptian deities were recognized and revered within the confines of Greek sanctuaries.

✧ Integration and Acceptance of Foreign Deities

This integration of foreign deities into local religious practice facilitated a unique form of cultural exchange. Greek and Egyptian worshipers had the opportunity to engage with gods beyond their traditional pantheon, fostering a rich, syncretic religious environment. As such, devotees of Zeus could offer their respects at an Egyptian temple to Zeus-Amun, while followers of Thoth might find themselves praying to a statue of Hermes-Thoth in a Greek temple.

✧ Implications of Cross-Cultural Worship

The implications of this cross-cultural worship were manifold. First, it fostered a degree of religious pluralism, encouraging the acknowledgment and reverence of foreign gods. Secondly, it promoted cultural integration and understanding between the Greeks and Egyptians, softening the boundaries between the two civilizations. Lastly, it engendered a sense of shared religious heritage, reinforcing the connections between the two cultures and their spiritual traditions.

Conclusion

In sum, the syncretism that took place during the Hellenistic period fundamentally reshaped the religious landscapes of Greece and Egypt. The mutual identification and worship of gods served as a potent symbol of cultural exchange and integration, fostering a unique, multicultural pantheon that celebrated diversity and promoted inclusivity.

Exercise: Reflect on the cultural and social implications of this religious syncretism. Consider its impact on individual worshipers and how it might have influenced their perception of foreign cultures. How did this cross-cultural worship contribute to the broader socio-cultural dynamics of the Hellenistic period? Discuss the potential challenges and benefits associated with such religious pluralism.

Interconnectedness and Universalism

✧ Syncretism: A Bridge between Cultures

One of the profound effects of syncretism during the Hellenistic period was the fostering of a sense of interconnectedness between distinct religious systems. This melding of Greek and Egyptian cosmologies, as exemplified in deities like Zeus-Amun and Hermes-Thoth, underscored the shared and universal aspects of divine reality. In essence, syncretism acted as a bridge, linking disparate religious and cultural traditions and highlighting their common elements.

✧ Universalism in the Hellenistic Period

This trend towards universalism was a distinctive feature of Hellenistic religion. The integration of foreign deities into local pantheons and the syncretic identification of gods across cultures effectively blurred cultural boundaries. What emerged was a more cosmopolitan understanding of divinity, which transcended individual cultures and local traditions.

✧ A Cosmic Perspective on Divinity

From a broader perspective, this cosmopolitan approach contributed to a more inclusive and universal perception of the divine. It acknowledged the diversity of religious expression while simultaneously emphasizing the fundamental unity underlying these diverse traditions. This universality did not negate the uniqueness of individual deities or cultural traditions; rather, it placed them within a broader, cosmic framework, reflecting a shared divine reality.

✧ Impact on Societal Coherence and Tolerance

Societally, this move towards religious universalism had significant implications. It fostered greater tolerance of foreign deities and cultures, reducing the likelihood of religious conflict. Moreover, by recognizing the shared elements in their religious traditions, Greek and Egyptian societies could find common ground, promoting societal cohesion and mutual understanding.

Conclusion

In summary, syncretism played a vital role in fostering a sense of interconnectedness and universalism in the Hellenistic period. By blurring the boundaries between distinct religious traditions and promoting a more cosmopolitan view of divinity, it contributed to a more inclusive and harmonious societal landscape.

Exercise: Consider the role of universalism in modern religious thought. Are there parallels between the religious syncretism of the Hellenistic period and contemporary trends in religious thought and practice? Discuss the potential societal benefits and challenges associated with religious universalism.

Political and Social Implications

✧   The Political Utilization of Syncretism

Syncretism offered Hellenistic rulers a potent tool to justify and reinforce their political power. By associating themselves with the divine, rulers could legitimate their authority and position themselves within a cosmic order that transcended mere mortal affairs. This strategic utilization of syncretism is vividly illustrated in the case of Alexander the Great. Upon his declaration as the son of Zeus-Amun at the Oracle of Amun at Siwa Oasis, Alexander not only affirmed his rule over Egypt but also reasserted his divine authority.

✧   Power, Prestige, and the Divine Right

The identification of a ruler with a god, or the claim of divine parentage, was a prevalent motif in the ancient world. By situating themselves within the divine cosmology, Hellenistic rulers could lay claim to a divine right to rule, a concept that conferred significant prestige and authority. This added a metaphysical dimension to political power, aligning temporal authority with a higher cosmic order.

✧   Social Implications of Divine Kingship

From a societal perspective, this divine kingship had profound implications. It served as a unifying force, promoting social cohesion by grounding political authority in a shared religious framework. This divine endorsement of political power also reinforced social hierarchies, providing a cosmic justification for societal inequalities.

✧   Influence on Cultural Identity and Cohesion

Beyond the political sphere, the syncretism of Greek and Egyptian cosmologies also had significant implications for cultural identity. The amalgamation of Greek and Egyptian religious traditions facilitated cultural exchange and mutual understanding, fostering a shared identity that transcended national boundaries. By incorporating elements of both Greek and Egyptian traditions, syncretism promoted cultural cohesion and unity amidst diversity.

Conclusion

In summary, syncretism was not merely a religious phenomenon; it was intricately entwined with the social and political fabric of the Hellenistic period. By intertwining the divine with the political, it reinforced the authority of rulers, promoted social cohesion, and shaped cultural identities.

Exercise: Examine other historical instances where religious beliefs and practices have been utilized for political purposes. Discuss the implications of this for societal cohesion and conflict, and the challenges it presents for the separation of religion and politics in modern societies.

Counterargument: The Persistence of Local Beliefs

✧ The Layered Landscape of Religion

The religious landscape of the Hellenistic period, while characterized by significant syncretic practices, was not one of wholesale change. Rather, it was a layered landscape, with syncretic beliefs and practices added onto a robust foundation of traditional and local religious customs. Despite the amalgamation of Greek and Egyptian gods and the importation of foreign deities, local gods and practices continued to play a significant role in both societies. This suggests a layered or palimpsestic model of religious change, where new beliefs and practices are layered upon, rather than replacing, existing ones.

✧ Persistence of Local Deities and Rituals

In both Greece and Egypt, local deities continued to be revered and local rituals upheld. These deities and rituals held significant cultural and historical importance, representing a continuity of tradition and heritage. In Greece, for example, the cult of Dionysius retained its vitality despite the emergence of syncretic deities. Similarly, in Egypt, the worship of Isis persisted and even flourished during the Hellenistic period.

✧ Syncretism and Cultural Resistance

The continued importance of local deities and practices indicates that syncretism was not a uniform or uncontested process. It was as much a site of cultural negotiation and resistance as it was a process of blending and amalgamation. Local populations, while incorporating foreign deities and practices into their religious systems, also asserted their own religious traditions and identities.

Conclusion

Therefore, understanding the religious landscape of the Hellenistic period requires a recognition of the intricate interplay between the local and the foreign, the traditional and the new. Syncretism, while transformative, was layered upon a robust substratum of traditional beliefs and practices, attesting to the dynamic and pluralistic nature of Hellenistic religion.

Exercise: Explore the dynamics of religious change and continuity in the Hellenistic period. How did local populations negotiate the influx of foreign deities and practices? To what extent did local and traditional beliefs resist or adapt to these changes? Consider how these dynamics illuminate the complexities of cultural exchange and religious transformation.

Conclusion: Impact and Legacy

Cultural Fusion and Religious Transformation

✧   Syncretism as the Engine of Religious Transformation

As we culminate our exploration of syncretism within the Hellenistic period, we cannot understate its profound implications on the religious landscapes of both Greece and Egypt. By fusing elements from the Greek and Egyptian pantheons, the practice of syncretism effectively transmuted the religious sphere into a melting pot of diverse and complex deities and practices.

Through this process, the religious landscape expanded beyond the traditional confines of individual cultures to accommodate a larger, more inclusive pantheon. This expansion was not merely quantitative, incorporating more deities, but also qualitative, fostering a transformative dialogue between differing religious ideologies and practices. It is in this fusion and dialogue that we observe the emergence of a unique, composite religious culture, characterized by its diversity and complexity.

✧   Pantheon Expansion and Interreligious Dialogue

The syncretic fusion of Greek and Egyptian gods, as epitomized in the composite deities of Zeus-Amun and Hermes-Thoth, led to a broadening of the existing pantheons. This expanded pantheon was not simply a collection of deities drawn from different cultures, but an intricate system of divine relationships and roles that reflected the intermingling of Greek and Egyptian cosmologies.

Beyond merely expanding the pantheon, syncretism also spurred a transformative interreligious dialogue. By conflating gods from different cultures, who were seen to embody similar domains or characteristics, syncretism effectively established a common ground for religious exchange and integration. As worshippers interacted with these syncretic deities, they were inadvertently participating in a cross-cultural religious discourse, which over time, led to a more nuanced and integrated understanding of the divine.

✧   The Emergence of a Complex Religious Tapestry

The result of this syncretic process was the development of a rich and complex religious tapestry during the Hellenistic period. This tapestry was characterized by its diversity, with deities from different cultures and traditions sharing the pantheon, and its complexity, manifested in the intricate relationships and interactions between these deities.

Through syncretism, religious practice in the Hellenistic period moved beyond the worship of individual deities towards a more systemic and relational understanding of the divine. Deities were not seen in isolation but as part of a larger, interconnected divine system that transcended cultural boundaries.

Exercise: Reflect upon the transformative impact of syncretism on the religious landscapes of Greece and Egypt. How did syncretism shape the development of religious practice in these cultures? In what ways did it alter the perception of the divine? How did the syncretic deities, such as Zeus-Amun and Hermes-Thoth, embody this transformation? Provide specific examples to substantiate your arguments.

Political Legitimization and Divine Authority

✧   Syncretism as a Political Mechanism

The realm of syncretism, while firmly rooted in the religious sphere, was by no means confined to it. In fact, in the Hellenistic period, it burgeoned as a potent socio-political instrument. The mingling of Greek and Egyptian deities served as a powerful vehicle for Hellenistic rulers to establish, consolidate, and legitimise their authority. This was achieved through their alignment with this divine cosmic order, signifying their ascendance from mere mortals to divine intermediaries.

In analysing this facet, it becomes clear that the creation of composite deities such as Zeus-Amun and Hermes-Thoth was not merely a theological venture, but one entrenched in the political machinations of the period. As these deities straddled the religious landscapes of both cultures, the rulers who associated themselves with these gods could leverage their authority across cultural boundaries, reinforcing their dominance.

✧   Divine Legitimisation and Power Consolidation

By positioning themselves within the divine cosmic order, Hellenistic rulers could weave a narrative of divine legitimacy around their rule. The rulers were no longer seen as merely powerful individuals or military victors, but as intermediaries or even incarnations of the divine. Their decisions, actions, and laws were imbued with a sense of divine sanction, making them not just the political, but also the spiritual leaders of their realms.

A prime example of this was Alexander the Great, who, during his visit to the Oracle of Amun at Siwa Oasis, was declared the son of Zeus-Amun. This association with the syncretic deity not only conferred divine legitimacy to his rule but also reinforced his authority over his newly conquered territories. Thus, the fusion of Greek and Egyptian deities served as a powerful political instrument, enhancing the rulers' power and influence.

✧   Far-reaching Implications on the Balance of Power

The political implications of syncretism were far-reaching, influencing the balance of power in the Hellenistic world. By associating themselves with syncretic deities, Hellenistic rulers could assert their authority over diverse cultural groups within their realms, enabling them to govern a diverse and multicultural society effectively. The adoption and propagation of syncretic deities also promoted cultural integration, thereby fostering social harmony and political stability.

Exercise: Examine the socio-political implications of syncretism in the Hellenistic period. How did rulers use syncretism to establish and consolidate their power? How did the identification of Greek and Egyptian gods affect the balance of power? Consider specific examples, such as the case of Alexander the Great being declared the son of Zeus-Amun. Also, consider the role of religious institutions and priests in this process. Were they merely pawns in the rulers' political games, or did they have a degree of agency in these developments? Provide supporting evidence for your arguments..

The Continuity of Local and Traditional Beliefs

✧   Continued Vitality of Local Deities

Despite the permeation of syncretism into the fabric of religious life during the Hellenistic period, it did not usurp or homogenize the religious landscape. Local deities retained their vitality and importance, continuing to be venerated and worshipped. This resilience is indicative of the deeply ingrained nature of local beliefs, as they were intertwined with communal identity, local history, and social structure.

For instance, even as Zeus-Amun was embraced, the worship of Zeus in his Greek form continued unabated, as did the worship of Amun in his original Egyptian context. Local cults and rituals persisted, often infused with a renewed sense of vitality, as they were incorporated into the larger cosmopolitan framework of Hellenistic religion.

✧ Layered Nature of Religious Change

The survival and continued relevance of local religious traditions underscore the complex and layered nature of religious change during the Hellenistic period. The adoption of syncretic deities did not replace local practices, but rather, it overlaid them, creating a nuanced and diverse religious landscape. This highlights the fact that religious change was not a simple process of replacement or supersession, but one of addition and layering, reflecting the multifaceted nature of religious expression.

✧ Resilience in the Face of External Influences

The resilience of local religious traditions in the face of syncretism testifies to the enduring strength of these traditions. Despite the proliferation of new syncretic deities and practices, local beliefs held their ground, demonstrating the deep-rooted nature of these traditions within the cultural and societal fabric. Local religious traditions, in their persistence, provided a sense of continuity and stability amidst the rapid changes of the Hellenistic period.

Exercise: Examine the endurance of local religious traditions in the face of syncretism during the Hellenistic period. How did these traditions adapt and persist amidst the influx of new religious ideas? Investigate specific examples of local deities or practices that maintained their vitality and importance during this period. What factors contributed to their resilience? How did local populations negotiate the tension between local and syncretic religious forms?

Consider also the implications of this persistence for our understanding of religious change. How does the survival of local religious traditions challenge or complicate our understanding of religious syncretism? How can we reconcile the simultaneous existence of local and syncretic religious forms within the same cultural context? Reflect on these questions and support your arguments with examples and evidence from primary and secondary sources.

The Legacy of Hellenistic Syncretism

✧ Influence on the Roman Period and Early Christian Thought

The syncretic practices of the Hellenistic period had a significant and lasting impact on the religious and philosophical landscape of the subsequent Roman period and the early Christian era. The cosmopolitanism engendered by Hellenistic syncretism was readily embraced by the Roman Empire, which incorporated a myriad of local deities and practices from its vast territories into the Roman pantheon. This practice of religious syncretism became a central feature of Roman religious policy, facilitating the pacification and integration of conquered peoples.

Furthermore, Hellenistic syncretism had a profound impact on early Christian thought. Christian thinkers of the early centuries AD, living in the largely Hellenised Eastern Roman Empire, drew on the philosophical and religious milieu of their time, which was significantly shaped by Hellenistic syncretism. The development of Christian theology was heavily influenced by Greek philosophy, which had itself been transformed by the influx of Eastern religious ideas during the Hellenistic period.

✧ Persistence of Hermeticism and its Impact

The impact of Hellenistic syncretism can also be traced in the continued influence of Hermeticism, a philosophical and religious tradition rooted in the worship of the syncretic deity Hermes-Thoth. Hermeticism, with its emphasis on the pursuit of wisdom and understanding of the cosmos, profoundly influenced Western esotericism. Its texts, attributed to Hermes Trismegistus ("Thrice-Greatest Hermes"), were central to the philosophical discourse of the Renaissance, inspiring movements like Renaissance Hermeticism.

Renaissance Hermeticism emphasized the harmony of religion and science, a philosophical stance that deeply influenced luminaries such as Marsilio Ficino and Giordano Bruno. Moreover, Hermetic thought played a significant role in the development of Rosicrucianism and Freemasonry, influencing their symbolism and rituals.

Even in the modern world, Hermeticism continues to inspire various esoteric and new-age movements. Its focus on spiritual transformation and the pursuit of hidden knowledge resonates with contemporary spiritual seekers, ensuring the enduring relevance of this ancient tradition.

Exercise: Delve into the lasting impact of Hellenistic syncretism on the Roman period, early Christian thought, and the subsequent philosophical and religious traditions. How did Hellenistic syncretism shape the religious policy of the Roman Empire? In what ways did it influence the development of early Christian theology?

Explore also the enduring influence of Hermeticism. How did Hermetic thought shape the intellectual landscape of the Renaissance? What impact has it had on Western esotericism and contemporary spiritual movements? In your analysis, provide specific examples and draw on both primary and secondary sources. Reflect on these questions and support your arguments with evidence from scholarly literature.

Conclusion

In essence, the phenomenon of syncretism in the Hellenistic period represents a complex and dynamic process of cultural interaction and exchange. It played a pivotal role in shaping the religious, social, and political landscapes of Greece and Egypt, leaving a lasting legacy that continues to enrich our understanding of ancient religions and cultures.

Exercise: Reflect on the long-term impacts and legacy of Hellenistic syncretism. How did syncretic practices in the Hellenistic period influence later historical periods and religious movements? How does this legacy inform our understanding of the processes of cultural interaction and exchange in historical contexts?

Reflection on the lasting impact of these cross-cultural interactions on the religious landscapes of the Mediterranean and North Africa.

Mediterranean Religious Landscape and the Persistence of Syncretic Traditions

✧   The Enduring Resonance of Hellenistic Syncretism in the Roman Pantheon

The Hellenistic period, replete with the syncretic amalgamation of Greek and Egyptian deities, is a defining chapter in the history of the Mediterranean's religious landscape. This era, characterized by the fluid and inclusive nature of religious practices, set a significant precedent for the Roman period that followed. The Romans, true to their pragmatic ethos, adopted and adapted the Hellenistic method of incorporating local deities into their pantheon. This strategic adoption contributed significantly to the religious pluralism of the Roman Empire, marking a noteworthy manifestation of Hellenistic syncretism's enduring impact.

In this context, it is crucial to understand that the Romans did not merely copy the Hellenistic pantheon but applied the principle of syncretism to assimilate diverse deities from their vast empire. This religious pragmatism became an effective tool for cultural assimilation, fostering a sense of unity within the diverse imperial territory.

✧   Religious Pluralism and the Emergence of New Religions

The culture of religious pluralism and openness to syncretism, characteristic of the Hellenistic and Roman periods, created a fertile ground for the advent and spread of new religions in the Mediterranean world. Mithraism, originating from Persia, the cult of Isis from Egypt, and ultimately, Christianity, gained significant traction in this religiously diverse environment.

These new religions often drew upon and transformed pre-existing deities and sacred sites, a process that mirrors the syncretic practices of the Hellenistic period. For instance, the mystery cult of Mithraism, popular among the Roman military, is believed to have absorbed elements of Greek, Roman, and Eastern deities. Similarly, the cult of Isis, an Egyptian goddess, was Hellenized and later Romanized, reflecting the continuity of syncretic processes across these cultural shifts.

✧   Christian Transformation of Pre-existing Deities and Sacred Sites

A pivotal aspect of the Hellenistic syncretic legacy lies in the transformation that occurred with the rise of Christianity. Early Christian communities, while formulating their unique identity, also engaged with the existing religious landscape. Many early Christian saints' cults can be seen as continuations of ancient local deities, albeit under a new guise. A classic example of this phenomenon is the cult of Saint Brigid in Ireland, which shows a significant overlap with the pre-Christian goddess Brigid.

Similarly, the transformation of pagan sacred sites into Christian churches is a widespread practice that signifies the continuance of religious traditions and sacred geography under new religious paradigms. The Pantheon in Rome, originally a temple for all Roman gods, was converted into a Christian church, exemplifying this process.

Exercise: Conduct a detailed exploration of the continuity and transformation of religious practices from the Hellenistic period to the Roman era and the rise of Christianity. Evaluate the degree of syncretism involved in the rise of new religions like Mithraism and the cult of Isis in the Mediterranean world. Also, investigate the Christian transformation of pre-existing deities and sacred sites. What kind of cultural and religious negotiations does this transformation entail? Utilize archaeological, literary, and historical sources to substantiate your analysis.

Impact on North African Religious Practices

✧ The Imprint of Hellenistic Syncretism in Egyptian Religion

In the sphere of North African religions, particularly in Egypt, the Hellenistic policy of syncretism had an enduring influence, deeply ingraining itself into the religious fabric of the region. This policy, adopted by the Greek Ptolemaic dynasty that ruled Egypt, advocated for the integration of Greek deities into the Egyptian pantheon, thus instigating a profound cultural and religious exchange.

The creation and widespread worship of Serapis, a syncretic deity designed to amalgamate Greek and Egyptian religious traditions, is a testament to the efficacy of this policy. The Ptolemaic rulers, aiming to unify their diverse subjects under a common religious banner, conceived of Serapis by combining attributes of Greek and Egyptian gods. Alongside Serapis, the cult of Isis, an Egyptian goddess who absorbed some features of Greek goddesses, found followers not only in Egypt but throughout the Roman Empire, marking a striking example of Hellenistic syncretism's far-reaching impact.

✧ Continuity and Adaptation: Ancient Egyptian Traditions in New Religious Contexts

Even with the advent of Christianity and later Islam, ancient Egyptian religious traditions demonstrated remarkable resilience, persisting and adapting through syncretic processes. Coptic Christianity, a distinctive Christian tradition that developed in Egypt, provides a compelling example of such religious continuity and transformation.

Coptic Christianity is widely recognized for its incorporation of elements reminiscent of ancient Egyptian beliefs. These include the usage of the ancient Egyptian language in liturgical contexts and the persistence of certain motifs and symbols, such as the ankh, a symbol of life in ancient Egyptian religion, in Christian contexts.

Similarly, in the realm of Islam, folk religious practices in Egypt show a notable degree of syncretism. These practices often combine orthodox Islamic beliefs with local traditions, including those with ancient roots. Such practices, although sometimes contested by orthodox interpretations, underscore the enduring influence of the Hellenistic legacy of syncretism.

Exercise: In the light of the examples discussed above, analyze the lasting impact of Hellenistic syncretism on Egyptian religious practices. How did the Ptolemaic policy of syncretism shape the religious landscape of Egypt? To what extent can we see the persistence of ancient Egyptian traditions in later religious phenomena, such as Coptic Christianity and folk Islam? Use archaeological, historical, and anthropological sources in your analysis to trace the continuity and transformation of religious practices in Egypt from the Hellenistic period to the present.

Exercise: Investigate in detail the continuing impact of Hellenistic syncretism on the Mediterranean and North African religious landscapes. Explore the transformation of local deities and sacred sites within the context of Christianity and the emergence of new religions like Mithraism and the cult of Isis. What are the distinguishing characteristics of these syncretic processes?

In the context of North Africa, analyze the enduring influence of Hellenistic-Egyptian syncretism on local religious practices, both in historical and contemporary terms. What are the manifestations of this influence in Coptic Christianity and folk Islam in Egypt? Consider these questions and support your analysis with primary and secondary sources from various academic disciplines, including theology, archaeology, and history.

An invitation to reflect on the wider implications for understanding the nature of cultural exchange and religious syncretism.

The Phenomenon of Syncretism: A Broader Reflection

The Hellenistic era, characterized by the profound blend of Greek and Egyptian religious frameworks, signals a critical juncture in the historical development of religious identities and practices. The phenomenon of religious syncretism that marked this period elucidates the complexities inherent in the understanding of cultural exchanges and religious amalgamations, propelling us to delve into some fundamental questions concerning the fluidity of religious identities, the dynamics of cultural interchange, and the resilience of religious traditions in response to socio-political transformations.

✧ Religious Syncretism and Fluidity of Religious Identities

The religious syncretism of the Hellenistic period serves as a compelling example of the permeable and flexible nature of religious systems. Despite the seemingly rigid boundaries that frequently typify religious identities' discourse, the amalgamation of Greek and Egyptian gods during the Hellenistic era denotes an impressive degree of fluidity and intersectionality. The creation of new, syncretic deities such as Serapis, the blending of Greek Zeus and Egyptian Amun, demonstrates the readiness of religious systems to absorb, blend, and transform elements from one another.

This willingness to fuse elements from different religious traditions fundamentally challenges any attempt to compartmentalize religious systems into discrete, insulated categories. The clear-cut borders often perceived or theorized in religious discourse are, in reality, much more porous, facilitating cross-pollination of ideas, practices, and divinities.

✧ Questioning the Boundaries

The fusion of Greek and Egyptian deities during the Hellenistic period illustrates the extensive blending and overlapping of religious identities. This phenomenon of syncretism raises fundamental questions about the very concept of distinct religious identities. Do rigid boundaries between different religious systems truly exist, or are they constructs that are routinely transcended in the reality of religious practice and belief?

It could be postulated that the boundaries separating different religious systems are not immutable barriers but rather flexible interfaces facilitating cultural and religious interchange. The Hellenistic period provides ample testimony to this fluidity and adaptability, with the creation of syncretic deities and the mutual incorporation of religious practices and ideas. This suggests that religious systems are not rigidly defined entities, but rather, fluid and adaptable structures that can absorb, integrate, and reconfigure external influences.

✧ Religious Identity: A Layered Construct

Religious identity, as indicated by the syncretism witnessed during the Hellenistic era, could thus be considered a layered construct, shaped not merely by a single, homogenous religious tradition but by the intertwining and amalgamation of various traditions. This dynamic nature of religious identity signals the inherent flexibility of religious systems and their capacity to adapt and evolve in the face of socio-cultural and political changes.

Exercise: Reflect on other historical or contemporary instances that display a comparable degree of religious syncretism to that witnessed during the Hellenistic period. What do these instances reveal about the nature of religious identity and the fluidity of religious systems? How do they illuminate the mechanisms of cultural exchange and the adaptability of religious traditions in response to changing socio-political contexts? Endeavor to integrate insights from diverse fields, such as witchcraft, Wicca, neo-paganism, Divination, Herbalism, Shamanism, Ecospirituality, and Ancient Greek Magic in your exploration of these questions.

Cultural Exchange as a Dynamic Process

Moreover, the Hellenistic example underscores the dynamics of cultural exchange. This exchange was not a simple, one-directional process, with one culture imposing its religious system on another. Instead, it was a complex, reciprocal process, involving selective adaptation, mutual influence, and creative reinterpretation. The Ptolemaic rulers, for example, did not simply impose Greek gods on their Egyptian subjects; instead, they created new, syncretic deities that resonated with both Greek and Egyptian religious traditions.

Adaptability and Resilience of Religious Traditions

Furthermore, the persistence of local Egyptian religious traditions, even as they were incorporated into the syncretic Hellenistic religious system, highlights the adaptability and resilience of religious traditions in the face of socio-political changes. Religious traditions, as this example shows, are not static entities; they evolve, adapt, and reinvent themselves in response to new circumstances.

Exercise: Reflect on the wider implications of the Hellenistic example for understanding the nature of cultural exchange and religious syncretism. How does the Hellenistic experience of syncretism challenge conventional understandings of religious boundaries? How does it illustrate the dynamics of cultural exchange and the adaptability of religious traditions? In your reflection, consider other historical or contemporary examples of cultural exchange and religious syncretism, comparing them with the Hellenistic case.

Conclusion: Summation of the Roles and Significance of the Primeval Gods

Recapitulation of the Chapter's Cardinal Points

This chapter aimed at elucidating the profound and multifaceted roles of the primeval gods within the complex tapestry of ancient Greek religion and mythology. These deities, representing elemental forces and cosmic principles, occupied a paramount position in the pantheon and the collective religious consciousness of the ancient Greeks. The first section of this chapter elucidated the individual roles and attributes of key primeval gods, namely Chaos, Gaia, Uranus, Tartarus, Eros, Erebus, and Nyx.

Chaos, often conceived as the primordial emptiness from which all things emerged, symbolizes the unfathomable mysteries of the universe's origin. Gaia, embodying the Earth, signifies fertility and the inexhaustible source of life. Uranus represents the sky and the celestial realm. Tartarus embodies the abyss and the underworld. Eros, the primal force of attraction and desire, catalyzes creation and change. Erebus and Nyx, symbolizing darkness and night respectively, are manifestations of the mysterious, hidden, and enigmatic aspects of existence.

The subsequent sections delved into the interconnectedness and interdependence of these primeval gods, illuminating the intricate cosmological web that they collectively weave. Moreover, this chapter explored their influence on later Greek mythology, revealing their enduring legacy in the genealogy of gods, the cosmogonic myths, and the moral and philosophical ideas permeating ancient Greek society.

The Primeval Gods' Collective Impact on Ancient Greek Religion and Mythology

The primeval gods, in their collective capacity, indubitably exerted a profound influence on ancient Greek religion and mythology. They shaped the Greek cosmogony, providing explanations for the origins and workings of the universe, and gave form to the abstract concepts and phenomena of nature, thus making them accessible to human understanding and manipulation.

These deities were pivotal to the narrative structure of Greek mythology. They established the genealogy of the gods, serving as progenitors of the divine pantheon. The dichotomy and interplay between Gaia and Uranus, for instance, set the stage for the succession myth, a recurrent theme across different Greek myths involving a struggle between an older generation of deities and a younger one.

Moreover, their presence pervaded ancient Greek religious thought and practice. The primeval gods, as embodiments of elemental and cosmic forces, were omnipresent in every facet of Greek life and worldview, influencing the way the Greeks perceived and interacted with the world around them. Their stories provided ethical and philosophical lessons, shaping societal values and norms.

In summary, the primeval gods served as pillars of Greek religious and mythological thought, providing a cosmological framework, supplying a genealogical base for later divinities, and offering ethical and philosophical guidance. Their stories offer intriguing insights into how the ancient Greeks sought to comprehend their world and their place within it, reminding us of the enduring power and appeal of myth in making sense of the cosmos.

Exercise: Reflect on the roles of primeval gods in other cultures' mythologies. How do they compare to their Greek counterparts in terms of attributes, functions, and impact on their respective societies? What insights can be gleaned from these comparisons about the nature of religion and mythology, the human quest for understanding the cosmos, and the cultural differences and commonalities in this quest?

Recapitulation

Key Takeaways from the Chapter

The analysis presented within this chapter illuminated the profound influence and nuanced roles of the primeval gods within the religious and mythical landscape of ancient Greece. These deities, embodying cosmic principles and elemental forces, established the foundational narrative framework for Greek cosmogony, and their attributes and relationships elucidated the Greek understanding of the universe's origin, operation, and the abstract dimensions of existence.

The exploration of individual primeval deities—Chaos, Gaia, Uranus, Tartarus, Eros, Erebus, and Nyx—revealed the diverse functions they fulfilled within Greek mythology. From representing primal emptiness to symbolizing Earth's fertility, from governing the celestial sphere to overseeing the chthonic depths, and from personifying attraction to embodying darkness and night, these deities painted a diverse and intricate tableau of cosmic existence.

The interconnectedness and interdependence of these primeval gods were highlighted, showing that they collectively wove an intricate cosmological web. Their influence permeated the subsequent layers of Greek mythology, shaping the genealogies of gods, cosmogonic narratives, and even the moral and philosophical ideas of ancient Greek society.

The primeval gods' collective capacity, as the forebears of divine genealogies and the architects of cosmic order, exerted an immense influence on Greek religious thought and practice. By personifying natural phenomena and cosmic forces, they were omnipresent in the ancient Greeks' worldview, influencing their interaction with the world around them and providing a narrative structure for understanding the universe's complexities.

Connection to Upcoming Content in Chapter 4: Heroes and Demigods: A Study of Heroic Figures in Greek Mythology

As we transition into the subsequent chapter—Heroes and Demigods: A Study of Heroic Figures in Greek Mythology—it is essential to recall the importance of the primeval gods within the genealogical structure of Greek mythology. The primeval gods form the lineage from which subsequent deities, heroes, and demigods spring forth, their actions setting in motion a series of events leading to the exploits and tribulations of Greek heroes and demigods.

The heroic figures, who form the focus of the ensuing chapter, are deeply entwined within this mythological lineage and cosmic order established by the primeval gods. These heroes navigate a world shaped by the divine dictates of these gods, their destinies influenced by their relationships with the deities, and their trials and triumphs reflective of the moral and philosophical lessons embedded in these primeval narratives.

Moreover, the duality and conflict inherent in the narratives of the primeval gods, such as the struggle between Gaia and Uranus, reappear in the heroic myths in various forms. Heroes often find themselves caught in the interplay of cosmic and elemental forces, their quests serving as a microcosm of the struggles of the gods.

Therefore, an understanding of the primeval gods, their roles, attributes, and the cosmological order they represent, is instrumental for a profound comprehension of Greek heroic mythology. As we delve into the intriguing realm of heroes and demigods, let us bear in mind the broader mythological canvas set by the primeval gods and the insights it provides into the adventures, trials, and tribulations of these heroic figures.

Exercise: Reflect on how the primeval gods' narratives provide context and depth to the tales of Greek heroes and demigods. Can you identify instances where the trials and tribulations of these heroic figures echo the struggles and themes present in the stories of the primeval gods? How do these recurring themes contribute to the coherence and richness of Greek mythology as a whole?

Chapter 5: The Lesser-Known Deities: A look at lesser-known gods, their roles, and the significance of these lesser deities in the daily life of ancient Greeks.

In the rich tapestry of ancient Greek mythology, many a deity presides over a realm of life, each contributing to the all-encompassing understanding of existence that the Greeks espoused. While much attention has been given to the more familiar Olympians, a comprehensive exploration of the ancient Greek religious mindset necessitates an examination of the less celebrated, yet integral, divinities. This chapter, hence, seeks to shine a light upon the lesser-known deities of the Greek pantheon and to delve into the nature of their roles, the scope of their influence, and their bearing on the daily lives of the ancient Greeks.

The deities we shall explore are diverse in their dominions, ranging from Hecate, the goddess of magic and witchcraft, to Eirene, the embodiment of peace. Despite their relative obscurity in the popular recounting of Greek mythology, these deities were central to the spiritual understanding and daily practices of the ancient Greeks. By examining these lesser-known gods and goddesses, we might gain a more nuanced comprehension of the depth and intricacy of the ancient Greek religious landscape, beyond the exploits of Zeus, Athena, and other prominent Olympians.

These lesser-known deities wielded considerable influence in domains that were integral to the ancient Greeks. Their dominions often represented essential facets of daily life and society: health, sleep, youth, vengeance, peace, and the magical and supernatural. As such, these deities were not mere footnotes in the vast annals of Greek mythology, but active participants shaping the ancient Greeks' worldview and daily existence.

It is important, therefore, that we illuminate these figures, their roles, and their impact. Not only will we gain a richer understanding of the multifaceted nature of Greek mythology, but we will also uncover the depth of wisdom the ancients derived from these deities, which in turn influenced their philosophy, ethics, and their understanding of the world. Through this exploration, we invite you to delve into the intricate interplay between the divine and the mundane, the known and the unknown, the celebrated and the overlooked, as we navigate the complex religious life of the ancient Greeks.

In embarking on this exploration, we shall witness that these deities, despite their relative obscurity, hold a mirror to the ancient Greeks' values, fears, hopes, and understanding of the cosmos, offering us an in-depth and multifaceted perspective of a civilization whose influence reverberates through the ages. Thus, the lesser-known deities, in all their diverse glory, form an integral part of our exploration of the ancient Greek pantheon, inviting us to delve into the rich, intricate, and diverse religious landscape of ancient Greece.

Lesser-Known Deities in the Ancient Greek Pantheon

The grandeur of the ancient Greek pantheon extends well beyond the paramount Olympian deities. While the prominence of Olympians such as Zeus, Hera, Athena, and Poseidon is unquestionable, they form but one facet of a diverse and expansive divine ensemble. To truly apprehend the depth and richness of the Greek spiritual imagination, one must traverse beyond these familiar figures and into the realms of the lesser-known deities who populated the religious consciousness of the ancient Greeks.

The term 'lesser-known' does not denote inferiority in status or importance, but rather refers to those deities less frequently spotlighted in popular renditions of Greek mythology. These divinities, despite their relative obscurity, played essential roles in various aspects of life, embodying and governing domains that were integral to the daily existence and socio-cultural fabric of the ancient Greeks. Ranging from personifications of abstract concepts to patrons of specific human activities, these deities offered explanations for natural phenomena, moral and ethical guidance, protection, and a sense of connectedness to the cosmos.

Hecate, for instance, stood at the crossroads of life, death, and magic, while Pan, the rustic god of shepherds and flocks, was celebrated in the wilderness, embodying the wild and fertile aspects of nature. Eirene brought forth the blessings of peace, and Asclepius held sway over healing and medicine. Nemesis meted out retribution for hubris, and Eris stirred the pot of discord. Hypnos governed the realm of sleep, offering mortals respite from their waking lives, while his brother Thanatos personified the inevitable end of life.

In their plurality and diversity, these deities represent the myriad concerns, hopes, and fears of the ancient Greeks, illustrating the ways in which the divine was intimately woven into the fabric of everyday life. They offer insights into the ancient Greeks' understanding of morality, ethics, the natural world, and the human condition, thereby augmenting our understanding of ancient Greek culture, society, and worldview.

This chapter thus aims to highlight the roles and significance of these lesser-known deities, examining the nature of their worship, the scope of their influence, and their impact on the daily lives of the ancient Greeks. In doing so, we endeavor to provide a more comprehensive and nuanced perspective on the Greek pantheon and the ways in which the divine permeated every aspect of life in ancient Greece. By journeying into the realms of these lesser-known deities, we open up a broader vista on the rich and intricate tapestry of ancient Greek religious belief and practice.

Presentation and description of selected lesser-known deities

In this section, we delve into the specifics of selected lesser-known deities, offering detailed portraits of these divine entities and exploring their roles, attributes, mythological associations, and influence on the daily life of the ancient Greeks.

Hecate: Hecate, the goddess of magic, crossroads, ghosts, and necromancy, was a complex and multifaceted figure. She was often depicted holding torches, a key, and a dagger, symbols of her dominion over liminal spaces and her power to grant or deny access to hidden realms and knowledge. Although Hecate was not an Olympian, Zeus, recognizing her power, granted her authority in the heavens, the earth, and the sea, making her one of the only deities with dominion in all three realms. While she was feared as the leader of ghosts and a practitioner of witchcraft, she was also revered as a powerful protective deity who could bestow prosperity and blessings upon those who honored her.

Pan: Pan, the god of shepherds, hunters, and rustic music, was a pastoral deity often associated with the untamed aspects of the natural world. Half-man and half-goat, Pan embodies the wild, unbridled forces of nature. Despite his uncouth and even terrifying appearance - the term 'panic' derives from the fear he was said to instigate - Pan was also a figure of mirth and celebration, known for his playful music and lascivious pursuit of nymphs. His worship was particularly prevalent in rural areas, where his influence over the fertility of flocks and crops was crucial.

Eirene: Eirene was the personification of peace and abundance. One of the Horae, or Seasons, Eirene was depicted as a young woman carrying a cornucopia, a symbol of plenty, and a scepter, an emblem of authority. Eirene's role was essential in the socio-political context of ancient Greece, a civilization marked by frequent warfare. She represented the ideal state of affairs in a war-weary society, embodying the harmony and prosperity that ensues in the wake of conflict.

Asclepius: Asclepius, the god of medicine and healing, was a significant figure in ancient Greece, where health and well-being were fundamental concerns. His worship was widespread, with numerous sanctuaries and healing centers known as Asclepieia. The practice of incubation, wherein supplicants would sleep in these sacred spaces in the hopes of receiving a healing dream or vision, testifies to the god's direct involvement in health matters.

Nemesis: Nemesis, the goddess of retribution, played an important role in maintaining the moral and social order of ancient Greek society. She was invoked as the force that restored balance when someone experienced excessive good fortune or committed grievous wrongs. Nemesis ensured that no mortal or deity could escape the consequences of their actions, thereby upholding the value of justice in Greek culture.

Eris: Eris, the goddess of discord and strife, is best known for her role in initiating the Trojan War. Her power to incite conflict made her a feared figure. Nevertheless, she was also recognized as a necessary part of life and existence. Strife could lead to positive outcomes, such as stirring individuals or societies to address injustices or overcome complacency.

Hypnos and Thanatos: Hypnos, the god of sleep, and Thanatos, the god of death, were brothers and shared dominion over human mortality. Hypnos was seen as benign, providing rest and respite, while Thanatos was feared as the inexorable end of life. They represent the Greek understanding of life's cycle and the dual aspects of mortality: rest and termination.

Each of these deities, despite their relative obscurity, held significant sway over aspects of life that were integral to the ancient Greeks. Their stories and attributes reveal the complexity and diversity of the Greek pantheon, providing rich insights into the multi-layered spiritual landscape of ancient Greece.

Mythological stories associated with each deity

The interconnection between the mythological narratives of the ancient Greek world and the lesser-known deities whose purview expanded into the daily life of the society unveils the indissoluble bond between these entities and the cultural fabric of that time. Each deity, despite the lack of frequent depiction in grand epics, upheld particular aspects of life and society, with their stories illuminating their roles, significance, and influence.

Hecate: Hecate figures prominently in the myth of Demeter's search for Persephone. As the maiden was seized by Hades and taken to the underworld, Hecate, the goddess of the crossroads and boundaries, stood as a silent observer. Later, she joined Demeter, providing vital assistance in the frantic search for the missing Persephone. Upon Persephone's subsequent residence in the underworld for part of the year, Hecate became her attendant and companion. This narrative emphasizes Hecate's association with the underworld, liminal spaces, and transitions.

Pan: Pan's unique origin story is pivotal to his character and role. As the offspring of Hermes and a nymph, Pan was born fully grown and with the attributes of a goat, a sight that led his mother to flee. Hermes, however, was delighted with his son and presented him to the other gods, who also found favour with Pan. This narrative emphasizes Pan's nature as a rustic, wilderness-loving deity, a master of music, and an entity capable of inducing panic.

Eirene: The goddess of peace, Eirene, holds a significant place in mythology through symbolism rather than specific narratives. Frequently portrayed carrying the infant Ploutos, the god of wealth, her imagery emphasizes the idea that peace leads to prosperity. This serves as an ideological narrative promoting societal harmony.

Asclepius: Born of a mortal woman, Coronis, and the god Apollo, Asclepius' myth involves his education under the centaur Chiron, who taught him the secrets of medicine. Asclepius' ability to heal and even resurrect the dead ultimately led to his demise, as Zeus struck him down for disrupting the balance between mortality and immortality. This narrative underscores Asclepius' significance as the bringer of healing and resurrector, impacting the ancient Greek perception of health and illness.

Nemesis: Nemesis, the goddess of retribution, features significantly in the tale of Narcissus, a man of extraordinary beauty who rejects all those who love him. Nemesis, responding to the plea of one heartbroken suitor, leads Narcissus to fall in love with his reflection. Unable to obtain the object of his desire, Narcissus ultimately fades away, emphasising Nemesis's role as an executor of divine punishment.

Eris: As the goddess of strife and discord, Eris is pivotal to the myth leading to the Trojan War. Outraged at being uninvited to the wedding of Peleus and Thetis, she tosses a golden apple inscribed "to the fairest" among the goddesses, inciting a dispute between Hera, Athena, and Aphrodite that eventually leads to the legendary conflict.

Hypnos and Thanatos: Hypnos (Sleep) and Thanatos (Death), twin brothers in myth, feature together in the Iliad, where they are tasked with carrying the body of the dead Sarpedon back to his homeland. This illustrates their complementary roles as bringers of rest and death.

Each of these narratives adds depth to the complexity of these lesser-known deities, shedding light on their integral roles within the ancient Greek pantheon and society. Further exploration of these stories aids in the development of a comprehensive understanding of ancient Greek culture and the multifaceted nature of its mythology.

The Roles of Lesser-Known Deities

The pantheon of lesser-known deities in ancient Greek mythology embodies a complex web of roles that often intersect, creating a comprehensive and nuanced tableau that shapes and reflects the multifaceted nature of the ancient Greek society. Their influence extends from the cosmic balance of the universe to everyday human life, displaying the ancient Greeks' profound and pragmatic recognition of divinity.

Hecate: As the goddess of magic, crossroads, and liminal spaces, Hecate held a multifaceted role. She was an intermediary between the mortal world and the divine or supernatural realms. Her association with crossroads underscores her function as a guide in decision-making, and her mastery over magic reflects her domain over occult knowledge and the manipulation of natural laws. Her role was to guide, protect, and even punish individuals who strayed into her dominion without the necessary respect or precaution.

Pan: Pan embodies the forces of the wilderness and the rustic milieu. As the god of shepherds, flocks, and mountain wilds, Pan's role was to preside over the pastoral aspects of life, ensuring the safety and prosperity of livestock, which were vital to the ancient Greek economy. His association with panic and fear can be seen as a reflection of the unpredictable dangers of the wilderness.

Eirene: Eirene, as the goddess of peace, represented a societal ideal in ancient Greece. She embodied tranquillity, prosperity, and the harmonious functioning of society. As such, her role was to preserve the peace and ensure a state of prosperity within the community, a critical element in the development and survival of the city-state.

Asclepius: As the god of medicine, Asclepius's primary role was healing. His influence penetrated deeply into daily life, with his temples serving as ancient healing centres. His symbolism extends to the snake, a common symbol in healing rituals, reflecting his role as a restorer of health and a symbol of hope for the sick.

Nemesis: Nemesis functioned as the implementer of divine justice. She ensured that happiness and unhappiness were duly allocated, that hubris did not go unchecked, and that mortals did not escape their due. Her role was to maintain a balance, a concept intrinsic to the ancient Greek worldview.

Eris: The goddess of strife and discord, Eris, represented the destructive aspects of conflict. Her role was not merely to incite disagreement but also to underline the negative consequences of disharmony, thereby acting as a cautionary figure in the collective consciousness of the Greeks.

Hypnos and Thanatos: As personifications of sleep and death, respectively, Hypnos and Thanatos had complementary roles. Hypnos represented rest and rejuvenation, a daily retreat from the toil of life, while Thanatos personified the inevitable end that awaits all mortals, symbolising the final rest. Their roles emphasize the cyclical nature of life and existence.

These lesser-known deities, through their distinct and significant roles, constituted an integral part of the ancient Greek religious and cultural framework. Their influence imbued various aspects of life, from the mundane to the profound, providing the Greeks with a comprehensive and complex understanding of their existence within the universe. The acknowledgment and appreciation of these lesser-known deities thus provide invaluable insights into the breadth and depth of ancient Greek religion and mythology.

Examination of the specific roles, responsibilities, and domains of influence of the selected deities

As we delve deeper into the complex tapestry of the ancient Greek pantheon, it becomes evident that each deity, irrespective of their popularity, possessed distinctive roles, responsibilities, and spheres of influence that had significant implications for the ancient Greeks. A detailed exploration of these aspects facilitates an in-depth comprehension of their religious perception and societal structure.

Hecate: Although a lesser-known deity, Hecate played a crucial role in the ancient Greek religion and was associated with the domain of magic, crossroads, and liminal spaces. Hecate's responsibilities included guiding souls to the afterlife, a task of immense significance. Furthermore, her influence permeated every crossroad, symbolic of life's important decision-making junctures, manifesting her as an omnipresent divine guide. Her dominion over magic imbued her with an aura of mystery, respect, and a modicum of fear, underlining her significant influence on the ancient Greeks' daily lives.

Pan: Pan's role as the god of shepherds, flocks, and the rustic wilds positioned him as an indispensable figure for the agrarian society of ancient Greece. His responsibilities encompassed the protection and prosperity of livestock - an economic linchpin for many ancient Greek communities. His influence in the pastoral realm signified the divine's presence even in the humblest of settings, reinforcing the Greeks' inherent connection to nature.

Eirene: Eirene was tasked with the responsibility of upholding peace, a coveted state of being in the oftentimes tumultuous ancient Greek city-states. Her domain stretched over societal harmony, reflecting in the law-abiding citizens' conduct, peaceful resolutions of disputes, and general prosperity of the community. She was a beacon of tranquillity, her influence keenly sought and highly revered.

Asclepius: As the deity of medicine and healing, Asclepius held an essential role in the ancient Greeks' health and well-being. His responsibilities spanned diagnosis, treatment, and recovery, turning his temples into hubs of healthcare and sanctuaries of hope. His serpentine staff, the Rod of Asclepius, remains an enduring symbol in the medical field, attesting to his timeless influence.

Nemesis: Nemesis embodied divine retribution, responsible for dispensing justice to those exhibiting hubris or ignoring their societal and moral obligations. Her domain underscored the importance of humility and righteousness, discouraging disproportionate pride or gain. Her role subtly shaped the ancient Greeks' moral compass and societal behavior.

Eris: Eris, the goddess of discord, although not an ideal figure, served a crucial role in highlighting the consequences of conflict and disharmony. Her responsibilities lay not in causing strife but in representing its destructive effects, making her a cautionary figure to avoid rather than to appease.

Hypnos and Thanatos: Hypnos, the personification of sleep, and Thanatos, the embodiment of death, had domains that were intrinsically linked to the human condition. Hypnos was responsible for providing mortals with nightly respite, while Thanatos represented the inevitable finality of life. Their roles resonated deeply with the ancient Greeks, offering both comfort and a sobering reminder of life's cyclical nature.

Through this comprehensive examination of their specific roles, responsibilities, and domains, we gain profound insights into the intricate workings of the ancient Greek religion and the deities' pervasive influence on society. These lesser-known gods served critical functions and catered to various facets of life, contributing to a holistic religious framework that encapsulated the ancient Greeks' existence.

Discussion on the diversity and specialization of functions in the Greek pantheon, exemplified by these lesser-known gods

The multifaceted nature of the Greek pantheon is a testament to the ancient Greeks' understanding of the world around them and the divine's role within it. The wealth of deities, both major and lesser-known, echoes the nuanced complexity of the world, reflecting a multitude of aspects - from the mundane to the profound, the physical to the abstract. This section delves into the remarkable diversity and specialization of functions within the Greek pantheon, utilizing the examples of the lesser-known gods explored in this chapter.

Diverse Range of Functions

The ancient Greeks had deities presiding over almost every conceivable aspect of their lives, resulting in a wide array of domains. The diversity of these gods' functions suggests an understanding that the world consists of interconnected spheres, each with its unique significance. Consider, for instance, the god Pan, a protector of shepherds and rustic landscapes, reflecting the value of agriculture and the rural life in ancient Greek society. Simultaneously, Hecate, the goddess of magic and crossroads, represents the mystical and uncertain aspects of life.

From Eirene, the goddess of peace, to Eris, the goddess of discord, the ancient Greeks acknowledged and revered the dualities inherent in life. Through Asclepius, they paid homage to the curative sciences, while through Hypnos and Thanatos, they confronted the everyday realities of sleep and death. This wide array of gods denotes an intricate understanding of various life aspects, each holding its distinct importance.

Specialization of Functions

In addition to diversity, the Greek pantheon also reveals a striking level of specialization. Each god did not merely preside over a broad aspect of life but often had a uniquely defined role within that aspect. This is exemplified by Asclepius, who was not just a deity of health but specifically the god of medicine and healing. Similarly, Nemesis was not merely a goddess of justice; she represented divine retribution for excessive pride or unjust gains.

This degree of specialization suggests that the ancient Greeks perceived the divine as intimately involved in every life facet, down to the most minute details. It underlines a profound conviction in divine omnipresence and the gods' power to intervene in the mortal world in very specific ways.

Interactions and Interdependencies

The pantheon's diversity and specialization also resulted in an intricate web of relationships among the gods, mirroring the interdependencies in the natural and societal world. For example, the domains of Hypnos and Thanatos, sleep and death, are intimately linked, symbolizing the constant dance between life's transitory rest and its final cessation.

Furthermore, some gods served as counterpoints to others, embodying opposing aspects of existence. Eirene and Eris, representing peace and discord, respectively, are a fitting illustration of this dichotomy, highlighting the Greeks' recognition of life's intrinsic dualities.

In conclusion, the diversity and specialization of functions within the Greek pantheon, particularly among the lesser-known deities, serve as a microcosm of the complex, multifaceted nature of existence as perceived by the ancient Greeks. The pantheon's intricate structure paints a vivid portrait of a society that sought to understand and venerate the divine in every aspect of life, thereby weaving a vibrant tapestry of religiosity intricately linked with daily life and societal structures.

The Significance of Lesser-Known Deities in the Daily Life of Ancient Greeks

Despite the prominence of the Twelve Olympians in our contemporary understanding of ancient Greek religion, the lesser-known deities played an indispensable role in the daily life of the ancient Greeks. Their areas of influence often covered the more immediate, practical aspects of existence - aspects which, though mundane, formed the fabric of everyday life. This section explores the significance of these lesser-known deities in ancient Greek daily life, shedding light on how the divine was woven into the mundane in Greek society.

Interactions with the Divine in Daily Life

In ancient Greece, the divine was not confined to the ethereal realm. Instead, the gods permeated every aspect of life, influencing a person's day from dawn to dusk. The lesser-known deities often governed more specialized, practical domains compared to the major gods, bringing them closer to the ordinary person's daily experience. The goddess Hestia, for example, presided over the hearth and home, crucial elements of domestic life, while the god Hermes, though part of the major pantheon, had dominion over commerce and was a daily presence in the lives of traders and merchants.

Religious practices such as prayers, offerings, and small household rituals played a substantial part in daily life, often directed towards these lesser-known gods. An individual might invoke Asclepius when seeking healing, or call upon Nemesis to avenge a perceived slight. Thus, the lesser-known deities were inextricably linked with the ebb and flow of daily life.

Socio-Cultural Context and Symbolism

The lesser-known deities also served as vital societal and cultural symbols, representing a wide array of human activities, values, and aspirations. Their various attributes and stories were embedded in the societal discourse, shaping values, norms, and expectations. For instance, Eirene, the goddess of peace, was more than a divine figure; she embodied a societal ideal, symbolizing the aspiration for harmony and balance.

These gods, therefore, had an important function as cultural signifiers. Their myths and stories were not mere entertainment but carried a wealth of symbolic meaning that imparted social mores and norms. These narratives, when narrated in public spaces or during festivals, served as shared cultural knowledge, helping to shape societal values and norms.

Lesser-Known Deities and their Relationship with Major Gods

The lesser-known deities often had familial or other connections to the more prominent gods, thereby strengthening the pantheon's overall narrative coherence. These relationships also underscored the interdependence of various aspects of life, reflecting the interconnected nature of the divine and the mundane. For example, Asclepius, the god of medicine, was the son of Apollo, who was associated with healing among his other domains.

In conclusion, the lesser-known deities, in their interaction with the daily life of the ancient Greeks, were a testament to the pervasive presence of the divine in the mundane. Their areas of influence, covering a diverse range of human experience, ensured that the divine was never a remote concept but a tangible, everyday presence. The function of these gods extended beyond the religious realm, symbolizing societal ideals and values, and contributing to the rich tapestry of Greek cultural narrative.

Examination of how lesser-known deities influenced day-to-day aspects of Greek life, customs, and beliefs

The lesser-known deities of the ancient Greek pantheon were deeply intertwined with the quotidian aspects of life, shaping not only the daily activities and routines of individuals but also the wider fabric of Greek society, customs, and beliefs. This section provides an in-depth examination of the multi-faceted influence these lesser-known deities had on the daily life, customs, and belief systems of the ancient Greeks.

Influence on Daily Routines and Activities

The lesser-known deities held sway over specific, often narrowly-defined domains of life that nonetheless had a profound impact on day-to-day activities. From the moment an ancient Greek individual awoke to the time they retired to sleep, the presence of these deities could be felt.

For instance, the god Hypnos, personifying sleep, had an inherent presence in people's nightly routines. The god Pan, associated with wilderness and rustic music, was felt by shepherds tending to their flocks, as well as anyone strolling through the countryside. Even mundane activities such as weaving, overseen by the goddesses, the Moirai, became infused with religious significance, thereby imbuing daily life with a sense of the divine.

Shaping Customs and Festivals

The influence of these deities extended beyond individual routines to communal customs and traditions. Seasonal festivals and community gatherings were often dedicated to lesser-known deities. Consider the Anthesteria, a festival held in honor of Dionysus, god of wine and merriment but not an Olympian. These events played a crucial role in maintaining social cohesion and expressing communal identity.

Furthermore, many traditional customs originated from myths involving lesser-known deities. For example, the custom of placing a coin in the mouth of a deceased person for the ferryman Charon originated from the belief in Charon's role in transporting souls across the river Styx to the afterlife.

Impact on Beliefs and Moral Frameworks

Beliefs in these lesser-known deities also impacted the moral and ethical frameworks within ancient Greek society. Deities like Nemesis (retribution) and Dike (justice) personified moral values and norms, providing divine backing for societal expectations of fair conduct. Belief in these deities enforced moral behavior, given the divine consequences attached to violating these principles.

Furthermore, deities like Tyche (luck) and Ananke (necessity) represented the acceptance of chance and inevitability in life, subtly shaping the Greeks' world-view and attitudes towards fate and personal agency. The influence of these deities, therefore, extended to shaping the philosophical and ethical underpinnings of society.

In conclusion, the influence of the lesser-known deities permeated the fabric of ancient Greek life, from daily routines to societal customs and belief systems. While not as prominent as the major gods, these deities played a crucial role in intertwining the divine with the mundane, thereby imbuing every aspect of life with religious significance. In their specificity and ubiquity, they provided a rich, multifaceted divine landscape that profoundly shaped ancient Greek society.

Exploration of the interplay between divine and mundane: how the Greeks perceived and invoked these deities in daily activities, celebrations, and rituals

In the Greek worldview, the divine was not a realm separate from the mundane. Instead, it was intimately linked to and involved in daily life, activities, and events. Lesser-known deities, with their specific domains and responsibilities, played pivotal roles in such integration, transforming common daily experiences into acts of religious significance. This section will explore the confluence of the divine and the mundane, highlighting how the Greeks perceived and invoked these lesser-known deities in their everyday lives, during celebrations, and within rituals.

Invocation in Daily Activities

The sacred was invoked in the everyday activities of ancient Greeks, from waking to retiring, by paying tribute to various deities. Deities such as Eos (Dawn) and Selene (Moon) were invoked daily at sunrise and sunset, respectively. Activities such as farming, fishing, and weaving were performed with an awareness of the deities who oversaw them - Demeter (Agriculture), Poseidon (Seas), and the Moirai (Fate). By acknowledging the gods in these activities, mundane tasks were transformed into acts imbued with divine presence and significance.

Perceived Presence in Celebrations and Festivals

Lesser-known deities were a central feature of Greek celebrations and festivals. For instance, the Anthesteria, a spring festival celebrating the maturation of wine, was held in honor of Dionysus. The rural deity Pan was celebrated during the rustic festival of the Lupercalia. These festivals were not only times of merriment but also significant religious occasions, which facilitated communal bonding and reaffirmed shared beliefs and customs. In this manner, the presence of these deities added a divine dimension to communal gatherings and celebrations.

Participation in Rituals

The interplay between divine and mundane was especially pronounced within the context of Greek rituals. The rituals offered a structured way for individuals and communities to interact with the divine. Lesser-known deities often figured prominently in these rituals. For example, Hekate, goddess of magic and crossroads, was frequently invoked in household protection rites and spells. In the ritual of the dead, Charon, the ferryman of Hades, was appeased with obol coins. These rituals provided a means of propitiating the gods, seeking their favor, or preventing their disfavor, and underscore the integral role these deities played in the spiritual lives of the Greeks.

Symbiosis between Divine and Mundane

Thus, through the invocation of these deities, the Greeks created a symbiosis between the divine and mundane. The divine was not relegated to an abstract, distant realm but was instead manifest in the material world, actively shaping and being shaped by human activities and experiences. This integration of divine and mundane not only lent a profound sense of sanctity to the everyday life of ancient Greeks but also created a vivid and dynamic spiritual landscape where humans and gods were in constant interaction.

In summary, the perception and invocation of lesser-known deities in everyday activities, celebrations, and rituals demonstrate the remarkable integration of the divine into the mundane in ancient Greek culture. It underscores the role of these deities in shaping the Greeks' world-view, their customs, and their socio-cultural identity. The daily invocation and the routine rituals provide a fascinating glimpse into how religion and daily life were inextricably intertwined in ancient Greek society.

Case Studies: Cults and Worship of Lesser-Known Deities

The plethora of deities in the Greek pantheon allowed for a rich tapestry of religious practices, and even lesser-known deities had specific cults dedicated to their worship. This section delves into a few selected case studies to provide a comprehensive understanding of how such cults operated and the role they played in the cultural and religious landscape of ancient Greece.

The Cult of Hekate

Hekate, the ancient Greek goddess of magic, witchcraft, crossroads, and ghosts, held a significant position in the pantheon despite her lesser-known status. Her domains were varied and extended into realms that were considered liminal, ambiguous, or boundary-crossing, hence making her a peculiar figure of veneration. Her cult was characterized by distinctive rituals, public and private, and the symbology associated with her added layers of complexity to her worship.

Household Veneration

At the domestic level, Hekate was acknowledged as a protector of the household, particularly the entranceway, a liminal space marking the threshold between private and public. Small shrines known as Hekataea were often placed near the household doors, indicating her role as a guardian against ill-omened spirits and malevolent magic. The Deipnon, a monthly ritual on the dark moon's eve, involved purifying the house and leaving offerings, often 'Hekate's Supper', at the crossroads or the house entrance to appease the goddess. This offering consisted of food that was considered ritually impure and thus not eaten by the humans, thereby drawing a clear boundary between the human and the divine.

Public Worship and Associations

Publicly, Hekate was recognized as a potent deity with control over land, sea, and sky, and her worship extended to several city-states in ancient Greece. Most notable was her veneration in Athens, where a sanctuary was dedicated to her at the Agora, a significant public space, reinforcing her association with communal safety and welfare.

Hekate's close association with crossroads, boundary markers (herms), and liminal spaces accentuated her nature as a liminal deity. She was believed to inhabit the thresholds, the spaces in-between, making her a mediator and a guide between the realms of the living, the divine, and the dead. Consequently, she was frequently invoked in rites of passage and magic rites that sought to manipulate boundaries, further testifying to her role as the deity of transitions and marginal spaces.

Hekate and Magic

Given Hekate's association with witchcraft and magic, she was a central figure in Greek spellcraft and divination. She was frequently invoked in 'binding spells' (defixiones) and love charms, and her approval was sought in necromancy, a form of divination that involved summoning the dead. Hekate's affinity with the darker aspects of the supernatural also marked her as a chthonic deity. Hence, she was often associated with rituals related to death and afterlife, thereby bridging the boundary between the living and the dead.

Symbolism and Iconography

In her iconography, Hekate was often depicted with torches, keys, and daggers, symbols that encapsulated her multifaceted nature. The torches represented her role as an illuminator and guide in dark times, the keys symbolized her authority over thresholds, and the dagger was a symbol of protection.

The cult of Hekate illustrates the elaborate and nuanced ways in which the ancient Greeks interacted with their deities, attributing them with specific roles within their societal and religious framework. Her worship offers an intriguing exploration into the concept of liminality in religion, and the intricate relationship between household rituals, public rites, and magic practices in the formation of religious traditions in ancient Greece.

The Worship of Asclepius

Asclepius, the son of Apollo and the mortal princess Coronis, emerged as a significant deity within the Greek pantheon, embodying the divine aspect of healing and medical practices. The adoration for Asclepius extended to include various methods of worship, from sacrificial rituals to the establishment of Asclepieia, sacred healing temples. The worship of Asclepius bears testament to the integration of spiritual beliefs and medical intervention in ancient Greece, illustrating the pervasiveness of divine influence in societal activities.

Asclepieia: Sanctuaries of Healing

Asclepieia, the healing temples dedicated to Asclepius, became the nexus of healthcare and spiritual worship, not only in Greece but also in the broader Hellenistic world. These temples were often constructed in serene locations, close to healing springs or surrounded by natural beauty, thereby creating an atmosphere conducive to recuperation. The best-known Asclepieion was in Epidaurus, which became a significant healing center in the ancient world.

These sanctuaries were not merely places of worship but functioned as ancient hospitals where the sick could stay and receive treatment. They included dormitories for the patients, theaters for entertainment, athletic facilities for physical rehabilitation, and libraries for the recording of medical cases and treatments. This combination of religious, therapeutic, and leisure facilities marks the Asclepieia as a unique amalgamation of the divine and the medical.

Rituals and Practices

The principal ritualistic practice associated with the Asclepieia was incubation, or 'enkoimesis.' The devotees, after a period of fasting, bathing, and sacrificing, would sleep within the temple precinct, hoping to receive a dream revelation from the god, which usually took the form of a healing prescription. These dream revelations were termed 'iatromanteia', and priests, often referred to as 'Asclepiads', would help interpret them.

Sacrifices also played a pivotal role in the worship of Asclepius. These usually consisted of roosters, a symbol of human vigilance and recovery from illness. It is noteworthy that these sacrifices were not consumed by the worshippers, differentiating them from the feasting that usually followed a sacrifice in Greek religious practices.

The Serpent Symbol

The serpent is a significant symbol in the cult of Asclepius, embodying regeneration and healing due to its ability to shed its skin. Sacred, non-venomous snakes were kept in Asclepieia and were involved in healing rituals, often slithering over sleeping patients during the incubation process. This practice underscored the symbolic interplay between the divine and medical healing.

Asclepius and Greek Society

The cult of Asclepius had a profound impact on Greek society, reflected in the societal appreciation of health and wellness. The integration of religious worship within health practices indicates the significance of divine intervention in Greek societal norms. Moreover, the vast network of Asclepieia and the well-documented healing inscriptions (iamata) suggest a systematic, organized approach to healthcare, guided by both religious and empirical principles.

In conclusion, the worship of Asclepius provides a fascinating insight into how ancient Greek society bridged the gap between the divine and mundane, particularly in the realm of health and medicine. It illuminates the profound role that religious beliefs played in shaping societal attitudes towards health and wellbeing.

The Cult of Pan

Pan, a rustic deity adored by shepherds, hunters, and other rural populations, was an intriguing figure within the Greek pantheon. Unlike the majority of Greek deities who resided on Mount Olympus, Pan made his home in the mountainous regions and caves of Arcadia, an isolated and bucolic area of the Peloponnese. Despite this rustic setting, the worship of Pan extended far beyond pastoral landscapes, penetrating into urban life and illustrating the permeation of religion across socio-economic boundaries.

Rustic Celebrations and Rituals

Pan was traditionally revered through practices that mirrored his rural, rustic persona. His devotees engaged in lively dances and robust music, notably the playing of Pan pipes, an instrument that the god himself was said to have invented. Such celebrations were usually held in natural settings, close to caves, forests, or mountain pastures, reflecting the deity's affinity for the wilderness.

Sacrificial rites played an integral role in the worship of Pan. Goats, symbolic of the deity due to his half-goat, half-human form, were the typical offering. These sacrifices were often accompanied by libations of milk and honey, further emphasizing the agrarian nature of his worship.

Sanctuaries of Pan: Between the Wild and the City

The primary sanctuary of Pan was nestled in the wilderness of Arcadia, reflecting the god's connection with remote and untamed landscapes. Nonetheless, Pan's worship was not confined to such rural spaces. The god had a significant sanctuary in

Athens, situated at the base of the Acropolis, suggesting that the adoration for Pan was not restricted to the countryside but was a part of urban religious life as well.

Pan in Athenian Society

The inclusion of Pan in Athenian worship demonstrates the deity's broader societal significance. According to the historian Herodotus, Pan's cult was established in Athens following the Battle of Marathon, where Pan supposedly appeared and induced panic among the Persian ranks, leading to a Greek victory. This tale underscores the manner in which religious beliefs could be shaped and adapted in response to historical events, reinforcing the intimate bond between religion and societal development.

Pan: A Mediator Between Man and Nature

The reverence for Pan underscores the ancient Greeks' recognition of the intrinsic connection between human beings and nature. Pan, being a deity of rustic and wild settings, served as a mediator between humans and the natural world. His worship reflected a deep-seated belief in the sanctity of the environment and its significance in daily life and well-being.

In conclusion, the cult of Pan provides a vivid example of how Greek religious practices and beliefs could transcend geographical and social boundaries. The worship of this rustic god in both the countryside and the city underscores the intricate relationship between the divine, human society, and the natural world in Greek religious consciousness.

The Cult of Eileithyia

Eileithyia, the Greek goddess of childbirth and midwifery, held a distinctive position in the lives of ancient Greek women. Her sphere of influence directly correlated with crucial biological and societal milestones in a woman's life, emphasizing the integration of divine figures into the intimate and domestic facets of Greek society.

Domestic Worship and Life Cycle Rituals

The worship of Eileithyia was primarily domestic, closely aligned with the familial sphere. This goddess was called upon at significant points in a woman's reproductive life cycle, which included the onset of menstruation, the process of childbirth, and rituals surrounding postpartum recovery.

The onset of menstruation, marking a girl's transition to womanhood, was an occasion for invoking Eileithyia's protection. She was further invoked during childbirth, a time fraught with danger for both mother and child in ancient Greece. Eileithyia's favour was sought to ensure a safe delivery and the survival of the mother. Post-birth rituals, vital for the purification of the mother and the protection of the newborn, also included offerings to Eileithyia.

Shrines of Eileithyia: Between the Public and Private

Shrines dedicated to Eileithyia often found their place within or near birthing rooms, demonstrating the close link between domestic spaces and the divine. These shrines were spaces of worship, prayer, and offering, reflecting the Greeks' desire for divine intervention during critical life events.

In addition to these domestic shrines, there were also public sanctuaries dedicated to Eileithyia. These were often visited by women hoping for a safe childbirth, where they would make votive offerings, such as small terracotta figurines representing pregnant women or nursing mothers. One of the most notable public sanctuaries of Eileithyia was located in Crete, an island often considered to be her birthplace in myth.

Eileithyia: A Female Deity for Women's Concerns

The cult of Eileithyia underscores the existence of deities assigned specifically to women's issues in the Greek pantheon. This association emphasizes the role of women in societal continuity and the divine recognition of female life events. It also reflects the inherent dangers of childbirth in ancient times and the necessity for divine protection and intervention.

In summary, the cult of Eileithyia exemplifies the intersection of the divine with the most intimate aspects of human life, specifically the feminine sphere. The practices surrounding her worship highlight the Greek belief in the permeation of the divine into every facet of life, from the public to the private, from the community to the individual, and from the mundane to the crucial milestones in life.

Concluding Remarks: Cults and Social Cohesion

These case studies present a multifaceted view of the diverse ways in which lesser-known deities were worshipped and how their cults permeated different aspects of Greek life. They underscore the specialization of functions in the Greek pantheon and illustrate how these deities fulfilled critical roles in society, fostering a sense of cohesion and shared identity among their worshippers.

Such cults not only allowed individuals to seek divine intervention for specific needs but also fostered community bonding, mediated social tensions, and reinforced shared values and norms. They were central to the communal fabric of ancient Greece and contributed significantly to the dynamic interaction between the divine and mundane, profoundly influencing the sociocultural ethos of the time.

The detailed exploration of these case studies helps students gain an in-depth understanding of how the worship of lesser-known deities was structured and the significant role such cults played in Greek society. It serves as a basis for further discussion on the nuanced interplay of religion and society in ancient civilizations, offering valuable insights into their belief systems, practices, and cultural identities.

Discussion of archaeological, literary, and historical evidence for the worship of selected lesser-known deities

In the study of the divine and its worship in ancient Greece, scholars rely on an array of sources, spanning archaeological findings, literary accounts, and historical records. These diverse sources afford a comprehensive, albeit not always unambiguous, view of how the Greeks interacted with their pantheon, including the lesser-known deities.

Archaeological Evidence

Archaeological discoveries represent a rich repository of physical and tangible evidence for the veneration of lesser-known deities, contributing significantly to our understanding of the intimate relationship between the ancient Greeks and their gods. These invaluable traces, manifested as material remains from antiquity, offer a dynamic and tactile window into the religious practices and beliefs of this period.

✧ Material and Iconographic Evidence

In the context of the cult of Hekate, a wide range of material and iconographic evidence supports the historical documentation of her worship. The archaeological record includes numerous terracotta statuettes and votive reliefs recovered from sanctuaries, private dwellings, and particularly at crossroads. These depictions often present Hekate as a three-bodied or three-headed figure (known as the Triple Hekate), each facing a different direction — a reflection of her role as a liminal goddess, protector of boundaries and crossroads. Some depictions also include torches, keys, and dogs, all traditional symbols associated with the goddess.

Additionally, archaeological remains have unearthed objects that suggest the practical components of worship. These include tables or altars used for the preparation of meals for the Deipnon, the ritual supper offered to Hekate on the eve of the new moon. This evidence confirms not just the occurrence of this ritual, but also its pervasive nature, as these tables have been found in multiple locations throughout Greece, indicating a wide-ranging and uniform practice.

✧   Healing Sanctuaries and Votive Offerings

Turning to the god of healing, Asclepius, archaeological evidence becomes a vital tool for exploring the practical aspects of healing cults in the ancient world. The sanctuaries of Asclepius, known as Asclepieia, serve as remarkable evidence of the interweaving of healing and religious practices.

Excavations of these sites, most notably at Epidaurus, Kos, and Pergamon, have brought to light a plethora of votive offerings, objects dedicated to the god in expectation of or in gratitude for healing. Remarkably, many of these offerings are anatomical models made of various materials such as terracotta, bronze, or marble. These anatomical votives, often depicting the afflicted part of the body — be it a leg, an arm, or even internal organs — give us a tangible sense of the types of ailments for which supplicants sought divine intervention, as well as the personal and intimate nature of their devotion.

✧   Temples, Altars, and Inscriptions

Beyond the specific cults of Hekate and Asclepius, the landscape of ancient Greece was dotted with numerous temples, altars, and other sacred spaces dedicated to lesser-known deities. Many of these remain in varying states of preservation and provide valuable insights into the architectural styles, locational choices, and the overall prominence of these deities.

Inscriptions, often found on stone steles or metal tablets, also constitute a significant part of the archaeological record. They can offer insights into the administrative aspects of cult practices, the nature of individual supplications, and even the sociopolitical implications of religious devotion. For instance, the Athenian Treasury at Delphi, though dedicated to the well-known deity Apollo, features numerous inscriptions revealing the patronage of lesser-known deities, confirming their active veneration.

In conclusion, archaeological evidence plays an indispensable role in our understanding of the worship of lesser-known deities in ancient Greece. It bridges the temporal divide, allowing modern observers to glimpse the spiritual lives of individuals in antiquity, while also reminding us that our current interpretations are largely built upon the physical remains of the past, always subject to further discovery and reinterpretation.

Literary Evidence

Literary evidence constitutes a rich tapestry of information that illumines the complex web of interactions between human beings and the divine realm in ancient Greek society. These textual materials, ranging from mythology to poetry, drama, philosophical treatises, and historical accounts, provide a nuanced view of the cultural and religious contexts within which these deities were venerated.

✧   Cosmological and Mythological Literature

A critical source of information about the pantheon of Greek deities is Hesiod's "Theogony," a foundational text of Greek cosmogony and theogony. Though the work is primarily concerned with the genealogy of the gods and the creation of the universe, it also provides invaluable insights into the functions and attributes of the lesser-known deities.

Eileithyia, the goddess of childbirth and labour pains, is mentioned several times in "Theogony." Hesiod identifies her as the daughter of Hera and Zeus, thereby underscoring her significant lineage. In addition, the text notes that she is invoked by women in labour, confirming her role in aiding childbirth.

✧   Pastoral and Dramatic Literature

Pan's pastoral character and his relationship with the natural world are documented in various literary sources. In Theocritus's "Idylls," a collection of short pastoral poems, Pan is frequently depicted as the companion of shepherds, highlighting his rural, rustic nature. His character, often portrayed playing the syrinx (a type of panpipe), and his intimate relationship with the natural environment underscore his role as a pastoral deity.

In addition, Pan's association with Dionysian rites is recorded in dramatic literature. In Euripides's "The Bacchae," Pan is represented as a deity involved in the orgiastic rituals characteristic of the worship of Dionysus, the god of wine and ecstasy. This depiction indicates an intersection of cultic practices and hints at a fluidity within the Greek pantheon.

✧   Historical and Philosophical Texts

Historical and philosophical texts also serve as important repositories of information about the cults and beliefs associated with lesser-known deities. For instance, in his "Histories," Herodotus records numerous rituals, sacrifices, and festivals associated with various deities, revealing the rich diversity of Greek religious practice. In addition, the works of Plato and Aristotle offer insights into how philosophical thought interacted with and influenced religious beliefs and practices.

It is crucial to remember, however, that literary evidence often reflects the biases and objectives of the authors and the sociocultural contexts within which they were writing. Thus, while such evidence is vital for our understanding of the veneration of lesser-known deities in ancient Greece, it must be considered alongside and in dialogue with archaeological and other forms of evidence. The symbiotic relationship between these various forms of evidence allows for a comprehensive and nuanced understanding of the diverse and rich tapestry of ancient Greek religion.

Historical Evidence

Historical evidence provides a valuable counterpart to archaeological and literary sources, elucidating the practices, customs, and societal context associated with the worship of lesser-known deities. This form of evidence frequently comes from inscriptions, which serve as historical records that capture a snapshot of religious and social life in ancient Greece. In particular, inscriptions found on durable materials such as stone or metal, have weathered the passage of time and offer a wealth of information about rituals, festivals, and the administrative aspects of religious practices.

✧   Healing Inscriptions from Epidaurus

An illuminating example of historical evidence comes from Epidaurus, the most important sanctuary dedicated to Asclepius, the god of healing. Here, healing inscriptions or 'iamata' were discovered, which detail the miraculous cures performed by the god, illustrating the hopes and beliefs of the people seeking relief from various maladies. These inscriptions are not only testament to the god's perceived power and mercy, but they also shed light on the societal understanding and treatment of illness in ancient Greece.

The 'iamata' are typically brief, recounting the patient's name, ailment, the dream in which Asclepius provided the cure, and the method of treatment. These narratives thus provide first-hand accounts of the process of incubation, where suppliants would sleep within the temple in hopes of receiving a divine dream revelation for their cure. It also underscores the role of dreams as a medium for divine-human communication in the ancient Greek worldview.

✧   Inscriptions Related to Other Deities

Historical evidence related to other deities such as Hekate, Eileithyia, and Pan also exist, further enriching our understanding of their worship. For instance, inscriptions discovered in the vicinity of crossroads, a significant locale associated with Hekate, often contain invocations to the goddess, testifying to her widespread veneration as a protective deity.

Inscriptions and dedicatory plaques found near childbirth rooms or domestic spaces often invoked Eileithyia, thereby providing tangible evidence of her role as a protector during childbirth.

Evidence for the rural deity Pan is often found in inscriptions from rural sanctuaries and caves, which attest to the rituals and festivals in his honor.

✧   Historical Evidence in Context

While historical evidence provides valuable insights into the religious practices and societal context of ancient Greek society, it should not be considered in isolation. Instead, it is crucial to integrate these findings with archaeological and literary evidence for a comprehensive understanding of the multi-faceted nature of ancient Greek religious worship. The synthesis of these diverse forms of evidence allows us to more fully comprehend and appreciate the complex religious landscape of ancient Greece, including the significant roles played by lesser-known deities in the everyday life of the Greeks.

In Conclusion

Through the triangulation of archaeological, literary, and historical evidence, we can construct a more nuanced understanding of the veneration of lesser-known deities in ancient Greece. It is a reminder of the depth of Greek religiosity, which extended beyond the twelve Olympian gods to encompass a multitude of deities, each serving a particular purpose and reflecting the intricate mosaic of Greek religious belief and practice. However, as with all historical analyses, this understanding is continually subject to revision and refinement as new discoveries are made and interpretations evolve.

Examination of regional variations in worship and representation

Ancient Greece was not a monolithic culture but rather a collection of city-states (poleis), each with its unique customs, traditions, and practices. Accordingly, the worship of the deities, including the lesser-known ones, varied widely across regions, reflecting localized interpretations and manifestations of divinity. This chapter will explore these regional variations, considering how geography, local culture, and history influenced the representation and worship of selected deities. We shall examine four examples: Hekate, Asclepius, Pan, and Eileithyia.

Hekate

The multifaceted character of Hekate, a chthonic deity associated with magic, witchcraft, and crossroads, found diverse expressions across various regions, reflecting the adaptation and transformation of her persona within local religious frameworks.

In **Athens,** Hekate's role was markedly domestic, as she was invoked in private households during the Deipnon ritual. This practice took place on the eve of the new moon, when the Athenians would purify their homes and prepare a meal—referred to as Hekate's suppers—to leave at the crossroads. This ritual was believed to propitiate the goddess and ward off malevolent spirits that might enter the household. The intimate connection between the goddess and the Athenian households underlines her function as a protective deity, involved in the day-to-day survival of her worshippers.

The Hekate of **Alexandria**, a city known for its confluence of diverse cultures, was a more cosmopolitan version of the goddess. Under the Hellenistic influence, her image transformed: she was often depicted in triple form, signifying her power over the earth, sea, and sky—a significant expansion from her earlier association primarily with the crossroads. This artistic and symbolic representation of Hekate illustrates the syncretic nature of Alexandrian religion, where Egyptian, Greek, and other foreign elements intermingled to create unique divine figures and cult practices.

Hekate's origins can be traced back to **Anatolia** (modern-day Turkey), where she held a distinct role compared to her Greek counterparts. Here, Hekate was revered as a prominent mother goddess figure. Her cult was closely tied with nature and fertility, and she was often invoked for prosperous harvests and the overall well-being of the community. The evolution from a fertility goddess in Anatolia to a deity of crossroads and witchcraft in Athens and finally, to a universal figure in Alexandria, underscores the fluidity and adaptability of divine identities in response to cultural and regional needs.

These regional variations of Hekate's worship practices not only demonstrate the localized adaptations of divine figures but also illuminate the intricate complexities of ancient religious beliefs. Studying such changes offers valuable insights into understanding the multi-layered fabric of Greek religion and its inherent flexibility to accommodate the evolving spiritual and pragmatic requirements of its followers.

Exercise for Further Reflection

Compare and contrast the worship of Hekate in Athens, Alexandria, and Anatolia. How do these variations reflect the different socio-cultural contexts of these regions?

What does the evolution of Hekate's image—from a household deity in Athens to a universal goddess in Alexandria   tell us about the changing dynamics of Greek religious practices?

Reflect on Hekate's Anatolian origins as a fertility goddess. How might these origins have influenced her later Greek persona? How do they complicate our understanding of her role within the Greek pantheon?

Engage in detailed research and critical thinking to delve deeper into these questions, further enhancing your understanding of the multifaceted nature of Greek religion.

Asclepius

The practice and conception of the healing god Asclepius's worship present intriguing regional variations, demonstrating the capacity of Greek religious practices to morph and adapt to different sociopolitical contexts.

Epidaurus, located in the Peloponnese, held the preeminent sanctuary of Asclepius. This place became a significant healing center, attracting individuals from far and wide seeking divine intervention for their ailments. The worshippers would perform sacrifices and undergo a ritual of incubation, where they would sleep within the temple, hoping to receive a dream revelation that would provide a solution to their malady. This dream, believed to be sent by Asclepius himself, was interpreted the following morning by the temple priests who would then suggest a suitable course of treatment.

The city of **Rome** provides an intriguing example of how the worship of Asclepius was adapted to cater to the distinct cultural and political ethos of the Romans. Asclepius, known as Aesculapius in Rome, was introduced to the city during a devastating plague in 293 BC. Following an incubation dream, it was decreed that a cult statue of the god should be brought from Epidaurus. The god's arrival and the subsequent cessation of the plague enhanced his prestige and cemented his position within the Roman pantheon. However, the Romans, renowned for their military prowess, also associated Asclepius with military victory. This syncretic understanding led to a unique blend of medical and martial worship, as the god was invoked not only for health but also for protection in battles.

Thus, the regional variations in the worship of Asclepius underline the flexible and adaptive nature of Greek (and later Roman) religious practices. These practices were not rigid or unchanging; rather, they were continuously evolving, shaped by diverse social, political, and environmental factors.

Exercises for Further Reflection

Explore the reasons for the differences in the worship of Asclepius in Epidaurus and Rome. How did local conditions and needs shape the deity's image and cult practices?

Discuss the process through which Asclepius was assimilated into the Roman pantheon. What factors contributed to his acceptance and his unique martial associations in Rome?

Compare the role of Asclepius in the Greek and Roman religious context. How did the transition from a Greek city-state system to the vast Roman Empire influence his worship and reputation?

Pursue in-depth research and engage in critical analyses to understand the complexity and dynamism of ancient religious practices and their profound impact on societal functioning.

Pan

The god Pan, epitomizing the spirit of the untamed wilderness, shepherds, and flocks, presents a compelling case study of regional variations in worship and representation in the ancient Greek world.

Rural **Arcadia,** nestled in the central Peloponnesian mountains, was recognized as Pan's primary sanctuary. Here, in these wild and rugged highlands, the deity was revered for his association with pastoral life and the wilderness, reflecting the region's primary modes of subsistence: shepherding and hunting. The Arcadians, living closely with nature, held Pan in high regard as the divine embodiment of their lifestyle and livelihood. In this context, Pan was often depicted with hunting dogs or amidst rural landscapes on vases and sculptures, exemplifying his role as a protector of shepherds and hunters.

However, Pan's worship was not confined to Arcadia or rural spaces alone. His influence extended to the urban center of **Athens**, a testament to the god's broad appeal and the fluidity of Greek religious practices. Pan's establishment in Athenian religious life is attributed to the events following the Battle of Marathon (490 BC) during the Persian Wars. According to Herodotus, Pan appeared to the Athenian courier Pheidippides, promising assistance to the Athenians in their battle against the Persians. After the Athenians' victory, they recognized Pan's aid by establishing a sanctuary for him on the northwestern slope of the Acropolis. Thus, even in the heart of this bustling city-state, Pan, a rustic deity, found a place of reverence, reflecting the rich, multidimensional nature of Greek religion.

Exercises for Further Reflection

Analyze how geographical context, lifestyle, and socio-political events influenced the worship and representation of Pan in Arcadia and Athens. How did these variations reflect the complexity and diversity of ancient Greek society?

Consider the reasons for Pan's acceptance and integration into Athenian religious life. What does this reveal about the Athenian attitude towards foreign or unconventional gods?

Discuss the possible connections between Pan's rustic character and the Athenians' victory at Marathon. How did this association contribute to his sustained reverence in an urban context?

By scrutinizing these regional variations, one can gain deeper insights into the dynamic and complex fabric of ancient Greek religion, society, and identity.

Eileithyia

Eileithyia, the divine midwife, personifies an integral aspect of women's lives in ancient Greece: childbirth. The variations in her worship across different regions provide a window into the multifaceted perceptions of this critical life event and the female divine's role therein.

Crete, an island with its unique cultural traditions, is considered Eileithyia's birthplace in some myths. Here, the goddess was often worshipped as a divine couple with her consort. This Cretan interpretation may reflect a broader view of childbirth as a process involving both feminine and masculine elements. Excavations of Cretan sanctuaries have uncovered double axes and other votive offerings related to fertility and childbirth, further attesting to Eileithyia's importance on the island. Also noteworthy is the "Dictaean Cave," one of the most significant Cretan cult places associated with Eileithyia's birth, a location deeply rooted in local mythology and religious practice.

On **mainland Greece,** Eileithyia's worship frequently intersected with that of Hera and Artemis. This syncretism reflects the complex and multifaceted nature of childbirth and the female divine in Greek religion. Hera, as the queen of the gods and the goddess of marriage, represented the societal expectation of women to become wives and mothers. Artemis, although primarily a virgin goddess of the hunt and wilderness, paradoxically also had strong associations with childbirth and was believed to aid women in labour. Eileithyia, in connection with these two deities, was often invoked during childbirth to ensure safe delivery and the mother's survival, a critical concern in a world without advanced medical care. Therefore, while maintaining her distinct identity, Eileithyia also became part of a divine trio overseeing different childbirth aspects, illuminating the Greeks' comprehensive understanding of this life event.

Exercises for Further Reflection

Contrast the representation of Eileithyia in Crete with her worship on mainland Greece. How do these regional variations reflect local cultures and societal values related to childbirth?

Explore the relationship between Eileithyia, Hera, and Artemis. What does this divine trio tell us about the ancient Greek understanding of childbirth and femininity?

Reflect on the significance of archaeological evidence, such as the Dictaean Cave and the discovered votive offerings, for our understanding of Eileithyia's worship in Crete.

In comprehending these regional variations in Eileithyia's worship, we gain a broader understanding of the diversity and adaptability of Greek religious practices, reflecting the complex interplay of locality, culture, and spirituality.

Interplay of Local and Pan-Hellenic Elements

The ancient Greek religious landscape, rich and diverse, encapsulated an intriguing dichotomy. On the one hand, it was characterized by a Pan-Hellenic religious framework consisting of a shared pantheon of gods and goddesses, universally recognized festivals, and certain common religious customs and beliefs. Simultaneously, the specificities of local geographies, cultures, and historical experiences imbued the religious practices of each city-state with distinct flavors, fostering a plurality of worship even within the shared framework.

Understanding this interplay of local and Pan-Hellenic elements necessitates an exploration of two significant processes: **Syncretism** and **Adaptability**.

Syncretism, the amalgamation of different religions, cultures, or schools of thought, played a vital role in bridging the gap between local and universal elements in Greek religion. The ancient Greeks were highly receptive to incorporating new gods into their pantheon, especially those of foreign origin. The introduction of such deities was often followed by a syncretic process whereby these new deities were identified with one or more existing Greek gods, acquiring new attributes in the process. Such syncretic trends could be seen in the worship of Hekate, who, despite her foreign origin, was integrated into the Greek pantheon and identified with Artemis and Selene.

Adaptability of religious practice also contributed significantly to the interplay between the local and the Pan-Hellenic. Greek deities, while part of the shared pantheon, did not have rigid, universally accepted characteristics. Instead, their personalities, attributes, and the modes of their worship were highly flexible and adapted according to the local context. For instance, Pan, though universally recognized as a pastoral deity, was also perceived as a powerful god in Athens, where he was honoured for his assistance in military victory.

Exercises for Further Reflection

Choose two lesser-known deities discussed in this chapter and explore the evidence for syncretism in their worship.

Reflect on the reasons why the Greeks might have been so receptive to the syncretic processes. What does this tell us about their society and religious attitudes?

Explore the concept of adaptability in Greek religious practice. How did the Greeks adapt the characteristics and modes of worship of their deities according to local context?

This dynamism in Greek religious practice, marked by the ability to integrate and adapt, speaks volumes about the versatility of Greek religion and its intrinsic capacity to respond to the needs of different communities while maintaining a common religious language. It underlines the complexity of Greek religious beliefs, which, though stemming from a shared pantheon, could develop distinct expressions and variations rooted in the local socio-cultural milieu.

In Closing: A Call for Further Research

While we have made substantial strides in understanding the nuanced nature of religious practice in ancient Greece, much remains to be explored. Future research could probe deeper into the socio-cultural factors driving these regional variations, the relationship between major and minor deities within regional cults, and how these relationships influenced local social and political structures. It is within this complex, multi-layered interplay of the local and the universal that the richness of ancient Greek religion truly unfolds.

Exercise for Further Reflection

How did the representation and worship of Hekate vary across different regions in ancient Greece?

Discuss how local culture and history in Epidaurus and Rome shaped the perception and worship of Asclepius.

Explore the variations in Pan's worship in rural Arcadia and urban Athens. What do these differences tell us about the ancient Greeks' relationship with the natural world?

How do regional variations in the worship of Eileithyia reflect differing local interpretations of the childbirth process?

Reflect on these questions, engage in further research if necessary, and attempt to articulate thoughtful, nuanced responses. It is through this process of inquiry and reflection that we deepen our understanding of the diverse religious landscape of ancient Greece.

Conclusion: The Overlooked Richness of the Greek Pantheon

This exploration into the worship and representation of lesser-known deities in the ancient Greek pantheon has navigated a rich tapestry of regional variations, syncretism, and adaptability. The specific case studies of Hekate, Asclepius, Pan, and Eileithyia offered a window into the multiplicity of Greek religious practice, which, despite operating within a shared Pan-Hellenic framework, displayed remarkable diversity reflecting local contexts, needs, and traditions.

The examination of archaeological, literary, and historical evidence highlighted the extensive, yet often overlooked, influence of these lesser-known deities on Greek religious life. The evidence presented not only served to corroborate the existence of these deities and their worship but also offered insights into the rituals, festivals, and administrative aspects of religious practices.

The interplay of local and Pan-Hellenic elements, realized through processes of syncretism and adaptability, underscored the dynamic nature of Greek religious practice. Despite the existence of a shared pantheon, the deities were not rigid, universally accepted entities but rather malleable figures capable of assuming various forms and attributes according to the local socio-cultural context.

Reflection on the Importance of Lesser-Known Deities in a Comprehensive Understanding of the Greek Pantheon

Often, the narrative of ancient Greek religion is dominated by the 'Olympian' gods and goddesses – those deities residing on Mount Olympus under the rule of Zeus. While the significance of these deities is undeniable, a comprehensive understanding of the Greek religious landscape necessitates an exploration into the realm of lesser-known deities.

The roles these deities played in various aspects of daily life, from Hekate's protection of households to Asclepius's healing abilities, from Pan's association with rusticity to Eileithyia's help during childbirth, reveal a religion deeply interwoven with the realities of human existence. Their cults addressed aspects of life that were beyond the realm of the Olympian gods, resonating closely with the immediate environment, concerns, and experiences of their worshippers.

Moreover, the study of lesser-known deities is crucial for understanding the intricate dynamics between local and Pan-Hellenic religious practices. The adaptability of these deities to local contexts and their syncretism with other gods and goddesses offer unique insights into the dialogic nature of Greek religion, where local religious traditions engaged with a broader shared religious language.

By venturing into the diverse and often overlooked world of lesser-known deities, one encounters a nuanced religious practice, reflecting both the shared cultural heritage and the regional diversity of ancient Greece. The richness of the Greek pantheon lies not only in the splendour of its Olympian gods but equally in its multitude of lesser-known deities, each contributing uniquely to the complex mosaic of ancient Greek religious life.

Exercises for Further Reflection

Reflect on why the lesser-known deities might have been overshadowed by the Olympian gods in our understanding of ancient Greek religion.

Discuss how studying lesser-known deities changes our perception of the ancient Greek religious landscape.

Explore the importance of regional diversity in understanding Greek religion. How does it affect our understanding of Greek culture and society?

Exercises and Discussion Questions

Understanding the Deities: Describe the characteristics and worship practices associated with Hekate, Asclepius, Pan, and Eileithyia. How do these lesser-known deities contribute to the richness of the Greek pantheon?

Examining the Evidence: Discuss the various types of evidence available for studying the worship of lesser-known deities in ancient Greece. How does each type of evidence contribute to our understanding of these deities and their cults?

Regional Variations: Explain how the worship and representation of Hekate, Asclepius, Pan, and Eileithyia varied across different regions of Greece. What factors might have contributed to these variations?

Interplay of Local and Pan-Hellenic Elements: Reflect on the interplay between local and Pan-Hellenic elements in the worship of lesser-known deities. How does this dynamic interaction shape our understanding of Greek religious practice?

The Role of Lesser-Known Deities: Discuss the importance of lesser-known deities in a comprehensive understanding of the Greek pantheon. How does focusing on these deities enrich our understanding of ancient Greek religion?

Potential Research Topics and Projects

Syncretism in Greek Religion: Conduct a research project on the phenomenon of syncretism in Greek religion, focusing on one or more lesser-known deities. Explore how these deities were combined or assimilated with other deities in different regions of Greece.

Deity and Society: Choose a lesser-known deity and explore how their worship reflects the social, cultural, or environmental characteristics of a specific region in ancient Greece.

Comparative Study: Compare the worship of a selected lesser-known deity in two different regions of Greece. Analyse the differences and similarities in their worship and discuss the reasons for these variations.

Deities and Ritual Practices: Investigate the rituals associated with a chosen lesser-known deity. How do these rituals reflect the deity's characteristics and role in Greek religion?

Beyond Greece: Research how the worship of a selected Greek deity was adapted in the Roman context. Discuss the changes in the deity's characteristics and worship practices and analyse the reasons for these modifications.

Chapter 6: Household and City Gods: An exploration of the deities related to domestic life and the city, like Hestia, and their religious and cultural importance.

In the vast pantheon of the ancient Greeks, a segment of deities was intricately tied to the daily lives of individuals and communities. These deities, often overlooked in traditional narratives, were deeply embedded in the societal fabric and operated in tandem with the rhythms of domestic life and civic duty. The influence of these household and city gods spanned across various spheres of life, from the hearth's warm glow to the bustling marketplace, from the cornerstone of a new home to the city's protective walls. This chapter invites an exploration into these intimate divinities, focusing on the cultural and religious importance of these gods within the tapestry of the ancient Greek world.

We commence with Hestia, the goddess of the hearth, home, and family. Referred to as the 'first and last', Hestia's place at the heart of the home and in the civic center made her an indispensable part of Greek life. Moving from the hearth to the broader domestic sphere, we encounter various minor deities, each overseeing a specific facet of household activities.

Then, we venture beyond the individual home and examine city gods, with an emphasis on Athena, the patron goddess of Athens, reflecting on her multifaceted role as a deity of wisdom, warfare, and crafts, embodying the city's civic identity and aspirations.

We consider the compelling dynamics between private and public spaces and the gods that govern them, and trace the interconnections between individual households and the larger community through the lens of shared religious experiences. To comprehend these dimensions, we adopt a multifaceted approach, drawing upon archaeological, literary, and historical evidence to illuminate our understanding of these domestic and civic deities.

The aim of this chapter is not only to provide an overview of these deities and their significance but also to provoke a deeper understanding of ancient Greek religious practice. By focusing on these everyday deities, we gain insight into the daily life and societal structure of ancient Greece, thereby shedding light on the intricate relationship between religion, culture, and the quotidian rhythms of life.

As we move through this chapter, let us engage in this fascinating exploration, probing the depths of ancient Greek society, where gods and mortals coexisted in a delicate balance of power and respect, each shaping the other in their shared journey through life's complexities.

I. Introduction
A brief overview of the theme of the chapter: the importance and roles of household and city gods in ancient Greece.

Household Deities

The ancient Greek pantheon comprises a myriad of deities, each with their unique portfolios, ranging from the omnipotent gods who governed cosmic phenomena to the lesser-known divinities associated with quotidian aspects of life. This chapter will focus on the latter category, particularly the household gods who governed the intimate sphere of the oikos or the household.

The household, in ancient Greek society, served as the fundamental unit of society, the microcosm of the polis or city-state. It was within this domestic setting that individuals first encountered and engaged with the divine, an engagement that was integral to maintaining familial prosperity and warding off potential calamity. Household deities, therefore, represented the sanctity of familial and domestic life, overseeing everything from the health of family members to the successful management of the household.

The preeminent among these deities was Hestia, the virgin goddess of the hearth, architecture, and the right ordering of domesticity and family. Her flame, present in every household and city hearth, symbolised more than mere physical warmth; it was a sacred representation of communal solidarity and familial continuity. However, alongside Hestia existed a host of other household deities such as the Agathos Daimon, a good spirit bringing luck and prosperity, the Keres, the spirits of violent death, and the Moirai, commonly known as the Fates, who controlled the metaphorical thread of life of every mortal from birth to death. Each of these deities performed specific roles that intertwined with the daily life in a typical Greek household, thus providing a comprehensive divine framework that catered to every possible domestic need and concern.

Through an exploration of these household deities, this chapter aims to elucidate the profound religious significance of the domestic sphere in ancient Greek society and how these deities were worshipped in a personal and intimate manner, a contrast to the state-controlled worship of the Olympian gods. Drawing upon archaeological, literary, and historical evidence, we will probe the rituals, beliefs, and practices associated with these deities, providing an encompassing overview of household religion in ancient Greece. This exploration will underscore how religion permeated every aspect of Greek life, from public affairs to private matters, and how the Greeks sought divine assistance, guidance, and protection in their everyday life, thus offering fresh insights into the lived religion of the ancient Greeks.

Hestia: Goddess of the Hearth and Home

Among the pantheon of ancient Greek deities, Hestia, the goddess of the hearth, the domestic order, and family, holds a distinctive position. Despite her absence from many of the dramatic mythological narratives that feature her Olympian counterparts, Hestia was intimately woven into the fabric of daily life and worship, serving as a constant, gentle presence in both the private domicile and the public polis.

The hearth was both physically and symbolically at the center of the home in ancient Greece. It provided warmth, light, and was the site where meals were cooked; therefore, it was crucial for physical sustenance. Simultaneously, it was the focus of communal gathering and familial identity, giving it an irreplaceable role in constructing social bonds and continuity. Hestia, as the personification of the hearth, was the guardian of this integral domestic space, the sacred flame, and the tranquillity and order of home life. Her role is further accentuated by her name, derived from the Greek word ἑστία (hestía) which literally means "hearth" or "fireplace".

Her importance transcended the private sphere and extended into communal and civic life. Each city-state, or polis, had a public hearth that housed Hestia's sacred flame. The eternal fire in the prytaneion, the building where important civic functions took place, symbolized the unity and vitality of the community. Similarly, colonies would take the flame from the hearth of their mother city to establish a connection with Hestia in their new settlement, manifesting the idea of continuity and shared identity.

The worship of Hestia was embedded in daily routines. The first part of every meal was offered to her, a practice that reinforced her role as the provider and protector of sustenance. Additionally, her blessings were sought during various domestic events, including the birth of children and the welcoming of guests, signifying her all-encompassing protective role. Notably, Hestia received the first and last offering at every public sacrifice, further emphasizing her prominence in Greek religious practice.

While there are few surviving dedicated temples or statues of Hestia, this should not be seen as a reflection of her significance. Instead, it is testament to her unique mode of worship, which was integrated into the daily life and routines of the Greeks, rather than being marked by grandiose ritual or architectural monumentality.

Hestia's character and representation, as a benign, non-partisan deity, largely devoid of the dramatic mythological narratives that are associated with other deities, presents a model of divine worship that is grounded in the appreciation of everyday life and basic human needs. The understanding of Hestia's role and worship offers valuable insights into the lived religion of the Greeks and underscores the fundamental religious concept that the divine permeates all aspects of life, including the mundane.

The mythology of Hestia

Hestia's mythology is unique among Greek deities. Unlike many other Olympian gods whose narratives are filled with feuds, rivalries, and dramatic exploits, Hestia's mythology is marked by its tranquillity and lack of conflict. This absence of dramatic narrative reflects her character as a goddess of peace, order, and stability. Nevertheless, her mythological character and attributes have profound implications for understanding the essential elements of Greek religious thought and practice.

According to Hesiod's "Theogony," Hestia was the first-born child of the Titans Cronus and Rhea. In an attempt to prevent a prophecy that predicted his downfall at the hands of his offspring, Cronus swallowed each of his children as they were born. Hestia, being the first swallowed, was the last to be disgorged when Zeus, who had been saved and raised in secret, forced his father to regurgitate his siblings. Thus, in the order of 'release', Hestia was the last born and therefore is often referred to as both the oldest and the youngest of the six principal Olympian gods.

Despite being an eligible maiden goddess, Hestia remained perpetually virginal. Both Poseidon and Apollo sought her hand in marriage, but she refused and, instead, asked Zeus to let her remain an eternal virgin. Zeus consented, granting her the honor of being worshipped in all households and having a place in the center of the home, further cementing her status as a domestic deity. This perpetual virginity further symbolizes her integrity, self-sufficiency, and uncompromised nature, aspects that are integral to the stability and sanctity of the hearth and home.

Hestia's mythology underscores her impartial and non-confrontational nature. Unlike many of her Olympian counterparts, she had no direct involvement in the affairs of humans, nor did she partake in the cosmic disputes that often roiled Olympus. This neutrality is consistent with her function as the goddess of the hearth, a symbol of home, hospitality, and communal solidarity, and is immune to the conflicts and disruptions that define other deities' mythological narratives.

While Hestia's mythology may seem understated compared to the dramatic tales of Zeus, Apollo, or Hera, it is this very tranquillity and steadfastness that underscores her importance. Her unchanging and peaceful character speaks to the Greeks' yearning for stability, peace, and order in their daily lives. Her mythology should be interpreted as a testament to the importance the Greeks placed on the sanctity of the home and the bonds of community and family. It underscores the belief that the divine could be found not just in the extraordinary but also in the simple, daily aspects of life.

Hestia's religious and cultural significance

Despite her quiet presence in mythology, Hestia played an essential role in the religious and cultural life of ancient Greece. As the goddess of the hearth, home, and family, her influence permeated the intimate aspects of daily life, from domestic rituals to the civic ceremonies that upheld the social order.

Hestia's most significant religious role was as the goddess of the hearth, a focal point in the Greek home. The hearth served practical needs of cooking and heating, but it also held a symbolic role as the heart of the familial and communal unit. Daily offerings were made to Hestia at the hearth; a portion of every meal was dedicated to her, symbolising her involvement in and blessing over the daily sustenance of life. Hestia's hearth was also where families conducted domestic rites, such as those concerning marriage, childbirth, and death, marking critical life transitions. Thus, through her association with the hearth, Hestia presided over the crucial milestones of individual and familial life.

Moreover, Hestia's flame was central to the concept of 'xenia' or hospitality, a vital aspect of Greek social ethics. The hearth was often the space where guests were received, emphasizing a safe and sacred space for the visitor. By extending hospitality, the host honoured Hestia, ensuring her protection and blessings for the household.

Hestia's influence extended beyond the confines of the home to civic life as well. In every city-state ('polis'), there was a public hearth in the 'prytaneion' or town hall, where Hestia's flame was kept burning perpetually. This public hearth served as a symbol of the collective civic identity, a point of commonality for the polis's inhabitants. It was a place where civic rituals took place and where communal meals were shared. Moreover, when colonists set out to establish a new city, they would take the flame from their city's prytaneion to ensure continuity and Hestia's protection in their new settlement. In this manner, Hestia served as a vital link between the private domestic sphere and the public civic sphere, emphasizing the interconnectedness of home, community, and the polis.

Despite her low-profile mythology, Hestia's religious and cultural significance was far-reaching. Her sphere was the everyday, the mundane, the household, but these were the very spaces where life happened and society was structured. In every fire that was kindled and in every home that was established, Hestia was invoked, not in the lofty spaces of grand temples but in the intimate corners of everyday life. Thus, Hestia's significance is a testament to the belief that the divine permeated all aspects of existence, binding together the home, the community, and the broader cosmos in a continuous cycle of reverence and reciprocity.

The role of the hearth in Greek households

In the ancient Greek world, the hearth served as the central axis of both domestic life and religious observance, its role blending the practical and the symbolic, the mundane and the sacred. The hearth, or 'estia' in ancient Greek, was much more than a functional appliance for cooking and heating; it was a potent symbol of home, family, and community, sanctified by its association with the goddess Hestia.

From a practical perspective, the hearth was integral to the daily life of an ancient Greek household. Situated centrally in the house, it was the place where meals were cooked and the home was warmed, particularly in the colder months. It was a gathering place for the family, the scene of storytelling, conversation, and shared meals.

However, it is the symbolic role of the hearth that truly underscored its centrality in Greek life. As the heart of the home, the hearth represented family continuity and unity. The fire that burned there was a tangible link between the generations, passed down from ancestors and to be passed onto descendants. The perpetuation of this flame signified the survival and continuity of the familial line.

Furthermore, the hearth held religious significance. It was the household's primary religious altar where daily offerings were made to Hestia, the goddess of the hearth. Every meal began and ended with a portion dedicated to Hestia, a ritual that brought the divine into the realm of the everyday. Other domestic rites, such as those marking births, marriages, and deaths, were conducted at the hearth, each a critical transition point sanctified under Hestia's purview.

The hearth's religious function was not confined to the familial or domestic sphere. In every city-state, a public hearth was maintained in the 'prytaneion' or town hall, where Hestia's flame was kept perpetually burning. This communal hearth symbolised civic unity and served as the focal point for civic ceremonies. When new colonies were established, fire from the mother city's prytaneion was transported to the new settlement's hearth, a ritual that ensured continuity, conveyed legitimacy, and invoked Hestia's protection.

Thus, the hearth served as a vital nexus in Greek households and city-states, binding together the realms of the practical and the symbolic, the familial and the civic, the human and the divine. It was in the glow of the hearth that the daily life of the Greeks was illuminated, warmed, and sanctified. The hearth was the silent witness to the ebb and flow of life, a constant presence in the ever-changing cycle of existence, much like the goddess it embodied—Hestia.

Archaeological and literary evidence of Hestia's worship

While the figure of Hestia does not dominate the dramatic narratives of mythology as some other Greek deities do, the evidence for her worship, both archaeological and literary, reveals her profound presence in the everyday life of the ancient Greeks. These sources provide a richer, more nuanced understanding of her role in Greek society, religion, and culture.

✧   Archaeological Evidence

Archaeological evidence for Hestia's worship is intrinsically tied to domestic and civic hearths. However, as these hearths were typically made of perishable materials, they are seldom preserved in the archaeological record. Instead, archaeological evidence for Hestia's cult primarily comes from the 'prytaneia' of Greek city-states, where the communal hearth was maintained. Excavations of these structures provide insight into the rituals associated with Hestia.

For instance, at the prytaneion of Olympia, a central hearth was found with a base of ashes, thought to be the remnants of the perpetual fire kept in Hestia's honour. Similarly, the prytaneion of Delphi featured a hearth without a chimney, suggesting the presence of a symbolic fire rather than a practical one. Other public buildings, such as the Council House of Athens, contained inscriptions dedicated to Hestia, confirming her association with civic spaces.

Moreover, archaeological finds have uncovered terracotta figurines, statuettes, and reliefs depicting Hestia. Although not as prevalent or elaborate as those of other deities, these items testify to her veneration. Hestia is typically depicted as a veiled woman, holding a sceptre or a flower, occasionally by a hearth or with a kettle, reflecting her domestic connotations.

✧ Literary Evidence

The literary corpus of ancient Greece provides further evidence of Hestia's importance. Despite her relatively muted presence in epic narratives, her significance is manifest in the repeated invocation of her name in prayers, oaths, and dedications, often as the first and last deity to be acknowledged.

Homer, for example, references Hestia in the 'Odyssey', linking her with Zeus and Athena as the primary recipients of sacrificial offerings. He portrays her as the first to receive offerings at feasts, signifying her integral role in ritualistic practices.

Hesiod's 'Theogony', a genealogical account of the gods, describes Hestia as 'the first-born child of wily Cronus and youngest too', and as 'the first and last', suggesting both her primacy and enduring presence in the divine hierarchy.

Additionally, in the works of the tragedians, Hestia is invoked in the context of household affairs, oaths, and hospitality. In 'Oedipus at Colonus' by Sophocles, for example, Oedipus cries out to 'Queen Earth and gentle Hestia', affirming her compassionate and nurturing aspect.

Thus, archaeological and literary sources collectively reveal a tapestry of Hestia's worship and cultural significance that spans both public and private spheres. These evidences depict Hestia as a deity deeply woven into the fabric of Greek life, one who presided over the fundamental aspects of their existence—home, family, community, and the cycles of daily life.

Other Household Deities

Beyond Hestia, the goddess of the hearth, the Greek pantheon housed a number of other deities intimately associated with the domestic sphere. While not always as widely venerated as their Olympian counterparts, these lesser-known deities were intrinsically woven into the fabric of everyday life, overseeing a variety of household affairs. Understanding these household deities requires a simultaneous appreciation of their individual characteristics and their collective role in enhancing the sanctity of the Greek home.

The concept of the household gods, or 'ktesios theoi', consisted of a diverse array of entities that were the patrons of everything from familial relationships, childbirth, and child-rearing, to the home's physical structures, and even to the mundane activities such as meal preparation and weaving. These deities, including Zeus Ktesios, Apollo Agyieus, the Agathos Daimon, and the complex array of ancestral spirits or 'herois', were venerated through both communal and individual rituals, integrating the sacred into the quotidian and contributing to a holistic religious experience that pervaded every facet of daily life.

This exploration of other household deities aims to underscore their significance in the domestic sphere, in contrast to the more extensively discussed public or civic gods. It seeks to elaborate how these deities were understood, invoked, and appeased, as well as how they were represented in literature, art, and archaeological evidence. By considering the diverse range of their responsibilities and the variety of forms they took, we can gain insights into the multifaceted nature of ancient Greek religion, shedding light on how religion and domesticity were inextricably linked in the Greek worldview.

Furthermore, this section intends to examine how the worship of these household deities paralleled, and occasionally overlapped with, the veneration of the more famous gods of the Greek pantheon. In doing so, we can begin to unpack the complex, layered nature of Greek polytheism, which was characterized not merely by a hierarchical pantheon of gods, but by a vibrant, diverse, and highly localized network of divine beings that attended to all aspects of human life.

In the subsequent sections, we will delve into a detailed discussion of some of these other household deities, their mythology, their roles in the daily lives of the ancient Greeks, and their cultural significance within the broader framework of Greek religion and society. By doing so, we will uncover the rich tapestry of divine entities that occupied the Greek household, each contributing their unique threads to the fabric of Greek domestic life.

The role and significance of other deities tied to domestic life, such as the Agathos

In the labyrinthine system of ancient Greek religious thought, domestic life was peppered with divine presence, turning the everyday into a sequence of sacred moments. Aside from Hestia, a constellation of other household deities emerged, among which the Agathos Daimon was of noteworthy importance.

The Agathos Daimon, literally translating as the 'Good Spirit', held a significant place in the Greek domestic pantheon. This deity, often envisaged in the form of a snake, was seen as a protective spirit that brought prosperity and good fortune to the household. Unlike the omnipotent Olympians, the Agathos Daimon was more intimately connected to individual homes and families, symbolising a personal and protective divine presence that was unique to each household.

This entity was venerated through monthly domestic rituals, typically during the Deipnon, the last meal of the lunar month, which marked a time of transition and was significant in purifying the household. Libations of unmixed wine and plates of food were routinely offered to this deity as a form of respect and in hope of future blessings. Such rituals underscore the integration of the divine into mundane tasks, making the everyday sacred and the sacred everyday.

The belief in the Agathos Daimon also reflects the profound ancient Greek conviction that the divine can and does interact in the most intimate spaces of human life. This deity, along with others like Zeus Ktesios, protector of the household's property, and Apollo Agyieus, guardian of the entrance, underscored the view that the gods were not remote entities, only concerned with grand cosmic affairs, but they were also immanent, permeating the smallest details of everyday life.

This approach to religion provided the ancient Greeks with a sense of security and control in a world where so much was unpredictable and potentially perilous. The belief in, and the associated rituals dedicated to these domestic deities, constituted mechanisms of managing the uncertainties of life. By seeking the favour of these gods through regular household rituals, the Greeks believed they could influence the otherwise capricious forces that shaped their lives.

Beyond the household, certain deities were also associated with broader aspects of the city. Athena Polias, the city protector, and Zeus Herkeios, protector of the household's boundary, are noteworthy examples. These deities indicate the gradient nature of Greek religion, where the divine influence extended from the deepest corners of the home to the broad city borders.

Hence, understanding these lesser-known household deities offers a richer, more nuanced view of the ancient Greek religious landscape. Their veneration indicates a religion that was highly contextual, deeply personal, and intricately woven into the fabric of everyday life. By acknowledging these gods, we gain a deeper understanding of how the Greeks perceived their world, a place fraught with uncertainty, yet made navigable through the protective and personal guidance of the household gods.

Daimon, the Keres, and the Moirai

The ancients considered the household a nexus of divine influences, and among these, the Daimon, the Keres, and the Moirai held roles of particularly intricate complexity. These entities, while not gods in the traditional sense, were nonetheless imbued with divine characteristics, navigating the spaces between human agency and divine will, offering an elaborate interpretation of fate, fortune, and destiny in the ancient Greek worldview.

✧   Daimones

The term 'Daimon,' far removed from its later Christian demonisation, held a more nuanced role in the ancient Greek cosmology. Encompassing a range of spirit entities, the term was inherently ambivalent, reflecting the multifaceted aspects of divine influence within daily life, from the benign to the malicious.

One might envision the concept of daimones as a complex spectrum, reaching from the benevolent protective spirits, such as the Agathos Daimon, to malevolent entities that brought about calamity and misfortune. Indeed, one could argue that the daimones personified the inexplicable forces that dictated the fluctuating fortunes of human life in the ancient Greek worldview.

◆   Benevolent Daimones: The Agathos Daimon

Among the benevolent spirits, the Agathos Daimon deserves particular attention. Often represented as a snake, it was a domestic entity believed to bring good fortune and prosperity. Every household honoured their Agathos Daimon, often with offerings of wine during meals, solidifying the link between daily life, the household, and the spiritual realm. In this capacity, the Agathos Daimon was an integral part of household religiosity, acting as a divine guardian and bestowing blessings upon the family.

◆   Malevolent Daimones: Spirits of Misfortune

On the other end of the spectrum, malevolent daimones were perceived as the bringers of catastrophe and ruin. Illness, crop failure, loss of social standing — such misfortunes were often attributed to the malefic influences of these malign spirits. Hence, the daimones, in this context, can be viewed as personifications of human anxiety and fear towards unpredictable and uncontrollable forces of life.

◆   Daimones in Plato's "Cratylus"

Plato's work "Cratylus" provides an illuminating perspective on daimones. According to Plato, daimones were a special category of divine entities, serving as intermediaries between the human and the divine realms. They communicated the prayers and offerings from humans to the gods and conveyed divine messages and decrees from gods to humans. This mediating role is significant, as it introduces a level of interactivity into the sacred. Such a perspective furthers the dissolution of strict boundaries between the divine and the mundane in Greek religious thought.

In conclusion, the concept of daimones offers a window into the Greek understanding of divine influence within daily life. Their ambivalent nature, swinging between benevolence and malevolence, reflects the complexity of life's fortunes in the ancient worldview. Daimones were not merely spiritual entities but embodied the multifaceted experiences of human life, intertwining the divine and the mundane in a continuous exchange.

✦   Keres

In stark contrast to the ambivalence of daimones, the Keres held an undisputedly ominous position within the Greek spiritual pantheon. These dark spirits of death, doom, and violent fatality were decidedly malignant, looming at the threshold of life and death, ready to claim the souls of those whose time had come. Often portrayed as gruesome women clad in blood-soaked attire, the Keres were harbingers of violent and untimely death, emphasizing the unpredictability and volatility inherent to human existence.

◆   Imagery and Representation of Keres

In visual depictions, the Keres often took the form of ghastly women, exuding an aura of dread and despair. Their imagery, deeply embedded in the cultural memory of ancient Greece, was potent and evocative. Dressed in bloody garments, equipped with talons as sharp as a hawk's, and often brandishing an amphora — a vessel for storing life's essence — they symbolized the violent end that they were believed to deliver.

Moreover, the Keres were frequently portrayed in battlefield scenes on ancient pottery, hovering over the warriors like gruesome vultures, ready to snatch the souls of fallen heroes. These depictions emphasize the inextricable link between the Keres and violent death, further reinforcing their dread-inducing persona.

◆   Symbolic Function of Keres

Although they may seem to represent mere personifications of death and destruction, the Keres' role was profoundly symbolic, reflecting deep-seated cultural beliefs about life and mortality. They embodied the ancient Greeks' recognition of life's precariousness and unpredictability, manifesting the brutal interruptions to the ordinary flow of life.

The Keres personified the cruel inevitability of death, but they also represented an understanding of existence itself as unpredictable, fragile, and subject to forces beyond human control. The ever-looming presence of the Keres was a potent reminder of mortality, a stark symbol of the capricious whims of fate that could, without warning, alter the course of life.

In conclusion, the Keres, in their gruesome glory, are not merely spirits of death and doom but embody a complex understanding of life, mortality, and the human condition. They serve as stark reminders of the uncertainty of existence, the inevitability of death, and the continuous human struggle against the whims of fate.

✧ Moirai

The Moirai, more familiar to English-speaking audiences as the Fates, stood as the embodiment of destiny in Greek mythology. This triumvirate of goddesses — Clotho, the Spinner; Lachesis, the Allotter; and Atropos, the Inexorable — wielded unchallenged control over the lifespan and fate of each individual. From the moment of birth, when Clotho spun the thread of life, to the inevitable end, when Atropos decisively cut it, the Moirai dictated the course of existence with unwavering authority.

◆ A Cosmic Framework Beyond the Gods

Their dominion was of such magnitude that it was deemed inescapable even by the gods themselves. This belief suggests the existence of an overarching cosmic framework, a predestined order to the universe that was impervious to divine intervention. The Moirai, in this regard, were not merely goddesses of fate but represented a fundamental principle of the Greek cosmos — an inexorable order and inevitability.

◆ The Complex Interplay of Fate, Chance, and Personal Action

However, alongside this seemingly deterministic worldview, Greek culture also acknowledged the critical role of personal choices and actions, a concept well-documented in Greek heroic literature. Heroes, despite knowing their fated end, could make decisions that influenced the course of their journey, embodying the tension between destiny and individual agency.

Thus, the Moirai, in their inescapable authority, did not merely impose an inflexible future. Instead, they personified the ancient Greeks' understanding of existence as a rich tapestry woven from threads of predestination, randomness, and personal action. Each person's life, therefore, was a unique fabric, spun, measured, and ultimately cut by the Fates, but also shaped by their own hands.

In summary, the Moirai, despite their grim role, personified a nuanced philosophy of life. The inevitable intervention of fate, the uncertainty of chance, and the potential for personal agency coalesced in their mythos, mirroring the complex interplay of forces that the Greeks believed to shape an individual's journey through life.

Conclusion

In assessing the importance of daimones, Keres, and the Moirai, one unearths rich insights into the profound and intricate theological and philosophical terrain of ancient Greek society. These entities are not merely fantastical figures from a bygone era; they serve as lenses through which we can scrutinize the Greeks' perceptions of reality, mortality, fate, and the delicate dance between human autonomy and divine decree.

The daimones, embodying an entire spectrum of moral ambivalence, stand as mediators between the human and divine realms, encapsulating the Greeks' recognition of a multi-tiered cosmos. The Keres, harbingers of violent death, reflect an acute awareness of life's precariousness and the unanticipated forces that can abruptly curtail existence. The Moirai, unfaltering in their dominion over individual destiny, underscore the concept of an overarching cosmic order, unassailable even by divine powers.

✧ A Window into Ancient Greek Worldview

By studying these deities, we apprehend a society grappling with existential questions, seeking to comprehend the capriciousness of existence, the inevitability of mortality, and the influence of unseen forces on human lives. They embody an acknowledgment of the paradoxical nature of life, wherein individuals navigate a complex web of personal agency, chance, and fate.

✧ Relevance to Contemporary Studies

For contemporary scholars, the value of exploring these entities lies not merely in the elucidation of antiquated religious practices or myths. It facilitates a deeper comprehension of the human endeavor to rationalize the inexplicable and to seek patterns amidst chaos — an endeavor that transcends cultural and temporal boundaries.

Consequently, the analysis of these household deities serves a dual purpose. Firstly, it enhances our understanding of ancient Greek culture, religion, and philosophy, contributing to the field of classical studies. Secondly, it enriches broader sociocultural and religious studies, offering timeless insights into the human quest for understanding and control in a seemingly chaotic world.

In conclusion, daimones, Keres, and the Moirai, far from being mere mythological curiosities, serve as key pieces of a larger puzzle. They elucidate the intricacies of ancient Greek thought, their struggle with existential dilemmas, and their attempts to comprehend and influence their world — a struggle that, in many ways, continues to mirror our own.

Their depiction in Greek mythology and literature

In the grand tapestry of Greek mythology and literature, daimones, Keres, and the Moirai have their unique threads woven intricately into the narrative fabric, painting a vivid picture of the unseen spiritual realities acknowledged by the ancient Greeks.

✧ Daimones in Greek Mythology and Literature

The presence of daimones in the literature of ancient Greece points towards an intriguing aspect of their cultural and religious milieu, presenting these entities as intermediaries between the human and the divine.

Homer, often considered the foundational figure of Greek literary tradition, refers to daimones in his seminal works. In the "Iliad" and the "Odyssey," these beings possess divine or semi-divine attributes and play pivotal roles in influencing human affairs. They are often depicted as messengers of the gods, signifying the close interrelation between humans and the divine in the Greek worldview. They are also recognized as formidable forces capable of affecting natural phenomena and altering the course of events, attesting to the dynamism attributed to these spiritual entities.

Hesiod's "Works and Days" offers another perspective on daimones. He depicts them as the spirits of the men of the Golden Age who continue to dwell on earth, overseeing human actions and dispensing wealth. This paints a benevolent image of daimones, presenting them as guardian spirits of humanity who perpetuate the ideals of a past golden era.

In the philosophical literature of ancient Greece, the concept of the daimon is further nuanced and expanded upon. Plato's works are particularly instructive in this regard. In his dialogue "Symposium," the character of Socrates introduces the concept of a personal daimonion. This daimonion, according to Socrates, prevents him from making wrong decisions. This is a significant departure from the more communal nature of daimones in other Greek literature and introduces the idea of a personal spiritual entity. It suggests that daimones could not only oversee broad aspects of human life but also guide individual moral conduct.

These different depictions of daimones demonstrate the fluidity and complexity of this concept in ancient Greek literature. They exemplify the belief in the interconnection between the human and divine realms and illuminate various aspects of Greek theology and anthropology. This underlines the central role daimones played in Greek culture, influencing both collective societal norms and individual ethical choices.

✧ Keres in Greek Mythology and Literature

The Keres, with their grim and menacing attributes, feature prominently within Greek literature, especially in relation to warfare and death. These entities, symbolizing the gruesome aspect of mortality, play crucial roles in several important works.

In Homer's "Iliad", a foundational work of Greek epic poetry, the Keres are personified as remorseless spirits that thrive in the carnage of warfare. They wait for the opportunity to carry away the souls of fallen warriors, depicting a terrifying image of death on the battlefield. This depiction of the Keres creates a harrowing metaphor for the violent demise that awaits many characters in the narrative, contributing significantly to the epic's overarching themes of heroism, fate, and mortality.

Hesiod, another monumental figure in the literary tradition of ancient Greece, includes the Keres in his "Theogony," an extensive poetic work presenting a genealogy of the gods. In his account, the Keres are introduced as the offspring of Nyx, the personification of night. This parentage symbolically links the Keres with the obscurity and dread associated with darkness and death. As the daughters of Night, they are inherently connected to the realm of the unknown, thereby embodying the frightening and inscrutable aspects of mortality.

These references to the Keres in the works of Homer and Hesiod underscore their cultural significance as personifications of death and violence. They are not simply embodiments of demise, but rather integral elements of a wider cosmological and philosophical system, intertwining the physical and the metaphysical, the known and the unknown, the living and the dead. The study of the Keres, therefore, reveals significant aspects of how the ancient Greeks comprehended and articulated the concept of mortality.

✧   The Moirai in Greek Mythology and Literature

The Moirai, or the Fates, are ubiquitous throughout Greek literature, embodying the concept of destiny and the inflexible course of life and death. Their presence and function in these narratives underscore the ancient Greeks' understanding of destiny as an inalterable path prescribed at the time of one's birth.

In Homer's "Iliad," one of the earliest and most influential works of Western literature, the Moirai are portrayed as unyielding figures who establish the fate of mortals at the time of their birth. Homer provides detailed descriptions of the functions of each of the three Moirai: Clotho spins the thread of life at the birth of an individual, Lachesis measures the length of this thread to determine the span of one's life, and Atropos, the most feared of the three, decides the manner of each person's death and ends their life by cutting the thread. This tripartite division of labor among the Moirai encapsulates a comprehensive view of an individual's life journey from birth to death.

In the realm of tragedy, one of the most prominent genres of ancient Greek literature, the Moirai often feature as significant elements driving the plot forward. They serve as dramatic devices to underline the unavoidable nature of destiny, even in the face of human effort to alter it. A notable instance of this appears in Sophocles' "Oedipus Rex," where the Moirai dictate a dire prophecy for the protagonist, Oedipus. Despite his best attempts to avert this prophecy, Oedipus inadvertently fulfills it, leading to a tragic narrative of self-destruction and sorrow. This utilization of the Moirai in the plot underscores the tragic tension between human free will and predetermined fate, a central theme in many Greek tragedies.

These examples from Homer's epic and Sophocles' tragedy highlight the pivotal role of the Moirai in ancient Greek literature. They serve not only as personifications of destiny but also as essential narrative elements that shed light on the ancients' perception of life, death, and the often futile struggle against the preordained course of existence. The Moirai, thus, represent a crucial intersection of mythology, philosophy, and literature in ancient Greek culture.

Conclusion

The depictions of daimones, Keres, and the Moirai in Greek mythology and literature reveal important aspects of ancient Greek spiritual understanding and their perception of life, death, and fate. They offer rich insights into how the ancient Greeks interpreted the presence of these spiritual entities in their daily lives and their influence on human destiny. For contemporary scholars, these portrayals provide valuable resources for studying the religious, philosophical, and socio-cultural dimensions of ancient Greek society.

City Deities

The ancient Greek pantheon comprised not only the divine entities overseeing natural phenomena, heroic exploits, and domestic life but also a significant number of deities associated with specific geographical locales. These city deities, embodying the spirit and identity of a city-state or 'polis', played an essential role in ancient Greek religious practice and civic identity. This chapter aims to provide an exhaustive analysis of these city deities, assessing their roles, worship, and significance in both the religious and social domains of the ancient Greek world.

Conceptually, city deities can be seen as an extension of the inherent anthropomorphism of Greek religion, which sought to project human characteristics and societal structures onto the divine realm. Just as households had their protective spirits, like Hestia, so did cities have their guardian deities. This confluence of divine and civic representation was not merely a religious tenet but also a reflection of the political, social, and cultural realities of the polis.

Foremost among these city deities were the patron gods and goddesses, who were believed to watch over the city, aid in its prosperity, and protect it from harm. Athena, the patron goddess of Athens, and Apollo, the patron god of Delphi, are exemplary instances of such protective deities. Their veneration was not confined to the construction of monumental temples or the performance of grand rituals but also permeated the daily life of the citizens, being intertwined with the city's collective identity and civic pride.

However, the realm of city deities was not restricted to these high-profile gods and goddesses. It also included a plethora of lesser-known deities and spirits, each associated with specific aspects of city life. Deities like Tyche, the goddess of fortune, were often seen as overseeing the destiny of the cities. Local nymphs and other nature spirits were also integrated into the divine hierarchy of the city, guarding over its natural resources and geographical features.

This chapter will dissect the various dimensions of these city deities, delving into their unique roles and attributes, forms of worship, and their depiction in ancient Greek art and literature. Furthermore, it will also explore how these deities were instrumental in shaping and reflecting the civic identity and societal norms of the ancient Greek polis. Through a comprehensive study of city deities, we can gain invaluable insights into the nexus of religion, society, and politics in ancient Greece, thereby enriching our understanding of this remarkable civilization and its enduring legacy.

Athena: Patron Goddess of Athens

Athena, known by many titles such as Pallas Athena and Athena Parthenos, stands as one of the most celebrated deities in the Greek pantheon. Daughter of Zeus, born fully armed from his forehead, she is the embodiment of wisdom, strategic warfare, and crafts. This chapter focuses on her special role as the eponymous patron goddess of Athens, the epicentre of ancient Greek civilization.

Athena's association with Athens is most vividly demonstrated in the city's foundational myth. As relayed by Apollodorus and other ancient sources, both Athena and Poseidon, god of the sea, vied for the position of the city's patron deity. In a divine contest, each presented a gift to the city's inhabitants. Poseidon struck his trident into the ground, from which sprang a saltwater spring, symbolizing naval power. Athena, on the other hand, produced an olive tree, a symbol of peace, prosperity, and resilience. The citizens of Athens, led by their king, Cecrops, chose Athena's gift, and thus the city was named after her.

This founding narrative not only substantiates Athena's role as Athens' divine protector but also encapsulates the city's identity and values: wisdom, peace, and prosperity over raw power and dominance, represented by Poseidon. Furthermore, Athena's gift of the olive tree, a crucial resource for food, oil, and timber, underlines Athens' economic vitality in the ancient Mediterranean world.

The worship of Athena in Athens was marked by grandeur. Her primary shrine, the Parthenon, atop the city's Acropolis, held a monumental statue of the goddess, crafted by the renowned sculptor Phidias. Festivals such as the Panathenaia were held in her honour, which involved sacrifices, athletic competitions, and a grand procession that reinforced both religious devotion and civic solidarity.

However, Athena's influence extended beyond grand temples and festivals. She was a constant presence in the lives of Athenians, embodying the ideals and aspirations of the city and its people. Her image adorned coins, pottery, and public buildings, making her an integral part of the city's visual culture. In literature and philosophy too, Athena's wisdom and strategic prowess were often invoked as guiding principles.

This chapter will delve into Athena's multi-faceted role as the patron goddess of Athens, exploring her religious, political, and cultural significance. It will also examine her depiction in art and literature, providing a comprehensive understanding of her centrality in the Athenian societal and spiritual landscape. By studying Athena's patronage, we can glean valuable insights into the interplay of religion, society, and identity in ancient Athens, further deepening our understanding of this remarkable polis and its enduring legacy.

The mythology and various aspects of Athena

Athena, emerging fully formed and ready for battle from the head of Zeus, is an iconic image that illustrates her status as a divine entity associated with wisdom and warfare. She was regarded as a virgin goddess, which signified her autonomy and independence within the Olympian hierarchy. Her birth narrative reflects the ancient Greek conception of wisdom - sudden, acute, and powerfully transformative.

As the Goddess of Wisdom, Athena was revered for her intellectual faculties and strategic acumen. In Homer's "Iliad," Athena is a crucial divine ally of the Greeks, aiding heroes like Odysseus and Achilles with strategic counsel. Her domain extended beyond military strategy to encompass wisdom in its broadest sense, including the realms of craft, invention, and knowledge. Thus, Athena personified the intellectual and creative prowess that defined Athenian culture.

Athena's warlike aspect is somewhat paradoxical. Unlike Ares, the god of war who personified the chaotic and destructive nature of battle, Athena represented the strategic and disciplined side of warfare. She was depicted armed, often with the aegis, a mythical shield associated with Zeus and covered with the skin of the divine goat Amalthea, displaying the Gorgon Medusa's head, a potent symbol of protection and deterrent against reckless aggression. This martial aspect underscores her role as a defender, both of individual heroes and the city-state of Athens.

Athena's role as patroness of crafts is also significant. She was known as Ergane, the worker, patronising various forms of artisanal work, especially those associated with domestic life, like weaving. The myth of Arachne, who challenged Athena to a weaving contest and was subsequently turned into a spider, highlights the goddess's authority over crafts and the dangers of hubristic challenges to divine supremacy.

Moreover, Athena was seen as a goddess of justice and righteous conduct, often intervening in mortal affairs to maintain order and fairness, as seen in Aeschylus's "Eumenides," where she establishes the Areopagus, a homicide court in Athens. Her role in this capacity underscores the value placed on lawful conduct and the importance of justice in Athenian society.

The mythology of Athena presents a multifaceted character of power and wisdom, skill and strategy, justice and peace. Her vast portfolio of roles and responsibilities captures the breadth of attributes and ideals admired and aspired to in Athenian society. This chapter will delve further into each of these aspects, considering their significance within both the religious context and the wider societal values and norms of ancient Athens. Through the lens of Athena, we can glean a nuanced understanding of how the divine mirrored and reinforced the cultural and intellectual landscape of one of history's most influential civilisations.

Athena's relationship with Athens: her role as a deity of wisdom, warfare, and crafts

Athena's intrinsic association with the city of Athens transcends mere titular attribution; she was the spiritual embodiment of the city's identity, its societal values, and its cultural ethos. This multifaceted deity wielded her influence in various arenas, notably wisdom, warfare, and crafts, embodying aspects of life that Athenians held in high regard.

As Athena Polias, 'Athena of the city', she was the divine guardian of Athens, her wisdom symbolising the rational and intellectual virtues that the city espoused. Athena's wisdom, however, was not confined to the philosophical or the abstract; it was eminently practical, bearing upon matters of state, justice, and civil organisation. Athenian lawgivers and statesmen sought her counsel, emblematised by the construction of the Erechtheion, a temple on the Athenian Acropolis dedicated to Athena Polias, demonstrating the reciprocal relationship between the city and the goddess, wherein the sacred and secular were inextricably linked.

In her capacity as Athena Promachos, 'Athena who fights in the front line', she personified the martial spirit of Athens, not through brutish strength or mindless aggression, but through strategy, discipline, and honourable conduct. Athena's martial aspect was celebrated annually during the Panathenaia, a grand festival involving athletic and military contests. The citizens would also offer her a new woven robe, or peplos, for her statue, underlining the intersection of her roles in warfare and craftsmanship.

Crafts and artisanal skills were another domain in Athena's capacious portfolio. As Athena Ergane, 'Athena the Worker', she patronised and protected various crafts, highlighting the reverence Athenians had for craftsmanship and skilled labour. Weaving, in particular, was under her auspices, embodying not just the domestic life and economy of Athens, but also artistic creativity and cultural memory, as traditional stories and myths were often depicted in woven fabrics.

In these myriad roles, Athena was not merely a remote divine figure but an active participant in the life of the city, her influence pervading the public and private, the political and domestic, the intellectual and practical spheres of Athenian life. Her multivalent character embodied the complex tapestry of Athenian culture, reflecting the aspirations, values, and ideals of this ancient society.

By studying Athena's roles, we gain insights into the Athenians' collective self-perception, their social norms, and their cultural practices. We glimpse the profound ways in which the divine was woven into the fabric of daily life, shaping and reflecting societal values and behaviours. Thus, Athena serves as an invaluable lens through which we can explore the complex dynamics of religion, culture, and identity in ancient Athens.

Archaeological and literary evidence of Athena's worship

The worship of Athena, given her multifarious attributes, permeated various aspects of Athenian life. This pervasiveness is evidenced in both the physical remains of ancient Athens and the rich corpus of Greek literature.

✧ Archaeological Evidence

The Acropolis, the physical and spiritual centre of Athens, serves as a testament to the profound reverence the Athenians held for Athena. Dominating this sacred precinct is the Parthenon, a monument of unsurpassed architectural and artistic grandeur, dedicated to Athena Parthenos, 'Athena the Virgin'. The temple housed a colossal chryselephantine statue of the goddess, created by Phidias, which symbolised her guardianship over the city. The temple's frieze depicted the Panathenaic procession, a key religious event in honour of Athena, illustrating the city's collective homage to their patron deity.

Another important monument is the Erechtheion, dedicated to Athena Polias. It housed the ancient wooden statue of Athena, considered the palladium of the city. This old image, purportedly fallen from the heavens, was believed to hold a potent connection with the goddess, thus serving as a focal point of her cult.

Artefacts such as pottery, votive offerings, and inscriptions also provide insights into Athena's veneration. Votive statues and reliefs found on the Acropolis represent a tangible testament to individual and public piety towards Athena. They often depict the goddess in her various roles and attributes, underscoring her diverse aspects acknowledged and revered by the Athenians.

✧   Literary Evidence

Greek literature abounds in references to Athena's worship. Epic poets like Homer, while not Athenian, provide valuable insights into her divine persona and her interaction with mortals. In the "Odyssey", Athena's guidance and protection of Odysseus attest to her role as a goddess of wisdom and strategic warfare.

Tragedians like Sophocles and Euripides also reference Athena's cult. In "Oedipus at Colonus", Sophocles describes the rites performed at the sacred grove of Athena near Athens, reinforcing the goddess's protective role.

Histories, too, bear testament to Athena's worship. Herodotus narrates how the Athenians, before the Battle of Salamis, received an oracle suggesting they seek refuge in the 'wooden walls' - interpreted as their ships - hinting at Athena's strategic wisdom in warfare.

Such rich archaeological and literary evidence collectively illuminate our understanding of Athena's integral role in Athenian religious life. By exploring these remnants of antiquity, we gain a deeper appreciation of Athena's diverse aspects, the fervour of her worship, and the profound manner in which she shaped, and was shaped by, the civic and cultural identity of ancient Athens.

Other City Deities

While Athena undeniably stands as the iconic symbol of Athens, it is important to acknowledge the pantheon of deities who were also accorded venerations in various other Greek cities. Such deities, with their unique attributes and mythological associations, exercised profound influences on their patron city's cultural, political, and social life.

Apollo: God of Delphi

The ancient city of Delphi, with its sprawling vistas of the surrounding valleys and mountains, stands as a testament to Apollo's prominence and influence in the Greek world. According to ancient narratives, Apollo, the multifaceted god of prophecy, music, healing, and the sun, is said to have established his oracle at Delphi, following the slaying of Python, a monstrous serpent guarding the spot.

✧   The Oracle and the Pythia

The central figure in the oracular procedures was the Pythia, a woman selected from the locals, who served as Apollo's mouthpiece. Seated on a tripod in the adyton, the innermost sacred area of the temple, she entered a trance-like state, induced perhaps by the ethylene gases emanating from the ground, and delivered cryptic prophecies. These prophecies, usually interpreted by priests, guided key decisions, spanning issues from personal dilemmas to significant political and military strategies.

The narratives of Herodotus, the 'Father of History,' abound with instances where Delphic prophecies shaped history. For example, his account of Croesus, the King of Lydia, who misunderstood the oracle's prophecy leading to his downfall, underscores the crucial and sometimes cataclysmic role the oracle played in decision-making.

✧   The Pythian Games and the Myth of Python

The mythological narrative of Apollo's slaying of Python forms a crucial backdrop to the Pythian Games. This quadrennial festival, second in prestige only to the Olympic Games, included not only athletic contests but also musical and dramatic competitions, reflecting Apollo's patronage of music and arts. Participants from different city-states congregated in Delphi, participating in an event that celebrated the cultural unity of the Greek world.

✧   Archaeological Evidence of Delphi's Significance

The archaeological evidence from Delphi further underscores its significance in the Greek world. The Sacred Way, leading up to the Temple of Apollo, is lined with treasuries and statues, erected by various city-states and individuals as offerings to Apollo. They aimed to gain divine favour and to conspicuously display their piety and prosperity.

The most renowned among these is the Athenian Treasury, built to commemorate their victory at the Battle of Marathon. It was lavishly adorned with reliefs depicting various mythological scenes, including the exploits of Theseus and Heracles.

The sheer number of inscribed tripods, ex-voto offerings, and architectural monuments stand as a testament to the importance of Apollo's oracle, not merely as a religious institution but also as a hub of cultural, political, and economic exchange.

In essence, Delphi, the centre of the world according to Greek myth, not only encapsulates Apollo's significant role in Greek religion and society but also represents the interconnectedness of religion, politics, and culture in the ancient Greek world. The oracle influenced decision-making processes, while the Pythian Games celebrated cultural unity, and the rich archaeological evidence attests to Delphi's widespread influence and prestige.

Artemis: Goddess of Ephesus

In the Greek city of Ephesus, nestled in what is now western Turkey, a unique manifestation of the goddess Artemis, known as Artemis Ephesia, was fervently revered. While the Olympian Artemis was predominantly recognized as the virginal huntress and the protector of young animals, her Ephesian counterpart embodied an array of attributes often associated with earth and fertility goddesses.

✧ Artemis Ephesia and the Symbolism of Fertility

Ephesian Artemis stands distinct from her Olympian version in her visual representation. Unlike the lithe, athletic figure of the Olympian Artemis, the iconic statue of Artemis Ephesia, found in the vast Temple of Artemis, portrays her as a hieratic figure adorned with numerous egg-shaped ornaments. Scholars have interpreted these as symbols of fertility. Some have read them as multiple breasts, signifying her as a nurturing deity, while others suggest they may be bull testes, connecting her with animal fertility. The ornamentation below her waist, featuring images of animals and bees, further associates her with nature and fertility.

✧ The Temple of Artemis at Ephesus

The grandeur of her temple at Ephesus, one of the Seven Wonders of the Ancient World, offers a testament to the influence and popularity of Artemis Ephesia. Rebuilt three times over the centuries after successive destructions, the temple was a monumental structure, dwarfing other Greek temples in its size and splendor. The temple was not only a place of worship but also a major commercial and social hub, housing valuable works of art and serving as a marketplace.

✧ Artemisia: A Celebration of the Goddess

Artemisia, the annual festival held in honour of Artemis Ephesia, further underscores her far-reaching influence. This festival attracted devotees from across the Greek world, underlining her importance beyond the local context of Ephesus. The festivities likely involved grand processions, sacrifices, theatrical performances, and athletic contests, similar to other city-state festivals.

In conclusion, Artemis Ephesia, with her distinct iconography and the grandeur of her temple, offers fascinating insights into the localized adaptations of Greek deities. The importance placed on fertility and nature in her worship, the opulent Temple of Artemis, and the widely attended Artemisia festival collectively contribute to a rich tapestry of religious practices in Ephesus, highlighting the dynamic nature of ancient Greek religion.

Demeter and Persephone: Goddesses of Eleusis

The ancient city of Eleusis, located approximately 22 kilometers northwest of Athens, held a unique place in Greek religious life. The city was celebrated as the epicenter of the cult of Demeter and Persephone (also known as Kore), the goddesses associated with fertility and the cycle of the seasons. Eleusis is perhaps best known for the Eleusinian Mysteries, enigmatic rituals of profound spiritual significance that evolved around the myth of Persephone's abduction by Hades, the God of the Underworld, and Demeter's ceaseless quest for her daughter.

✦   The Mythological Background

According to the myth encapsulated in the 'Homeric Hymn to Demeter', Persephone was gathering flowers when Hades seized her and took her to the Underworld to be his bride. Distraught, Demeter searched for her daughter across the earth, neglecting her duties as the goddess of agriculture, resulting in a widespread famine. Finally, an agreement was made for Persephone to spend part of the year with Hades in the Underworld and part with Demeter on earth. This cyclical narrative was understood as an allegory for the changing seasons, with Persephone's descent and ascent symbolizing the death and rebirth of vegetation.

✦   The Eleusinian Mysteries

The Eleusinian Mysteries, held annually, were intended to prepare the initiated for a blessed afterlife by revealing sacred truths encapsulated in this myth. The exact nature of these truths is largely unknown due to the oath of secrecy taken by initiates, but ancient testimonies consistently associate the Mysteries with a hope for a better fate in the afterlife.

The celebrations, lasting approximately a week, comprised two parts. The 'Lesser Mysteries', held in the spring in Athens, were seen as a preparation for the major event. The 'Greater Mysteries' were held in the autumn at Eleusis and involved a procession from Athens to Eleusis, followed by several days of rituals, including sacrifices, purification rites, and the secretive initiation ceremony held within the Telesterion.

✧   The Telesterion and Other Archaeological Evidence

The Telesterion, a large initiation hall, was the focal point of the Eleusinian sanctuary. Archaeological evidence suggests that it could hold several thousand initiates. Although its exact interior arrangement remains a mystery, it is known that the focal point was the 'Anaktoron', where the high priestess, the Hierophant, revealed the sacred objects and performed the rituals.

The sanctuary also included a Plutonium, a cave associated with the entrance to the underworld, and other structures such as the Roman-era initiates' lodgings, the Sacred House, and the Kallichoron well, where Demeter was said to have sat in her mourning.

In conclusion, the cult of Demeter and Persephone at Eleusis represents a significant facet of Greek religious life, providing a unique blend of myth, ritual, and hope for the afterlife. Its popularity and enduring influence are evidenced by its continuous operation from the Mycenaean period until the late Roman Empire, emphasizing its pan-Hellenic appeal and its resonance with profound human concerns about life, death, and divine justice.

Poseidon: God of Corinth

Corinth, a significant city-state during the Classical period of ancient Greece, was strategically located on the narrow isthmus that links the Peloponnese with the rest of Greece. Its advantageous position and seafaring heritage led to its association with Poseidon, the god of the sea, earthquakes, and horses. Corinthian coins frequently featured Poseidon's symbolic trident, underscoring his importance to the city-state. Additionally, Poseidon was worshipped as the presiding deity of the Isthmian Games, a major athletic and musical festival held in his honour.

✧   Poseidon's Temple on the Isthmus

The archaeological remains of Poseidon's temple on the Isthmus bear witness to the maritime deity's paramount importance in Corinth. The temple, surrounded by pine and cypress trees, once housed a gold and ivory statue of Poseidon seated in a chariot drawn by hippocamps, mythical sea-horses, indicating the city's maritime prowess and its reverence towards Poseidon.

The temple was also an important gathering place for worshippers during the Isthmian Games, the athletic and musical festival held every two years. The games, second in prestige only to the Olympic Games, included a wide range of contests such as chariot racing, pankration, and musical competitions, alongside religious rituals in honour of Poseidon. Winners were rewarded with a crown of celery or pine, symbolic of the Isthmus' verdant landscape.

✦ Historical Testimony: Pausanias' Description of Greece

Pausanias, a second-century AD traveller and geographer, offers valuable details about the temple of Poseidon and the Isthmian Games in his work, 'Description of Greece'. He narrates the founding myth of the Games, linking them to the hero Melicertes, whose body, according to legend, was discovered at the Isthmus by his mother Ino. Ino and Melicertes were subsequently deified as Leucothea and Palaimon and were revered alongside Poseidon at the Isthmus. The Palaimonion, an underground chamber dedicated to Palaimon, was believed to be the site where the hero's body was discovered, further attesting to the intricate web of divine and heroic cults in Corinth.

✦ Cultural Impact and Significance

As the guardian deity of Corinth, Poseidon's cult significantly influenced the city's cultural and religious landscape, paralleling Athena's influence in Athens. However, the emphasis on Poseidon's maritime aspect and the interweaving of his worship with local heroes and myths exemplify the localised nature of Greek religious practices. Each city-state moulded their chief deities to reflect their unique socio-cultural contexts, demonstrating a synthesis of pan-Hellenic and local religious traditions. This dynamic interplay between the local and the universal is a significant characteristic of ancient Greek religion, enriching our understanding of its diversity and complexity.

Discussion on the significance of deities tied to the city, such as Zeus Polieus, Tyche, and Hecate

As we delve further into the interaction between urban spaces and divine entities in ancient Greek culture, we must consider deities whose jurisdictions are explicitly tied to the city and its activities. In this discourse, we turn our attention to three such divinities: Zeus Polieus, Tyche, and Hecate. Each of these gods and goddesses has unique characteristics and domains, contributing distinctively to the cityscape.

Zeus Polieus: The Guardian of the Polis

The epithet of 'Polieus', as we previously noted, is etymologically linked to the Greek word 'polis' or city, embodying Zeus' protective and supervisory role over city-life. The veneration of Zeus Polieus as a divine custodian, resonates profoundly with the political and social fabric of the city-states, predominantly Athens and Crete. The deity's image intricately entwines the city's political health with its spiritual wellbeing, illustrating how seamlessly the religious and the civic spheres coalesced in ancient Greece.

An annual festival, known as the Dipolieia, held in Zeus Polieus's honour in Athens, is of special significance. This festival featured the Bouphonia, a ritual sacrifice of an ox. According to the ancient historian Porphyry, an ox was led to a ceremonial trough filled with water and barley. If the ox ate from the trough—an act interpreted as consent—it was then sacrificed. The axe used in the killing was immediately cast aside, symbolically representing a crime committed.

The participants would then abscond, ostensibly leaving the 'murder' weapon with the 'victim'. A simulated judicial proceeding followed, with all the implements used in the ritual—the axe, the knife, the water, and the barley—being put on 'trial'. Unsurprisingly, the inanimate axe was found 'guilty', and the community absolved itself of the act of violence, restoring its moral and religious equilibrium. The ritualistic killing and subsequent exoneration hint at the paradox of sacred violence—a necessity to appease the gods yet a deed requiring purification.

Such an elaborate ceremony is instructive in several ways. First, it reveals the psychological and ethical tensions inherent in sacrificial rites, as well as the inventive ways the community found to reconcile them. Second, it brings to light the use of legal metaphors in religious ceremonies, thus demonstrating the interplay of civic and divine law. Lastly, it allows us to examine the societal norms surrounding guilt, innocence, and responsibility.

In Crete, too, Zeus Polieus was invoked as a guardian deity. Inscriptions from the city of Dreros dating to the 7th century BCE speak of a "horos", a boundary marker, associated with Zeus Polieus, suggesting a protective role in territorial demarcation. Interestingly, here Zeus Polieus is paired with Athena, indicating local variations in cult practices and divine associations.

In conclusion, the analysis of Zeus Polieus and the rituals associated with him provides a compelling lens through which to explore the complex interactions between the sacred and the secular, the individual and the community, and the human and the divine in the context of the ancient Greek city-state. It further encourages students to ponder the universality of such paradoxes and confrontations in other religious and cultural contexts.

Tyche: The Goddess of Fortune

In the tapestry of Greek mythology and religion, Tyche, the goddess of fortune, occupies a pivotal role. Often perceived as an unpredictable deity who wielded control over an individual's or a city's fortune, Tyche's worship was interlaced with the citizens' hopes, fears, and their sense of place in the universe.

Tyche's iconic representation, a figure adorned with a mural crown and holding a cornucopia, encapsulates her significance. The mural crown, resembling city walls, symbolises her protection of the polis, while the cornucopia, a horn overflowing with fruits and grains, embodies prosperity. Her iconography, hence, paints a picture of a deity who safeguards cities and bestows blessings of fortune upon them.

Tyche's veneration surged notably during the Hellenistic period, an epoch marked by significant political and social upheaval. In an era of fluctuating fortunes, where city-states grappled with new political realities and individuals faced changing social dynamics, Tyche's influence grew exponentially. Her sway over luck and fortune resonated with the prevailing sense of uncertainty and the heightened reliance on fate's caprices.

Certain cities, most notably Antioch and Alexandria, boasted of a special relationship with Tyche, acknowledging her as their guardian deity. Antioch's famous Tetrapylon, a monument located at the city's crossroads, housed a renowned statue of Tyche crafted by the eminent Hellenistic sculptor Eutychides. Seated on a rock, with the river-god Orontes at her feet, this representation of Tyche became an emblem of the city's identity and aspiration.

The cult of Tyche invites us to probe deeper into the interplay of human agency and divine providence, an intersection that Greek society continually negotiated. It presents an opportunity to explore how religious beliefs shape, and are shaped by, broader social and cultural contexts. The figure of Tyche, therefore, extends beyond religious symbolism, opening avenues for philosophical discussions and debates on determinism and free will, chance and causality.

In conclusion, the study of Tyche and her cult offers insights into the Hellenistic world's religious life and socio-cultural dynamics. It encourages students to question and understand how societies across time have negotiated the balance between human agency and divine intervention, a theme that resonates in contemporary religious and philosophical discourse.

Hecate: The Boundary Keeper

Hecate, often categorised as a liminal deity in the vast Greek pantheon, presided over boundaries, crossroads, magic, and the spectral realm, making her an intriguing figure within the socio-religious fabric of ancient Greek cities. She held an essential, albeit ambivalent, position within Greek religious observance, not as a central, public deity but as a guardian of the peripheries, both literal and metaphorical.

Hecate's most distinctive connection was to crossroads, liminal spaces that symbolised choice, uncertainty, and transition. These crossroads were often marked by shrines or statues of Hecate, termed 'Hecataea', highlighting her role as a guide and protector at such decision points. In addition, Hecataea were commonly installed at the entrances of homes and cities, further affirming Hecate's association with liminality and transition.

Moreover, Hecate's connection with magic and witchcraft, as evidenced in literary sources like Apollonius Rhodius' 'Argonautica' and Theocritus' 'Idylls', placed her in a unique position of power and reverence. She was often invoked for protection against malign forces, thereby serving as a divine buffer against the unseen and the unknown.

The worship and veneration of Hecate, therefore, reveal the complex interplay between urban spaces and religious practices. The presence of Hecataea at city outskirts, thresholds, and crossroads underscores Hecate's role as a boundary-keeper. It manifests a distinctive nexus between the 'polis' (city) and 'chōra' (countryside or unclaimed land), with Hecate mediating the transition from one to the other. Such a perspective aligns closely with modern geographical and anthropological theories regarding the symbiotic relationship between humans and their environment, and the socio-cultural significance of boundaries and transitional spaces.

In summary, Hecate's cult, focused around boundaries and transitional spaces, invites students to examine the intricate relationship between the physical landscape, human settlement, and religious practices. Through her, we can explore the socio-cultural meanings that ancient societies attached to their spatial realities and delve deeper into how such meanings shape and are shaped by religious observances. By doing so, we engage in a dialogue that reaches beyond the realm of ancient history, touching upon contemporary issues of space, culture, and identity.

Each of these deities illustrates the diversity and complexity of city deity worship, revealing the intricate ways in which religious practices intersected with daily life, political organisation, and the physical environment. Moreover, the study of these deities can illuminate broader questions about human agency, fortune, ritualistic violence, and the urban-rural divide, offering rich material for further research and discussion.

Their roles in protecting the city and ensuring its prosperity

City deities in ancient Greece were often perceived as divine patrons, their roles intricately linked with the protection, sustenance, and prosperity of the cities they presided over. The cults of these deities, tailored to reflect and reinforce the socio-political and economic realities of each polis, offered a spiritual framework that underpinned civic life, thereby contributing to the city's well-being and success.

Zeus Polieus, as we have previously discussed, symbolised political authority and was invoked as the guardian of the polis. His worship, manifested in rituals like the Bouphonia, reinforced social cohesion and endorsed the sanctity of community life, thereby contributing to political stability and civic harmony. Furthermore, Zeus, as the sky god and the controller of weather, was also vital for agriculture, a significant source of sustenance and economic prosperity.

Tyche, the goddess of fortune, embodied the whims of fate that could impact a city's prosperity. Cities sought her favour to ensure bountiful harvests, success in warfare, and overall good fortune. The rise in Tyche's veneration during the Hellenistic period reflects an acute awareness of the precariousness of fortune and the role of divine will in influencing human affairs. Thus, Tyche's cult played a critical part in managing collective anxieties and fostering a sense of optimism and resilience.

The goddess Athena, the divine patron of Athens, was another pivotal city deity whose spheres of influence encompassed wisdom, warfare, and crafts. Her association with these domains had a profound impact on Athens' cultural, military, and economic aspects. The Panathenaic Festival, a grand citywide celebration held in her honour, not only fostered civic unity but also reinforced Athens' image as a centre of cultural and intellectual excellence.

In the peripheries of the cities, Hecate stood as the guardian of boundaries, her presence providing a supernatural bulwark against malign forces. She controlled the delicate balance between the known (the city) and the unknown (the wilderness), effectively protecting the city from potential harm. Her role underscores the psychological comfort derived from demarcating and controlling liminal spaces, thus contributing to a sense of safety and orderliness within the city.

In conclusion, city deities played a multifaceted role in the protection and prosperity of the polis, addressing both tangible and intangible aspects of city life. Their worship functioned as a form of social contract between the city and the divine, an agreement rooted in reciprocity and mutual sustenance. Understanding these dynamics enables us to comprehend the mechanisms by which religion permeated public life in ancient Greece, and offers valuable insights into the ways societies use belief systems to negotiate their realities.

Regional variations in the worship of city gods

The worship of city gods in ancient Greece, while demonstrating shared pan-Hellenic characteristics, also showcased considerable regional variations. These variations manifested in the selection of the city deity, the rituals performed, the attributes emphasised, and the iconography adopted, reflecting the interplay between local cultural, socio-political, and environmental factors and broader Greek religious practices.

Athens' patron deity, Athena, was primarily revered as a goddess of wisdom and strategic warfare, aspects that resonate with Athens' reputation as a hub of intellectual activity and its formidable military prowess. The Panathenaic Festival, unique to Athens, encapsulates this distinct worship mode, combining military processions, athletic contests, and the presentation of a new peplos (garment) to Athena's statue.

In Corinth, a city-state renowned for its naval power, the primary city deity was Poseidon, the god of the sea. The Isthmian Games, held in his honour, underscored the city's maritime identity. Similarly, in Sparta, a city-state famed for its military discipline, the dual worship of Artemis Orthia and Athena Chalkioikos reflected the city's martial ethos and the important role of women in perpetuating Spartan societal values.

The city of Ephesus in Asia Minor revered Artemis Ephesia, a variant of Artemis significantly different from her Olympian counterpart. Unlike the huntress Artemis venerated in the mainland, Artemis Ephesia was a nature and fertility goddess, her worship reflective of the indigenous Anatolian traditions and the city's agrarian economy.

In the city of Delphi, the cult of Apollo was intertwined with the Delphic Oracle, which attracted pilgrims from across the Greek world seeking divine guidance. This unique institution, inextricably linked with the city's identity, underscores the variety in Greek religious practices, transcending the local-global dichotomy.

These regional variations in the worship of city gods underline the adaptability and dynamism inherent in Greek religious practices. They illustrate how each city moulded its spiritual landscape in alignment with its cultural ethos and societal needs, creating a multifaceted, localised interpretation of pan-Hellenic deities. Further studies into these regional variations can shed light on the complexities of religious syncretism, the role of environment in shaping religious practices, and the intersectionality of religion, politics, and culture in ancient societies.

The Interplay between Household and City Gods

In ancient Greek society, the sacred landscape was not confined to grand temples or public shrines. It permeated all aspects of life, extending into the household. Each home hosted its protective deities, typically Hestia, goddess of the hearth, and Zeus Herkeios, protector of the courtyard, alongside the family's ancestral spirits, the Agathos Daimon and the Lares. The worship of these household gods, performed through daily rituals and offerings, assured the household's prosperity and safety.

Household gods and city gods, rather than functioning in separate domains, exhibited a complex, intertwined relationship. This connection is discernible in two main dimensions: the reciprocal influences in their worship and the shared goals of safeguarding the community.

Firstly, the worship of household gods often mirrored the veneration of the city deity. The celebrations of city festivals often began with rituals at home. For instance, during the Athenian Panathenaic Festival, each family offered sacrifices to Athena at their household altar before joining the grand procession to the city's acropolis. This practice indicates how public and private religious activities were inextricably linked, creating a seamless spiritual continuum that pervaded the entire polis.

Secondly, both household and city gods were seen as guardians of their respective communities. The household gods protected the family and ensured its welfare, while the city deity safeguarded the entire polis, defending it against external threats and bestowing prosperity. This shared protective function underlines the complementary roles of household and city deities within the broader framework of Greek religious practices.

The interaction between household and city gods provides a unique lens to understand Greek religion's deeply integrated nature. It illuminates how spiritual life seamlessly blended public and private spaces, reflecting the societal belief that the divine was immanent in all aspects of existence. Further exploration into this theme can offer insightful perspectives on the communal nature of ancient Greek society, the intersection of private and public life, and the role of religion in shaping societal norms and behaviours.

Examination of the dynamics between private and public worship

The analysis of private and public worship in ancient Greece provides an intricate perspective on the collective religious mindset, as these two dimensions of spirituality were deeply interconnected and mutually influential. Such analysis, indeed, contributes significantly to our understanding of the broader sociocultural dynamics of the time.

Private Worship in the Domestic Sphere

In the domestic sphere, the veneration of gods took place daily. Small-scale sacrifices were offered at the home's altars to the household gods such as Hestia, the goddess of the hearth, Zeus Herkeios, the protector of the household, and the Agathos Daimon, a protective spirit. These acts of piety were integrated into the daily routines and underlined the household's continued goodwill to the gods. They were largely informal and involved individual family members or the entire household.

Public Worship in the Civic Sphere

In contrast, public worship was grand and periodic, involving collective rituals and sacrifices at city temples during religious festivals. The celebrations could last several days and often included processions, feasts, athletic competitions, and theatrical performances. This collective worship served not just as religious rites but also as opportunities for civic bonding, socialization, and the reinforcement of societal norms.

Interplay between Private and Public Worship

The dynamics between private and public worship were not dichotomous but symbiotic. For instance, during city-wide festivals, the festivities often began with individual households making offerings at their home altars, after which they would join the public processions and rituals. Furthermore, the private household rituals provided a continuous form of piety between the more infrequent city-wide festivals. This interplay elucidates the permeation of religious worship throughout all aspects of ancient Greek life.

The conceptualization of private and public worship as separate entities is a modern perspective. For the ancient Greeks, religious worship was an inherent part of life, woven into the very fabric of their societal structure. As such, the dynamics of private and public worship in ancient Greece could be better seen as a fluid continuum rather than separate, discrete entities.

The study of these dynamics serves as a focal point for the broader exploration of social norms, civic identity, familial roles, and the intersection of personal and public life in ancient Greek society. As a point of reflection, one might consider how these dynamics compare and contrast with contemporary forms of worship and their role in the societal fabric.

Shared religious experiences that connected individual households to the larger community

In the sphere of ancient Greek society, religious experiences were multifaceted in nature, encapsulating both private household rituals and public city-wide celebrations. These dimensions of worship were not isolated phenomena, but rather mutually reinforcing elements that fostered a sense of belonging, both at the familial level and within the larger community.

Festivals and Public Celebrations

Public celebrations, such as city-wide festivals, represented significant shared experiences. These included grand events like the Panathenaia in Athens, the Dionysia, or the Olympic Games, where citizens from different social strata and households came together to honour the gods. It was in these collective celebrations that the unity of the polis was most vividly manifested.

The festivals, marked by sacrifices, processions, athletic competitions, and theatrical performances, were not only religious occasions but also social events, fostering a sense of community and shared cultural identity. These public expressions of piety often began at a domestic level, with individual households making preliminary offerings at their home altars before joining the city-wide celebrations.

Household Rituals and Domestic Worship

While household rituals were primarily conducted in the private sphere, they played a vital role in binding the community. These everyday acts of piety towards household gods, such as Hestia, Zeus Ktesios, and the Agathos Daimon, conveyed a shared religious tradition and reinforced communal norms and values.

In particular, lifecycle rituals, such as births, marriages, and deaths, had both private and public elements. For instance, during weddings, the marital rites performed within the home were followed by a procession through the city streets, effectively tying the family event to the broader community.

Sacred Spaces

Sacred spaces, such as temples, shrines, and sanctuaries, served as important loci for shared religious experiences. While these spaces were central to public worship, they also facilitated personal expressions of devotion, such as individual prayer and the offering of votive gifts.

In conclusion, the intricate interplay between private and public worship in ancient Greece facilitated shared religious experiences that served to integrate individual households into the larger community. This multifaceted religious landscape underscores the permeative nature of religion in ancient Greek society, shaping and reflecting the communal ethos. In comparing these practices with contemporary religious cultures, students may reflect on how shared religious experiences continue to inform societal bonds and communal identities.

Conclusion: Reflecting on the Importance of Household and City Gods

The interplay between household and city gods in ancient Greek religion presents a fascinating study of the symbiotic relationship between individual households and the larger city-state community. The multiplicity of gods and goddesses worshipped at both the household and city level reflects the complexity and diversity of Greek society and its religious practices.

City gods, such as Athena Polias in Athens or Zeus Polieus, played an essential role in shaping the collective identity and communal ethos of a city-state. Their worship, through grand festivals and public rituals, served to unify the community, fostering shared cultural values and a sense of belonging among the citizens. Moreover, city gods often encapsulated the distinct characteristics or aspirations of the city-state, with their worship serving as a declaration of civic pride and identity.

Household gods, on the other hand, served a more intimate function. Deities like Hestia, Zeus Ktesios, and the Agathos Daimon were invoked in daily household rituals, offering protection and blessings on the familial unit. The sanctity of these domestic rituals reflected the importance of the family as the fundamental societal unit in ancient Greek society.

Nevertheless, the distinction between household and city gods was not rigid, as the ancient Greek religious experience was deeply interconnected. Household rituals often served as the foundation for city-wide celebrations, while the worship of city gods was also reflected in individual homes. This dynamic interplay between the domestic and public spheres of worship led to a cohesive religious framework, wherein shared experiences connected individual households to the larger community.

In reflecting upon the importance of household and city gods, we perceive a multifaceted religious landscape that intricately wove together the private and public spheres of ancient Greek life. It is a testament to the pervasiveness and societal significance of religion in this historical context. This intricate network of religious devotion offers us a lens through which we may comprehend the societal structures, values, and shared cultural experiences of ancient Greece. These insights also invite comparative analyses with other historical or contemporary religious cultures, highlighting the universal human endeavor to navigate the complexities of communal and individual existence through the prism of religious expression.

Through this study, it is hoped that students are inspired to delve deeper into the captivating realm of ancient Greek religion, fostering critical thinking, and expanding their understanding of historical and cultural diversity. This understanding can be a cornerstone in the development of mutual respect for diverse religious traditions and cultural expressions, a crucial aspect of global citizenship in our increasingly interconnected world.

Recap of the key points discussed in the chapter

The discussion in this chapter has traversed a variety of topics within the realm of ancient Greek religion, providing insights into the complex interplay between household and city deities and the roles they played in both private and public religious life. Herein, we encapsulate the salient points:

The Significance of Household Gods: Deities such as Hestia, Zeus Ktesios, and Agathos Daimon were intrinsically tied to the household, a crucial societal unit in ancient Greece. These gods were invoked for protection, prosperity, and domestic harmony.

The Role of City Gods: Each Greek polis typically had a patron deity, which personified the aspirations and ethos of the city-state. Celebrations and rituals devoted to these deities, such as Athena Polias in Athens or Zeus Polieus, were pivotal in defining communal identity and fostering civic unity.

Regional Variations in Worship: The worship of deities demonstrated considerable regional variation, reflecting the unique cultural, socio-political, and environmental contexts of different city-states. This underlines the flexible and locally adaptive nature of Greek polytheism.

Interplay between Household and City Gods: An intriguing symbiosis was observed between household and city gods, reflecting the interconnectedness of private and public spheres in religious practices. Shared religious experiences and festivals often served as a bridge, connecting individual households to the broader community.

The Dynamics of Private and Public Worship: The interface between domestic and communal religious activities provides an invaluable perspective on the social structure and cultural norms of ancient Greek society. The analysis of these dynamics allows us to comprehend the religious life of the ancient Greeks on both an individual and collective scale.

Shared Religious Experiences: These experiences, whether in the form of household rituals or city-wide celebrations, provided a collective framework for expressing religious devotion. They played a significant role in strengthening communal bonds, enhancing social solidarity, and defining a shared cultural identity.

Reflecting on these key points can help us understand the multifaceted religious landscape of ancient Greece and appreciate the profound impact of these practices on the fabric of Greek society. This, in turn, provides a rich context for the continued exploration of ancient cultures, offering valuable insights into the complexities of human society and cultural expression across historical periods.

Reflection on the essential role of household and city gods in understanding ancient Greek religion and society

Through the lens of historical analysis and cultural interpretation, it becomes abundantly clear that the integral role of household and city gods in ancient Greek society extends beyond mere religious observance. Their presence and veneration reflected not just the belief systems, but also the socio-political structures, communal identities, and cultural mores of the Greek polis, thereby offering a more nuanced understanding of the ancient Greek world.

From a sociological perspective, household gods such as Hestia, Zeus Ktesios, and Agathos Daimon were pivotal in perpetuating the norms of familial hierarchy and domestic life. They underpinned the sanctity of the oikos, the household, as a fundamental societal unit, reinforcing the values of unity, stability, and mutual obligation. Their veneration was a continuous practice, intricately woven into daily life, and as such, can be seen as a reflection of the sustained importance of tradition and continuity in Greek society.

City gods, on the other hand, were representative of communal identity and civic pride. They were the divine embodiment of the polis, its achievements and aspirations. The shared veneration of city gods, particularly during public festivals and rituals, served to enhance civic solidarity and foster a sense of belonging. In this light, they functioned as vital pillars of communal cohesion, reinforcing social order and collective morality.

The examination of regional variations in the worship of deities reveals the flexible and localised nature of Greek polytheism. The distinctive characteristics and attributes assigned to the same god in different regions reflect the adaptability of religious beliefs to local cultural, environmental, and socio-political contexts. This illustrates the inherent dynamism within the ancient Greek religious system, allowing us to appreciate its complexity and resilience.

The interplay between household and city gods underlines the interconnectedness of private and public spheres in the Greek religious context. This symbiotic relationship provided a comprehensive framework for religious observance, simultaneously addressing personal concerns and communal obligations. The analysis of this interplay offers insights into the complexities of ancient Greek society, enabling a more profound understanding of its structures and dynamics.

Thus, the study of household and city gods provides a multifaceted perspective on ancient Greek religion and society. Their veneration illuminates the intersection of personal devotion, familial duty, and civic responsibility, showcasing the intricate web of relationships that structured Greek life. By examining these dynamics, we gain a more profound appreciation of the spiritual underpinnings of Greek society, as well as the sociocultural complexity that characterised this significant period in human history.

Chapter 7: The Nature Deities: Overview of Pan, the nymphs, and other gods and spirits associated with natural phenomena and landscapes.

From the Olympian pantheon to the most obscure daimones, gods and spirits pervaded every layer of ancient Greek life. Among these divine entities, nature deities occupied a particularly prominent position, influencing not merely the Greeks' religious imagination but also their understanding of the natural world and their place within it. In this chapter, we will delve into the vibrant and complex realm of these nature deities, exploring how they were conceived, venerated, and incorporated into everyday life and grand cosmic narratives alike.

We will focus our exploration on Pan, the goat-footed Arcadian god, and the nymphs, ethereal spirits of the natural world. These figures represent two key types of nature deities, each embodying a different relationship between humanity and the environment. Pan, often seen as a wild yet benign presence, personifies the Greeks' apprehension and fascination with the wilderness, while the nymphs, as the spirits of trees, springs, mountains, and other geographical features, epitomise the life-giving and unpredictable facets of nature.

In addition, we will cast our gaze on other nature deities and spirits associated with specific natural phenomena and landscapes, from the icy breath of Boreas, the god of the North Wind, to the nurturing embrace of Gaia, the Earth herself. Their myriad stories and rituals shed light on how the Greeks sought to comprehend and negotiate their intricate, multifaceted relationship with the natural world.

In exploring the complex tapestry of myths, iconography, and cult practices surrounding these deities, we hope to discern the threads of ecological wisdom, societal norms, philosophical musings, and spiritual longing woven into it. Furthermore, we aim to highlight the interplay between these nature deities and human society, reflecting on how they shaped and were shaped by human activities ranging from agriculture to navigation.

Ultimately, this chapter seeks to guide readers through the verdant landscape of Greek nature deities, inviting them to engage with the rich tapestry of mythology, cultic practices, and philosophical underpinnings these deities encompass. As we embark on this journey, we will not only unravel the complexities of ancient Greek religion but also gain fresh insights into the timelessly profound human quest to find divinity in the heart of nature.

Brief overview of the role of nature deities in ancient Greek religion

The pantheon of ancient Greek religion was not limited to the well-known gods and goddesses who resided on Mount Olympus. An array of nature deities, each presiding over different aspects of the natural world, constituted an integral part of this multifaceted religious landscape. From the highest mountains to the deepest rivers, from the densest forests to the most fertile fields, every corner of the Greek world was deemed to be under the influence of one or more of these divinities.

While the Olympian gods were seen as the movers and shakers of the cosmos, bestowing order and justice, the nature deities represented a different facet of divinity. Often embodying the unpredictable and mysterious forces of nature, they were simultaneously seen as life-giving and destructive, benevolent and dangerous. These dual aspects of nature deities were reflected in their worship and representation, often involving rituals and offerings intended to win their favour or avert their wrath.

Pan, the god of shepherds and flocks, of mountain wilds, hunting and rustic music, is a significant figure in this context. Although not an Olympian, he was widely venerated in rural areas, especially in Arcadia, his reputed birthplace. His image—half-man, half-goat—captures the primal, chaotic essence of the wilderness, offering insights into the Greeks' conceptualisation of the human-nature divide.

The nymphs, in contrast, were more benevolent and intimately connected to specific locales. As minor deities of nature, they were associated with various natural features such as groves, springs, mountains, and caves. The nymphs were often invoked as nurturers and protectors, and many localities claimed a particular group of nymphs as their own. They served as a bridge between the human and divine realms, weaving the sacred into the fabric of everyday life.

The worship of nature deities, therefore, was not merely a reflection of ancient Greeks' spiritual beliefs but also a way of navigating their relationships with the environment. Whether it was seeking Pan's assistance for a successful hunt, propitiating the nymphs for a bountiful harvest, or consulting an oracle of Gaia for crucial decisions, these rituals embedded a sense of divine immanence in the natural world, making it a living participant in human affairs rather than a passive backdrop.

However, it's essential to remember that the worship and understanding of nature deities were far from monolithic, mirroring the geographical, cultural, and temporal diversity of the ancient Greek world. This diversity, along with the multifaceted narratives and symbolism associated with these deities, offer a rich and nuanced lens through which we can explore ancient Greek society's perceptions and interactions with the natural world.

In the subsequent sections, we will delve deeper into the mythology and cult practices associated with Pan and the nymphs, as well as other nature deities, to better understand their roles and significance in ancient Greek religion. Along the way, we will also consider the insights they provide into broader issues such as the human-nature relationship, community identity, and ecological sustainability.

Scope of the chapter and key questions to be explored

This chapter will undertake a comprehensive exploration of the nature deities of ancient Greek religion, primarily focusing on the god Pan, the nymphs, and other gods and spirits associated with natural phenomena and landscapes. The discourse will revolve around an examination of these divinities' mythology, iconography, cult practices, and the socio-cultural contexts in which they were worshipped.

Among the key questions to be explored are:

How were nature deities such as Pan and the nymphs represented in ancient Greek mythology and iconography? What attributes, characteristics, and associations did they possess, and what do they tell us about the Greeks' understanding and personification of nature?

What were the rituals, ceremonies, and cult practices associated with the worship of nature deities? How did these practices reflect and influence the Greeks' interactions with their natural environment?

How did the worship of nature deities vary across different regions and periods in ancient Greece? What factors influenced these variations, and what implications do they hold for our understanding of regional identities and inter-regional connections in the ancient Greek world?

What roles did nature deities play in the broader religious, social, and cultural contexts of ancient Greek society? How did they interact with other divine entities and with human communities?

How can we interpret the ancient Greeks' relationship with nature and the environment through the lens of nature deities? How do these interpretations contribute to contemporary debates and discussions on ecology, environmentalism, and human-nature relations?

In answering these questions, we will not only deepen our understanding of nature deities and their significance in ancient Greek religion but also illuminate broader aspects of ancient Greek culture and society. We will particularly emphasise the ways in which the worship of nature deities shaped and reflected the Greeks' perceptions of and interactions with their natural environment, providing valuable insights into their ecological consciousness and ethos. By doing so, this chapter aims to further enrich the scholarly dialogue on ancient Greek religion and its multifaceted interconnections with the natural world.

Pan: The Arcadian God of Nature

Pan, whose name literally translates to "all" or "everything" in ancient Greek, holds a significant place within the pantheon of deities, primarily associated with wild nature, shepherds and flocks, hunting, and rustic music. As the Arcadian god of nature, Pan exemplifies the wilderness's untamed beauty and mystery, embodying the ancient Greeks' complex relationship with their natural surroundings.

Mythological and Iconographic Representation of Pan
In mythology, Pan is typically depicted as the son of Hermes and a nymph, born in the remote, mountainous region of Arcadia. Uniquely half-human and half-goat in appearance, Pan exhibits a strikingly theriomorphic (animal-like) countenance in contrast to the predominantly anthropomorphic Greek gods. This form – the horned head and torso of a man and the lower body and legs of a goat – bespeaks a deity deeply intertwined with the wild and unstructured side of nature, a stark contrast to the cultivated landscapes of the polis.

Pan's iconographic representations further underscore these associations. He is often portrayed playing the syrinx, or panpipes, a musical instrument that he himself is said to have invented. This association with music underscores Pan's connection to the harmony and melody inherent in the natural world, seen as a reflection of cosmic order.

Cult Practices and Worship of Pan

Cult practices dedicated to Pan were markedly distinct from those of Olympian gods. His worshippers often gathered in caves and grottos, sites emblematic of the untamed wilderness that Pan personified. Ritual practices included music, dancing, and sacrifices, usually of goats, symbolising a return to the primordial, unstructured aspects of existence momentarily liberated from the strictures of societal norms.

In Athens, the cult of Pan achieved significance after the Battle of Marathon (490 BCE), where Pan was believed to have instilled 'panic' (a term derived from his name) among the invading Persians, leading to their defeat. Following this, a sanctuary dedicated to Pan was established on the north slope of the Acropolis, indicating the incorporation of this rustic deity into the urban religious landscape.

Pan in Regional and Socio-cultural Contexts

Pan's popularity across Greece was not universal. His primary locus of worship remained in Arcadia, a region that, due to its mountainous terrain and relative isolation, preserved a more traditional, rural way of life. Here, Pan was integral to the pastoral lifestyle, offering protection to shepherds and their flocks.

However, Pan's reach extended beyond Arcadia into other regions of Greece, where his image and mythology were often adapted to local contexts. As previously noted, in Athens, Pan was celebrated as a martial deity, a sharp diversion from his Arcadian persona. These regional variations underline the fluidity of ancient Greek religious practices, shaped and reshaped by local socio-cultural dynamics.

Pan and the Natural World: Ecological Implications

The figure of Pan offers profound insights into the ancient Greeks' understanding of and interaction with their environment. Pan embodies the wild and untamed aspects of nature, simultaneously enchanting and terrifying, fertile and chaotic. His worship reflects a profound respect for the natural world's autonomy and a recognition of the essential interdependence between human society and its environment.

By venerating a deity so intimately connected with the wilderness, the Greeks acknowledged the intrinsic value of nature beyond human utility. This perspective, offering a deep ecological consciousness, may provide thought-provoking implications for contemporary environmental discourses, reminding us of the critical need for harmonious human-nature relations.

In conclusion, Pan, the Arcadian god of nature, stands as a compelling symbol of the intricate ties between the natural world and the cultural imagination. Through the lens of Pan's worship, we gain a richer understanding of the ancient Greek ethos towards nature, revealing a complex web of reverence, fear, and symbiosis.

Origins and major myths associated with Pan

As we venture further into the world of Pan, the Arcadian god of nature, we must delve into the myths and stories that defined him. Pan's origins are entrenched in a rich tapestry of narratives that underscore his significance within the Greek mythological corpus and help us better understand the cultural values and ideologies that shaped these tales.

Birth and Origins of Pan

The lineage of Pan and the circumstances of his birth, as recounted in various versions of Greek mythology, provide significant insights into his characterization as a nature deity. The inherent inconsistencies in these accounts echo the fluid and multifaceted nature of the deity himself, just as they do for many other figures in the mythological pantheon.

✧   Parentage of Pan

Pan, in Greek mythology, is uniquely positioned due to his parentage, a hybrid being borne out of a pairing that converges the structured Olympian pantheon and the untrammeled, vibrant realm of nature. His father, Hermes, is an Olympian god, the child of Zeus himself and Maia, one of the Pleiades, signifying the sphere of celestial divinity. His mother, frequently identified as the nymph Dryope, on the other hand, signifies the terrestrial and the chthonic, the domain of nymphs, spirits, and natural forces.

Pan's dual heritage from these contrasting domains is manifested in his unusual physique. Unlike most Greek gods who are depicted in human form, Pan is presented as a creature that straddles the human and animal realms. He possesses the upper body of a man and the hindquarters of a goat, a juxtaposition that visualises the coalescence of civilised and wild aspects of his character. This dual nature is reflective of his parents: the Olympian divinity from Hermes and the wild and natural spirit from Dryope.

This bi-fold manifestation is essential to understanding Pan's role within the Greek pantheon. He does not reside exclusively in the celestial heights of Mount Olympus nor is he entirely of the earth. Instead, Pan, like the crossroads he frequents, stands at the juncture of these realms, bridging the gap between the wild and the civilised, the earthly and the divine. He navigates these liminal spaces, just as his father Hermes navigates between the mortal and divine worlds, suggesting a thematic continuity within this divine lineage. This crucial role underscores the importance of

Pan's unique status within the divine hierarchy and underpins many of his interactions and influences within the human world, which we shall delve into further in subsequent sections of this chapter.

◆ Lineage and Symbiosis of the Olympian and Chthonic Elements

In the most frequently cited mythos, Pan is the offspring of the Olympian messenger god Hermes and a nymph, most often identified as Dryope. This lineage represents a profound symbiosis of Olympian and chthonic elements. Hermes, a son of Zeus, embodies the divine, Olympian order. He is known for his capacity to move between the celestial, terrestrial, and underworld realms, delivering messages and conducting souls to the afterlife. His dynamic role underscores the permeability and interconnectedness of these spheres. Dryope, a nymph, symbolizes the raw, natural world. As a nymph, she belongs to the vast cohort of minor deities associated with specific locales in the natural environment: trees, mountains, streams, and more.

From this intersection, Pan emerges, embodying both the structured divine order and the untamed, vibrant pulse of nature. His lineage thus presents a harmonious convergence of two contrasting facets of the Greek spiritual cosmos.

◆ Physical Manifestation and the Dual Nature

Pan's birth narrative underscores his uniqueness. His goat-like features, particularly his hindquarters, tail, and horns, combine with his human upper body and head to create an unconventional visage. This stark departure from the typical anthropomorphic depiction of the Greek gods underscores Pan's duality—part god, part beast. His unique form reflects the dual aspects of his parentage and foreshadows his role as a deity straddling two worlds: the civilized, associated with the structured divine order, and the wild, connected to the raw pulse of nature.

◆ The Liminal Deity

Much like his father Hermes, Pan navigates liminal spaces, functioning as a bridge between the wild and the civilized, the earthly and the divine. His physical form, a fusion of human and animal traits, is a visual representation of these dual roles. He is neither entirely of the celestial heights of Mount Olympus nor solely of the earth. Instead, he stands at the juncture of these realms, embodying the intersectionality of the natural world and the divine order.

Pan's prominent role in the Greek pantheon and his influence within the human world cannot be understated. His unique status within the divine hierarchy allows him to oversee and influence a broad spectrum of phenomena, from the serenity of pastoral landscapes to the unpredictable wilds of the mountains and forests. This expansive purview makes Pan one of the most multifaceted deities in the Greek pantheon, a figure that simultaneously embodies harmony and discord, tranquility and terror, civilization and wilderness. In the following sections, we shall delve into the complexities and contradictions of Pan, exploring how this liminal deity shaped and was shaped by the ancient Greeks' perceptions of the natural world.

✧   Reaction to Pan's Birth

The initial reactions to Pan's birth, particularly from his mother Dryope, are telling. The myth recounts that Dryope, confronted by her child's hybrid form, was terrified and fled. This flight illustrates the fear that the untamed wilderness, personified in Pan, could inspire. It offers an echo of the broader Greek worldview, wherein the wilderness was often seen as a place of potential danger and chaos, in stark contrast to the relative safety and order of the polis (city-state).

Hermes, however, is said to have reacted with delight at the sight of his son. He joyously presented Pan to the Olympian gods, who are also described as being pleased by the unusual god. This episode illustrates the acceptance of the wild, untamed aspects of nature within the divine order, reminding us that the ancient Greek perception of nature was not solely one of fear, but also one of awe, respect, and even joy.

The reactions to Pan's birth were a study in contrasts, revealing prevailing attitudes toward wilderness and natural phenomena in ancient Greece. The retelling of these events provides crucial insights into how the Greeks navigated their relationship with nature and how Pan served as a symbol for the myriad and often conflicting sentiments associated with the natural world.

◆ Dryope's Fear and the Wilderness as Other

Dryope's response to her son's unusual appearance offers a valuable insight into the ancient Greeks' perception of the wilderness. Pan's hybrid form, simultaneously man and beast, engendered fear, prompting his mother to flee. Her reaction can be interpreted as a reflection of the broader Greek worldview. The wilderness, synonymous with Pan, was often viewed as a realm of potential danger and chaos, a stark counterpoint to the relative safety and order of the polis, or city-state. The Greeks, valuing order and fearing the unpredictable, might have regarded the untamed aspects of nature with a certain degree of trepidation. This fear, symbolized by Dryope's flight, demonstrates the cultural and psychological distance that separated civilization from wilderness.

◆　Hermes' and Olympians' Delight and the Reverence for Nature

Conversely, Hermes' reaction to Pan's birth—his delight, rather than dread—serves to balance this perspective. The god Hermes was unphased by his son's peculiar form; instead, he embraced Pan's difference and presented him with pride to the other Olympian gods. The gods' acceptance of Pan—half god, half beast—suggests a contrasting viewpoint, one that highlights the reverence and fascination ancient Greeks also held towards the untamed aspects of nature.

In this context, Pan's reception among the gods represents an acknowledgment of the wild's vital role within the cosmological order. The Olympian gods, while embodying order and civilization, recognized the importance of the wilderness and the natural world. Their acceptance of Pan is a testament to this understanding and respect. The wilderness, represented by Pan, was not only feared but also valued for its inherent vitality, beauty, and the sense of awe it could inspire.

Through the lenses of Dryope's fear and Hermes' delight, we glimpse the dualism inherent in the Greek perception of nature. This dichotomy, marked by both dread and reverence, highlights the complex and multifaceted relationship between the ancient Greeks and their natural environment, a relationship embodied by Pan, the god who straddles these two worlds. The following sections will continue to explore these themes as we delve into Pan's various myths, his cult worship, and his enduring influence on cultural perceptions of nature.

✧　Pan's Birthplace: Arcadia

The remote and rugged region of Arcadia is regarded as Pan's birthplace, which is central to his association with wilderness, pastoral life, and the ruggedness of the untamed world. Arcadia, characterised by its mountains, dense forests, and wild landscapes, reflects Pan's uncontrolled and primitive nature. This was a place on the margins of the civilized Greek world, where wilderness was more prominent than man-made structures, and where a deity such as Pan could reign.

In essence, the multifaceted accounts of Pan's lineage and birth serve as rich narrative devices, shaping his identity and sphere of influence. They embody the complex interplay between civilisation and wilderness, order and chaos, fear and delight. These dichotomies, personified in Pan, offer a unique lens through which to view the ancient Greeks' relationship with and understanding of the natural world.

◆ Arcadia as Pan's Birthplace: Symbolizing the Untamed World

The birthplace of a deity in the Greek pantheon is not simply a geographical location but also a symbolic landscape that reflects and reinforces the character and domain of that deity. In Pan's case, the Arcadian region, a wilderness on the periphery of the civilized Greek world, underscores his affiliation with the untamed facets of nature.

◆ Arcadia: Between Civilization and Wilderness

Arcadia, Pan's reputed birthplace, is a remote and rugged region. Characterised by mountainous terrains, dense forests, and wild landscapes, it is a testament to the untamed world. Arcadia's geographic features - the daunting heights of its mountains, the impenetrability of its forests, the capriciousness of its wilderness - reflect Pan's untamed, primal nature. The landscapes of Arcadia serve as an emblem of Pan's dominion over wilderness and the untamed.

Arcadia is unique as it lies at the fringes of the Greek world. This liminal space, where wilderness supersedes man-made structures, serves as the perfect realm for a deity like Pan. It provides an environment where the Arcadian Pan could hold sway, reflecting the dichotomy between the wild, untamed aspects of nature and the civilised Greek society. It also underscores the link between geographic location and identity in Greek mythology.

◆ The Narrative Device of Birthplace and Lineage

The narratives of Pan's birth and lineage serve a crucial purpose beyond simply recounting his origins. They frame Pan's identity, highlighting his unique status as a bridge between civilisation and wilderness, the ordered world of human society and the unpredictable realm of nature. His parentage - Hermes, the Olympian, and Dryope, the nymph - along with his birth in Arcadia, personify the interplay between order and chaos, human and nature, fear and delight.

These contrasting dichotomies provide a rich narrative texture and afford a unique perspective on the ancient Greeks' understanding of their relationship with the natural world. Pan, as the embodiment of these dichotomies, personifies the tension and synergy between civilisation and wilderness. As we continue to explore Pan's myths, cult, and influence, this dynamic interplay becomes more apparent, offering profound insights into the worldviews and value systems of the ancient Greeks.

Major Myths Associated with Pan

A range of myths associated with Pan further elucidates the character and domains of this multifaceted god. One of the best-known tales is the creation of Pan's signature musical instrument, the panpipes (syrinx). According to the myth, Pan pursued the beautiful nymph Syrinx, who, desperate to escape his advances, was transformed into a stand of reeds by her sisters or by the river nymphs. When Pan's breath swept across the reeds, they emitted a haunting melody. Enchanted, Pan fashioned an instrument from the reeds, which he named Syrinx in honor of his unattainable love.

This tale underscores Pan's intimate connection with nature and his role as the patron of rustic music, his melodious pipe symbolizing the music inherent in the natural world. Additionally, it provides a prime example of the recurring motif in Greek mythology where pursuit and transformation converge, often revealing complex dynamics of desire and resistance.

Another significant narrative centers on Pan's role during the Persian Wars. According to Herodotus, Pan appeared to the courier Pheidippides, who was en route from Athens to Sparta before the Battle of Marathon, promising assistance to the Athenians in their fight against the Persians. Indeed, at Marathon, Pan was said to have instilled "panic" (a term derived from his name) among the Persian ranks, contributing to the Athenians' victory. Following the war, Pan's cult was introduced into Athens, illustrating how the god's protective role in warfare was recognized alongside his traditional domains of nature and pastoral life.

Pan and the Satyrs

Although not a major myth in its own right, the association of Pan with the satyrs - woodland spirits renowned for their love of music, dance, and wine - is an important aspect of his mythological characterization. Like Pan, the satyrs are theriomorphic, often depicted with horse-like tails and ears, and sometimes with similar goat-like features. Their association with Pan is indicative of his leadership over the wild aspects of nature, emphasizing the more carefree, hedonistic, and chaotic elements that he and his retinue embody.

◆ Pan and the Satyrs: Leadership over Wild Nature

The mythology of Pan is suffused with vibrant characterisations, symbolic associations, and narrative devices that convey a spectrum of messages and themes. One of the more significant facets of his mythos is his affiliation with the satyrs, the woodland spirits revered for their proclivity for music, dance, and libation.

◆ The Satyrs: Theriomorphic Companions of Pan

The satyrs are theriomorphic entities, often portrayed with distinctive equine tails and ears, and occasionally sharing the caprine features that characterise Pan. These creatures are typically depicted as vivacious and unrestrained, mirroring Pan's uncontrolled, exuberant essence. The inclusion of the satyrs in Pan's narrative amplifies the untamed, ecstatic aspects of nature that he governs.

Satyrs, in their depiction, serve as a significant extension of Pan's image. They encapsulate the indulgent, hedonistic, and unrestrained elements that Pan embodies, thus emphasizing his rule over the untamed facets of the natural world. The association of Pan with these theriomorphic entities further delineates the boundary between the human and the wild, underscoring the complex interface that Pan navigates as a deity.

■ Pan: A Leader among the Wild

The interaction between Pan and the satyrs is more than a mere affiliation; it signifies Pan's authority over these wild spirits. They dance, sing, and celebrate in his company, often following his lead in merriment and music. This narrative of leadership amplifies the chaotic, joyous, and at times, frightening facets of the natural world over which Pan presides. It underscores his role as a deity who commands not just the geographical wilderness, but also the wild, untamed forces represented by the satyrs.

By exploring the relationship between Pan and the satyrs, we illuminate the deity's command over both the geographical wilderness and the unpredictable, often hedonistic forces of the natural world. This perspective offers valuable insights into the ancient Greeks' nuanced understanding of the natural world and the balance and interplay between order and chaos, discipline and indulgence, fear and ecstasy. These complexities will be further explored in subsequent discussions on Pan's myths and cults.

Pan and the Moon Goddess Selene

In a lesser-known myth, Pan is linked romantically with the moon goddess Selene. He reportedly wooed her by disguising his goat form with a white fleece, evoking images of light and darkness, wilderness and the celestial, in their union. The story, though not as prevalent as others, suggests Pan's reach beyond his earthly domains, hinting at a potent symbolism encompassing both the terrestrial and celestial realms.

In sum, the myths of Pan offer an extraordinary window into the character of this unique god and the cultural context from which his worship arose. His narratives, rich with symbolism and layered with meaning, underscore the complexities inherent in humanity's relationship with the natural world, simultaneously capturing the whimsy, fear, desire, and respect that characterized this interaction in the ancient Greek world.

◆   Pan and Selene: The Union of Wilderness and the Celestial

Despite the plethora of myths associated with Pan, his relationship with the moon goddess Selene is less commonly known. This coupling, however, presents a captivating melding of the terrestrial and the celestial, hinting at Pan's reach extending beyond his typical rustic dominion.

◆   A Lesser-Known Courtship: Pan and Selene

According to this narrative, Pan sought to win the affections of Selene, the moon goddess known for her luminous beauty. To achieve this, Pan adopted a disguise by covering himself with a white fleece, thus softening his caprine features. This ruse draws intriguing parallels between Pan's earthiness and Selene's radiant celestiality. The white fleece not only masked his animal form but also reflected the shimmering luminescence associated with the moon, bridging the gap between the terrestrial and the celestial, and between the untamed wild and the divine order.

◆   The Symbolism of Pan and Selene's Union

The mythology surrounding Pan and Selene's union is noteworthy for the potent symbolism it represents. This relationship allows for the juxtaposition of light and darkness, wilderness and celestial order, thus situating Pan within a broader cosmic framework. Pan's attraction to Selene could be interpreted as the eternal allure of the distant and the divine, while his successful courtship signifies the potential of the earthly and untamed to touch the lofty spheres of celestial order.

Though not as prominent as other narratives in Pan's mythology, this tale illuminates a different aspect of Pan's character. It underscores his adaptability, shrewdness, and the breadth of his influence, extending from his rustic domains to the celestial heights. Moreover, it re-emphasizes his dual nature, as a deity straddling two realms, much like his theriomorphic form straddles the human and the animal worlds.

◆　　　Implications of the Pan-Selene Myth

In conclusion, the narratives surrounding Pan provide a multi-dimensional understanding of this unique god and the cultural milieu from which his worship emerged. These stories are awash with symbolism, with each layer of meaning contributing to a nuanced depiction of Pan and his role within the Greek pantheon. They underscore the complexities inherent in humanity's relationship with the natural world, capturing a spectrum of emotions—whimsy, fear, desire, and respect—that characterized ancient Greek interaction with nature.

The myth of Pan and Selene, while less prominent, lends itself to a rich analysis of the multifaceted ways in which terrestrial and celestial entities intersect, shedding light on the ancient Greek understanding of the cosmos and their place within it. The following sections will delve deeper into the worship and cult of Pan, providing further insights into the significance of this complex and captivating deity.

Iconography and symbolic attributes of Pan

As we delve further into the rich tableau of Pan's mythology, it is critical to consider his visual representation in ancient art, and the connotations of his symbolic attributes. These visual markers and symbols not only shape our understanding of Pan's role within the Greek pantheon but also offer insights into the broader cultural and religious contexts of the ancient Greek world.

Anthropomorphic Fusion

The physical depiction of Pan is as distinct and complex as his lineage and myths suggest. Pan is characteristically represented in theriomorphic form, a fusion of human and animal, his upper body reminiscent of a mature man while his lower half is unequivocally that of a goat. This combination signifies Pan's unique position as a mediator between the civilised and the wild, the human and the animal.

✧　　　Anthropomorphic Fusion in Pan's Iconography

Anthropomorphic fusion, a concept epitomised in Pan's iconography, encompasses the blending of human and animalistic features, leading to the creation of hybrid forms. Pan's representation, as both man and beast, is a poignant embodiment of this artistic and conceptual amalgamation.

✧   Delineation of Pan's Form

When we speak of Pan's representation, it is essential to first clarify the dual facets of his form. Pan's upper half is distinctly human. He is often portrayed with the torso of a mature man, complete with a full beard—an atypical representation considering the ancient Greek gods are generally depicted in the bloom of youth. In contrast, his lower body exhibits goat-like characteristics, including hindquarters and cloven hooves, reflecting an undomesticated, primal aspect.

✧   Symbolism and Significance

The fusion of human and animal within Pan's figure holds profound symbolism. The human part of his form aligns him with the civilised world and establishes his divine kinship. Simultaneously, his caprine features tie him closely to the wild and unregulated aspects of the natural world. Thus, Pan's theriomorphic form stands as a testament to his lineage, mirroring the junction of the celestial and terrestrial spheres in his parentage, while also emphasising his role as an intermediary between civilisation and wilderness.

✧   Connection to Shamanic Traditions

When we explore this concept in a broader perspective, the anthropomorphic fusion of Pan bears striking resemblances to figures in shamanic traditions worldwide, where the shaman, a spiritual mediator, often adopts animal forms or attributes to traverse between different realms of existence. In this context, Pan's hybrid form can be seen as a potential representation of similar transcendent capabilities.

✧   Counterpoint in Greek Art

The representation of Pan's theriomorphic form is noteworthy, particularly when considered in the wider context of Greek art. Typically, Greek deities were represented in fully anthropomorphic forms, adhering to idealised human aesthetics. The marked departure in Pan's depiction can be seen as a conscious artistic and narrative choice, serving to highlight his unique role within the Greek pantheon.

✧   Implications for Nature-Culture Dynamics

The anthropomorphic fusion in Pan's depiction serves as a potent symbol of the ancient Greeks' understanding of the interaction between nature (wild, chaotic, and untamed) and culture (civilised, orderly, and human-centric). The liminality of Pan, oscillating between the cultured and the wild, is a physical manifestation of this ongoing negotiation. It provides us with valuable insight into how the Greeks perceived, negotiated with, and contextualised 'wilderness' within their socio-cultural and religious frameworks.

In conclusion, Pan's distinctive theriomorphic form is a visualisation of his inherent dualities—wild yet cultured, earthly yet divine. His representation demonstrates a deep symbiosis of apparent contradictions, reflecting not only his personal attributes and domain but also the broader conceptual dichotomies prevalent within the ancient Greek worldview. A study of this anthropomorphic fusion, therefore, not only illuminates our understanding of Pan as a deity but also provides significant insights into the socio-cultural constructs of the ancient world.

Pan's Caprine Features

Pan's caprine (goat-like) features are not limited to his lower body. His ears and horns are those of a goat, further emphasising his animalistic nature. Horns in various cultural contexts can represent fertility, strength, and virility, connoting Pan's affiliation with the primal and procreative forces of nature.

A closer examination of Pan's caprine attributes—his ears, horns, and lower body—sheds light on an essential aspect of Pan's characterization. Each attribute contributes to the imagery of the untamed, the primal, and the raw, underscoring the potency of Pan's connection to the natural world.

✦   Detailed Caprine Traits

Beyond his hybrid bipedal stance, Pan's depiction regularly includes a pair of goat ears protruding from his head and two prominent horns that crest above his brow. His caprine lower body is complete with cloven hooves, an unmistakable mark of his animalistic attributes.

✦   Symbolic Importance of Horns

Horns, in various cultural contexts, have deep-rooted symbolic associations. In the ancient world, horns were frequently used as symbols of fertility, virility, and strength—potent life forces that Pan, as a god of the wild, embodies. Horns also signify sovereignty and divinity in several ancient cultures, pointing to Pan's place within the divine hierarchy.

✦   Goat Symbolism and Pagan Traditions

The goat itself holds special significance in many pagan traditions. As one of the earliest domesticated animals, goats have been seen as embodiments of survival and adaptability. Their association with wild and mountainous landscapes echoes Pan's own domain. Moreover, goats were frequently used in fertility rites and seasonal ceremonies, reflecting Pan's connection to nature's cyclical processes.

✧　　Pan in Ecospirituality

From the perspective of ecospirituality, which explores the spiritual connections between humans and the natural world, Pan's caprine features can be seen as an embodiment of nature's untamed vitality. His horns and goat legs symbolise the unbroken, primal connection between the divine and the raw, untamed aspects of nature.

✧　　Implication for Wiccan and Neo-pagan Interpretations

In the modern context, the Wiccan and Neo-pagan interpretations of Pan emphasise his caprine aspects to highlight his links to fertility, raw sexual energy, abundance, and the unrestrained forces of nature. This focus offers a fresh perspective on the symbolism of Pan's goat-like attributes, aligning them with themes of liberation, joyous self-expression, and alignment with natural cycles.

✧　　Pan's Caprine Features: A Summary

Pan's goat-like attributes, particularly his horns, serve as profound symbols, representing not just his wilderness domain but also various themes of fertility, strength, and virility. They underscore the link between the earthly and the divine, reflecting the primal forces that drive life. These caprine features deepen our understanding of Pan as an entity embodying the untamed and the primal, an ambassador of the wild in the realm of the gods, and further emphasise his unique position in Greek mythology. Therefore, a careful study of these symbolic representations allows for a broader understanding of Pan's persona and the cultural context that shaped it.

Portrayal of Age

While many Greek gods are portrayed in the flush of eternal youth, Pan is often depicted as a mature man, occasionally even with the hint of age—another notable deviation from conventional divine representation. This mature depiction may link to themes of wisdom associated with age, perhaps suggesting a deep, innate knowledge of the natural world and its cycles.

In the vast repertoire of Greek mythology, immortality often translates into a representation of eternal youth among the deities. In striking contrast to this norm,

Pan is consistently portrayed as a mature figure, sometimes even hinting at an advanced age. This peculiarity in Pan's depiction is significant, and it prompts us to delve deeper into the symbolism and cultural interpretations associated with this mature representation.

✧   Detailed Description of Pan's Age in Art

A careful examination of Pan's portrayals in Greek and Roman artwork reveals a deity not captured in the bloom of youth, as is typical for the Olympian gods. Instead, Pan is depicted as a mature man, his features often etched with lines that hint at the passage of time. His visage is typically adorned with a thick beard, further enhancing his mature appearance.

✧   Symbolism of Maturity and Age

Age in the classical world was associated with wisdom and experience, carrying the weight of knowledge amassed over time. Pan's mature depiction could thus be linked to a deeper, innate understanding of the natural world, its processes and cycles, far beyond superficial beauty and ephemeral youth. In this regard, Pan may embody the wisdom of the wild—an intuitive, primal understanding of life's rhythms and the ebb and flow of nature's myriad cycles.

✧   Shamanistic Interpretation

Drawing parallels with shamanistic traditions, Pan's mature portrayal can also signify the archetype of the wise elder or the shaman, a mediator between the physical and spiritual realms. Shamans, like Pan, often inhabit liminal spaces and carry the wisdom of both worlds. Pan's advanced age might symbolise his long-standing communion with natural and spiritual elements, reflecting a shaman-like mastery over the secrets of the natural world.

✧   Implications for Ecospirituality and Magic in Ancient Greece

From an ecospirituality perspective, the wisdom attributed to Pan through his mature depiction emphasises the deep respect and reverence for the natural world's inherent wisdom. Similarly, in the context of ancient Greek magic practices, an aged Pan might symbolise the acquisition of arcane knowledge and secrets of the earth, positioning him as a deity with profound esoteric associations.

✧   Neo-Pagan and Wiccan Interpretations

Within the neo-pagan and Wiccan interpretations, Pan's age is often seen as a testament to his status as the 'Horned God,' a deity of nature, wilderness, and the life cycle. This characterisation aligns with the depiction of Pan as a mature, even aged figure, symbolising the full cycle of life, acknowledging not just birth and growth but also maturity and the inevitable approach of death.

✧   Pan's Age Depiction: A Summary

The portrayal of Pan as a mature figure, in contrast to the youthful depictions of many Greek gods, adds another layer of complexity to his characterisation. His age suggests a deep, abiding connection to the rhythms of the natural world, the wisdom of the wild, and the understanding of life's cyclical nature. This aspect of Pan's depiction provides further insight into his unique role in Greek mythology and his enduring relevance in contemporary spiritual and ecological discourse.

The Syrinx

One of Pan's most emblematic attributes is the Syrinx, or Pan flute. This instrument, fashioned from reeds of different lengths, has its origins in a myth where Pan pursued the nymph Syrinx, who transformed into reeds to escape his advances. Pan's association with the Syrinx, therefore, does not merely reinforce his musical inclinations but also serves as a symbol of his unrequited desires and his connection with the natural world.

The syrinx, or Pan flute, is a crucial element in the iconography of Pan, reflecting multifaceted aspects of his character and narrative. It is more than a mere musical instrument; it is imbued with layers of symbolism that narrate a myth, express Pan's passions, and exemplify his profound connection with the natural world.

✧   The Syrinx in Art and Literature

Depictions of Pan often show him holding or playing a syrinx, a set of hollow reed pipes of varying lengths. The instrument is intimately associated with him and serves as a reliable visual identifier in Greek and Roman art. In literature, the syrinx appears in various myths and pastoral poems, further solidifying its relationship with Pan.

✧   Origins of the Syrinx: The Myth of Pan and Syrinx

The syrinx is entrenched in mythological narrative. The story of its origin revolves around Pan's pursuit of the nymph Syrinx, who sought to evade his advances. She was transformed into reeds by her sisters or river nymphs, depending on the version of the tale. When the wind blew through the reeds, they produced a melancholic sound that captivated Pan. Unable to distinguish Syrinx from among the reeds, he gathered some of various lengths and bound them together to create the first syrinx. Thus, the instrument serves as a symbol of Pan's unrequited love and longing for Syrinx.

✧　　Symbolism and Associations of the Syrinx

Beyond its mythic origin, the syrinx also symbolizes Pan's harmonious relationship with the natural world. Crafted from reeds, the syrinx embodies the wild, untamed landscapes that Pan inhabits and rules over. It signifies his ability to create harmony from the elements of nature, highlighting his role as a pastoral deity and his domain over shepherds and flocks.

The haunting music produced by the syrinx, melancholic and enchanting, further mirrors Pan's multifaceted nature. It is reflective of his joy and hedonism, as well as his capacity to instil panic and fear.

✧　　Interpretations in Neo-Paganism, Wicca, and Shamanism

In Neo-Pagan, Wiccan, and Shamanistic traditions, the syrinx takes on additional interpretations. It is viewed as a tool for invoking elemental spirits, particularly of air and earth, the wind being the breath that gives voice to the reeds, grounded in the earth. As such, it becomes an instrument of magic and ritual, symbolizing communication with the natural and spiritual realms.

✧　　Influence on Ecospirituality and Herbalism

From an ecospiritual perspective, the syrinx, made from natural materials and producing music that echoes nature's sounds, epitomizes the deep connection between humanity and the environment. Similarly, in the realm of herbalism, the reeds used in the syrinx's creation represent adaptability and survival, linking back to Pan's association with the resilience of nature.

✧　　The Syrinx in Pan's Iconography: A Summary

The syrinx, as part of Pan's iconography, provides a potent symbol layered with meaning. Its narrative origin reveals a tale of desire and transformation, while its form and function speak of harmony with nature and the music of the wild. Whether viewed from a traditional mythological perspective or through the lens of modern spiritual and ecological practices, the syrinx is an essential key to understanding the complexities of Pan's character and cultural significance.

The Shepherd's Crook

Another common emblem found in depictions of Pan is the shepherd's crook, symbolising his role as a pastoral god. This emblem underlines Pan's connection with shepherds and the rustic life, reaffirming his place as a protector of livestock and patron of the countryside.

The shepherd's crook is an emblem of considerable significance in the iconography of Pan. This object, a common tool for shepherds in ancient Greece and beyond, enhances Pan's role as a pastoral deity and underscores his connection to the rustic life.

> ✧ Depictions of the Shepherd's Crook

In ancient Greek and Roman art, Pan is often depicted holding a shepherd's crook—a staff with a hooked end. The object serves as a visual identifier for his pastoral nature. The shepherd's crook appears in various forms, from simple wooden staves to more ornate depictions encrusted with jewels or made of precious metals in later periods, mirroring societal changes and evolving artistic styles.

> ✧ Symbolism of the Shepherd's Crook

As a symbol, the shepherd's crook underscores Pan's status as a protector of shepherds and their flocks. The crook itself is a tool used by shepherds to manage and protect their sheep, allowing them to guide lost sheep back to the fold or to defend the flock from predators. Its presence in depictions of Pan reinforces his association with these pastoral duties, further grounding his image in the realm of the rustic and the wild.

> ✧ The Shepherd's Crook in Context of Pan's Nature

The pastoral aspect of Pan's nature, represented by the shepherd's crook, creates an interesting contrast to his wild, untamed side. This tool of control and protection juxtaposes his chaotic aspects, providing a balanced image of a god who personifies both the untamed wilderness and the managed pastoral landscapes.

✧   Interpretations in Neo-Paganism and Ecospirituality

In modern spiritual traditions, including Wicca and Neo-Paganism, the shepherd's crook often symbolizes guidance and protection, linking back to its original function. It can also represent leadership and the responsibility of leading others with care and wisdom, mirroring the role of Pan as a guide in the wilderness.

From an ecospiritual perspective, the shepherd's crook, a tool crafted from the materials of the Earth, emphasizes humanity's reliance on nature for survival and well-being. This reading aligns well with Pan's character as a figure representing a harmonious, albeit raw and untamed, relationship with the natural world.

✧   The Shepherd's Crook in Pan's Iconography: A Summary

In the intricate tableau of Pan's iconography, the shepherd's crook offers a potent symbol of his pastoral dimension. It serves to articulate Pan's role as protector and guide, contrasting and balancing his wild and chaotic aspects. Both a practical tool and a symbol of divine function, the shepherd's crook provides a crucial link between the rustic life and the divine world, underscoring the duality inherent in Pan's nature and mythology.

Association with Satyrs

Pan's association with the Satyrs—the riotous, woodland spirits—is another significant aspect of his iconography. They are often portrayed alongside him in scenes of revelry and music, reinforcing Pan's role as a hedonistic deity of the wilds, untamed by civilised norms.

Pan's association with the Satyrs, the hedonistic and often debauched woodland spirits, forms a significant aspect of his iconography, contributing to his overall image as a wild and unpredictable deity. The satyrs, like Pan, embody the spirit of the untamed wilderness, the love for music, and the embrace of sensual pleasures.

✧   Satyrs in Classical Mythology and Art

Satyrs in Greek mythology are often portrayed as companions of Dionysus, the god of wine, fertility, and ecstasy. In visual representations, they are usually depicted as half-human, half-beast, with equine tails and ears, and sometimes with similar goat-like features to Pan, highlighting their theriomorphic nature. Satyrs are renowned for their love of music, dance, wine, and sexual pursuits, elements that align them closely with Pan's character.

✧   The Iconography of Pan and Satyrs

Satyrs frequently feature in scenes alongside Pan, often participating in activities reflective of their shared wild and hedonistic attributes, such as music-making, dancing, and drinking. They appear as members of Pan's retinue, reinforcing his status as a leader of the wild aspects of nature. Scenes featuring Pan and satyrs reveling together not only emphasise the wild, joyous, and hedonistic aspects of these characters but also serve to accentuate Pan's exceptional status as a deity who, unlike other Olympians, freely mingles with these lower-class deities or spirits.

✧   The Symbolic Significance of Satyrs in Pan's Myths

The presence of satyrs in Pan's myths and iconography intensifies his connection with the wild and chaotic facets of nature. Their hedonistic and untamed behaviours align with Pan's own tendencies, offering a mirror through which we can explore the complex character of this pastoral god. They underscore themes of unbridled joy, primal lust, raw emotion, and the power of music, elements inherent in Pan's persona.

✧   Pan, Satyrs and the Wilderness in the Context of Neo-Paganism

In modern neo-pagan traditions, the image of Pan and his satyr companions are often used to represent the untamed forces of nature and the unapologetic pursuit of life's pleasures. They serve as reminders of the wild, primal energy within us all, and the importance of music, dance, and revelry in celebrating life and connecting with the natural world.

✧   The Association of Pan with Satyrs: A Summary

The association of Pan with the satyrs serves as a potent symbol of his wild, chaotic, and hedonistic nature. It reflects his status as a deity of the wilderness, the untamed, and the pastoral. The presence of satyrs in Pan's iconography and myths deepens our understanding of his character, emphasising his raw and primal energy, his music, his lust, and his unapologetic delight in life's pleasures. In essence, the relationship between Pan and the satyrs provides a fascinating glimpse into the complex, multifaceted persona of this unique Greek deity.

Connection with Nymphs

Images of Pan in the company of nymphs are also prevalent in ancient art, reflecting his erotic aspect and his interaction with these nature spirits. These depictions highlight the underlying themes of desire, pursuit, and occasionally, evasion—a dynamic reflective of Pan's unfettered, natural forces, and their interplay with the broader ecosystem.

Pan's frequent association with nymphs, the divine spirits of nature in ancient Greek mythology, is a prominent feature of his iconography. This relationship, often portrayed in artistic and literary representations, embodies not only Pan's erotic aspect, but also his integral connection to the natural world, delineating the complex interplay of desire, pursuit, and evasion that unfolds within these interactions.

✦　Nymphs in Greek Mythology and Art

Nymphs in Greek mythology are female nature spirits often associated with specific localities such as woods, mountains, streams, and meadows. They embody the beauty, fertility, and wildness of the natural world, and like Pan, exist on the periphery of the divine and human realms. In visual art, they are typically portrayed as young, beautiful maidens, often observed in the company of deities associated with nature and wilderness.

✦　Pan and Nymphs in Classical Iconography

In visual representations, Pan is often portrayed amidst nymphs, emphasizing his robust sexual nature and his deep connection with the wilderness. These depictions often involve scenes of pursuit, reflecting the nature of Pan's interactions with these spirits—charged with desire, yet often met with evasion. This dynamic reflects Pan's raw, untamed desires and their interplay with the natural world.

✦　Symbolic Interpretations of Pan's Interactions with Nymphs

The recurrent narrative of pursuit and evasion between Pan and the nymphs symbolizes the unpredictable, often chaotic, nature of primal desires. Moreover, it serves as a metaphor for the intricate relationships within ecosystems, where the dynamic of pursuit and evasion is a fundamental principle of survival. In a broader perspective, these depictions resonate with the perennial human experiences of desire and rejection, love and loss.

✦　Pan and Nymphs in Modern Interpretations

Modern reinterpretations, such as in neo-pagan traditions, often view Pan's interaction with nymphs symbolically, representing the wild, untamed aspects of our nature and the natural world. They remind us of the primal forces within us, the intrinsic link between desire and freedom, and our integral connection with the earth and its cycles.

✧   Pan's Connection with Nymphs: A Summary

Pan's association with nymphs in iconographic representations emphasizes his wild, sexual nature and his intrinsic connection with the natural world. These scenes, often filled with desire, pursuit, and evasion, echo the ebb and flow of life's forces, the primal urges that drive existence, and the complex dance of relationships within the broader ecosystem. In essence, Pan's connection with nymphs in his iconography offers profound insights into understanding the multifaceted character of this intriguing Greek deity.

Implications of Pan's Iconography

In conclusion, the visual representation of Pan and the symbols associated with him paint a compelling portrait of this deity. From his hybrid form to his connection with the Syrinx, every attribute carries significant implications, reinforcing and elaborating upon Pan's multifaceted character and his role within the Greek pantheon. The exploration of Pan's iconography also underscores the broader thematic interplay between civilisation and wilderness, highlighting the boundaries and intersections of these two spheres as perceived in the ancient Greek worldview.

Worship and cult of Pan: Sanctuaries, rituals, and festivals

The worship of Pan, as with any deity of the ancient Greek pantheon, is a multifaceted aspect encompassing various elements such as sanctuaries, rituals, and festivals. This chapter will delve into the specifics of these components, providing an in-depth understanding of the practices associated with the worship of Pan.

Sanctuaries of Pan

One of the key locations of Pan's worship was the Arcadian region in Greece, where his primary sanctuary was located at the foot of the Lycaeus mountain. Here, the natural setting - a cavernous landscape adorned with lush vegetation - accentuated Pan's affinity with the wilderness. Temples dedicated to Pan were not grand, marbled edifices like those dedicated to Olympian gods but were often grottoes, caves, or other naturally occurring structures. In Athens, the sanctuary of Pan was established in a cave on the northwestern slope of the Acropolis, further underscoring his connection with rustic, wild spaces.

Pan's sanctuaries hold an eminent position in the realm of his worship, being primary locations of religious activity and tribute. These sacred sites, commonly placed in rustic settings, embody Pan's affinity with the wild, exhibiting both his primal nature and the ancients' perception of the divine in relation to the natural world.

✧   The Arcadian Sanctuary

One of Pan's key sanctuaries was nestled in the Arcadian region in Greece, specifically at the base of Mount Lycaeus. This location, known as one of the oldest and most revered of the Pan cult centers, boasts a landscape that is markedly cavernous and verdant. The naturalness of this environment served to highlight the deity's quintessential nature as a wilderness god. It is not without reason that Pan's sanctuary was placed here, for Arcadia itself is deeply tied to the wilderness, both in topography and cultural reputation. The relationship between the Arcadian sanctuary and Pan's rustic disposition is a testament to the ancient Greeks' understanding of the unity of the divine and natural realms, both of which are bound by an inherent, pervasive sacredness.

✧   The Athenian Sanctuary

In contrast to the rural landscape of Arcadia, the bustling city of Athens also housed a sanctuary dedicated to Pan. This sanctuary, rather than being an elaborate temple of marble and stone like those of the Olympian gods, was situated in a cave on the northwestern slope of the Acropolis. The cave's location juxtaposed against the magnificent Acropolis provides a striking emblem of Pan's liminal status, bridging the wild with the civilised, the rustic with the urban. The choice of a cave as a sanctuary site further underscores Pan's integral connection with the wild and untamed, a place that, despite its position in the heart of a metropolis, was a clear nod to the deity's untamed and rustic nature.

✧   Other Pan Sanctuaries

Pan's sanctuaries were not confined to these two notable locations. Across Greece, there were various sites where Pan was worshipped, from Delphi to Marathon. These sites, while geographically dispersed, shared the common trait of being tied to the natural landscape. Caves, springs, and groves were among the common places where Pan was venerated, reaffirming the significant connection between the deity and the wild.

✧   Architectural and Symbolic Aspects

Interestingly, these sanctuaries were often marked by simplicity, contrasting with the grandiosity of other godly edifices. The choice to celebrate Pan in such natural settings might have been influenced by the desire to preserve the raw, unadulterated aspects of the natural world that Pan embodied. The architectural simplicity of Pan's sanctuaries, paradoxically, serves to communicate a powerful symbolic message about Pan's essence, his sphere of influence, and the way in which the Greeks understood and interacted with the divine.

Conclusion

In conclusion, an exploration of Pan's sanctuaries, their location, structure, and symbolic implications, offers a profound insight into Pan's divine profile as well as ancient Greek religious practices. These sanctuaries, placed within the bosom of nature, not only serve to reinforce Pan's image as the god of the wild but also provide a snapshot of the intricate nexus between the divine, the natural, and the human as conceived by the ancient Greeks.

Rituals and Offerings

Rituals in honor of Pan involved various offerings, the nature of which often reflected the deity's pastoral connections. Incense, fruits, honey, and even small cakes called 'panspermia', which were made from a mixture of grains and pulses, were common offerings. Animal sacrifices were also prevalent, primarily involving livestock such as goats and sheep. Additionally, the practice of 'truphē', or the fattening of animals for sacrifice, was linked to the worship of Pan, reinforcing his role as a pastoral deity. Ritual dances and music, especially the playing of reed pipes or the Syrinx, were also integral aspects of Pan's worship, echoing his mythological association with merriment and music.

Rituals and offerings made in Pan's honour held immense significance in his worship, shedding light on the deity's pastoral characteristics, his connection with the wilderness, and his role as a divine force of merriment. These practices also reflect broader themes prevalent in ancient Greek religion, from the nature of sacrificial offerings to the symbolic potency of music and dance.

✧ Offerings of Produce

As the god associated with rustic abundance and pastoral wealth, Pan's rituals often involved the offering of produce reflective of his sphere. These offerings commonly comprised incense, fruits, and honey, emblematic of nature's bounty. The gifting of these items served as an act of reciprocity, thanking Pan for the successful harvest and continued fertility of the lands.

Particularly noteworthy is the offering of small cakes known as 'panspermia'. These cakes were concocted from an amalgamation of different grains and pulses, signifying a literal and symbolic harvest. The 'panspermia' offerings thus acted as a microcosm of the agricultural abundance overseen by Pan, making them apt tributes to his divine oversight of the rustic sphere.

✧   Animal Sacrifices

Alongside these more pastoral offerings, the worship of Pan frequently encompassed the practice of animal sacrifice, with livestock such as goats and sheep playing a prominent role. Given Pan's iconographic representation as a half-goat deity and his significant links to shepherding, the choice of these particular animals for sacrifice establishes a symbolic resonance.

Additionally, the practice of 'truphē', or the ritual fattening of animals for sacrifice, was closely tied to Pan's worship. This practice once again highlights Pan's association with the pastoral realm and the prosperous yield it symbolizes.

✧   Ritual Music and Dance

Music and dance, inherent in the majority of ancient Greek religious rites, held a particular significance in Pan's worship, resonating with his mythological association with joyous music and revelry. The playing of the reed pipe, or Syrinx—Pan's musical instrument par excellence—formed a cornerstone of these rituals.

The act of making music in Pan's honour served not only as an offering but also as a symbolic reenactment of the deity's own mythical actions. The auditory aspect of this tribute, the captivating melody produced by the Syrinx, adds an additional layer of sensory engagement, immersing the worshippers in an all-encompassing spiritual experience.

Conclusion

In summary, the varied rituals and offerings dedicated to Pan offer a multi-dimensional understanding of his worship, amplifying his ties with nature, merriment, and pastoral life. These practices also provide profound insights into the broader spectrum of ancient Greek religious customs, highlighting the importance of symbolic resonance, reciprocity, and sensory engagement in their interaction with the divine. Furthermore, it should be noted that these rituals were not static, but evolved over time, shaping and being shaped by shifting societal norms and religious interpretations.

Festivals

Several festivals were celebrated in honor of Pan, most notably the 'Lupercalia' in Rome, which although dedicated to the Roman deity Lupercus, is thought to have been influenced by the worship of Pan due to the significant overlap in their spheres of influence. The festival involved rites of purification, fertility rites, and a distinctive footrace where young men would run around the city boundaries, striking bystanders with strips of goat hide, believed to confer fertility.

The 'Rural Dionysia' was another festival where Pan was prominently featured. As part of the Dionysiac retinue, Pan was invoked and celebrated during this annual event that celebrated the cultivation of vines.

✧ Lupercalia: An Intersection of Worship

Lupercalia was an archaic festival observed in Rome, traditionally associated with Lupercus, a pastoral god akin to Pan. Notwithstanding its primary affiliation with Lupercus, the Lupercalia bore striking parallels with the rites associated with Pan, suggesting significant cross-cultural influence.

The festival, celebrated on the ides of February, involved elaborate rites of purification and fertility. Commencing with the sacrifice of goats and a dog at the cave of Lupercal (the purported nursing place of Romulus and Remus), the festival was marked by the participation of Luperci—priests of Lupercus. Following the sacrifice, these priests would smear their foreheads with the sacrificial blood, which was subsequently wiped off with wool soaked in milk, eliciting laughter—a detail reminiscent of the merriment associated with Pan.

One of the most distinctive aspects of the Lupercalia was a footrace that ensued post the sacrificial rites. Young men, or Luperci, would run about the city boundaries, striking bystanders—especially women—with strips of goat hide, known as februa. This practice, believed to confer fertility and prevent sterility, was symbolic of the fertility aspect of Pan's and Lupercus' worship.

✧ Rural Dionysia: Celebrating the Vine Cultivation

The Rural Dionysia was an annual event that celebrated the cultivation of vines, which, in the agrarian societies of ancient Greece, was an occasion of significant importance. Pan's association with this festival is indicative of his involvement with the pastoral and the wild, serving as the intermediary between wilderness and cultivated land.

As part of the Dionysiac retinue, Pan was invoked and celebrated during the Rural Dionysia. Given his reputation for merriment and his association with wilderness, his presence complemented the nature of this festival—an event marked by joyous procession, phallic songs, dramatic performances, and a general air of jubilation.

Notably, the Rural Dionysia was also a testament to the reconciliation of opposites: the cultivation of the wild (vineyards) for a product of civilisation (wine), a dynamic that is present in the persona of Pan himself—half wild goat, half civilised man.

Conclusion

In conclusion, the festivals of Lupercalia and Rural Dionysia showcase the multiple dimensions of Pan's worship, whilst also offering insights into how Greco-Roman societies navigated their relationship with nature, fertility, and civilization. The blend of joyous celebration with profound spiritual practices underlines the ancients' capacity to create religious rituals that touched every facet of their lives, from the mundane to the extraordinary, embodying the dichotomy of their existence in the intersection of civilisation and wilderness. As students, you might ponder upon this intricate interplay of opposites and how it reflected in their understanding of divinity. Exercises in the following section invite you to explore this concept further.

Implications and Significance

The various practices associated with the worship and cult of Pan serve to further underline the deity's dual roles as both a rustic, wilderness-associated deity and as a liminal figure straddling the world of humans and the divine. Furthermore, the deeply symbolic nature of the rituals, offerings, and festivals associated with Pan offers valuable insights into the ways in which the ancients perceived and interacted with the natural world, and how they conceptualised the relationships between the divine, the human, and the natural realms.

✧   Pan: A Rustic and Liminal Deity

Pan, in his rustic and wilderness-associated form, represented the unbound aspects of nature and its raw, instinctive forces. This archetype manifested in his various attributes such as his goat-like form, his syrinx, and his residence in Arcadia, a region known for its untamed landscape. In this capacity, Pan was a potent symbol of the wild that existed outside the boundaries of human civilisation, and yet was intrinsic to it.

However, Pan was not only the embodiment of the wilderness, but also served as a liminal deity. He straddled the boundary between the human and the divine world, as well as the intersection between the civilised and the wild. The liminal status of Pan is further exemplified in his physical form, which combines human and animal elements, symbolising a union of civilisation and wilderness. This dichotomy in Pan's character affirms the ancient Greek perception of a complex interrelationship between these spheres of existence.

✧   Interactions with the Natural World

The practices associated with Pan's worship, including rituals, offerings, and festivals, offer invaluable insights into the ancients' relationship with the natural world. Animal sacrifices, the use of natural cave formations as sanctuaries, the celebration of Rural Dionysia to honour the cultivation of vines, and the association of Pan with natural and pastoral elements, all underscore a deep and intrinsic connection between the human and natural realms. It suggests an understanding of coexistence and mutual dependency, an acknowledgment that the cultivation of nature is a process of collaboration and respect, rather than domination.

✧   Relationships between the Divine, Human, and Natural Realms

The cult of Pan allows us to better comprehend the multifaceted relationships between the divine, human, and natural realms in the ancient Greek mindset. As a rustic god of the wild, Pan was not ensconced in the remote heavens but resided amidst nature, and as a consequence, was much closer to the human realm. His worship, often marked by merriment and festivity, embodied a divine-human interaction that was not merely reverential but also partook of camaraderie and joy.

Furthermore, through the symbolism associated with Pan, we discern a worldview that does not segregate the divine, the human, and the natural into isolated categories, but perceives them as interconnected and interdependent. This perception has profound implications, not merely for understanding ancient Greek religion and society, but also for contemporary debates surrounding environmental ethics, anthropocentrism, and the role of spirituality in ecological conservation.

Conclusion

The worship and cult of Pan provide us with a nuanced understanding of ancient Greek beliefs, their perception of the divine and human worlds, and their interaction with nature. Pan, as a deity, encompasses and celebrates contrasts—wilderness and civilisation, merriment and terror, human and divine, thereby epitomising the multifaceted nature of existence. In comprehending these aspects, students are encouraged to recognise the complexity of the ancient worldview and its relevance to the pressing ecological and ethical debates of our contemporary world.

Pan's influence on the Greek perception of wilderness and pastoral landscapes

Pan, the rustic god, plays a pivotal role in the conceptualisation of wilderness and pastoral landscapes in the ancient Greek mindset. The Arcadian deity's attributes and the practices of his cult highlight the deep interconnections between nature, society, and the divine as conceived by the ancient Greeks, thereby providing significant insights into their worldviews.

The Wilderness and Pan

Wilderness, in the ancient Greek perspective, was not merely an unchartered physical realm, but also a conceptual space representing the untamed and unpredictable aspects of nature and existence. Pan, the deity with the torso of a man and the lower body of a goat, was a perfect embodiment of this wilderness. His hybrid form, neither fully human nor fully animal, suggested a being who exists at the periphery of the human world, yet is deeply integral to it.

In the worship and mythology associated with Pan, the wilderness was not seen as a hostile or menacing entity, but a necessary contrast to civilised life. Pan's character, imbued with merriment and pastoral peace on the one hand, and irrational fear ('panic') on the other, encapsulated the dual aspects of the wild – its serenity and its unpredictability. Thus, through Pan, the Greeks personified and engaged with the wilderness, recognising its essential role in their existence.

✧   The Wilderness in the Ancient Greek Perspective

To appreciate the influence of Pan on the ancient Greek perception of the wilderness, it is imperative to first consider what the term "wilderness" meant within this cultural context. Wilderness, as understood by the Greeks, was not merely defined by geographical and topographical features. It encompassed an abstract plane, representative of a profound metaphysical realm that was unfettered by human intrusion. This wilderness constituted the untamed and unpredictable facets of existence, a space where the rational and structured sensibilities of civilisation receded to make way for the raw, natural order of life.

✧   Pan - Embodiment of the Wilderness

Within this context, Pan, with his goat-like lower body and human upper form, was an embodiment of the wilderness. His hybrid form underscored his liminality, serving as a potent symbol of a creature that was neither wholly human nor wholly beast, but a composite of both. Pan's physical attributes designated him as a being perched on the periphery of the human world while being deeply woven into its fabric, creating a bridge between humanity and the wilderness.

His dwelling places, too, were indicative of his connection to the wilderness. As established, Pan's sanctuaries were not built within city limits but rather in caves, grottoes, and the foothills of mountains, places intrinsically associated with the wild. Thus, Pan represented a conduit between the human and natural worlds, and his spaces were points of interaction where individuals could engage with the wilderness.

✧   Mythology and Worship: Engaging with the Wilderness through Pan

Pan's character, as depicted in myth and worship, allowed the ancient Greeks to interact with the wilderness on a symbolic level. Despite his wild and untamed nature, Pan was not portrayed as a menacing figure. Rather, he was seen as embodying an essential aspect of existence that offered a necessary counterpoint to the constraints of civilised life.

On the one hand, Pan was known for his merriment, his music, and his pastoral tranquillity, encapsulating the serene and peaceful facets of the wild. He was a god to be celebrated and enjoyed, one who invoked the inherent joy of living in harmony with nature.

On the other hand, Pan was also associated with a unique form of fear, referred to as 'panic'. This fear, characterised as a sudden, irrational terror that could seize individuals without warning, symbolised the unpredictable and sometimes unnerving elements of the wild. This duality, tranquillity, and fear together embodied the multifaceted essence of the wilderness.

In the worship of Pan, the Greeks enacted a symbolic dialogue with the wilderness, negotiating its unpredictable and chaotic elements while embracing its peaceful and nourishing facets. Through the medium of Pan, they acknowledged and embraced the wilderness, not as a hostile, alien realm, but as an integral, necessary part of their world, thus crafting a nuanced and complex relationship with the natural world around them.

This comprehensive understanding of Pan's relation to the wilderness allows for a deeper appreciation of his role and offers a broader framework to study the intersection of Greek society, religion, and the environment. The interface of these elements, represented through the figure of Pan, offers valuable insights into the ancient Greek worldview, enriching our understanding of their culture and their perception of the wilderness.

The Pastoral Landscape and Pan

Pastoral landscapes represented the idyllic, peaceful coexistence of humans and nature. These landscapes were spaces where the rigorous demarcations between the civilised and the wild blurred into a harmonious blend. As a pastoral deity, Pan personified this symbiosis. He was the god of shepherds and flocks, of mountainous wilds and lush, green meadows - spaces that were as much human as they were natural.

The pastoral landscape, symbolised by Pan, embodied the ancient Greek ideal of 'Golden Age' – a time of harmony between humans and nature. Pan's music, often portrayed in art and literature as a symbol of unity and peace, resonated with the tranquillity and harmony that characterised this pastoral ideal.

✧   The Pastoral Landscape in the Ancient Greek Perspective

The ancient Greeks held a distinctive perception of pastoral landscapes, envisioning them as utopian spaces that portrayed a peaceful coexistence between humans and nature. These landscapes constituted a realm where the rigorous dichotomy of civilised and wild blurred into a harmonious synthesis, thereby encapsulating the ideal balance of humanity's habitation with the natural world.

Pastoral landscapes, thus, were more than mere physical spaces - they were mental constructs and philosophical ideals, providing a prototype of ecological harmony and an optimal state of existence. Within these spaces, humans, while maintaining their rural livelihoods, coexisted and interacted with nature without disrupting its intrinsic order.

✧   Pan - The Personification of Pastoral Landscape

Pan, as a pastoral deity, emerged as the personification of this idyllic union between humans and the natural environment. His traditional role as the god of shepherds, goats, and sheep, entrenched him within the fabric of rural life. Simultaneously, his affinity for the wild, signified by his association with mountainous wilds, caves, and verdant meadows, underscored his connection to the natural world.

This dual association, with both human pastoral activity and the untrammeled wild, rendered Pan the symbolic manifestation of the pastoral landscape. He was a figure that stood at the crossroads of the human and natural domains, embodying their potential for harmonious coexistence.

Pan, Music, and the Pastoral Ideal

Further, the association of Pan with music, specifically the syrinx or panpipes, served as an eloquent symbol of unity and peace. The music of Pan, often depicted in visual and literary art forms, was conceived as an auditory expression of the tranquillity and harmony intrinsic to the pastoral ideal. The enchanting melodies from Pan's pipes were said to soothe both wild animals and humans, uniting them in a shared experience of auditory pleasure, thereby furthering the symbiotic spirit of the pastoral landscape.

The pastoral ideal represented by Pan was reminiscent of the Greek mythological concept of the 'Golden Age.' This was a primordial era of peace and abundance, a time when humans and nature were envisaged as existing in a state of perfect harmony, without strife or struggle for dominance. Through Pan, this pastoral 'Golden Age' found its emblem, facilitating an understanding of the delicate balance between human activity and the preservation of the natural world.

In conclusion, Pan's connection with the pastoral landscape illuminates an essential aspect of Greek cultural and religious ethos. His role as a mediator between the human and the natural, civilised and wild, reveals the Greek appreciation for harmony and balance, and their understanding of humanity's place within the larger ecological system. This perspective, emblematised in the figure of Pan, offers a profound insight into the Greek vision of a sustainable and harmonious coexistence with nature. It underscores the importance of this vision in their cultural, religious, and societal paradigms.

The Influence of Pan on Greek Environmental Ethos

Pan's character and attributes impacted the Greek perception of wilderness and pastoral landscapes, shaping their interactions with the natural environment. The Pan-inspired ethos recognised the value of wilderness not merely as a resource to be exploited but as an essential component of existence that needed to be engaged with, respected, and preserved. The pastoral ideal propagated by Pan encouraged sustainable practices and cohabitation, fostering an inherent conservationist perspective.

✧ The Wilderness, Pastoral Landscape, and Greek Environmental Ethos

The attributes and character of Pan significantly influenced the development of the Greek environmental ethos. The wilderness, as envisaged through the prism of Pan's character, was not merely a chaotic, untamed space but an essential facet of the natural world, possessing its own intrinsic value and beauty. This perspective helped cultivate an appreciation for the wilderness in the Greek consciousness, shaping their interactions with the natural world in a manner marked by respect, curiosity, and a sense of belonging.

Simultaneously, the pastoral landscapes, often symbolised by Pan, were envisaged as serene, harmonious spaces where humans and nature coexisted symbiotically. This vision nurtured a more sustainable approach to natural resources, with practices guided by the principles of balance, moderation, and respect for the natural order.

✧ Pan - Inspiring a Conservationist Perspective

The various narratives, rituals, and iconography associated with Pan, therefore, fostered an inherent conservationist perspective. This perspective saw the environment not merely as a resource to be exploited but as an integral component of existence. This ecological consciousness encouraged a sense of stewardship, where the objective was not only to utilise natural resources for human needs but also to ensure their preservation and regeneration.

✧ Implications of Pan's Influence on Greek Environmental Ethos

In sum, the influence of Pan, a deity intrinsically tied to both the wilderness and the pastoral landscapes, cultivated a distinctive environmental ethos in ancient Greece. His sphere of influence, embracing both the rustic wilderness and the bucolic pastoral realm, symbolised the ideal equilibrium between humans and the environment.

The importance of maintaining this balance became a central tenet of the Greek environmental ethos, promoting a lifestyle that, while making use of the gifts of nature, sought to do so in a manner that preserved and respected the natural world. This principle resonates with modern-day concepts of sustainability and ecological balance, demonstrating the enduring relevance of the lessons gleaned from the ancient worship and mythology of Pan.

It is noteworthy to consider how this ecological consciousness, which was so deeply woven into the fabric of Greek religious and cultural practices, could potentially offer a lens through which to view contemporary environmental challenges. Reflecting upon the ancient Greek environmental ethos inspired by Pan might guide us towards fostering a more sustainable and respectful relationship with the environment in our current times.

Critiques and Counterarguments

While Pan's influence on Greek perceptions of nature is evident, it is crucial not to oversimplify these interactions or view them through an idealised lens. Other factors, including socio-economic dynamics, other religious and cultural beliefs, and the harsh realities of survival and expansion, often led to practices that were at odds with the harmonious model represented by Pan.

The cult of Pan, while acknowledging the interconnectedness of the human and natural realms, also reinforced the hierarchy between them, with humans often seen as superior. For instance, the practice of animal sacrifice, a significant part of Pan's worship, reflects this anthropocentric worldview.

✦　Balancing Perspectives: The Influence of Socio-economic Dynamics and Other Religious Beliefs

In analysing Pan's influence on Greek perceptions of wilderness and pastoral landscapes, it is crucial to balance the idealised pastoral vision with the realities of ancient Greek society. Socio-economic dynamics, including the necessity of agriculture, hunting, and expansion for survival and prosperity, often dictated interactions with the natural world. Even as Pan's cult celebrated the harmony between human and nature, these realities invariably led to exploitation of the environment, sometimes on a significant scale.

Similarly, the Greek pantheon was a complex network of deities, each with their own spheres of influence. While Pan's domain was largely pastoral and wilderness, other deities like Demeter and Dionysus had strong associations with agriculture and cultivation - realms that necessitated the taming of the wild for human purposes. The influence of these and other deities would also shape the Greek relationship with the natural world, sometimes in ways that were incongruous with the ideals embodied by Pan.

✧ Anthropocentrism in Pan Worship

It is also noteworthy to mention that the worship of Pan, while emphasising harmony with nature, also reinforced an anthropocentric worldview. Humans were the central agents in the rituals and practices associated with Pan's cult, indicating a belief in human superiority or control over nature.

The practice of animal sacrifice, a significant part of Pan's worship, is an example of this perspective. Even as Pan's iconography and narratives emphasised symbiosis, the act of sacrifice underscored human dominance over animals, using them as offerings to please the divine.

✧ Re-evaluating the Greek Environmental Ethos

Thus, while the influence of Pan did encourage a sense of respect and appreciation for the wilderness and pastoral landscapes, it is critical to place this within a broader context that also recognises the more complex and occasionally contradictory aspects of Greek interactions with the environment. To do so allows for a more nuanced understanding of the ancient Greek environmental ethos and highlights the multifaceted nature of human-environment relationships.

Reflecting on these critiques and counterarguments does not diminish the importance of Pan's role in shaping the Greek perception of the wilderness and pastoral landscapes. Rather, it provides a more comprehensive and realistic picture of the complexities involved in the human-nature dynamics in ancient Greek society. In doing so, it reminds us that environmental ethics is not a monolithic concept but a complex field shaped by a myriad of factors and perspectives.

Conclusion

The figure of Pan thus presents a complex and nuanced lens through which to examine the ancient Greek perception of wilderness and pastoral landscapes. While acknowledging the critical influences and the ideal of harmonious coexistence that Pan represents, it is also vital to consider the broader socio-cultural context, conflicting practices, and inherent contradictions that marked the human-nature dynamics in ancient Greece.

As students engage with these complexities, they are encouraged not only to gain an understanding of ancient Greek beliefs but also to critically evaluate contemporary attitudes towards the environment and our role within it. The intersection of mythology, environmental perception, and conservation ethics presents a rich field of study with the potential for generating insightful discussions and critical thinking.

Discussion on Pan's roles as a deity of fertility, music, and panic

As a pastoral deity, Pan is indelibly associated with the concept of fertility. Fertility in this context is not solely concerned with procreation, but extends to the fecundity of the earth and its life-sustaining capacities. As the protector of shepherds and their flocks, Pan's connection with fertility was readily apparent in the healthy growth and propagation of livestock under his aegis.

Moreover, the lush wilderness, teeming with life, further reflected Pan's status as a fertility god. Pan's fertility aspect also extended to his role in Dionysiac rites, known for their fertility connotations. In art and literature, Pan is often depicted in sexually suggestive poses, highlighting his association with carnal fertility.

From an agricultural perspective, Pan's relationship with fertility bears a close connection with the vital cycle of growth and harvest. Despite his primary association with wilderness, Pan's influence spilled over to the cultivated land, reinforcing the blurred demarcation between the pastoral and the agricultural in ancient Greek society.

Pan, Music and Merriment: Cultural and Aesthetic Dimensions

Music forms a central theme in the mythos and cult of Pan, resonating with his vivacious and merry nature. Pan was credited with the invention of the syrinx, or panpipes, a musical instrument fashioned from reeds. The enchanting melodies played on this instrument were believed to bring joy, instigate dance, and even charm the natural world into a harmonious rhythm.

Pan's association with music and merriment fostered an aesthetics of harmony and accord, encapsulating the vision of a world in sync with itself. The universality of this aesthetic vision underscores music's ability to transcend the human realm and resonate with the broader cosmos, thus reflecting an interconnected worldview.

Pan and Panic: Fear, Chaos, and the Wild Unknown

Despite the merriment and harmony that Pan is often associated with, a diametrically opposite aspect forms an integral part of his deity - that of irrational fear or panic. The term 'panic' itself is etymologically linked to Pan, stemming from the Greek 'Panikon Deima'.

This connection between Pan and panic is emblematic of the unpredictable and chaotic aspects of the wilderness, as well as the anxiety that comes with stepping into the unknown. Pan's ability to instigate sudden, groundless fear among travellers, especially in lonely and desolate places, embodies this aspect.

Pan's association with panic, thus, serves as a constant reminder of the dual nature of the wild - tranquil yet unpredictable, beautiful yet terrifying. It represents the delicate balance between the idyllic and the chaotic, between the known and the unknown.

Synthesizing Pan's Multi-faceted Roles

Analyzing Pan as a deity of fertility, music, and panic demonstrates the complex, multi-layered nature of his character. His associations span from the serenity of pastoral landscapes to the unpredictability of the wild, from the joy of music to the fear of the unknown. Pan's character provides a comprehensive lens through which the intricate interplay between humans, the environment, and the divine can be examined.

As a fertility deity, Pan was a symbol of life and sustenance. As a patron of music, he represented harmony and joy. As a harbinger of panic, he epitomized the chaos and fear inherent in the wild. Each of these roles tells us something about how the ancient Greeks perceived and interacted with the world around them, reflecting an array of attitudes and beliefs that ranged from appreciation and love for the natural world, to respect and fear of its unpredictable powers.

Each role of Pan is inextricably tied to the others, creating a composite picture of a deity who encapsulates the tension between order and disorder, joy and fear, life and its cessation. In each of these dynamics, we see a deity who personifies the forces of nature in all their awe-inspiring multiplicity.

In conclusion, through a comprehensive exploration of Pan's roles as a deity of fertility, music, and panic, we not only gain insight into the multi-dimensional character of this rustic god, but also into the intricate tapestry of cultural, religious, and environmental perceptions that defined ancient Greek society. Pan's deity, therefore, serves as a complex symbol of the interplay between humans, nature, and the divine in the ancient world, offering a nuanced perspective that continues to resonate in contemporary discourse on human-nature relationships.

The Nymphs: Spirits of Nature

In the dense and diverse pantheon of ancient Greek mythology, the nymphs hold a unique place as divine beings intimately tied to nature and the elements. As minor deities or spirits, they represent different aspects of the natural world - springs, rivers, mountains, trees, and more. Their origin is as diverse as the elements they represent, born from the various gods and goddesses of the Greek pantheon.

As denizens of the wilderness, nymphs are often associated with places that were regarded as rich in spirit and beauty, but also potentially perilous. Their role as intermediaries between the divine, human, and natural realms underscores the interconnected worldview prevalent in ancient Greek society.

The Many Forms of Nymphs

Nymphs are characterised by a multiplicity of forms, each tied to a specific aspect of the natural environment. Naiads, for instance, were nymphs of fresh water - fountains, wells, springs, streams, and brooks. Nereids were sea nymphs, daughters of the sea god Nereus. Dryads and Hamadryads were associated with trees and forests, particularly oaks. Oreads presided over mountains and gorges, while Meliae were nymphs of the ash tree, from which mankind was said to have been created.

Each type of nymph was a personification of the vital force of the element they represented, embodying its unique qualities and influences. Nymphs were often depicted as beautiful young maidens, reflecting the ancient Greek association of beauty with goodness and divinity.

The Role and Influence of Nymphs

The nymphs played a crucial role in the everyday life and religious practice of the ancient Greeks. As protectors of specific localities, they were often invoked for their beneficence and propitiated with offerings and rituals. They were believed to have power over fertility, growth, and nourishment, in line with their close association with the life-giving aspects of nature.

At the same time, the nymphs' intimate connection with certain places imbued these locales with a divine presence, thus sanctifying the natural environment. Springs, groves, and caves where nymphs were thought to dwell became places of worship, often marked by an altar or a dedicated sanctuary.

Nymphs in Literature and Art

The nymphs were a popular subject in Greek literature and art, serving as muses to poets and artists. Their representation varied, sometimes depicted as playful and carefree beings, at other times portrayed as elusive and withdrawn. In both cases, their portrayal served to emphasise the intrinsic beauty and mystery of the natural world.

Their frequent appearance in Greek mythology, including in the works of Hesiod and Homer, underscores their cultural significance. They are often portrayed interacting with gods and mortals, featuring in various myths as consorts, companions, or in some cases, adversaries.

Nymphs: Embodiment of the Greek Perception of Nature

The nymphs, in their various forms and roles, exemplify the complex and nuanced Greek perception of nature. As divine embodiments of natural elements, they express an inherent respect and reverence for the environment. Their veneration indicates an awareness of the inherent sacredness of the natural world, the need for its preservation, and the interdependence of all life forms.

Yet, the nymphs also reflect a recognition of the unpredictability and potential danger of the natural world. Their dual nature - beneficial yet capricious - mirrors the ambivalent relationship humans often have with the environment, fluctuating between dependence and fear, between exploitation and conservation.

Through the lens of the nymphs, we can better understand how the ancient Greeks perceived, interacted with, and sought to control their natural environment. Their belief in nymphs reveals a worldview that, while acknowledging the power and independence of nature, also attempts to negotiate and manage this power through ritual and narrative.

Critiques and Counterarguments

However, it would be an oversimplification to view the nymphs solely as benign nature spirits. Many stories describe nymphs as alluring and dangerous, capable of leading men astray or driving them mad. These narratives point to a more complex understanding of the nymphs, revealing societal attitudes about gender, power, and the relationship between humans and the natural world.

Furthermore, the existence of different types of nymphs, each associated with a particular aspect of the environment, suggests a certain level of fragmentation in the

Greeks' understanding of nature. It's worth questioning to what extent this fragmented perception might have influenced their interactions with the environment, and how it reflects broader Greek views about the world and their place in it.

In conclusion, through an in-depth examination of the nymphs in Greek mythology, we not only gain insight into the ways the ancient Greeks personified and engaged with the natural world, but we also gain a better understanding of how these beliefs reflect and shape cultural attitudes towards nature, the divine, and the relationship between them. The nymphs, in their diversity and complexity, offer a rich and multifaceted perspective on ancient Greek environmental ethos and worldview.

Definition and categorisation of nymphs

In the vast tapestry of ancient Greek mythology, nymphs were generally understood as minor female deities associated with natural elements. Etymologically, the term 'nymph' comes from the Greek word 'νύμφη', which means young woman or bride. Unlike major deities, nymphs were typically tied to specific locations or features in nature. They were considered to be both immortal and ageless, often portrayed as beautiful young maidens, reflecting Greek ideals of beauty and femininity.

Nymphs held a complex role within the Greek pantheon. They were not worshipped in the same manner as the major Olympian gods, but their presence in the landscape of Greek mythology was ubiquitous and significant. As spirits of nature, nymphs were believed to inhabit, animate, and personify different facets of the natural world, from woodland groves and mountain peaks to flowing rivers and deep caverns.

Categorisation of Nymphs

The nymphs were not a monolithic group but were categorised into various types based on the particular element of nature they were associated with. This categorisation mirrored the ancient Greeks' intricate understanding of the natural world and their desire to give a divine aspect to each of its components.

> ✧　Water Nymphs

Water nymphs, commonly known as Naiads, inhabited fresh water sources such as springs, rivers, fountains, lakes, and marshes. Their existence was intrinsically tied to their water body, which they were believed to control and protect. Examples of Naiads include the Pegaeae (spring nymphs), the Potameides (river nymphs), and the Limnades or Limnatides (lake nymphs).

Oceanids and Nereids were nymphs of the sea, with the former representing the larger body of the ocean, while the latter were associated with the more specific Mediterranean Sea.

A. Naiads

The Naiads, often regarded as the quintessential water nymphs, were associated with fresh water bodies - springs, rivers, fountains, lakes, and marshes. These water bodies were essential to the life-sustaining cycles of the ancient Greek landscape, providing the vital resources of drinking water and irrigation for agriculture. Consequently, the Naiads were revered for their power to control and protect these invaluable water sources.

Different types of Naiads were assigned to the diverse water bodies. Pegaeae, for instance, were the guardians of springs. Springs, with their constant and mysterious source of water, were often considered sacred and were central to many local cults. Potameides presided over rivers, entities that had a major influence on human settlements, navigation, and agriculture. Limnades or Limnatides, nymphs of lakes, underscored the Greeks' awareness of various types of freshwater bodies, each with its distinct characteristics.

The relationship between the Naiads and their corresponding water bodies was often perceived as a form of symbiosis. The Naiads, as the animating spirits of the waters, derived their identity and existence from the water bodies, while in return, they bestowed the waters with life, movement, and divine aura.

B. Oceanids and Nereids

While Naiads ruled the freshwater bodies, the vast realm of the sea was assigned to the Oceanids and the Nereids. The Oceanids, daughters of the titan Oceanus and his sister Tethys, personified the enormous and unpredictable body of the world-ocean, a concept in ancient cosmology that encircled the earth. They were innumerable, a thousand according to Hesiod's 'Theogony', representing perhaps the countless aspects and moods of the sea, and its many currents, waves, and tides.

The Nereids, fifty in number, daughters of Nereus (the old man of the sea) and Doris (an Oceanid), were nymphs of the Mediterranean Sea. In contrast to the vast and somewhat impersonal world-ocean, the Mediterranean Sea had a more direct influence on the lives of the Greek people. It was their primary avenue for trade, travel, exploration, and military expeditions. The Nereids, thus, were more directly involved in human affairs compared to the Oceanids.

A notable Nereid was Thetis, the mother of the Trojan War hero, Achilles. She represents the integration of the nymphs into major mythological narratives and their influence on human destinies.

Both the Oceanids and Nereids, by representing different aspects of the sea, encapsulated the Greeks' recognition of the sea's importance, its manifold nature, and its potent influence on their lives and civilization. They personified the ancient Greeks' fear, respect, and awe for the sea, underscoring the inherent connection between human societies and their marine environment.

In conclusion, water nymphs, through their association with various bodies of water, underscored the importance of water in the life and survival of ancient Greek societies. They acted as mediators between humans and the vital, yet potentially dangerous, powers of nature, and through them, the ancient Greeks sought to understand, personify, and ultimately influence these natural forces. The water nymphs thus serve as powerful symbols of the human-nature interaction in Greek mythology and religion.

✧   Land Nymphs

Dryads and Hamadryads were tree nymphs, spirits who lived within trees, particularly oaks. The life of a Hamadryad was connected with the tree they inhabited; if the tree died, so did the nymph. Similarly, Oreads were mountain nymphs who personified the rugged peaks and gorges.

A. Dryads and Hamadryads

Dryads, from the Greek 'dryas' meaning 'oak', were the nymphs of trees and forests. In a broader sense, Dryads encompassed all tree nymphs, but more specifically, they were associated with oak trees, a tree of great significance in various Greek myths and rituals. They were often depicted as beautiful maidens inhabiting the trees, symbolising the vital life force of the trees and their integral role in the ecosystem.

Hamadryads were a specific type of Dryads whose existence was intrinsically linked with a particular tree, often an oak. This notion of a shared life between the Hamadryad and its tree profoundly symbolised the concept of interdependence in nature. The life of a Hamadryad mirrored that of its tree; its youth, maturity, and ageing followed the life cycle of the tree, and if the tree were to die, the Hamadryad would perish too. This mythology may have encouraged a degree of conservation ethos, since the destruction of a tree signified the death of a divine entity.

It is worth noting that the perceived personhood of trees through their association with nymphs such as Dryads and Hamadryads underlines a form of early animism. It reflects a belief system that considered various elements of nature as animated and personified, thereby fostering a sense of respect and sanctity towards the environment.

B. Oreads

Oreads were the nymphs of the mountains, hills, and gorges - the rugged, often inaccessible features of the landscape. They were considered to personify the untamed and wild characteristics of these regions. Inhabiting the heights, far from human settlements, they signified the daunting yet majestic aspects of the natural world.

Oreads, like other nymphs, were known for their interactions with gods and humans. They were part of the retinue of the hunting goddess Artemis, reflecting the goddess's association with wilderness areas. These nymphs were also involved in various myths where their mountains served as arenas for divine or heroic exploits.

Oreads highlight the Greeks' awareness of the diverse aspects of their geography, acknowledging the mountains as entities with their distinctive ecology and persona. They also symbolise the human fascination with the lofty heights, often associated with sacredness, challenge, and a closer connection with the divine.

In conclusion, through Dryads, Hamadryads, and Oreads, the ancient Greeks recognised and respected the sacredness and vitality of their land, from the trees that provided them with essential resources, to the mountains that marked their landscapes. These land and tree nymphs, while embodying various aspects of nature, also underline the human tendency to personify and venerate nature, creating a divine bridge between the human world and the natural environment.

✧   Other Nymphs

Other types of nymphs include the Meliae (ash tree nymphs), Anthousai (flower nymphs), and Hesperides (nymphs of the sunset and the garden of the gods). These classifications further demonstrate the detailed taxonomy developed by the ancient Greeks to personify and divinise natural elements.

The ancient Greek pantheon consisted of a host of nymphs representing various natural phenomena, from specific types of trees and flowers to abstract concepts like sunset. The following are examples of these diverse nymph categories:

A. Meliae

The Meliae were the nymphs of the ash trees. According to Hesiod's Theogony, they sprang from the blood of the castrated Uranus (Heaven) when his son Cronus threw his severed genitals into the sea. The Meliae were particularly significant as they were associated with the ash tree, from which humans crafted their weapons and tools. Hence, they were not merely spirits of nature but also represented the utilitarian aspect of nature's resources.

B. Anthousai

Anthousai were flower nymphs who personified the beauty and transience of flowers. They were believed to transform into the flowers they guarded, essentially symbolising the ephemeral beauty of nature. The Anthousai remind us of the Greeks' appreciation for aesthetic beauty in nature, an appreciation that transcended into their art, literature, and mythology.

C. Hesperides

The Hesperides were the nymphs of the evening and the golden light of sunsets. They were entrusted with the care of the garden of the gods, where a tree bearing golden apples grew. This garden was located in the far western corner of the world, a place where the sun sets. The Hesperides, besides their association with the majestic vision of the sunset, symbolised the bounty of nature that the gods enjoyed. The golden apples were often seen as symbols of immortality and divine knowledge.

This taxonomy of nymphs, from the Meliae and Anthousai to the Hesperides, encapsulates the nuanced ways in which the Greeks perceived their natural environment. They understood the significance of each element of nature, acknowledging its utility, beauty, and symbolical potential. These nymphs reflect the integral role that nature played in Greek culture and religion, encouraging a degree of respect and conservation ethos towards the environment. They also underline the human capacity for personification and the human tendency to seek divine in the natural world.

These ancient beliefs offer modern readers a chance to reassess their relationship with nature, providing a platform for discussion on how ancient attitudes towards the environment can be reconciled with, and perhaps inspire, contemporary environmental perspectives.

Function and Role of Nymphs

Nymphs served as intermediaries between the human and divine realms, embodying the life forces within the natural world and often acting as divine attendants to greater deities. They were invoked as part of the religious practices connected to the places they inhabited. Their blessings were sought for various aspects of everyday life, from the fertility of the land and the safety of seafarers to the well-being and growth of children.

In many myths, nymphs were also seen as the consorts of gods and the mothers of heroes, further linking them to key narratives within the mythic tradition.

Understanding the Nymphs

Nymphs, in their numerous forms and roles, not only reveal the ancient Greeks' deep reverence for the natural world but also demonstrate their nuanced understanding of its different elements. The existence of different types of nymphs suggests a comprehensive system of divinity that accounted for the variety of natural phenomena experienced by humans. This categorisation and personification of natural elements facilitated a sense of connection and interaction with the environment, encapsulating a religious and cultural framework that placed nature at the heart of existence.

While we must be mindful of the potential for oversimplification, this study of nymphs provides a valuable lens through which to explore and understand the ancient Greek relationship with the natural world, and how this relationship was mythologised and ritualised. The nymphs, in their multiplicity and diversity, offer a profound insight into the interplay between human culture and natural phenomena, which was pivotal in shaping the beliefs, practices, and narratives of ancient Greek society.

Role of nymphs in Greek mythology and their associations with specific natural features

Nymphs, as semi-divine beings in Greek mythology, played a vital role in embodying the divine qualities attributed to nature. Their mythological narratives often elucidate the interactions between gods, humans, and the natural world, contributing to a complex network of beliefs, values, and perceptions surrounding nature.

These minor deities were associated with fertility and growth, typically depicted as beautiful maidens, embodying grace, youth, and allure - qualities that reflect the pleasing aesthetics of nature. This anthropomorphisation of nature facilitated a deeper connection between the Greeks and their environment, turning impersonal natural phenomena into entities with which they could interact.

In Greek mythology, nymphs were frequent companions of higher gods and goddesses, reflecting their integrative and supportive roles in the natural order. For instance, the Nereids, sea nymphs, were the attendants of Poseidon, the god of the sea. Dryads and Hamadryads, tree nymphs, were often seen with Artemis, the huntress goddess who roamed the forests. These associations underline the holistic perception of the natural world, where each element, each deity, has a role to play in the grand scheme.

Associations with Specific Natural Features

The different types of nymphs, categorised based on the natural elements they represented, depict an elaborate network of divine personifications mapped onto the Greek landscape. This taxonomy extended to all aspects of nature, from water bodies and mountains to specific kinds of trees and flowers, even abstract natural phenomena like the sunset.

Water nymphs, or Naiads, for instance, personified the life-giving and nurturing aspect of fresh water sources, often thought to have healing powers. Dryads and Hamadryads, on the other hand, were associated with trees, primarily oaks, thus symbolising the strength, endurance, and shelter provided by these trees.

The Anthousai, flower nymphs, epitomised the transient beauty of nature. The Hesperides, the nymphs of the evening and the golden light of sunset, symbolised the end of the day, the completion of a cycle, and the promise of another dawn. Each nymph, in their unique way, contributed to the personification of nature, allowing the ancient Greeks to perceive their environment as a realm filled with divine presence.

The personification and deification of natural elements through nymphs not only reflected the Greeks' reverence for nature but also affected their actions and attitudes towards it. They believed that displeasing a nymph could result in negative consequences. For example, failing to respect a water source, home to a Naiad, might lead to the drying up of that source or a decline in its healing properties.

This anthropomorphised and divinised view of nature encouraged a measure of respect and possibly fostered a rudimentary sense of environmental consciousness among the ancient Greeks. These perspectives provide a fascinating lens through which to examine the nexus of mythology, nature, and culture in ancient Greece and prompt us to reflect upon the ways in which our own narratives and beliefs about nature shape our interactions with it.

Discussion on the relationship between nymphs and other deities, notably Artemis

The relationships between nymphs and the greater deities in Greek mythology offer a fascinating perspective into how the ancient Greeks perceived the interconnectedness of nature and divinity. These minor nature deities served as companions, attendants, or handmaidens to more prominent gods and goddesses, reflecting the integrated hierarchy of the divine order within the natural world.

The Artemis-Nymph Connection

The relationships between Artemis, the virgin goddess of the hunt, wilderness, wild animals, and childbirth, and various nymphs, particularly the Dryads and the Naiads, is particularly noteworthy. Artemis, in her wild and untamed nature, was often accompanied by nymphs who mirrored her qualities. This divine assembly was seen as guardians of the wilderness, fostering growth, and ensuring the continuous cycle of life and death.

❖   Artemis and Nymphs: A Reflection of the Divine and the Wild

Artemis's associations with nymphs accentuate her role as a bridge between the wild and the divine. As a patron of both the untamed wilderness and the tamed animals, Artemis' domain was inherently paradoxical, embodying the interface between civilization and wilderness, order and chaos, and creation and destruction. The nymphs, by their very nature, mirror these dualities inherent in Artemis.

❖   Nymphs as Companions and Mirrors of Artemis

As mentioned earlier, nymphs, particularly the Dryads and the Naiads, were often depicted as Artemis's companions, with some myths portraying them as her hunting entourage. Their relationship was not one of servitude but camaraderie, born out of a shared love for the wilderness.

Moreover, nymphs were not merely passive followers but active participants in Artemis's realm. They played essential roles in nurturing the wilderness and promoting the cycles of growth and decay that Artemis presided over.

✧   Role in Fostering Life

The nymphs were seen as nurturing spirits, often associated with fertility and growth, mirroring Artemis's role as the protector of young creatures and the patron of childbirth. As tree nymphs, the Dryads embodied the life-giving aspect of nature, providing shelter and sustenance to the creatures of the forest. Similarly, the Naiads, as water nymphs, represented the vital life-sustaining force of water, essential for all living beings.

✧   Shared Guardianship of Wilderness

Together, Artemis and the nymphs were seen as guardians of the wilderness. Their combined efforts ensured the preservation and thriving of nature's wild spaces, promoting a balance between growth and decay, life and death, order and chaos.

✧   Partnership for Harmony in Nature

In summary, Artemis's connection with nymphs represented an alliance that reinforced the symbiotic relationship between different elements of the wild. They symbolized the harmony within nature, a balance of forces that allowed the wilderness to thrive. Through their association, the Greeks celebrated the divine in the natural world, acknowledging the sacredness inherent in every facet of the wilderness.

Dryads: The Tree Nymphs and Artemis

Artemis, known for her affinity with forests and woodland creatures, had a special connection with the Dryads, the tree nymphs. These nymphs, who personified the trees and the forest, were often depicted as Artemis's companions, joining her in her hunts and providing her with shelter and comfort in the wilderness.

This relationship underscores the harmony between the different facets of the wilderness. Artemis, as the huntress, represents the predator-prey dynamic, the cycle of life and death that propels nature. The Dryads, on the other hand, embody the quiet strength and endurance of trees, the life-giving and sheltering aspects of the forest. Together, they reflect a balanced view of nature, embracing both its tranquil and turbulent elements.

✧   Dryads and Artemis: An Intimate Bond

The affinity between Artemis and Dryads was not merely coincidental but represented an intimate bond between the deity and the spirits of the wilderness. In many ways, the Dryads were seen as an extension of Artemis herself, embodying her virtues of resilience, independence, and deep connection with the wild.

✧ Dryads: Extensions of Artemis's Wilderness

Dryads, or tree nymphs, were often considered Artemis's constant companions and confidantes. Given their shared dominion over the forest, their relationship was one of mutual respect and cooperation. The Dryads, each bound to a specific tree, personified the spirit of the forest - its calm, its strength, and its capacity to nurture life.

✧ Artemis: The Huntress and the Guardian

Artemis's role as a huntress is not just about predation but is also about maintaining balance within the ecosystem. This involves safeguarding the wilderness from excessive destruction and ensuring the cyclic renewal of life. In the process of executing her duties, Artemis regularly interacts with Dryads. Her role as the guardian of the wilderness is complemented by the life-sustaining roles of the Dryads.

✧ Harmony in Wilderness: Dryads and Artemis

Together, Artemis and the Dryads maintain the harmony and balance within the forest ecosystem. Artemis, with her bows and arrows, upholds the natural law of predation and death, essential for ecological balance. The Dryads, embodying the trees, provide shelter and sustenance, symbolising growth, life, and the enduring strength of nature. They represent two sides of the same coin – life and death, creation and destruction, growth and decay – and together, they exemplify the intricate balance that characterises the wilderness.

Mutual Respect and Cooperation

In summary, the relationship between Artemis and the Dryads is marked by mutual respect and cooperation, reflecting the interdependence that is inherent in nature. Artemis, in her capacity as the protector of wilderness, recognises and values the contributions of the Dryads. Similarly, the Dryads acknowledge Artemis's role in maintaining ecological balance. This dynamic underscores the harmonious coexistence and mutualistic interactions that pervade natural systems, reinforcing the belief that all elements of nature, however disparate, are interconnected and interdependent.

Naiads: The Water Nymphs and Artemis

The Naiads, nymphs of fresh water bodies, also shared a close relationship with Artemis. Water, being essential for life, was a crucial element in the wilderness that Artemis ruled over. The Naiads were said to provide fresh water for Artemis and her hunting dogs during their expeditions in the woods.

These water nymphs also had an essential role in Artemis's capacity as a goddess of childbirth. The Naiads were often invoked during childbirth to provide clean, healing water, reflecting the nurturing and life-sustaining aspect of water.

✧　　Naiads and Artemis: The Flow of Life

Naiads, being the nymphs of fresh water bodies, were seen as the living embodiment of the life-giving and sustaining properties of water. They were often considered as the intimate allies of Artemis, reflecting the goddess's close relationship with all forms of life in the wilderness.

✧　　Naiads: The Quenchers of Thirst

During her long hunting expeditions, Artemis and her companions, both divine and mortal, required sustenance and rejuvenation. Naiads, governing the rivers, springs, and other freshwater sources, were believed to provide the necessary hydration to Artemis and her hounds. These interactions highlight the interdependencies in the natural world and illustrate how different aspects of nature work in tandem.

✧　　Naiads in Childbirth and Artemis's Role as Protector

Beyond the hunt, Naiads also had an important role to play in Artemis's capacity as a deity of childbirth. Given the ancient belief in the healing and purifying properties of water, Naiads were often invoked during childbirth to provide a safe and clean environment. As such, they played a crucial part in reinforcing Artemis's role as a protector of women, particularly during childbirth.

✧　　The Nurturing Aspects of Water

By tying the role of Naiads to childbirth and the sustenance of Artemis and her entourage, the Greeks underscored the nurturing and life-sustaining aspect of water. Freshwater, under the care of Naiads, was not just a passive element but was recognised for its active role in maintaining life and ensuring well-being.

✧   Interconnected Roles

To conclude, the interconnected roles of Artemis, the huntress and protector of childbirth, and the Naiads, the nymphs of freshwater sources, exemplify the interweaving of various facets of the natural world. The mutual support and cooperation between them depict the inherent symbiosis and interdependencies in nature, highlighting the harmonious co-existence of diverse natural elements and beings.

Conclusion: A Symbiotic Relationship

The relationship between Artemis and the nymphs is a vivid representation of the symbiotic dynamics that characterise the ancient Greek perception of nature and divinity. Each entity, each deity, has its role in the larger ecological and divine framework. The greater goddess does not exist in isolation but is part of a complex network that includes the lesser deities or spirits, highlighting an integrated worldview.

This understanding of nature and divinity also reflects in the Greeks' cultural practices. The respect and reverence they showed towards these gods and spirits were not limited to grand temples but extended to every tree, every water source, every mountain peak, thereby infusing their daily life with a sense of the sacred.

Counterarguments and Areas for Further Discussion

While the relationships between Artemis and the nymphs appear to promote a balanced and integrated view of nature, it is essential to consider the broader social and cultural contexts. For instance, the gender dynamics at play in these narratives, with Artemis and the nymphs often portrayed in submissive or servile roles to male gods, reflect the patriarchal structures prevalent in ancient Greek society.

Furthermore, the anthropomorphic representation of nature, while facilitating a connection between humans and the environment, may also contribute to an anthropocentric worldview. By humanising nature, the Greeks could have inadvertently reinforced a sense of human superiority or entitlement, leading to exploitation or disregard for non-human entities.

These perspectives open up avenues for further discussion and critical analysis, allowing students to explore the multifaceted nature of mythological narratives and their implications on society and the environment.

Worship and veneration of nymphs: Sanctuaries, offerings, and local cults

The nymphs, despite their minor status in the hierarchy of Greek deities, commanded a unique position in the Greek religious landscape. With their close associations to specific natural features and their ubiquitous presence across the Greek world, nymphs were an integral part of local cults, public rites, and domestic rituals.

Sanctuaries of the Nymphs

✦ Nymphs and Natural Sanctuaries

Given their intrinsic connection with nature, many sanctuaries of the nymphs were naturally occurring sites such as caves, springs, trees, and groves. These locations were not just worshipped as the abodes of nymphs but were also believed to embody the nymphs themselves. The Cave of the Nymphs on Ithaca, mentioned in Homer's Odyssey, is one such example.

Indeed, the close association between nymphs and naturally occurring features such as springs, caves, trees, and groves had profound implications for the worship of these deities in the Greek world. These sites, while serving as sanctuaries for nymphs, were seen as more than just sacred habitats. The nymphs were believed to embody these sites, merging with the natural features themselves, which resulted in a unique form of worship that combined elements of nature veneration and deity worship.

Consider, for instance, the Cave of the Nymphs on Ithaca, a site mentioned in the Homeric Odyssey. In the narrative, upon his return to Ithaca, Odysseus hides his treasures in this cave, where the Naiads, the freshwater nymphs, were believed to reside. The cave is not merely a dwelling for the Naiads; it becomes an extension of their being, with the stalactites and stalagmites described as the nymphs' looms and distaffs, tools typically associated with women's craft in the ancient world. The cave becomes a sacred and animate space, its natural features infused with divine presence.

Springs, another common sanctuary for nymphs, particularly Naiads, illustrate a similar convergence of nature and divinity. Springs were often considered to be the outward manifestation of the nymphs' life-giving and healing power. They were sites of both physical and spiritual cleansing, where the pure, fresh water was perceived as a direct gift from the nymphs. Rituals and offerings at these sites underscored this belief, with libations and ablutions forming integral parts of the worship.

Similarly, trees and groves, especially those inhabited by Dryads and Hamadryads, were treated with great reverence. Certain tree species, notably the oak, were considered particularly sacred. The life force of a nymph was believed to be intertwined with that of her tree, blurring the boundaries between the tree as a natural object and as a manifestation of the divine.

These natural sanctuaries provided an accessible and tangible link between the human and divine realms, reinforcing the nymphs' roles as intermediaries between humans and the more remote, major deities. They were focal points for rituals and festivals, as well as for more personal acts of piety, embedding the worship of nymphs in both the communal and individual religious experiences of the ancient Greeks.

✧ Constructed Sanctuaries

There were also constructed sanctuaries and altars for the nymphs, especially in urban environments where natural features might not be readily available. These artificial sanctuaries were commonly located near or within other major sanctuaries, emphasizing the close ties between nymphs and the major deities.

In addition to their associations with natural sites, nymphs were also venerated in constructed sanctuaries within the urban fabric of Greek cities. These sanctuaries, though artificially created, did not dilute the nature-centric essence of the nymphs but rather adapted their veneration to an urban context, indicating the flexibility and adaptability of nymph worship.

One notable example is the Sanctuary of the Nymphs and Aphrodite on the South Slope of the Athenian Acropolis. Here, a naturally occurring cave was incorporated into a larger sanctuary complex, illustrating a blend of natural and built environments. The co-dedication to Aphrodite, the goddess of love and beauty, underscores the overlapping functions and shared characteristics of these female deities.

Altars dedicated to the nymphs were also common features in the precincts of major sanctuaries such as the Sanctuary of Zeus at Olympia and the Sanctuary of Apollo at Delphi. At Delphi, the renowned Castalian Spring was overseen by a group of water nymphs known as the Castalian Nymphs. Near this sacred spring, the rock of the Sibyl, another prophetic figure associated with the nymphs, was located.

In some urban contexts, sacred groves were artificially created for the veneration of nymphs, particularly the Dryads. These groves, often enclosed within larger sanctuaries, featured statues and altars dedicated to the nymphs. The veneration of the nymphs within these constructed environments underscores their importance within the Greek pantheon, their close associations with major deities, and their integral roles within both rural and urban religious life.

It is worth noting that these constructed sanctuaries were not merely poor substitutes for their natural counterparts but held their own significance. They provided a space for the expression of piety in environments where direct access to nature might be limited. Moreover, their incorporation within major sanctuaries indicates the reciprocal relationships between the nymphs and the more dominant deities, underscoring the nymphs' roles as intermediaries and facilitators within the larger Greek religious framework.

Offerings to the Nymphs

✧ Types of Offerings

Offerings to the nymphs generally reflected their nature and roles. Items associated with fertility, such as fruits, grains, and milk, were common, as were honey and wine, substances linked with joy and pleasure. Votives of a more personal nature, including clothing items and locks of hair, were also given, possibly as tokens of individual devotion or as part of rites of passage.

The diverse range of offerings made to nymphs underscores their multiple roles and associations within Greek mythology and religious practice. The offerings were largely agrarian, reflecting the nymphs' integral connections with fertility and abundance. Given their close association with various natural features and elements, it is unsurprising that many of the offerings involved elements derived directly from nature.

Fruits, grains, and milk were commonly offered to the nymphs, symbolic of their influence over growth, fecundity, and sustenance. These offerings can be seen as both a form of gratitude for past bounties and an appeal for continued abundance. This kind of offering is in line with the general ancient Greek practice of giving back to the gods a part of what they were believed to have provided.

Honey and wine, substances linked with joy, pleasure, and festive occasions, were also frequently given to the nymphs. This could be indicative of the nymphs' association with certain forms of revelry, further emphasising their connection with Dionysian festivities. Wine, a product of the vine—a plant requiring careful cultivation—might also represent the harmonious interaction of nature and human endeavour.

Additionally, offerings were not confined to agrarian produce or manufactured goods. Personal tokens, such as clothing items or locks of hair, were also dedicated to the nymphs. While seemingly unusual in comparison to the more traditional offerings, these personal tokens could serve as poignant symbols of individual devotion or be associated with particular rites of passage. For instance, locks of hair were often given during rites of passage, symbolising a form of personal sacrifice or transition.

The richness and diversity of the offerings made to the nymphs serve as testament to their complex roles within Greek religion and society. From elements of the earth to personal belongings, these offerings represented a dynamic relationship between the human and divine realms, mediated through the diverse figure of the nymph.

✦   The Significance of Offerings

The range and nature of these offerings underscore the close and personal relationship between humans and nymphs. They highlight the various roles of nymphs - as nurturers, healers, and protectors - and the manifold ways in which humans sought their favor.

The comprehensive spectrum of offerings presented to the nymphs reveals an intimate and multifaceted interaction between humans and these lesser deities of nature. It provides us with significant insights into how the nymphs were conceived and how their roles were appreciated within the Greek cultural milieu.

Being so intimately connected to everyday life and the natural environment, nymphs held a position that was at once more accessible and more directly pertinent to the common person than perhaps the lofty Olympian deities. The gifts given to them were not just tokens of reverence but also tangible means of communicating human needs, desires, and gratitude.

Nymphs were perceived as nurturers, their blessings and favor sought for a bountiful harvest or an abundant catch. Offerings of grains, fruits, and other agricultural produce not only served as a token of appreciation for their perceived role in agricultural fertility but also an appeal to their benevolent nature for continued abundance.

The roles of nymphs as healers were also recognized and celebrated. Springs and wells, often associated with nymphs, were considered to have healing properties. Offerings, especially personal ones like clothing or locks of hair, were likely left by those seeking or giving thanks for healing. In this context, the offering acts as a symbolic exchange, a pact of sorts, where the physical offering is an appeal or a thanksgiving for the nymph's intercession.

Furthermore, nymphs were seen as protectors, their favor sought for safe journeys, protection from wild animals, and even in matters of love and childbirth. The variety of personal tokens offered to nymphs underlines the deeply personal nature of the protection sought from these spirits of nature.

The active veneration and the significant diversity of offerings directed towards nymphs indicate their critical and active role in Greek religious and socio-cultural life. The nymphs, through their multiple roles, served as critical mediators between humans and the divine, providing a tangible and personal dimension to the human understanding and experience of the divine world.

Local Cults and Nymphs

✧ Cults Centred Around Specific Nymphs

Certain localities had cults centred around specific nymphs who were believed to be particularly active in their area. These nymphs might be associated with a particular spring, tree, or mountain, and were invoked for their power over local conditions, including fertility, health, and well-being.

Indeed, the close association of nymphs with specific localities often resulted in the development of local cults centered around particular nymphs who were believed to exhibit an especially influential presence in their respective regions. These local nymph cults were an integral part of the religious landscape in ancient Greece, reflecting a profound reverence for the divine within the natural world and the particularities of local geographic features.

It's critical to comprehend the rationale behind this localization of cult worship. The nymphs were perceived not only as divine entities but also as personifications of specific elements in the natural landscape. A nymph could embody a river, a tree, a mountain, or a spring, and her well-being was thought to be intrinsically linked to the health and prosperity of the feature she represented. Thus, these cults can be seen as attempts to propitiate these divine forces and ensure the local environment's fertility, stability, and overall well-being.

In these localized cults, the specific nymphs were often bestowed with names, either derived from the geographic features they were associated with or from the legends and myths that surrounded them. For instance, the Naiad nymph Arethusa was associated with a particular spring in the Peloponnese, while the Dryad nymph

Syke (Fig) was believed to inhabit a specific fig tree. The veneration of these nymphs usually took place at the site of their respective natural elements.

The locals would make offerings and perform rituals to seek the nymph's favor, asking for protection, healing, fertility, and other blessings. The offerings would typically be items that held local significance or were relevant to the nymph's nature and the favor sought. For instance, at a sacred spring, the locals might offer small silver or terracotta vessels as symbols of their gratitude for the clean water the spring nymph provided.

Moreover, the cults often involved communal festivities, dances, and feasts, reinforcing the social cohesion and collective identity of the local community. Thus, the localized nymph cults served not only religious and practical purposes but also played a crucial role in fostering and sustaining the local communities' socio-cultural fabric.

These cults' practices underscore the ancients' understanding of the symbiotic relationship between humans and the natural world. The nymphs, as personifications of nature, were respected, revered, and cared for, embodying the principle that the preservation and prosperity of nature are inextricably linked with human well-being. In this way, the local cults centred around specific nymphs were not just religious institutions; they also served as reminders of the delicate balance that exists between humans and the world they inhabit.

✦ Nymphs and Hero Cults

Nymphs were often associated with local hero cults. They were believed to be the nurses or mothers of these heroes, tying them into the local lore and adding a layer of divine sanction to the cult of the hero.

In the rich and diverse landscape of Greek mythology and religious practice, nymphs and heroes were often interconnected through complex familial and caretaking relationships, creating a unique interplay between mortal and immortal realms. This fusion is frequently observed within the context of hero cults, where nymphs assumed significant roles as either the mothers or nurses of these celebrated mortals.

The connection between nymphs and hero cults fundamentally served to legitimize the divine ancestry of the hero, further accentuating their extraordinary qualities and deeds, and imbuing them with a certain level of sacredness. At the same time, it reinforced the belief in nymphs as nurturing figures associated with fertility, growth, and care, crucial for human survival and prosperity.

An instance of such association can be found in the story of the renowned hero Achilles. In some variants of his tale, Achilles was the son of the Nereid Thetis, a sea nymph known for her wisdom and foresight. The divine lineage of Achilles from a nymph mother established his extraordinary abilities and heroic status. Simultaneously, it underscored Thetis' role as a protective mother who went to great lengths to try to preserve her son from his fated demise.

Nymphs were also often portrayed as nurses or caregivers of heroes, a role that was not only limited to biological offspring. For example, the Nymphs of Ida, known as the Idaians, were said to have nursed the infant Zeus, the future king of gods, providing him shelter and sustenance while hiding him from his father, Cronus.

Furthermore, these ties between nymphs and heroes were often integrated into the local lore and worship practices. Nymphs and heroes were frequently venerated together in joint cults, with shared sanctuaries and rituals. These cults reinforced the local identity and the unique cultural and religious landscape of a region, fostering communal solidarity and pride.

For instance, at the hero shrine of Erichthonius in Athens, the adjacent cave of the nymphs was a crucial part of the cultic practice. It was believed that the daughters of Cecrops discovered Erichthonius in this cave, where he was being nurtured by the local nymphs. The shared worship of the nymphs and Erichthonius at this site signified the intermingling of the divine, the heroic, and the local, thus sanctifying the entire locale and enriching its spiritual significance.

In conclusion, nymphs' involvement with hero cults indicates the multifaceted role of these divine beings in ancient Greek religious life. It demonstrates the integration of divine and mortal realms, emphasizes the nurturing attributes of nymphs, and provides local color to the universal phenomenon of hero worship. These intersections offer fertile ground for further investigation into the complexities of ancient Greek religious beliefs and practices.

Conclusion

The veneration of nymphs, as reflected in their sanctuaries, offerings, and local cults, provides a fascinating glimpse into the everyday spirituality of the ancient Greeks. More than just minor deities, the nymphs, with their close ties to the natural world and their involvement in various aspects of life, represent a form of divine presence that was immediate, tangible, and deeply personal.

Interpretation of the nymphs as embodiments of the life-giving and unpredictable aspects of nature

The nymphs, those female deities of lower rank in the Greek pantheon, have played a remarkable role in encapsulating the ancient Greek understanding and conceptualisation of nature. Known for their association with various elements of the natural world, these divine beings symbolised the fertile, life-giving aspects of nature while also embodying its unpredictable and often capricious character. This dual representation reflects the two-faced nature of the environment, which, while being a source of sustenance, is also a realm of untamed forces and unforeseeable changes.

Nymphs as Life-Giving Entities

Nymphs were widely perceived as life-giving entities, consistently associated with elements of nature that provide sustenance and foster growth. From the Naiads, or water nymphs, who presided over springs, rivers, and other freshwater sources, to the Dryads and Hamadryads, the tree nymphs that were intimately connected with the vitality of their trees, the nymphs epitomised the nurturing aspects of nature.

In the context of agriculture, for instance, nymphs were seen as protectors of the fields, ensuring their fertility. The Anthousai, flower nymphs, represented the beauty and ephemeral nature of flowers, symbolising the blossoming and decay inherent in the cycle of life. Meanwhile, the Meliae, or ash tree nymphs, were not only the nurturers of their trees but were also associated with the nurturing of man, for it was from an ash tree that the first human beings were believed to be born.

The very fabric of ancient Greek mythology is interwoven with the belief in nymphs as life-giving and nurturing entities. Such an association stems from their profound connection with various elements of the natural world that are vital for human life and civilization. The nymphs' distinctive roles and associations with specific natural elements brought them to the foreground in various spheres of human life in antiquity, most notably agriculture and survival in the wilderness.

The Naiads, or water nymphs, were embodiments of the freshwater bodies they inhabited, such as springs, brooks, rivers, and wells. These sources of water were essential for the survival of ancient communities, not just as a source of drinking water, but also for irrigation, bathing, and healing rituals. The Naiads, in their role as custodians of these water bodies, were thus venerated as life-givers, providing sustenance and vitality to humans and nature alike.

In a similar vein, the Dryads and Hamadryads, the nymphs of the trees, were seen as embodiments of the life-force within trees, particularly oaks in the case of Hamadryads. The life cycle of these nymphs was believed to be intrinsically tied to that of their trees, reflecting the cyclical nature of growth and decay inherent in all life forms. The reverence for trees, and by extension, these tree nymphs, reflects a recognition of their role in providing food, shelter, and other material needs.

In the realm of agriculture, one of the primary foundations of human civilization, nymphs were seen as potent guardians and nurturers. Their perceived influence over natural elements pivotal for successful crop growth led to their veneration as protectors of the fields, with rituals and offerings made to ensure the land's fertility and a bountiful harvest.

The Anthousai, the flower nymphs, despite their lesser-known status, played a unique role in symbolising the ephemeral yet cyclical aspect of life. They were associated with flowers, which, in their transient blooming and inevitable decay, offer a poignant representation of the life-death-rebirth cycle.

Not to be overlooked are the Meliae, the nymphs of the ash tree. In addition to their role as nurturers of their trees, they held a profound place in the creation myth of mankind. According to Hesiod's "Theogony," it was from the trunks of the ash tree, cared for by the Meliae, that the first mortals, known as the Silver Race, were born, establishing an enduring bond between mankind and nature.

In sum, the nymphs, in their various forms and associations, stood as personifications of nature's life-giving aspects, nurturing both human life and the natural world. The ancient Greek belief in these deities underscores a deep-rooted understanding and reverence for nature as a vital source of sustenance and growth.

The Unpredictability of Nature

However, the nymphs were not merely benign, nurturing figures. As with nature, they also had an unpredictable, often tempestuous side. For example, the Naiads, while often being invoked as healers and life-givers, could also inflict illnesses known as "nympholepsy" upon those who offended them. These conditions, often characterised by frenzy or melancholia, symbolised the mental disorientation and physical malaise that could be brought about by drinking from a contaminated water source.

Similarly, the Dryads, while often associated with the stability and longevity of trees, were also intimately connected with the death of these trees. In the case of

Hamadryads, the nymphs and their trees were believed to share the same lifespan - a powerful reminder of the fragility and impermanence inherent in life.

The nymphs' association with life's benevolence must not overshadow the acknowledgement of their unpredictability and potential for destructive force, in keeping with nature's dichotomy. Nature, while bountiful and nurturing, can also be volatile and unforgiving. The nymphs, as embodiments of natural elements, reflect this dual aspect.

The Naiads, nymphs of fresh water bodies, while typically venerated for their life-giving and healing attributes, were also known to inflict illnesses upon those who failed to respect them or their abodes. The maladies, broadly known as "nympholepsy", included a range of symptoms from disorientation to frenzied states or deep melancholia. Such afflictions could symbolise the tangible consequences of disrespecting nature, such as drinking from a contaminated water source, resulting in physical and mental distress. This dual nature of the Naiads underscores the capriciousness inherent in natural elements – vital for life yet potentially harmful if disrespected or misused.

Similarly, the Dryads and Hamadryads, tree nymphs, while often symbolising stability, endurance, and the life-sustaining properties of trees, were also tied to the trees' mortality. Particularly in the case of Hamadryads, the lifeline of these nymphs was inseparable from their associated tree. When the tree died, so did the nymph. This belief presents a stark reminder of the delicate balance of life and death in nature, reflecting not just the fragility of life but also the impermanence that underscores the very essence of existence.

Furthermore, certain types of nymphs, such as the Oceanids and Nereids, who represented larger and more formidable bodies of water, like the sea, were sometimes associated with natural disasters such as floods and storms, further underscoring the unpredictable and often dangerous aspects of nature.

The reverence and fear for nymphs therefore mirror the ancients' relationship with nature – a careful balance of reliance, respect, and wariness of its unpredictable power. Through their worship and myths surrounding nymphs, the ancients acknowledged nature's dual capacity to nurture and destroy, an understanding that nurtured their respect for the natural world and shaped their strategies for survival and growth.

In conclusion, the nymphs, in their diverse forms and representations, offer a comprehensive personification of the various aspects of nature, from its capacity to give and sustain life to its unpredictability and potential for destruction. They encapsulate the ancient Greeks' complex and nuanced understanding of the natural world and their place within it – a relationship characterised by a delicate balance of dependence, respect, and caution.

The Nymphs and the Wilderness

The portrayal of nymphs as inhabitants of the wilderness – those untouched, pristine spaces beyond the perimeters of human civilisation – further enhances their embodiment of the unpredictability of nature. The nymphs, as divine entities, inhabit the untamed outdoors, dwelling in forests, mountains, rivers, and caves. Their elusive character and tendency to retreat from human contact, as frequently depicted in mythological narratives, echo the elusive and often uncontrollable characteristics of nature itself.

Living in regions considered inaccessible or difficult for humans to traverse, nymphs can be seen as the personification of the elusive wild. In various myths, nymphs are represented as avoiding or fleeing from human interaction, a metaphorical parallel to humanity's struggle to gain dominion over and understand the capricious forces of nature.

For instance, the Oreads, mountain nymphs, personified the rugged, often inaccessible high terrains, while the Naiads and Oceanids, as water nymphs, represented the unpredictable and sometimes perilous nature of water bodies. The Dryads and Hamadryads, tree nymphs, were the embodiments of the enigmatic, deep forest, further from human habitation. Their elusive nature and the sacredness associated with their dwellings were perhaps indicative of the boundaries humans acknowledged between the civilised world and the untamed wilderness, between the predictable and the unpredictable, the known and the unknown.

The wilderness, thus, as the domain of the nymphs, symbolises those aspects of nature that remain beyond human control, despite continuous attempts to tame, understand, and exploit it. The wilderness is wild, free, and can be both nurturing and threatening, much like the nymphs who inhabit it. These characteristics resonate with the portrayal of nymphs as complex, multifaceted entities, reflecting the manifold facets of nature – its capacity to sustain and destroy, its tranquillity and tempestuousness, its predictability and capriciousness.

In summary, through their manifold associations with the natural world, nymphs serve as powerful personifications of the dichotomy inherent in nature – its nurturing, life-sustaining capacities juxtaposed with its unpredictable, often violent tendencies. This dual representation reflects the ancient Greek understanding of their complex and dynamic relationship with the environment. An understanding of nymphs offers a window into this ancient worldview and highlights the enduring human attempt to understand, navigate, and negotiate our place within the natural world. This understanding holds relevance even today as we grapple with our own relationship with the environment in an age of ecological change and uncertainty.

Other Nature Deities and Spirits

The study of nymphs allows us to embark on a broader exploration of deities and spirits associated with nature in ancient Greek and Roman culture. Besides nymphs, there are numerous other divine and semi-divine entities whose roles and representations are intimately connected with the natural world, including Pan, Gaia, Gaea, and the satyrs, among others. This chapter seeks to offer an in-depth examination of these deities and spirits, the elements of nature they are associated with, and their impact on human-nature relations in the ancient world.

Pan: The God of the Wild

Among the most notable nature deities in Greek mythology is Pan, the Arcadian god of the wild, shepherds, and flocks. Half-man, half-goat, Pan embodies the rustic, untamed aspects of the natural world. His domain extends to forests, mountains, and fields, where he frolics and makes merry, often causing a sense of unreasoning fear known as 'panic' in those who encounter him.

As the patron deity of shepherds, Pan also represents the symbiotic relationship between humans and the wilderness, as demonstrated by the pastoral lifestyle. Through Pan, the ancients conceptualised the delicate balance between the wild and the domesticated, encapsulating the necessity, yet inherent unpredictability, of interacting with the natural world.

Gaia: The Primordial Earth Goddess

Gaia, or Gaea, is the primordial earth goddess, representing the Earth itself in the Greek cosmology. As the mother of all life – gods, humans, and creatures alike – Gaia signifies the fertile, nurturing aspect of the Earth. Her function as the universal mother connotes the concept of 'Mother Earth', encapsulating the interconnectedness and interdependence of all life on our planet.

The reverence and worship of Gaia demonstrate the ancients' understanding of the Earth as the fundamental basis of existence and survival. This ancient recognition underscores the importance of respecting and preserving our environment, a notion that remains highly relevant in the context of contemporary ecological concerns.

Satyrs: Spirits of the Woodlands

Satyrs, like Pan, are half-man, half-goat beings associated with the untamed wilderness. Often depicted as followers of Dionysus, the god of wine and ecstasy, satyrs embody the primal, hedonistic aspect of nature. They are frequently portrayed in myths and art as indulging in revelry and pursuing nymphs, symbolising the wild, uncontrolled, and often chaotic facets of the natural world.

Satyrs' behaviour, in its extreme hedonism and disregard for social conventions, underscores the ancients' understanding of the wilderness as a space beyond the boundaries of civilised order. They serve as reminders of the untamed and often unfathomable aspects of nature, reinforcing the need for balance and respect in our interactions with the natural world.

Other Nature Spirits

The ancient world teems with a multitude of other nature spirits, each representing specific elements of the natural world. The Oreads are mountain nymphs, the Alseids are grove nymphs, and the Aegipans are sea-goats, to name but a few. Their multitude and variety underscore the ancients' perception of the natural world as animated and sentient, inhabited by divine entities that oversee its functioning and must be respected.

In summary, understanding these nature deities and spirits enriches our comprehension of how ancient cultures interacted with, respected, and often feared the natural world. These entities personify various aspects of nature, encapsulating its life-giving capabilities, its unpredictable demeanour, and its fundamental role in human existence. Such comprehension provides us with crucial insights into our ongoing relationship with nature, offering timeless wisdom for contemporary societies grappling with environmental challenges and the urgent need to promote sustainability and ecological balance.

Overview of deities associated with specific natural phenomena (e.g., Boreas, god of the north wind; Gaia, the personification of Earth)

A wide array of deities in the Greek and Roman pantheons is associated with specific natural phenomena. This connection imbues nature with a divine aspect, enhancing the significance of these phenomena in everyday life and broadening the context within which the ancients interacted with the natural world. This chapter aims to provide a comprehensive analysis of deities associated with particular natural phenomena, including Boreas, the god of the North Wind, and Gaia, the personification of Earth, among others.

Boreas: The God of the North Wind

Boreas, the North Wind, forms a critical part of the Greek pantheon of nature deities. As a member of the Anemoi, the wind gods, he represents a specific natural force, in this case, the chilling, powerful winds from the North. In iconography, Boreas often appears as a bearded, muscular man with wings, signifying his celestial origin and his ability to traverse the sky swiftly. His usual depiction as an older figure may reflect the harsh, sometimes harsh nature of the winds he symbolises.

The ancient Greeks perceived the winds as powerful natural forces that had the capacity to influence their lives profoundly. Boreas, in particular, was associated with the cold winds of winter. In terms of meteorology, these winds were essential to the climate of Greece, marking the onset of the winter season, a crucial period in the agricultural calendar. The ancients, therefore, revered Boreas as the embodiment of these critical seasonal changes.

However, Boreas was not solely a benign figure. His winds, while essential for the transition to winter, could also be destructive. Greek mythology contains stories of Boreas wreaking havoc, flattening grain fields with his fierce gusts, stirring up violent sea waves, and causing severe winter storms. This destructiveness is encapsulated in the myth of Boreas' abduction of Oreithyia, the Athenian princess, a narrative imbued with violence and force.

Nevertheless, the portrayal of Boreas is not merely a representation of nature's destructive power. Rather, it underlines the inherent unpredictability of natural forces, their potential to oscillate between nurturing and destructive, often without warning. This dual portrayal served as a reminder of the capriciousness of nature, prompting humans to maintain a cautious and respectful relationship with the natural world.

Moreover, Boreas' narratives often convey a deeper symbolic significance. The violent abduction of Oreithyia, for example, has been interpreted as an allegory for the forceful penetration of the cold winter winds into the land, a necessary albeit harsh aspect of the seasonal cycle.

In conclusion, through Boreas, the ancient Greeks personified and sought to comprehend the often unpredictable and potent forces of nature. By acknowledging their capacity for both creation and destruction, they recognised the complex, multifaceted relationship between humans and the natural world. Boreas, as the embodiment of the North Wind, stands as a potent symbol of nature's paradoxical aspects, encapsulating the necessity of balance, respect, and understanding in our interactions with the environment.

Gaia: The Earth Personified

As previously discussed, Gaia (or Gaea) is the personification of the Earth, often referred to as Mother Earth. As the primordial deity from whom all life sprang, Gaia represents the Earth's fertility and the interconnectedness of all life.

The veneration of Gaia underscores the ancients' profound respect for the Earth and the recognition of their dependence upon it for survival. This perspective holds a mirror to contemporary ecological thought, which stresses the importance of maintaining a sustainable relationship with our planet.

Helios and Apollo: Deities of the Sun

The sun, essential for life on Earth, has long been deified in various cultures. In Greek mythology, the sun god is Helios, often depicted driving a chariot across the sky. However, over time, many of the sun's attributes were assimilated into the god Apollo, who became associated with light, truth, and healing.

The sun's daily journey across the sky became a potent symbol of reliability, consistency, and enlightenment. The worship of sun deities underscores the fundamental human reliance on the sun for light, warmth, and the growth of crops, highlighting the sun's integral role in human survival.

Poseidon: God of the Sea

Poseidon, the mighty god of the sea, represents the ocean's vastness, power, and unpredictability. His temperamental nature, capable of stirring up storms and causing earthquakes (hence his epithet 'Earth-shaker'), embodies the chaotic and often destructive aspect of the sea.

Yet, Poseidon was also worshipped as a deity who provided seafarers with safe passage, a clear acknowledgement of the sea's importance for travel, trade, and sustenance. His dual aspect – as both the destroyer and the protector – underscores the complex, often ambivalent relationship between humans and the sea.

Pan and the Satyrs: Deities of the Woodlands

As noted previously, Pan and the satyrs, with their half-human, half-animal forms, personify the wilderness and its inherent wildness, unpredictability, and sensuality. These deities, often associated with Dionysus, the god of wine, fertility, and ecstasy, represent the untamed aspects of nature, the elements that resist domestication and control.

Their hedonistic and unruly behaviour serves as a reminder of the essential wildness of nature, pointing towards the necessity of balance, respect, and understanding in our interactions with the natural world.

In conclusion, the association of various deities with specific natural phenomena provides an intricate picture of how the ancients personified and interacted with nature. These deities and their narratives served to conceptualise and make sense of the complexities of the natural world, framing humans' relationships with their environment in terms that emphasised respect, balance, and interdependence.

Examination of spirits associated with particular landscapes (e.g., Oreads, mountain nymphs; Naiads, freshwater nymphs)

Oreads - Nymphs of the Mountains

The Oreads, from the Greek 'ὄρος' meaning 'mountain', are a class of nymphs who preside over the mountains, hills, and gorges. As spirits of high peaks and craggy cliffs, the Oreads embody the grandeur and majesty of these natural formations. They represent not just the physical attributes of mountains, but also the metaphysical associations of height, isolation, and divine proximity.

Mountain landscapes, owing to their altitude and often challenging terrain, were conceived as liminal spaces where the divine and human worlds intersected. Many significant Greek myths, including the titanomachy, and the narratives of deities like Zeus, emphasize this sacred connection. The Oreads, as inhabitants of these divine landscapes, signify this sanctity and the bridge they provide between the terrestrial and the celestial.

Moreover, mountains, with their elevated vantage points, symbolise the divine perspective, suggesting an association between the Oreads and the concept of wisdom. By residing in these lofty domains, the Oreads may represent an aspiration for knowledge, wisdom, and insight.

Naiads - Nymphs of Freshwater Sources

Naiads, derived from the Greek 'Ναϊάδες', are the nymphs who preside over freshwaters - springs, streams, fountains, lakes, and rivers. These nymphs are among the most frequently encountered in Greek mythology due to the ubiquity of water sources in the Greek landscape and the essential role of water in human life.

The Naiads, as freshwater nymphs, embody the nurturing, life-giving qualities of water. As natural wellsprings were often the primary sources of potable water for ancient communities, the Naiads' association with these sources underscores their essential role in sustaining life.

But water, like nature itself, can be unpredictable and volatile. While it is a source of life, excessive or misused water can lead to illness or death. Correspondingly, Naiads, while generally benevolent, could inflict illnesses, known as 'nympholepsy', on those who offended them or trespassed their domains. This dual nature serves as a stark reminder of the delicate balance that exists within nature.

Landscape Spirits - An Intersection of Physical and Spiritual Realities

In conclusion, both the Oreads and Naiads, like other landscape spirits, demonstrate the ancient Greeks' profound connection with their natural environment. Through these spirits, the Greeks personified specific landscapes and natural elements, thereby attributing a sacred significance to these entities and recognising their essential role in human existence.

Furthermore, these landscape spirits exemplify the ancient perception of nature as a potent force, embodying both life-giving nurturance and destructive potential. This understanding underscores the necessity of maintaining a respectful, harmonious relationship with the natural world, a perspective that remains relevant today.

As you engage with this chapter, consider the roles of Oreads and Naiads and their relevance to the ancient Greek understanding of the natural world. What do these entities symbolise, and how do they reflect the ancient Greeks' interaction with nature? What might we learn from these ancient perceptions, and how can we apply these insights to our current relationship with the environment?

Discussion on the symbolism and cultural significance of these deities and spirits

Ancient Greek deities and spirits, including those associated with natural phenomena and specific landscapes, often exhibit a complexity of symbolic representations. These figures embody not only the physical elements they are associated with but also reflect broader themes and ideologies of the societies that revered them. Through understanding the symbolic dimensions of these entities, we can glean significant insights into the ancient Greek world view, particularly regarding the human-nature relationship and socio-cultural norms.

Boreas and Gaia - Dual Perspectives on Nature

Take, for instance, Boreas, the god of the North Wind. On one level, Boreas represents the literal physical force of the northern wind. However, his symbolism extends far beyond this primary association. The harsh, cold winds Boreas embodies are indicative of the challenging and sometimes destructive side of nature, reminding us of the trials that the winter season presents in agricultural societies.

In contrast, Gaia, the primordial deity personifying the Earth, represents the nurturing, life-sustaining aspects of the natural world. As the ancestral mother of all life, she encapsulates the concept of fertility, abundance, and continuity, a stark contrast to Boreas' harsher representation.

These contrasting depictions underscore the ancient Greeks' recognition of nature's dual facets - both nurturing and destructive. Such understanding emphasises the need for respect, reverence, and a harmonious relationship with the natural environment, themes that permeate Greek mythology and religious practices.

Oreads and Naiads - Landscape Personifications

The Oreads and Naiads, mountain and freshwater nymphs, offer a different yet complementary perspective. As spirits associated with specific landscapes, they reflect the Greeks' deep connection to their immediate environment and their attempts to understand and engage with it on a spiritual level.

The Oreads, as mountain nymphs, could be seen as symbolising the awe-inspiring grandeur of the natural world, the pursuit of spiritual elevation, and perhaps the human longing for transcendence. Conversely, the Naiads represent the essential life-sustaining elements of nature and the delicate balance that must be maintained to ensure survival and prosperity.

The Broader Cultural Significance

The symbolic representations of these deities and spirits offer a lens into the Greeks' conceptualisation of the cosmos, where the divine and natural worlds were intimately intertwined. These figures also played integral roles in ritual practices, civic identities, and cultural narratives, reinforcing communal bonds and social norms.

For instance, specific deities and spirits were often invoked for protection or guidance in various aspects of daily life, from agriculture to warfare. Such practices highlight how religion and belief systems were intricately woven into the fabric of ancient Greek life, affecting social, economic, and political structures.

As you delve into this chapter, reflect upon the multi-layered symbolism of these deities and spirits. How do these figures reflect the ancient Greeks' perception of nature and their place within it? How might these symbolic understandings influence societal practices and values? Are there contemporary belief systems or ideologies that echo these ancient views? Engage with these questions to deepen your understanding and draw connections to broader themes in cultural history and philosophy.

The Interplay between Nature Deities and Human Society

The Theocentric Cosmology of Ancient Greece

The cosmology of ancient Greece was fundamentally theocentric, meaning it placed gods at the center of the universe and its interpretation. This perspective represented a world order in which gods and goddesses held dominion over all aspects of existence, both physical and metaphysical. This cosmology was far from a mere metaphysical abstract; it permeated all aspects of Greek life, shaping societal norms, influencing behavior, and defining a collective belief system.

Nature deities, a crucial element within this theocentric framework, personified various elements of the natural world. Each deity commanded specific realms of nature, imbuing every natural phenomenon with divine significance. The sky, the sea, the wind, rivers, mountains, trees - all were overseen by their respective deities, thus infusing the natural world with sacredness. This interpretation served to highlight the intimate relationship between humans and their environment, which was viewed not merely as a resource, but as a living entity suffused with divine forces.

The pervasiveness of these deities in Greek society is evident in their enduring presence across various societal domains. Mythology is rife with narratives involving nature deities, with stories showcasing their feats, relationships, and conflicts serving as rich sources of cultural and moral lessons. Religious rituals, too, prominently involved veneration of nature deities, whether it was the pouring of libations to the Naiads for clean water, or offering sacrifices to Zeus for favorable weather.

Moreover, civic practices and institutions were frequently associated with nature deities. For example, Athena, the patron goddess of Athens, who was associated with wisdom, warfare, and also with olive trees, was at the heart of Athenian identity and pride. Her symbol, the olive tree, was not just an economic asset but a divine gift, contributing to the sense of the sacred in everyday life.

In conclusion, the theocentric cosmology of ancient Greece, with its pantheon of nature deities, imbued all aspects of existence with divine significance. This viewpoint served as a powerful force in shaping societal norms, directing behaviors, and fostering a collective belief system deeply entwined with the natural world.

Nature Deities as Mediators and Regulators

Nature deities in ancient Greek cosmology served as vital intermediaries between humanity and the environment, embodying various natural phenomena and forces. These deities held jurisdiction over aspects of nature that were indispensable to the survival and prosperity of ancient Greek society, such as weather patterns, seasonal changes, and the availability of natural resources. The Greek reliance on agriculture, coupled with their extensive maritime activities, further amplified the significance of these nature deities.

Boreas, the god of the North Wind, was an essential figure within this pantheon. His arrival signaled the advent of winter, marking a period of scarcity and hardship but also a time for rest and renewal for the land. Boreas was thus both revered and feared, his power respected and his wrath dreaded. Through veneration of Boreas, the Greeks acknowledged the necessity of winter's trials, understanding them as part of the life-sustaining cycle of seasons.

In the same vein, the Naiads, nymphs of freshwater sources, were integral to daily life and survival. As the presiding spirits over springs, rivers, and wells, the Naiads were believed to control the supply of freshwater, a resource vital for agriculture, hydration, and sanitation. Their favor was sought to ensure the steady flow and purity of these water sources, reinforcing the societal understanding of nature as both provider and potential withholder.

Rituals of worship and propitiation dedicated to these deities underscored the profound respect ancient Greeks held for nature's power and the necessity of maintaining a harmonious relationship with it. This balance, precariously hinged on the whims of the deities, was key to human survival and societal progress. The religious practices therefore served not only as acts of reverence but also as mechanisms for managing ecological relationships, regulating resource use, and mitigating environmental uncertainties.

The role of these deities as mediators underlines a worldview that saw humanity as an integral part of nature, rather than its master. It fostered a sense of mutual dependence and respect between the human and natural worlds, a symbiosis that is perhaps even more resonant in our current era of ecological crises. By examining this interplay, we gain valuable insights into the ancient Greeks' sustainable practices and their efforts to negotiate their existence within the capricious realm of nature.

Social Rituals and Civic Identities

Nature deities in ancient Greece played crucial roles not only as representations of the natural world but also as focal points around which social rituals were organised and civic identities constructed. The spaces dedicated to these deities, such as temples, sacred groves, and sanctuaries, served as communal hubs around which societies formed and strengthened. These locations were often sites of ritualistic performance and communal interaction, thereby fostering a shared sense of identity and social cohesion among the populace.

A salient example of this dynamic can be seen in the Panathenaic festival honouring Athena, the goddess of wisdom, warfare, and handcraft, who was also associated with the olive tree. This grand festival was a major civic event in ancient Athens, featuring processions, sacrifices, athletic games, and artistic competitions. A significant part of the procession involved the presentation of a new peplos, or garment, to the statue of Athena, symbolising the community's devotion to the goddess.

The Panathenaic festival not only solidified the civic identity of the Athenians but also underscored the multifaceted role of Athena as a patron of various aspects of Athenian life. Moreover, her association with the olive tree highlighted this plant's economic and symbolic importance to Athens. The olive tree, offering food, oil, and wood, was a major resource for the Athenians, while the olive branch also served as a universal symbol of peace and victory. Therefore, the festival served to underline the intricate interdependencies between society, economy, and nature. The veneration of Athena, especially in her association with the olive tree, encapsulates the complex interface between societal, economic, and environmental realms. It reinforces the notion of a reciprocal relationship wherein the health and prosperity of society are closely tied to the well-being and sustainability of the natural environment.

The study of these rituals and their associated nature deities allows us to understand how the ancient Greeks perceived their environment, constructed their civic identities, and developed their societal norms. It further elucidates how they recognised and responded to the complex interplay of ecological, economic, and social factors in their daily lives.

Nature Deities in Cultural Narratives and Discourses

The nature deities of ancient Greece were integral components of cultural narratives and philosophical discourses, serving as potent symbols and metaphors through which complex ideas were explored and societal norms communicated. These deities were the protagonists of mythologies that carried important societal messages, communicated moral and ethical codes, and informed cosmological understandings.

In cultural narratives, nature deities often served as embodiments of certain societal values and cosmological concepts. For example, Gaia, the personification of the Earth, emerged as a central figure in Hesiod's "Theogony," an epic poem that provides a genealogical account of the divine world. As the ancestral mother from whom all life sprang, Gaia held a central position in the theogonic order. Her relationships with her offspring, particularly her Titans and the Olympian gods, formed the core narrative of the poem, which relayed complex themes such as power dynamics, familial relations, and cycles of creation and destruction.

Gaia's story in "Theogony" not only serves as a genealogical record of divine beings but also functions as an exploration of primordial power and order. In this context, Gaia represents the fundamental stability and order of the earth, serving as the fixed base upon which the drama of divine power plays out. At the same time, Gaia's role in the successive overthrow of Uranus, her husband, and Cronus, her son, by their offspring underlines the cyclical and often violent nature of power transitions, a theme that resonates with the unpredictable and sometimes destructive characteristics of the natural world.

In philosophical discourses, nature deities were used as vehicles to investigate more abstract concepts. For instance, in the pre-Socratic philosophical tradition, nature deities were often invoked in cosmological discussions about the origin and structure of the universe, facilitating explorations of complex ideas about chaos and order, permanence and change, and life and death. These deities also served to articulate the complex and multifaceted relationship between humans and the natural world, highlighting humanity's dependence on, and vulnerability to, the forces of nature, while simultaneously exploring the human capacity to understand, manipulate, and control these forces.

These cultural narratives and philosophical discourses form an integral part of our understanding of ancient Greek society. They offer valuable insights into the societal norms, values, and beliefs of the time, as well as the complex and nuanced ways in which the Greeks understood and interacted with their natural environment. Furthermore, they demonstrate the profound and pervasive influence of nature deities on the cultural and intellectual landscape of ancient Greece, underscoring the crucial role of these deities in shaping Greek society's worldview and ethos.

The Enduring Relevance of Nature Deities

The examination of nature deities and their diverse roles within ancient Greek society provides more than just a historical perspective; it forms a basis for understanding ongoing human relationships with the natural world. The symbology and cultural significance of these deities, embodying various elements and forces of nature, reveal how humans sought to make sense of and negotiate their place within the environment, a task that remains crucial today.

In ancient Greece, the human-nature relationship was fundamentally theocentric and symbolic, with deities standing at the crux of humanity's interactions with the natural world. Today, while the names and faces of deities have evolved, many societies continue to personify and venerate elements of nature, whether in the form of patron saints, totem spirits, or other religious and cultural figures.

From an environmental perspective, the respect and veneration accorded to nature deities underscore an understanding of nature as a force to be respected and protected. This understanding takes on increased relevance in the face of modern environmental challenges, such as climate change, deforestation, and biodiversity loss. As we navigate these crises, the ancient Greek attitudes towards nature remind us of the need for respect, balance, and harmonious coexistence with the natural world.

In the realm of societal practices and cultural narratives, the stories and mythologies surrounding nature deities continue to resonate. These narratives, centered on themes of power, transformation, life, and death, remain central to many cultural and artistic expressions, shaping our literature, art, and philosophy. The narratives continue to reflect and inform our perceptions of the natural world, contributing to discussions about human responsibility and agency in the face of natural forces and environmental change.

From a scholarly perspective, the study of nature deities in ancient Greece offers a template for interdisciplinary research. It invites a conversation between history, anthropology, environmental science, and religious studies, among other fields. This interdisciplinary approach allows for a richer understanding of how cultural, religious, and societal factors intertwine with environmental perceptions and practices, both in the past and the present.

As we reflect on the enduring relevance of nature deities, it is imperative to foster critical discussions about how these ancient understandings compare and contrast with contemporary views on nature and environment. In what ways do our current belief systems, scientific understandings, and societal practices reflect a shift from ancient perspectives, and in what ways do they continue to embody similar principles? Such discussions not only illuminate the continuity and change in human-environment relationships over time but also offer valuable insights as we navigate the environmental challenges of the present and future.

Reflection on how nature deities shaped the Greeks' understanding and interaction with the natural world

The pantheon of Greek mythology is replete with deities representing diverse natural phenomena, from overarching entities like Gaia, the personification of Earth, to specialized divinities like the Naiads and Oreads, nymphs presiding over freshwaters and mountains respectively. Through these figures, the Greeks sought to explain, regulate, and negotiate their interactions with the natural world. This chapter aims to provide an in-depth reflection on how these nature deities profoundly shaped Greek understanding of and interaction with the natural world, framing their environmental ethos, societal practices, and philosophical discourses.

Conceptualizing the Cosmos – The Natural World and Divine Order

The Greek understanding of the cosmos - the ordered and harmonious universe - was a theocentric and geocentric model where nature was not perceived as a separate entity, but intimately linked with divinity. This perspective was rooted in their mythology, as immortalized in their literature and arts.

In this cosmological framework, divine entities were both regulators and manifestations of natural phenomena, from the grandeur of earth and sky to the specificity of winds and water bodies. The gods did not merely preside over nature; they were intrinsically part of it.

Hesiod's "Theogony," one of the earliest and most significant Greek cosmogonic narratives, provides a salient illustration of this perspective. The narrative begins with Chaos, the void, or the gaping nothingness. From Chaos emerged Gaia (Earth), the foundational entity representing the entire physical world. Alongside Gaia, other primordial entities like Tartarus (the deep abyss used as a dungeon of torment) and Eros (representing love or the creative force of procreation) came into existence.

These primordial entities gave birth to a vast array of other deities and Titans, many of whom were personifications of natural phenomena. For example, Ouranos (the Sky) was Gaia's son and husband, reflecting the ancient perception of the inseparable bond between the earth and the sky. Similarly, entities like Okeanos and Tethys represented the world-encircling river and the nourishing aquifer, testifying to the importance of water bodies in Greek life and thought.

The family tree of gods as depicted in "Theogony" served not just as a genealogical record, but more importantly, as a conceptual map that ordered the cosmos. Each deity, representing a distinct aspect of the natural world, held a specific place in this divine hierarchy, which was mirrored in the earthly order.

By attributing divine significance to natural elements, the Greeks imbued them with sacredness, thereby dictating the moral and ethical parameters of human interactions with the environment. Respecting a forest was not just an ecological responsibility, but also a religious obligation to the tree nymphs, the Dryads. Overfishing could anger the sea god, Poseidon, bringing about his wrath in the form of destructive storms or sea creatures.

This deep intertwining of the natural and divine profoundly shaped the Greeks' understanding of the cosmos. It reinforced a worldview that recognized the inherent worth of the natural world, promoted the principles of balance and harmony, and shaped a society that sought coexistence with nature, rather than dominion over it.

The Socio-Religious Paradigm – Nature Deities and Greek Society

Nature deities were integral to the socio-religious practices of the Greeks. Deities like Demeter, the goddess of agriculture, and Dionysus, the god of vine, were revered in festivals such as Thesmophoria and Dionysia, reflecting the significance of agriculture and winemaking in Greek society. Temples, sacred groves, and sanctuaries dedicated to these gods functioned as communal spaces where societal norms were enacted and reinforced, tying civic identity to natural and divine elements.

Indeed, the role of nature deities in shaping the social and religious fabric of ancient Greek society cannot be overstated. Their omnipresence in religious rituals, festivals, and civic practices offered tangible evidence of the intimate relationship between human society, divine entities, and the natural world. This interdependence not only shaped the Greeks' understanding of the cosmos but also structured their socio-cultural norms, daily practices, and communal identities.

Deities like Demeter, the goddess of the harvest and grain, and Dionysus, the god of wine, vegetation, pleasure, and festivity, were central to Greek agricultural life. Demeter, with her daughter Persephone, symbolized the cyclical nature of growth, death, and rebirth associated with farming. The Thesmophoria, a festival held in her honor, was a significant event for married Athenian women, strengthening female social bonds and reinforcing gender roles within the societal fabric.

Similarly, Dionysus was not only the deity associated with winemaking but also with ecstasy and ritual madness. The Dionysia, a large festival in his honor, was an important cultural event that included not just wine-drinking and revelry, but also theatrical performances, where social norms could be inverted or critiqued.

In addition to these deities, lesser divine beings like the Nymphs, Satyrs, and Pan also played a role in daily life and local cults. Nymphs, in particular, represented various natural elements—Naiads for freshwater sources, Oreads for mountains, and Dryads for trees. Local groves, caves, or springs could be considered the dwelling place of these beings, infusing the local landscape with a sense of the sacred.

Temples, altars, sacred groves, and sanctuaries dedicated to these deities served as focal points of community life. They were venues for religious rituals, local festivals, and civic meetings, and they often housed artworks or treasuries reflecting the community's history and achievements. They also served as asylums, providing sanctuary to suppliants and reinforcing the age-old Greek value of hospitality.

This socio-religious paradigm, where deities, humans, and the natural world were interconnected, helped to forge a strong sense of community. Communal worship, shared rituals, and common sacred spaces fostered social cohesion, reinforcing a collective identity grounded in shared values, practices, and belief systems. Through these interactions, Greek society asserted its unity, continuity, and distinctiveness.

Therefore, the worship of nature deities was far more than an expression of primitive animism or superstition. Instead, it was a complex, multilayered system that linked the physical and the metaphysical, the individual and the community, the human and the divine. It fostered a holistic worldview where humans were integral parts of the natural world, bound by sacred obligations to the divine entities that embodied and governed it.

Articulating Ethos – Nature Deities in Cultural Narratives and Discourses

Nature deities permeated Greek cultural narratives and philosophical discourses, playing didactic roles and reflecting societal values. They were often protagonists in stories illustrating themes of power dynamics, hubris, justice, and reciprocity. These narratives encouraged respect for the natural order and warned against excessive human ambition. The tale of King Erysichthon, punished by Demeter for disrespecting her sacred grove, exemplifies the cultural ethos of respecting nature.

The narratives featuring nature deities indeed played an instrumental role in articulating and perpetuating Greek societal ethos, values, and worldview. Through these narratives, the Greeks not only expressed their understanding of the natural world but also navigated complex themes such as morality, power, ambition, and respect for the divine and natural order.

These stories were not just tales of gods and supernatural beings; they were cultural vehicles that communicated and preserved societal values across generations. They highlighted the virtues of piety, humility, respect for nature, and warned against the consequences of hubris and impiety. The narratives encoded societal norms and expectations, and their recurring themes provided a moral framework that guided the Greeks in their interactions with each other and with the natural environment.

Consider, for example, the story of King Erysichthon, mentioned in your question, who is known for his disrespect towards Demeter, the goddess of the harvest. The king violated the sanctity of Demeter's sacred grove by cutting down her beloved trees, ignoring the pleas of the Nymphs and even killing one of them. As a consequence, Erysichthon was cursed by Demeter with insatiable hunger, which eventually led to his downfall. The tragic end of Erysichthon served as a potent warning against the disrespect of the gods and the natural order they represent.

Similarly, the myth of Narcissus, a youth who fell in love with his own reflection in a pool and eventually died out of unrequited self-love, serves as a cautionary tale about self-absorption and neglect of others, including the nature spirits. The pool in which Narcissus saw his reflection was often considered as inhabited by a Naiad, a water nymph, symbolizing the living nature that he overlooked.

These stories, among many others, illustrate the multifaceted roles of nature deities in Greek cultural narratives. They were not only revered as the controllers of natural forces but also respected as the upholders of moral and societal order. By integrating these deities into their cultural discourses, the Greeks developed a comprehensive understanding of the world, where human society, natural environment, and divine order coexisted and interacted in harmony.

The influence of these cultural narratives extended beyond morality tales. They provided a framework for philosophical discussions, facilitating the exploration of complex concepts such as life and death, nature and culture, chaos and order, and the human-nature relationship. Philosophers such as Heraclitus, Empedocles, and Plato engaged with these narratives in their philosophical inquiries, further contributing to the integration of nature deities into Greek intellectual and cultural life.

The Dialectics of Control – Human Agency and Divine Will

Greek interaction with the natural world was characterized by a complex dialectic between human agency and divine will. While they attempted to control the environment – through agriculture, building projects, and warfare – they also recognized that many aspects of nature were beyond human control, governed by the gods. This led to a societal model that sought a harmonious coexistence with nature, embodied in their rituals and practices.

In the worldview of the ancient Greeks, there existed a distinct dialectic between human agency and divine will, particularly in relation to the control and interpretation of natural phenomena. This paradigm acknowledged the boundaries of human capabilities, simultaneously recognising the inevitable and powerful intervention of the divine.

On the one hand, the Greeks exerted their agency to manipulate their natural environment for survival and prosperity. They engaged in agriculture, exploiting the fertility of the earth (Gaia) and seeking the blessings of Demeter, the goddess of the harvest. The Greeks mastered seafaring, appeasing Poseidon, the god of the sea, to ensure safe voyages. Architectural endeavours, too, reflect human attempts to shape the environment, often invoking gods like Athena, the patron deity of Athens and the goddess of wisdom and strategic warfare.

On the other hand, the Greeks recognised the overarching power of divine beings in determining the course of natural events, an acknowledgment that induced both fear and reverence. Earthquakes, storms, droughts, and other natural disasters were perceived as manifestations of divine displeasure. The harsh, cold winds of winter, personified by Boreas, the North Wind, served as reminders of the formidable power of the divine that could not be tamed by human hands. Thus, the Greeks sought to placate these divine forces through rituals, offerings, and observance of sacred rules and boundaries (themis), to ensure favourable conditions and avert potential catastrophes.

This delicate equilibrium between human agency and divine control encouraged a societal model that underscored the importance of harmonious coexistence with nature, embedded within their socio-religious rituals, civic duties, and moral obligations. It fostered a culture of respect for the environment, careful resource management, and adherence to religious and societal norms. This nuanced understanding of the natural world and humanity's place within it, as mediated by the divine, was a key characteristic of Greek society and provides important insights for modern discussions on environmental ethics and sustainability.

Consider the Panathenaic Festival, where the Athenians celebrated Athena's birthday with a grand procession, music, athletic contests, and a significant offering of a new peplos (garment) to the goddess. The Athenians, under the patronage of Athena, demonstrated their skills, achievements and offered their respect and gratitude to the goddess, highlighting their recognition of Athena's favour in their prosperity. Simultaneously, the offering to Athena symbolised their acknowledgment of the divine intervention and control over their city's wellbeing.

As students engage with these historical and cultural perspectives, it is essential to consider how these ancient practices and understandings inform current interactions with the environment. In what ways does the concept of divine will and control continue to shape human actions towards nature? How can historical understandings of the divine-human-nature interaction inform modern environmental policy and practice? These reflections can encourage a more nuanced understanding of current environmental concerns and the development of holistic solutions.

Conclusion: The Enduring Influence and Contemporary Relevance

The ancient Greeks' relationship with their pantheon of nature deities, as we have discussed in this chapter, serves as an enduring template for studying human-environment interactions. These deities' symbolic roles in the Greeks' understanding of natural phenomena, their participation in societal rituals, their presence in cultural narratives and discourses, and their significance in the dialectics of control, present a complex, yet coherent, model of how human societies may perceive, interact with, and derive meaning from the natural world.

In the Greeks' theocentric cosmology, every aspect of the natural world, from mountains and rivers to trees and winds, was animated by a divine essence. Such a worldview fostered respect for nature and its many manifestations, discouraging exploitation and encouraging symbiotic relationships. This understanding, which facilitated a balance between use and preservation, is an idea that continues to be relevant today as we grapple with issues of sustainable development and environmental conservation.

Furthermore, the nature deities were integral to societal practices and the construction of civic identities. Celebrations in honour of Demeter, Dionysus, or Athena, among others, served not just as religious rituals but also as communal activities that reinforced societal norms and fostered social cohesion. These events emphasised the connection between humans, their societal lives, and the environment - a relationship that today is often overlooked or taken for granted. In our current era of growing social isolation and environmental disconnect, understanding this integrative approach can inspire practices that foster community building and environmental stewardship.

In cultural narratives and philosophical discourses, nature deities often embodied moral and ethical values, teaching lessons about power, ambition, justice, and reciprocity. Such stories illustrated the consequences of upsetting the natural or divine order, warnings that resonate powerfully in an age of anthropogenic environmental change. Today, as we witness the effects of climate change, deforestation, and biodiversity loss, these ancient narratives can serve as stark reminders of the need for humility, caution, and respect in our dealings with nature.

Finally, the Greek understanding of human agency vis-a-vis divine control over the natural world highlights the delicate balance that must be negotiated in our interactions with the environment. While technological advancements have given modern societies unprecedented power to exploit natural resources, we continue to grapple with the realisation that many aspects of nature remain beyond human control. As we face environmental crises that threaten the very survival of various forms of life on earth, the ancient Greek paradigm offers a salutary lesson on the importance of respectful coexistence with nature.

In conclusion, the Greeks' interactions with their nature deities illuminate various aspects of the human-environment relationship that are of enduring relevance. As we navigate our contemporary environmental challenges, the insights provided by these ancient practices offer a valuable lens through which to understand and perhaps reassess our own relationship with the natural world. As such, the continued study of these deities and their roles in ancient Greek society holds a significant place in the discourses of environmental humanities, ecological philosophy, and sustainability studies.

Engaging with the Topic: Discussion Questions and Exercises

How did the belief in nature deities shape Greek societal norms and practices related to the environment?

Compare the ancient Greek approach to nature with modern attitudes. What principles remain relevant, and what has changed?

Explore how the presence of nature deities in Greek narratives and philosophical discourses influenced their environmental ethos.

Consider the dialectics of control in the Greek understanding of the natural world. How did this affect their interaction with the environment, and what lessons can be drawn for contemporary society?

Remember, the exploration of these questions is not meant to yield definitive answers but to stimulate critical thinking and inspire further research into the fascinating interplay of religion, society, and the environment in ancient Greek culture and beyond.

Discussion on the role of nature deities in agriculture, navigation, and other human activities

In ancient Greece, a society that was predominantly agrarian and maritime, the nature deities performed a critical role in governing key activities such as agriculture, navigation, and weather patterns. The manifestations of these deities in the physical world underscored their importance in the everyday lives of the Greeks.

Agriculture and Nature Deities

Greek agriculture was intrinsically tied to nature deities, revealing an intimate link between agricultural practices, religious beliefs, and societal norms. Among the most significant of these deities was Demeter, the goddess of the harvest, grain, and fertility. Associated with the life-giving aspects of the earth, Demeter was revered as the provider of agriculture's bounty, with major festivals like Thesmophoria and Eleusinian Mysteries dedicated to her.

The Thesmophoria, for instance, was an annual women's festival held to ensure agricultural fertility. It celebrated the cycle of life and death, reflecting the agricultural cycle of sowing and harvesting. During the festival, rituals included the scattering of pig remains, which had been left in trenches, or megara, to decay, over fields to fertilize them. The rituals of the Thesmophoria, therefore, were inextricably tied to agricultural practices and encapsulated the ancient Greek understanding of the regenerative power of the earth.

Dionysus, the god of vine and wine, played a similar role in the cultivation of grapevines, an important agricultural and economic activity in ancient Greece. The festival of Dionysia, marked by processions, dramatic performances, and revelries, celebrated the cultivation of vines and the production of wine

.

Expanding on the role of nature deities in agriculture in ancient Greece indeed unveils the rich tapestry of their religious beliefs, economic activities, and societal structures. This section will delve deeper into these intricate connections, highlighting the profound significance of deities like Demeter and Dionysus in Greek agricultural practices and the broader societal implications.

✧ Demeter: The Divine Patron of Agriculture

Demeter, the Greek goddess of grain and fertility, played a pivotal role in Greek agriculture, offering a divine explanation for the cycle of planting, growth, and harvest. Venerated as the one who bestowed upon humanity the knowledge of agriculture, she held a prominent position in the Greek pantheon.

Her significance can be gleaned from the Eleusinian Mysteries, one of the most important religious rites in ancient Greece. The mysteries, shrouded in secrecy, offered the promise of a blessed afterlife, reflecting the perceived connection between agricultural cycles and life's mysteries of birth, death, and rebirth. Demeter's central role in these mysteries underscores her profound influence on Greek agriculture and the broader Greek worldview.

Similarly, the Thesmophoria was another annual festival dedicated to Demeter, celebrated exclusively by women. Rituals performed during this festival, like the scattering of decayed pig remains over fields, were more than mere superstitions. They signified a deep understanding of the earth's regenerative capacity and the organic cycle of decay and growth. This, too, manifested the intimate bond between the Greek people, their agricultural practices, and their religious beliefs.

✧ Dionysus: The God of Vine and Wine

Dionysus, the god of wine, vegetation, pleasure, and festivity, was another nature deity deeply intertwined with Greek agriculture. He was especially associated with the cultivation of grapevines, an activity of immense economic importance in ancient Greece. The significance of Dionysus extends beyond his association with wine and festivity, as he symbolized the beneficial, life-giving forces of nature, as well as its destructive aspects, such as madness and chaos.

The celebration of Dionysia showcased the importance of grape cultivation and wine production in Greek society. The festival involved the public procession of a phallus and a jar of wine, symbolizing fertility and the fruitfulness of the earth. The theatrical performances, a critical component of the Dionysia, originated as choral performances dedicated to Dionysus, eventually evolving into the Greek tragedy and comedy genres. Hence, Dionysus' influence was not confined to agriculture; he was pivotal in the development of Greek dramatic art.

✧   Reflections on the Role of Deities in Greek Agriculture

In conclusion, understanding the role of nature deities like Demeter and Dionysus in Greek agriculture offers vital insights into the broader societal and cultural practices of ancient Greece. These deities served as more than divine patrons of specific crops or practices. They symbolized the Greeks' recognition of the cyclic and regenerative aspects of nature, encapsulated in the agricultural cycle. Moreover, they facilitated the integration of economic activities into the societal and religious fabric of ancient Greece, ensuring a harmonious balance between practical needs and spiritual beliefs.

As we delve further into this topic, consider how this dynamic between religious beliefs and practical needs might manifest in contemporary societies. How have modern agricultural practices evolved in relation to societal beliefs and values? How might ancient Greek practices inform contemporary discussions on sustainable agriculture and ecological consciousness? Engaging with these questions can foster a deeper understanding of the enduring relevance of ancient practices and belief systems.

Navigation and the Worship of Sea Deities

Given Greece's geographical setting, with its extensive coastline and numerous islands, seafaring was an integral aspect of life, particularly for trade, fishing, and warfare. As such, the sea and its associated deities, such as Poseidon, the god of the sea, and Nereus, the old man of the sea, held substantial importance.

Poseidon was especially revered, as he held dominion over the seas. Sailors would offer sacrifices before embarking on journeys to appease him and ensure safe travels. The Isthmian Games, one of the four Panhellenic Games, held in honor of Poseidon, underscored his significance in the maritime culture of ancient Greece. Similarly, the Nereids, sea nymphs and daughters of Nereus, were believed to aid sailors and fishermen, further exemplifying the role of nature deities in navigation.

Navigating the vastness of the sea was a pivotal part of life for the ancient Greeks, given their geographic location at the confluence of three continents and amid the Aegean's island-studded waters. This section will illuminate the significant roles the sea deities, primarily Poseidon and the Nereids, played in Greek navigation, illustrating their influence on maritime practices and cultural discourses of ancient Greece.

✧   Poseidon: The God of the Sea

Poseidon, one of the three principal deities in the Greek pantheon alongside Zeus and Hades, was considered the master of the sea. To the seafaring Greeks, Poseidon was not merely a mythological figure but a real presence whose mood could determine the success of their voyages. He was simultaneously revered and feared, given his notorious temperament. He could either bestow calm seas and safe passage or unleash formidable storms and sea monsters.

The mariners often offered sacrifices to Poseidon before embarking on their journeys, invoking his goodwill for a safe and prosperous voyage. These rituals underscored the central place Poseidon occupied in the collective psyche of the Greeks, reflecting the intersection of their maritime activities, religious beliefs, and societal practices.

The Isthmian Games, one of the four major Panhellenic Games held in honor of Poseidon, provided further testament to the god's significant role. The games, held near the Isthmus of Corinth—an essential maritime passage—highlighted the strong association between the sea god and Greek navigation.

✧   The Nereids: Aid in Sea Navigation

While Poseidon was the primary sea deity, other lesser-known entities like the Nereids, the daughters of the sea god Nereus, also occupied an essential place in Greek seafaring traditions. Known for their beauty and benevolent nature, the Nereids were believed to assist sailors in distress, guiding them through turbulent waters. Their narratives often emphasized the unpredictable yet conquerable nature of the sea, infusing the Greek mariners with a sense of confidence and respect for the sea's might.

✧   Reflections on the Role of Deities in Greek Navigation

In sum, understanding the role of nature deities in Greek navigation reveals the deep-seated reverence for the sea that permeated Greek society. It illuminates how religious beliefs intertwined with practical activities, underscoring the symbiotic relationship between the human and divine worlds.

In their attempts to navigate the sea's dangers and uncertainties, the ancient Greeks invoked their gods' assistance, reinforcing the notion that the sea was as much a spiritual realm as a physical one. This perspective fostered a balance between human endeavours and respect for the natural world, a principle that holds lasting wisdom for contemporary discussions on human-environment interactions.

As you further contemplate this topic, consider how these ancient practices compare to contemporary approaches to navigation and sea travel. How have modern technological advancements changed our relationship with the sea? How might ancient Greek practices inform modern seafaring or contribute to broader environmental and ecological discussions? Engaging with these questions can stimulate critical thinking and foster a multidisciplinary understanding of these issues.

Weather Phenomena and Their Divine Patrons

Nature deities were also responsible for weather phenomena critical to both agricultural and maritime activities. The Anemoi, for instance, were wind gods who could bring favorable winds for sailors or destructive storms. Boreas, the north wind, was known for bringing the cold winter air, while Zephyrus, the west wind, was associated with the light spring breezes conducive to plant growth.

Similarly, Zeus, the king of the gods, held dominion over the sky and weather. He could bring nourishing rains for crops or unleash destructive thunderstorms, reflecting the capriciousness of weather phenomena and their profound impact on human activities.

✧   The Anemoi: Divine Patrons of the Winds

In the ancient Greek worldview, the four primary wind deities, collectively known as the Anemoi, held sway over the winds and, by extension, influenced weather conditions vital to human survival. Boreas, Notus, Zephyrus, and Eurus each represented a cardinal direction, with unique attributes and effects on weather patterns.

Boreas, the North Wind, was associated with the chill of winter, often depicted as a bearded man with shaggy hair, embodying the harshness of the winter months. Conversely, Zephyrus, the West Wind, was a harbinger of spring, bringing mild and refreshing breezes conducive to plant growth. Eurus, the East Wind, was considered unlucky and destructive, often associated with autumn's challenging weather, while Notus, the South Wind, was linked to the scorching heat of summer and the late-summer storms that often brought destruction.

These wind deities' characteristics illuminate the ancient Greeks' perception of different wind and weather patterns' effects on agriculture and seafaring. For instance, the arrival of Zephyrus was eagerly awaited for its beneficial impact on crops, while Boreas was both respected and feared for its potential to bring harsh winters that could threaten food security. Similarly, the favorable wind brought by some Anemoi was essential for successful maritime navigation.

✧ Zeus: Master of Weather Phenomena

As the king of the gods, Zeus held dominion over the sky and all meteorological phenomena. His control over elements such as rain, thunder, and lightning was often central to stories of reward and retribution. When pleased, Zeus could send beneficial rain that nourished the earth and contributed to abundant harvests. In contrast, his wrath could manifest in severe thunderstorms, droughts, or flooding, often interpreted as divine punishment for human transgressions.

Zeus' role as the controller of weather phenomena underlines the central theme of reciprocity in Greek religious belief and societal values. The capriciousness of weather, capable of both nurturing life and causing destruction, was thus seen as a reflection of divine will, influencing human conduct and societal norms.

✧ Reflections on the Role of Deities in Weather Phenomena

The roles that the Anemoi and Zeus played in controlling weather phenomena illustrate how the ancient Greeks interpreted and navigated their natural environment. They highlight the deep entwinement of religion, societal values, and practical activities, revealing a worldview that respected the power and capriciousness of natural phenomena.

As you delve further into this topic, consider how the ancient Greeks' approach compares with contemporary understandings of weather and climate. How has scientific progress influenced our interactions with and interpretations of weather phenomena? In light of current environmental crises, what insights can we glean from the Greek approach to nature and divinity? These are potent questions that invite reflection, facilitating a multidimensional exploration of human-environment relationships across time.

Conclusion: The Reciprocity of the Divine and Human

In examining the role of nature deities in agriculture, navigation, and weather control, one discerns a profound interplay between divine influence and human agency. The Greeks' worship of these deities demonstrates their recognition of the human dependence on nature's forces. Simultaneously, their religious rituals, encompassing offerings and sacrifices, display an attempt to negotiate with these divine forces, seeking their favor and mitigating their wrath.

This dynamic reciprocity illustrates the intricate and delicate balance in the Greeks' relationship with nature and the divine. It underscores the critical roles of nature deities in practical aspects of Greek life, informing not just their religious practices, but also their economic activities and societal organization.

Exercise:

Consider the following questions for further discussion and reflection:

How does the worship of nature deities reflect the Greeks' understanding of their environment and their place within it?

Can we draw parallels between the Greek approach to agriculture, navigation, and weather control and modern practices? If so, how do these compare, and what insights can we glean from these comparisons?

How does the Greeks' theocentric worldview influence their practical activities and societal norms? How does this compare with other societies, historical or contemporary?

How do the rituals and festivals dedicated to nature deities mirror the agricultural and maritime activities they govern? Consider factors such as timing, participants, and ritual practices.

By contemplating these questions, you can further deepen your understanding of the multifaceted role of nature deities in Greek society, the negotiation between human agency and divine will, and the enduring relevance of these relationships in our current ecological and societal contexts.

Analysis of the dichotomy between wilderness (as represented by nature deities) and civilisation

Nature Deities and Wilderness: The Embodiment of the Unruly

In ancient Greek society, nature deities often embodied the untamed wilderness. Pan, the god of the wild, shepherds, and flocks, personifies this connection. With his half-human, half-goat form, Pan was imagined as being at home in the wilderness, away from civilisation, in a world unmodified by human activity. His rustic appearance and playful, mischievous character reflected the unpredictable, often capricious elements of nature and its forces.

In addition to Pan, the nymphs, minor nature goddesses, were also embodiments of the wilderness. Nymphs personified various natural elements - from rivers and springs (Naiads), trees and forests (Dryads and Hamadryads), mountains (Oreads) to the sea (Nereids). Dwelling in these natural entities, they were integral components of the wilderness, far removed from human civilisation.

Indeed, the depiction of nature deities such as Pan and the nymphs in ancient Greek mythology underscored the understanding of wilderness as untamed, uncontrolled, and teeming with divine presence. These deities did not merely represent various natural elements; they were perceived as inherent parts of the wilderness, further bridging the divine and the natural world.

The figure of Pan, a deity with a distinctive half-human, half-goat form, emerged as an embodiment of the untamed wilderness. Pan was often portrayed as residing in remote, inaccessible locations such as caves or deep in the forests, away from the organized society of humans. His association with music, particularly the panpipe, and his notorious lasciviousness further emphasized his connection with uncontrolled natural and instinctual forces. The panic or fear (panikon deima) that he could instill was also seen as a manifestation of the unpredictable nature of the wilderness.

Similarly, the nymphs personified various elements of the natural world. The Naiads, for example, were thought to inhabit and govern freshwater sources like springs and streams. They were believed to have the power to bestow or withhold the freshwater, necessary for life and agriculture, underscoring their vital role in the natural world. Dryads and Hamadryads were linked to trees and forests, whereas Oreads were associated with mountains, highlighting the wide range of natural entities that were considered divine. These nymphs, in their distinct domains, personified the various facets of the wilderness and its numerous elements.

Furthermore, the often capricious and unpredictable behavior of these deities mirrored the unpredictability of the wilderness. They could be benevolent, granting favors and nurture to the ecosystem and humans alike. Yet, they could also be malevolent, unleashing natural disasters if disrespected or ignored, underlining the inherent volatility and untamed nature of the wilderness.

This perception of the wilderness, as represented by nature deities, allowed the Greeks to interact with the environment in a meaningful way, attributing natural phenomena to divine actions and fostering respect for the wilderness. It was a mode of understanding and interpreting the environment around them, translating the mysteries of the untamed wild into a cosmology filled with divine entities.

The Demarcation of Civilisation

Contrasting with the wilderness embodied by nature deities like Pan and the nymphs, ancient Greek society had its own markers of civilisation. These markers included urban development—represented by polis (city-states), architectural advancements, and man-made sanctuaries for the gods—political institutions, philosophical thought, and structured religious rituals. This demarcation between wilderness and civilisation reflected a dichotomy in ancient Greek societal understanding, emphasizing the human ability to structure, order, and derive meaning amidst the chaotic natural world.

The ancient Greeks, much like many other civilizations, drew a clear distinction between the organized world of the polis (city-state) and the untamed wilderness. This demarcation was not merely geographical or physical; it encompassed philosophical, societal, and religious dimensions, reflecting the complex ways in which the Greeks made sense of their environment and their place within it.

Urban development marked a significant delineation of civilization. The polis, characterized by its fortified city center (acropolis) and surrounding residential and agricultural land, was a principal manifestation of human organization and control over the natural environment. The architectural splendors of the polis – its temples, theaters, agoras, and gymnasia – were more than functional entities. They were symbols of human ingenuity and societal order, a stark contrast to the uncontrolled and unpredictable wilderness.

In particular, the construction of temples and sanctuaries dedicated to the gods in these city-states represented a significant overlap between civilization and the divine. These sacred spaces were distinct from the rest of the polis, offering a formalized setting for religious rituals, festivals, and sacrifices. Even though these temples were often associated with nature deities (such as the Temple of Artemis at Ephesus or the Temple of Poseidon at Sounion), their architectural design and ceremonial function were indicative of human control and order.

The demarcation of civilization was not limited to urban organization and architecture; it extended to the realm of thought and societal institutions. The birth of philosophy, for instance, was a testament to the intellectual dimension of this demarcation. Greek philosophers like Plato and Aristotle sought to derive order from chaos, emphasizing reason and rationality over the capriciousness associated with the wilderness. The formulation of political and legal systems, the codification of societal norms, and the establishment of educational institutions (such as Plato's Academy and Aristotle's Lyceum) were all manifestations of this intellectual and societal demarcation.

Simultaneously, structured religious rituals further emphasized this demarcation. These rituals brought order to the seemingly unpredictable divine world, with calendared festivals, sacrificial norms, and priestly administrations, all creating a sense of predictability and control, even in their engagements with the divine.

In summary, the demarcation of civilization in ancient Greece can be viewed as a testament to human agency and control. It marked the human ability to structure, order, and make sense of the world amidst the unpredictability of the natural environment. At the same time, it demonstrated the complex interplay between wilderness and civilization, a dichotomy that was central to the Greek understanding of the world.

Interactions and Interdependencies: Wilderness and Civilisation

Despite the apparent dichotomy, Greek civilisation was not separate from wilderness; instead, it had complex interactions and interdependencies with the wild. Wilderness areas were essential for resources, including food, water, and materials for building, all crucial for the growth and sustenance of civilisation. However, the wilderness, with its inherent unpredictability, could also pose threats, including natural disasters, which the Greeks often attributed to the displeasure of the gods.

Religious rituals, such as sacrifices and festivals, were crucial mediators in this human-wilderness relationship. They provided structured practices through which Greeks sought to appease the nature deities, negotiate their dependence on the wild, and attempt to mitigate the threats it could pose. Consequently, while nature deities represented wilderness and its chaotic, untamed aspects, they also played integral roles in the civic and religious life of Greek society.

The Pantheon of the Deities in Greek Religion

The Greeks' interaction with the wilderness, represented by the nature deities, was not one of simple dichotomy or antagonism, but rather of complex engagement and interdependence. Civilisation and the wilderness were intertwined, each shaping and being shaped by the other in a dynamic relationship.

The wilderness provided resources crucial for the maintenance and expansion of civilisation. From forests offering timber for construction and firewood, rivers and springs providing fresh water, to the untamed landscapes affording game for hunting and land for agriculture, the wilderness was a vital supplier. Even materials for artistic creations, such as pigments for painting and stones for sculpture, were procured from the wilderness. Thus, the wilderness was not merely a realm of the gods or a space distinct from the human civilised world; it was a vital part of the material and economic foundation of Greek civilisation.

However, the very resources that the wilderness provided also made human societies susceptible to the unpredictable and potentially destructive aspects of the natural world. Natural disasters such as earthquakes, droughts, storms, and floods, were seen as manifestations of the wilderness's capricious nature. These phenomena, frequently attributed to the displeasure or wrath of the gods, demonstrated the potential threats the wilderness could pose to Greek civilisation.

Religious practices played a crucial role in negotiating this intricate relationship between civilisation and the wilderness. Sacrifices, prayers, and rituals were often performed to honor the gods and goddesses of nature, not only out of reverence but also to appease them. These practices were thought to help avert natural calamities, ensure the continued provision of resources, and bring about favorable conditions for agriculture and other human activities.

Festivals, such as the aforementioned Thesmophoria dedicated to Demeter and the Dionysia in honor of Dionysus, while celebrated within the realm of the polis, revolved around themes and practices deeply tied to the wilderness. They often involved processions, dances, and other performances in outdoor spaces and highlighted agricultural cycles and the bounties of nature – elements characteristic of the wilderness.

Moreover, the intricate narratives and myths featuring nature deities further elucidated this complex relationship. They often depicted interactions between gods and mortals that underscored the interdependence between the wilderness and civilisation, serving as allegorical guides for how humans could navigate this relationship.

In conclusion, the wilderness and civilisation in ancient Greece, rather than being isolated or oppositional realms, existed in a state of dynamic interaction and interdependence. The nature deities, embodying the wilderness, were not just symbols of the untamed natural world; they were integral to the societal, religious, and even economic facets of Greek civilisation. This underscores the holistic understanding the Greeks had of their world, a world where the divine, the human, and the natural were inextricably intertwined.

Reflection: Wilderness and Civilisation in the Contemporary Era

The ancient Greek understanding of the dichotomy and interplay between wilderness and civilisation offers a template for examining similar concepts in the contemporary context. Consider the ongoing negotiation between uncontrolled nature and human societal order, especially in the face of climate change and environmental crises. What roles do modern 'nature deities'—be it in the form of nature-centric religions, environmental philosophies, or personified representations of natural entities—play in contemporary society?

In the face of current environmental challenges, how does society negotiate the dichotomy between wilderness and civilisation? Does this dichotomy still hold, or has our understanding of the relationship between humanity and nature evolved?

Further, reflect on how ancient Greek practices such as structured religious rituals and the personification of nature could inform modern approaches to environmental conservation and sustainability. These reflections will provide valuable insights into the enduring and evolving relationship between human societies and the natural world.

Conclusion

As we draw chapter seven to a close, it is essential to consolidate the rich tapestry of interconnections we have explored between the ancient Greeks, their pantheon of nature deities, and their engagement with the natural world. This complex network of relationships underscores the holistic worldview that was characteristic of ancient Greek society, where the divine, the natural, and the human were intimately intertwined.

At the heart of this worldview was the pantheon of nature deities, who, as we have seen, were not merely symbolic figures but were instrumental in shaping how the Greeks understood and interacted with their natural surroundings. These deities were imbued with the power to govern different facets of the natural world, such as the earth, the sea, the sky, the winds, and the wild. The ancient Greeks attributed their agricultural prosperity, success in navigation, and the unpredictability of weather phenomena to these divine entities, reflecting the multifaceted relationship between society and the natural world.

Simultaneously, these deities were intimately involved in societal and cultural processes. From the major civic festivals like the Thesmophoria and Dionysia to the philosophical discourses that employed them as didactic figures, the nature deities played an integral role in shaping Greek societal norms, values, and ethos. They were agents through which the Greeks articulated their understanding of the world, moral lessons, and societal values, providing cultural narratives that helped structure their societal ethos and worldview.

This relationship with nature deities and the natural world was also dialectical. While the Greeks sought to control their environment through agricultural practices, construction projects, and seafaring activities, they simultaneously acknowledged the limitations of their control and the ultimate authority of the divine. This recognition led to a societal model that sought to negotiate this dialectic between human agency and divine will and to strive for a harmonious coexistence with the natural world.

One of the most profound manifestations of this dialectic was evident in the dichotomy and interdependence between wilderness and civilisation. As we have seen, nature deities often personified the wilderness, signifying the unruly, untamed aspects of the natural world. At the same time, these deities were deeply implicated in the civilised realm of the polis through rituals, sacrifices, and festivals. This highlighted the inherent dynamic between civilisation and the wilderness - a relationship of simultaneous dichotomy and interdependence, of antagonism and negotiation.

Lastly, let us reflect on the enduring influence and contemporary relevance of this ancient worldview. The ancient Greeks' theocentric cosmology, socio-religious practices, cultural narratives, and dialectical interaction with the natural world provide a robust template for understanding human-environment relationships, which remains relevant today. In an age where environmental crises are increasingly prominent, the ancient Greeks' respectful engagement with nature, their recognition of the natural world's intrinsic value, and their acknowledgment of the limitations of human control offer valuable perspectives and lessons.

In the next chapter, we will delve further into the implications of these insights for contemporary practices and discourses, particularly those associated with neo-paganism, ecospirituality, and other nature-centric belief systems. As we do so, remember the key insights from this chapter and consider how they might enrich our understanding of these contemporary phenomena.

For further reflection, consider the following questions:

How might the ancient Greek understanding of nature deities inform contemporary environmental ethics?

In what ways does the dichotomy and interdependence between wilderness and civilisation manifest in modern societies?

How can the ancient Greek model of negotiating the dialectic between human agency and divine will be applied to contemporary issues related to environmental control and stewardship?

These questions will help you critically engage with the content of this chapter and foster a deeper understanding of the intricate relationship between humans, the divine, and the natural world.

Recap of the main points discussed in the chapter

Chapter 7 provided an in-depth exploration of the crucial role that nature deities played in ancient Greek society and their interactions with the natural world. The following are the central points we examined:

Articulating Ethos: Nature deities were integral in shaping societal values, norms, and cultural narratives in ancient Greece. They often functioned as didactic figures, elucidating moral lessons and articulating cultural ethos, particularly those related to power dynamics, hubris, justice, and reciprocity.

Nature Deities and Human Activities: Nature deities were deeply involved in human activities like agriculture and navigation. Deities like Demeter and Dionysus played key roles in agricultural practices, while sea deities like Poseidon and Nereus were central to seafaring activities. The Anemoi and Zeus governed weather phenomena critical to these human endeavours.

Dichotomy Between Wilderness and Civilisation: The Greeks conceptualized a dichotomy between the wilderness, often represented by nature deities like Pan and the nymphs, and human civilisation, marked by the polis, architectural advancements, and structured societal systems. This dichotomy underlined the Greeks' perception of their ability to order and manage the seemingly chaotic natural world.

Interactions and Interdependencies: Despite this dichotomy, the ancient Greeks recognized a deep interdependence between civilisation and the wilderness. They understood that while the wilderness offered vital resources, it also posed significant threats. Religious rituals and offerings to nature deities helped mitigate these risks and maintain a balance.

Dialectics of Control: The ancient Greeks navigated a complex dialectic between human agency and divine will. Despite attempts to control and harness the environment, they acknowledged that ultimate authority lay with the divine. This dialectic influenced a societal model that sought harmony with nature.

Enduring Influence and Contemporary Relevance: The Greeks' understanding and interactions with the natural world offer enduring insights into human-environment relationships. Their theocentric worldview and respectful engagement with nature are relevant in contemporary discourses, particularly amid current environmental crises.

The chapter invites us to reflect on these ancient practices, beliefs, and relationships, and consider their implications for our current engagement with the environment. Understanding these historical contexts helps enrich our understanding of contemporary phenomena and responses to modern environmental challenges.

Reflection on the enduring influence and relevance of nature deities in contemporary paganism, ecospirituality, and environmental discourse

The rich tapestry of ancient Greek religion and mythology, especially concerning nature deities, continues to influence contemporary movements and discourses. From the resurgence of neo-pagan practices to the burgeoning of ecospirituality, the narratives of nature deities remain impactful, facilitating our grappling with the ongoing environmental crisis.

Contemporary Paganism and Neo-Pagan Movements

In modern pagan and neo-pagan movements, the reverence for nature deities from various pantheons, including the Greek, is palpable. These movements often espouse a polytheistic or pantheistic worldview and hold sacred the immanence of divinity in nature. For example, practitioners may revere and invoke Demeter as a symbol of earth's fertility or venerate Dionysus to celebrate life's intoxicating beauty. Moreover, the seasonal celebrations of neo-pagan traditions often echo the agricultural cycles that were integral to ancient Greek religious festivals.

Ecospirituality

Ecospirituality, which bridges the gap between spiritual beliefs and environmental stewardship, also finds resonance with the respect and reverence accorded to nature deities in Greek mythology. Ecospiritual practices often emphasize interconnectedness with all beings and promote a holistic approach to the planet that transcends anthropocentrism. The ancient Greeks' understanding of their interdependence with the wild - as mediated by nature deities - can thus enrich these contemporary spiritual perspectives.

Environmental Discourse

In the broader environmental discourse, the narratives surrounding nature deities provide a powerful framework for reflecting on human-nature relationships. They remind us of the need to respect natural limits, celebrate the earth's bounties, and recognize our dependencies on ecological systems. In an age of climate change and biodiversity loss, these narratives could inspire more sustainable practices and attitudes, fostering an ethos of care, respect, and reciprocity towards the natural world.

In conclusion, the enduring influence of nature deities offers a fruitful ground for dialogue and reflection. These ancient narratives, intertwined with modern perspectives, can facilitate a deeper understanding of our place within the natural world and guide our actions towards more sustainable futures.

Suggestions for further reading and research

For those interested in deepening their understanding of the relationships between nature deities, ancient Greek society, and the natural world, the following resources may prove invaluable. They offer a variety of perspectives, incorporating classical studies, mythology, religion, and environmental humanities.

Burkert, Walter. "Greek Religion: Archaic and Classical." This seminal work provides a comprehensive overview of ancient Greek religion, including the role of nature deities in societal practices and understandings of the world.

Hughes, J. Donald. "Pan's Travail: Environmental Problems of the Ancient Greeks and Romans." Hughes' book offers an environmental history of ancient Greece and Rome, providing insights into how their environmental understandings influenced societal practices and belief systems.

Buxton, Richard. "The Complete World of Greek Mythology." Buxton's book is a great resource for understanding the complexities of Greek mythology, including the roles and symbolism of various nature deities.

Kearns, Emily. "The Heroes of Attica." Although Kearns' focus is primarily on heroes, she also provides useful insights into the religious practices and beliefs of ancient Athens, including the role of nature deities.

Pedersen, Roger S. "Classical Landscape with Figures: The Ancient Greek City and Its Countryside." Pedersen's work offers an intriguing examination of the relationships between the ancient Greeks and their natural landscape.

Naiden, F. S. "Ancient Supplication." This book provides a fresh perspective on the role of supplication in Greek society and its connection to the divine.

In addition to these books, students are encouraged to delve into scholarly articles from journals such as "Classical Antiquity," "The Journal of Hellenic Studies," and "The Classical Quarterly." Online databases like JSTOR and Project MUSE can also provide access to a plethora of resources for further research.

Exercises and Discussion Questions

The following exercises and discussion questions are designed to stimulate deeper consideration of the topics covered in this chapter and to promote engagement with these concepts in a critical and analytical manner. They can be used for independent study or as a basis for group discussion:

Exercises

Create a Chart: Develop a comprehensive chart that categorizes various Greek nature deities, their domains, and their roles in society and human activities. Include information on any associated rituals, festivals, or myths related to each deity.

Myth Analysis: Choose a myth featuring a nature deity, such as the myth of Demeter and Persephone or Dionysus and the sailors. Analyze the myth, examining how it reflects ancient Greek understandings of the natural world and the role of the deity within this context.

Compare and Contrast: Compare the role of nature deities in ancient Greek society with their roles in another ancient civilization (such as the Romans, Egyptians, or Celts). Identify any commonalities and differences, and reflect on what these might indicate about each society's relationship with nature.

Discussion Questions

How do you think the dichotomy between wilderness and civilization, as represented by nature deities, shaped ancient Greek society's understanding of the world and their place within it?

Consider the enduring relevance of nature deities today, particularly in modern pagan practices and environmental discourse. What similarities and differences can you identify between ancient and contemporary contexts?

Reflect on the role of nature deities in agricultural and maritime activities in ancient Greece. How might these relationships between the divine, the natural world, and human activity compare to the modern world's relationships with nature?

Explore the concept of the anthropomorphization of nature through deities. What might this reveal about how the ancient Greeks related to their environment?

Consider the function of rituals, sacrifices, and festivals in the Greek worship of nature deities. How might these practices have contributed to societal cohesion and identity in ancient Greece?

Reflective and analytical exercises to deepen understanding of the chapter's content

Journaling: Reflect on a nature deity (e.g., Demeter, Dionysus, or Poseidon) and their influence on Greek life, both as an embodiment of natural forces and as a societal guide. Write a journal entry from the perspective of an ancient Greek citizen experiencing a festival, such as the Thesmophoria or Dionysia. Describe the events, emotions, and thoughts evoked, focusing on how these practices demonstrate the relationship between nature, deities, and society.

Contextual Analysis: Analyze a piece of ancient Greek art (a statue, vase painting, or temple relief) that depicts a nature deity. In your analysis, consider the symbolic elements, the story or event being depicted, and what this reveals about the role of the deity and their connection to the natural world. Discuss how the artwork reflects ancient Greek perceptions of the divide between civilization and wilderness.

Historical Research: Research an ancient Greek city-state, like Athens or Corinth, and examine how its geographical location might have influenced the worship of specific nature deities. Consider the city's proximity to the sea, mountains, or fertile plains. Reflect on how these natural features and the corresponding deities may have shaped the city's culture, economy, and societal practices.

Comparative Reflection: Reflect on modern societal attitudes toward nature and environmental conservation. Compare these attitudes to the reverence and respect shown by ancient Greeks toward nature deities. Are there elements that could be beneficially incorporated into modern perspectives on nature and environmental stewardship?

Debate Exercise: Prepare a debate on the role of anthropomorphization in understanding and relating to natural forces. On one side, argue that personifying nature as deities enables a deeper connection and respect for the environment. On the other side, argue that anthropomorphization oversimplifies complex natural processes and could lead to a misunderstanding of the natural world.

Remember, these exercises are meant to stimulate critical thinking and personal reflection, helping you deepen your understanding of the content and apply the concepts in a broader context. It is as important to engage with these activities as it is to have a definitive answer.

Thought-provoking questions for classroom discussion

How did the Greeks' belief in nature deities shape their understanding and interaction with the natural world? Can we draw parallels to any modern practices or beliefs?

Discuss the role of nature deities in societal norms and ethics in ancient Greece. How did these deities and their associated myths serve as moral and ethical guides?

Explore the dichotomy between wilderness and civilization in ancient Greek society. How did the interaction with nature deities reflect this dichotomy?

Examine the role of festivals and rituals in Greek society. How did these practices reflect the Greeks' respect for and dependence on nature?

How were nature deities represented in Greek art and literature? What do these representations tell us about the Greeks' perceptions of the natural world?

Reflect on the relationship between human agency and divine will in Greek society. How did this relationship impact the Greeks' attitudes towards environmental control and manipulation?

Compare the role of nature deities in ancient Greece with their role in contemporary spiritual practices such as Wicca, neo-paganism, and ecospirituality. What similarities and differences can you find?

Analyze the concept of anthropomorphizing nature in the context of ancient Greece. What were the potential benefits and drawbacks of this practice?

How might the ancient Greek approach to nature and deities inform modern attitudes toward environmental sustainability and conservation?

How can an understanding of ancient Greek religious practices and their relationship with nature enhance our understanding of human-environment relationships in general?

These questions aim to stimulate thought and dialogue, encouraging a deeper understanding of the complex relationships between deities, nature, and society in ancient Greece. They also challenge students to connect these historical practices to contemporary environmental and spiritual discourses.